RESEARCH STORIES FOR LIFESPAN DEVELOPMENT

ALAN MORRISON

State University of New York at Plattsburgh

LARY SHAFFER

State University of New York at Plattsburgh

ALLYN AND BACON

Boston ▪ London ▪ Toronto ▪ Sydney ▪ Tokyo ▪ Singapore

Series Editor: *Tom Pauken*
Marketing Manager: *Caroline Croley*
Editorial-Production Service: *Omegatype Typography, Inc.*
Manufacturing Buyer: *Joanne Sweeney*
Cover Administrator: *Kristina Mose-Libon*
Electronic Composition: *Omegatype Typography, Inc.*

Copyright © 2002 Allyn & Bacon
A Pearson Education Company
75 Arlington Street
Boston, MA 02116

Internet: www.ablongman.com

Between the time Website information is gathered and published, some sites may have closed. Also, the transcription of URLs can result in typographical errors. The publisher would appreciate notification where these occur so that they may be corrected in subsequent editions.

Many of the designations used by manufacturers and sellers to distinguish their products are claimed as trademarks. Where those designations appear in this book, and Allyn and Bacon was aware of a trademark claim, the designations have been printed in initial or all caps.

Library of Congress Cataloging-in-Publication Data

Morrison, Alan.
    Research stories for lifespan development / Alan Morrison, Lary Shaffer.
        p.   cm.
    Includes bibliographical references and index.
    ISBN 0-205-34054-7 (alk. paper)
    1. Psychology—Research—Methodology.   2. Developmental psychology.   I. Shaffer,
Lary   II. Title.

BF76.5 .S433   2002
155'.07'2—dc21

                                                                                        2001018861

Printed in the United States of America

10   9   8   7   6   5   4   3   2   1   06   05   04   03   02   01

To my grandparents,
whose love and support has been unwavering.
A. P. M.

To master teacher David R. Shaffer,
an inspirational educator who accepts nothing short of excellence.
L. C. S.

And to our students
Pollis non docere scientiam

CONTENTS

CHAPTER TWELVE
Chip Off the Old Block   119

Genetics and psychological characteristics.

PART IV   LATER CHILDHOOD—7 YEARS TO 12 YEARS

CHAPTER THIRTEEN
Watching and Weighting   130

Childhood obesity and television watching.

CHAPTER FOURTEEN
Boldface Letters   140

Attributions and learned helplessness.

CHAPTER FIFTEEN
It All Adds Up   149

Ethnicity and academic performance.

CHAPTER SIXTEEN
Watch Yourself   159

Behavioral therapy and self-management.

PART V   ADOLESCENCE

CHAPTER SEVENTEEN
At a Loss for Words   171

Sensitive periods and language development.

PREFACE

The reason we wrote this book is to help students learn about the scientific approach to the study of human development. We started a few years ago by producing handouts that we could use in our own teaching. This duplicated material covered much of the usual content in human development while, at the same time, introducing the students to the fun and challenge of thinking critically about scientific findings. Even in the first days of using chapters in draft with classes, the rewards were substantial: interesting and active classes populated by students who learned to be intellectually critical.

This book has one overarching bias—science. Scientific practice will be the standard against which methods and findings will be judged. Sometimes you will find that we are a little sarcastic about things in human development that we consider to be muddleheaded and useless. That is what happens when you buy a book with an attitude. Psychology, as we know it, is a relatively young science, and like any other scientific field, it is constantly evolving. New ideas about behavior are being formulated while old ones are discredited. New scientific strategies are devised to test new hypotheses. Our goal is to help you to view the field of human development as it is today, not as it was years ago. Most psychology departments have a course in the history of psychology—this is not a text for that course.

We want you to be able to read the contemporary research literature and evaluate the assertions that are made. We also want you to be critical of statements about behavior made by the media, friends, family, and others. We want you to behave like scientific thinkers. We believe that through this book you will gain a valuable set of skills that you can take with you for use in other courses and in your life after college. It is our hope that after finishing this course you will ask critical questions when presented with the results of research findings.

You may wonder why we chose the particular research studies that are discussed in this book. Several criteria served as guidelines. First, we wanted the articles to be new so that they would represent the cutting edge of developmental research. Our own bias is toward empirical research, and we chose articles to represent our view of good science. We chose robust articles to try to give you good models of research. We have not been very critical of the studies we present, but we have used these studies to give you the tools you need to begin to make critical evaluations of any and all studies. After a few weeks we find that our own students begin to be critical of all the studies they encounter—those in the remainder of the book and studies from elsewhere. Because of practical limitations, there is no such thing as a perfect research study. We want you to be able to find and evaluate strengths and weaknesses in research.

Although it is important to learn to be critical, it is also important to be balanced in your critiques. For example, most studies might be criticized because their samples are fairly narrow and do not represent the diversity that is found in the world. Although this is correct and it does limit the ability to widely generalize findings, for many studies it is not a very important criticism. This book is intended to be a bridge to help you to read real journal articles. That is where the cutting edge of knowledge about human development is found. If you have questions about some topic in human development, that is where you should seek answers. We have described and simplified some of the methodology of studies discussed in the book. The research has been simplified but it has not been dumbed down.

This book does not contain lists of definitions for vocabulary words. It does not have condensed summaries of the material at the end of the chapters. However, any technical terms that are not found in a standard dictionary are defined for you in the text. You will have to use a dictionary to look up other words that you do not recognize. This book uses graphs, charts, and tables analogous to those found in the contemporary scientific literature. It will be your responsibility to interpret these figures and to extract the relevant information contained within them. In later chapters we often refer back to earlier sections where a concept was introduced. This will allow you to refamiliarize yourself with concepts if necessary. Furthermore, at the end of the chapters, we have included a section where we refer to the critical thinking toolkit items introduced in the chapter. A toolkit item refers to a skill or set of skills that you can learn and take along with you on your quest toward becoming a scientific thinker. We believe that these tools have a variety of applications and can be used on a daily basis in the real world (unlike that electric paper clip dispenser your Aunt Edna gave you).

Successive drafts of this book were used for several years with our human development classes at SUNY Plattsburgh. Earlier versions consisted of loose chapters with many errors that were given to the students as fast as we could write them. Subsequently, our students were joined in this enterprise by three other human development classes and their adventurous instructors: Mr. Jerimy Blowers at SUNY Plattsburgh, Dr. Sheila Clonan at Colgate University, and Dr. John Klein at Castleton State College in Vermont. We owe all the students in those classes, and in particular Mr. Gerald Tan, heartfelt thanks for their willingness to work with those drafts while we polished and reworked them.

We gratefully acknowledge the encouragement and support of University of Texas scholar Josh Duntley. He was initially responsible for the idea of a student-centered human development course in which students did most of the talking and, as a result, did a lot of learning. He has always been unafraid to point out fluff and foolishness in seemingly scientific sources. His work on four editions of an earlier human development book paved the way for this text.

We are grateful for a summer stipend from the Redcay Foundation at SUNY Plattsburgh that supported some of the writing of the book. Our department chair, Dr. William Gaeddert, made extra office space available for us and permitted us to teach the human development course repeatedly, giving us the opportunity to field test the book. Mrs. Judy Dashnaw, our department secretary, worked tirelessly and meticulously in the preparation of the teaching materials that accompany this book. Plattsburgh colleagues Dr. Tom Moran and Dr. Matt Merrens supported us with their enthusiasm and many hours of discussion about all aspects of this project. Dr. Katherine Dunham and Dr. Renee Bator cleared up our questions about the details of research methodology. The provost of our college, Dr. Cynthia Hirtzel, supported and encouraged our unusual teaching style by visiting our class. Mat Broderick joined us in teaching the class and helped to shape the teaching style and materials.

We cannot imagine how this book could have been written without the dedicated work of SUNY Plattsburgh interlibrary loan librarians Mary Turner and Cheryl Lafountain and document delivery librarian Cynthia Pratt. They located and copied hundreds of articles for us and we are deeply indebted to them for their painstaking work. Laura Patno, at the SUNY Plattsburgh college store, helped us to field test the book by overseeing the duplication of earlier drafts. Bryan Kieser, director of the Latin Translation department at Black Minorca Books and Latin instructor at SUNY Plattsburgh, kindly helped us with translations. *Semper paratus.* It is clear to us that the fine people who work at SUNY Plattsburgh sincerely want you to have the best possible learning experience, and we are proud to have such dedicated colleagues.

In addition, we would like to thank our reviewers for their thoughtful comments and suggestions: Sheila M. Clonan, Colgate University; and K. Laurie Dickson, Northern Arizona University.

CHAPTER 1

SOUND FAMILIAR?

In the past few decades, psychological research has dramatically expanded our understanding of the competence of small children. You can see the remarkable increase of new knowledge within this domain by looking at old books that discussed child development. Years ago, the classic textbook of psychology by Goodenough and Tyler (1959) had a large section on the first two years of life, which was primarily concerned with young children's performance of rather mundane physical skills. For newborns, these were behaviors such as reflex responses. For older children, basic behaviors such as walking and grasping were described. The primary discussion of cognitive or intellectual development in the first two years centered on the classic observations of the famous developmental psychologist Jean Piaget. However, even Piaget did not seem to appreciate the extent of cognitive competence that we now understand to be characteristic of a newborn baby.

Since that time, good research methodology has revealed that newborns possess some surprising abilities in a variety of domains. For example, Butterfield and Siperstein (as cited in Papalia & Olds, 1992) have shown that small infants prefer music to noise, can distinguish among colors (Teller & Bornstein, 1987), prefer their mother's face to that of a stranger (Walton, Bower, & Bower, 1992), prefer certain odors (Steiner, 1979) can imitate some adult facial expressions (Meltzoff & Moore, 1994), and show some rudiments of depth perception (Granrud, Yonas, & Peterson, 1984). These are a few examples of the many competent performances that carefully designed research has elicited from babies in the first few weeks or months of life.

The application of sophisticated research methodology to the study of infants has allowed for recent advances in our understanding of behavior, particularly the behavior of newborns. In this book we will highlight the methods and the findings of developmental research. The study at the center of this first chapter is an example of the research method called the *experiment*.

THE EXPERIMENT

The experiment is generally considered to be the most powerful single tool for scientific investigation. This is not to say that experiments are always better than other scientific approaches. A weak or badly designed experiment may produce results inferior to some other

Incorporating the research of I. Swain, P. Zelazo, and R. Clifton, "Newborn Infant's Memory for Speech Sounds Retained over 24 Hours," 1993, *Developmental Psychology, 29,* pp. 312–323.

research design, assuming, of course, that the other design has been carefully constructed and carried out. Because of ethical limitations, many questions cannot be studied using experiments.

Throughout this book, we are going to use the word *experiment* in a very restricted sense. In science, an experiment is one particular type of research design, not just any scientific attempt to investigate an idea. It is quite common, even within scientific writings, that a study is called "an experiment" when it is not. We want you to know the difference because it is a basic distinction for thinking clearly about psychology. Beyond scientific circles, the situation is even more chaotic when it comes to the word *experiment.* This word is commonly used in the vernacular to mean all sorts of things, none of which bear any resemblance to proper scientific use of this term. If your car does not start you may say that you are going to "do an experiment" to see if the source of this failure is a dead battery. Your experiment is to see if the headlights work, and then to try other electrical devices—windshield wipers, radio, and so on. If these devices operate properly, you might conclude that something else is wrong with the car. Basically your approach is to thrash around trying things until you either figure out what is wrong or you give up. This is what most of us do when faced with situations in ordinary life, but in science we do not call this procedure an experiment.

In science, an experiment is the approach a researcher uses when trying to find a cause-and-effect relationship between some objects or events. In an experiment, the researcher attempts to hold most aspects of a situation constant while making one or a few changes in a carefully prescribed manner. Following these careful changes, observations are made recording what has happened as a result. Because most factors are held constant over the entire experiment, the outcomes observed are presumed to be caused by the changes introduced by the researcher.

Let us say that you are a developmental psychologist who is interested in the memory ability of newborn children. You believe that newborns may be able to remember the sound of a word over a period of 24 hours. You could take this assumption, also known as a *hypothesis,* and perform an experiment to see whether you could support it. You would have to get permission to study newborns at a nearby hospital. Ideally, these newborns would be randomly selected from a large population of babies so that you would not have a biased sample of one type: big babies, little babies, full-term babies, premature babies, and so on.

Next, you randomly assign the babies to two groups. One group will hear a word repeated over and over and one group will not. Here random assignment is necessary in an effort to eliminate systematic differences between the two groups. Individual babies will be different in all sorts of ways, but, ideally, the only difference between all the babies in one group and all the babies in the other group would be whether they hear a repeated word. Because there may be some differences among the individual babies that are not obvious, you want these inconsistencies to be spread throughout your sample as uniformly as possible. Next, you actually run the experiment. Some babies are exposed to the word, perhaps repeated over and over, and some are not. The next day, a simple test is devised to see if the newborns who heard the word respond differently to it than babies who did not hear the word. This simple test might involve watching to see if each baby turns its head differentially when the sound it had heard the day before is played first in one ear and then in the other.

Think about the details of this experiment for a moment. How might it be improved? If you reflect on this, you will find there are many ways, both significant and insignificant, to include important details and to refine the quality of your observations. For example, you might want to be sure that the babies who do not hear a particular word on the first day are exposed to all aspects of the Day 1 experimental situation except hearing the word. This may include holding many aspects of the situation constant, such as handling by strange researchers. If you do not do this and the babies who heard the word react differently when the word is repeated the next day, your findings may have been the result of remembering the word or the differences may merely reflect having been handled more.

Unlike most psychology textbooks, we do not intend this book to be a dictionary of psychology. We assume that you will use standard dictionaries to look up words you do not know. However, there are some technical terms you will have to know in order to think critically about the experiment as a research design. Because these are used as technical terms and may not be found in dictionaries we will list them. Some basic components of the experiment are:

Independent variable. This is the situation the experimenter manipulates. In an experiment it is the difference created by the experimenter. It is referred to as independent, because it is supposed to be independent of other characteristics belonging to the participants. In our sample study of newborn memory, the independent variable was hearing or not hearing the repeated word. The independent variable is often abbreviated as IV.

Dependent variable. This is the outcome that is measured by the experimenter. It is called dependent because it is believed that it depends on the independent variable. In the newborn study, it was the reactions of the newborns when the word was played on the second day. The dependent variable is often abbreviated as DV.

Probability level. When differences are found between research groups in a study, a notation such as $p < .01$ often accompanies those numerical differences. This notation signifies the outcome of a statistical test performed to assess the likelihood that a finding was the result of the research manipulation, rather than chance variation. In the newborn study, if some babies turned toward the sound they had experienced the day before while others do not, a statistical test would be required to indicate the probability that the level of turning in response to the sound was greater than might be expected by random head turning. The p in the notation refers to probability. If the notation is $p < .01$, it means that the statistical test has indicated that the probability is less than 1 in 100 that the head turning observed was just random behavior. It is a convention in psychology that in order to be called *statistically significant,* the probability level of differences must be no greater than $p = .05$. This is a fairly strict criterion because it means that there is only 1 chance in 20 that the results are owing to chance factors.

Operational definition. When concepts are defined according to the procedures by which they are measured, they are said to be operationally defined. In the newborn study, the memory of the infants is operationally defined as differential head turning. We cannot really know what the baby remembers from one day to the next so we define memory in terms of some behavior that can be measured. In reading research studies you should evaluate operational definitions and ask yourself if they are adequate to provide a test of the hypothesis.

Experimental group. This is the group that receives the treatment. In the sample study, it was the group of newborns who heard the word on the first day.

Control group. This is a comparison group that does not receive the treatment, or gets a different treatment. In the newborn study, it was the group of babies who did not hear the word. In some studies, it is difficult to know which group is the experimental group and which is the control group because one group gets one treatment and one group gets another. In such a case, both groups may be called experimental groups.

Control. This refers to attempts to eliminate influences of factors other than the independent variable. In our study, randomized selection and randomized assignment to groups were types of controls. For another type of control, if we gave the babies who did not hear the word on Day 1 the same amount of handling by strange researchers, we would say we had "controlled for extra handling." Often, to control something in a study means to hold it constant across the different research groups. Think again about the newborn study and try to imagine a few more controls that would strengthen the study.

Confound. A study has a confound if there is some reasonable explanation for the measured level of the dependent variable other than the independent variable. If we had not controlled for the amount of handling, we would have had a confound. We would not have been able to determine if hearing words, amount of handling, or both caused differences in the dependent variable. We would say that our study was confounded. Often confounds are only discovered after a study is finished by someone who was not involved in the study. This person may be reading the study for the first time and is able to look at it from a new perspective.

Baseline. A baseline measurement is a measurement taken before any treatment is given. Baseline measurements are not restricted to research designs that are experiments. However, within experiments, baseline measurements are common where participants serve as their own control group—so called *within subjects designs.* Baseline data are collected to measure behavior before the application of the independent variable. Afterwards, the dependent measures may be compared to the baseline data to see what has changed.

In this book, we will be very careful when we use the word *cause.* Although this word is used very loosely by all of us in everyday life, in scientific discussions it should be used only when describing the outcomes of experiments, not findings from other research methods. You can see the reason for this in the previous descriptions. Unless most variables are controlled while one or a few are carefully manipulated, it is very difficult to say which variable was responsible for causing a particular dependent outcome.

Swain, Zelazo, and Clifton (1993) reported a carefully conducted study that contained some of the components of the hypothetical newborn experiment. They were interested in the ability of newborns to remember speech sounds over 24 hours within the first days of life.

Previous studies had shown that newborns could remember their mothers' voices, a conclusion reached because newborn babies demonstrated a preference for hearing their mothers, rather than strangers (DeCasper & Fifer, 1980). The babies could not have preferred their mothers' voices unless they remembered them, at least for a short while. It has even been suggested that memories start before birth: Newborns have been shown to recognize their mothers' voice, even when filtered or muffled, as it would have been in utero (Spence & DeCasper, 1987).

PARTICIPANTS

The participants in this study were 36 newborn infants. They were resident in their natal hospital at the time of the study. They were at least 24 hours old and had an average age of slightly less than 48 hours. They were all full-term infants, meaning that they were not premature; they were born an average of 38 weeks following conception. There had been no particular problems associated with their health either before or after birth. At birth, the *Apgar Scale* rating system is used to determine if a newborn has immediate problems that require attention (Apgar, 1953). It does this by assessing *a*ppearance (color), *p*ulse (heart rate), *g*rimace (reflexes), *a*ctivity (muscle tone), and *r*espiration (breathing). The total scale is scored from 0 to 10. A score of 7 or above is usually considered to be normal. All the newborns in this study had Apgar scores of 8 or higher. The babies were predominantly Caucasian and were from a wide range of socioeconomic levels.

A few other requirements were imposed on newborns in order to be considered for participation. They had to have been fed within one hour of testing and they had to have been asleep immediately before testing. Otherwise, babies might have tended to fall asleep during the testing session. Babies were eliminated from participation if they were fussy, drowsy, could not orient to stimuli, or could not complete the second part of the study the following day. Some babies could not participate because their parents would not give permission.

Looking at these requirements for participation, you can see that Swain et al. (1993) went to considerable lengths to control for outside sources of variability that might have affected the dependent outcomes of the study. If the newborns had not been similar at the start of the study, it might have been difficult to see the effects of the independent variable. Imagine that some of the babies were premature, some fussy, some sleepy, some hungry, and some not paying attention to stimuli. The chaos of differences would probably have created so much variability within the experimental and control groups that the effects of the independent variable would be difficult to see. This illustrates the importance of controlling many variables and manipulating one or a few in experimental methodology.

STUDY DESIGN

Cognitive research with newborns can be difficult because clever research strategies have to be devised to allow the researchers to draw confident conclusions about what the child knows. One of the primary methods for studying infants is called *habituation* (Zelazo,

Weiss, & Tarquinio, 1991). Habituation refers to the decreasing response rate to a stimulus following repeated presentation of that stimulus.

In a simple example, if you were to present a sound to a baby, the baby might well show some sign of attending to the sound. If you play the sound over and over (e.g., *ma, ma, ma, ma, ma*) the rate of responding is likely to decrease over repeated presentations. This is habituation. If you then change the sound (*ma, ma, ma, pa, pa, pa*) and the infant responds differently at the instant of change, you are probably safe in concluding that the infant can tell the difference between the sounds. You can be more confident in your conclusion if you have done this with a group of infants and have controlled for other variables that might have resulted in a change of response at the time the sound changed.

Two words were used as the primary stimuli by Swain et al. (1993): *tinder* and *beagle.* These were chosen because it was not likely that many of the newborns would have heard these words often, if at all, within the first days of life. These two words are also approximately the same length and are phonetically comparable in that they contain about the same number of sounds. A female researcher spoke them into a tape recorder at 2-second intervals, trying to make the presentation as uniform as possible from one utterance of a word to the next. The additional word *papa,* spoken by a computer-generated voice, was also used.

For the main comparison of the study, infants were assigned to one of three groups. Each group comprised 12 newborns:

> *No Change Group:* a group that was habituated to the same word on each of two successive days
>
> *Change Group:* a group that was habituated to a different word on each of two days
>
> *Age Control Group:* a group that was only habituated to a word on the second day

Half of the change group and half of the no change group were habituated to the word *beagle* on the first day of the study. The other halves of these groups were habituated to *tinder.* On the second day of the study, the change group heard a different word than had been heard on the first day and the no change group was habituated to the same word as on the first day. The age control group had no habituation the first day and was habituated to either *beagle* or *tinder* on the second day. Table 1.1 shows this pattern and several other aspects of the design of the study.

As you can see from Table 1.1 there were 30 trials for habituation on each day. Each trial consisted of the newborn hearing the stimulus word repeated continuously at 2-second intervals for a total of 30 seconds or until the infant turned toward or away from the sound for at least 3 seconds. Following these 30 trials, there was a delay of 145 seconds and then 5 more trials of repeated sounds were presented. At the end of Day 2, all babies were exposed to the novel stimulus, a computer-generated voice saying "papa" for five trials.

PROCEDURE

During the research manipulation for each infant, one experimenter held the baby. The baby was positioned at a 45-degree angle, facing the same way as the experimenter. There was an audio speaker on each side of the infant's head, about 30 cm from the infant's ears. These speakers were used to present the stimulus words. A second experimenter recorded the di-

TABLE 1.1   Research Design

	DAY 1				DAY 2				Novel
	Habituation		Recovery		Habituation		Recovery		
	Stimulus Word	No. of Trials	Delay (in sec.)	No. of Trials	Stimulus Word	No. of Trials	Delay (in sec.)	No. of Trials	No. of Trials
GROUP									
No Change	beagle	30	145	5	beagle	30	145	5	5
	tinder	30	145	5	tinder	30	145	5	5
Change	beagle	30	145	5	tinder	30	145	5	5
	tinder	30	145	5	beagle	30	145	5	5
Age control					beagle	30	145	5	5
					tinder	30	145	5	5

Source: From Swain, I., Zelazo, P., & Clifton, R. (1993). Newborn infant's memory for speech sounds retained over 24 hours. *Developmental Psychology, 29,* 314.

rection and duration of the infant's head turning. This data recording was accomplished by pressing silent buttons on a switch box connected to a computer that recorded the results. Both of these experimenters were unaware of the participant baby's group assignment. They were also unaware of the nature or source location of the stimulus word because they wore headphones that played a masking sound consisting of all three stimulus words at once. This sound interference was used to ensure that the two researchers could not know the nature of the stimulus and transmit, subtly or otherwise, this knowledge to the participant baby. In older literature, this situation would have referred to the researchers as being "blind" to aspects of the study. The American Psychological Association (APA) now suggests that it is preferable to avoid the word *blind* and use, instead, words such as *masked* or *unaware*. The publication manual of the APA sets guidelines for the conventions of publishing in most psychology journals (American Psychological Association, 1994).

A third experimenter was responsible for the other aspects of the study. This person assigned participants to groups, operated the tape recorder that presented stimulus words, and collected the data from the computer.

A baseline requirement for participation in the experiment was that infants needed to turn "toward the sound for 3 of 4 consecutive trials within the first 12 trials" (Swain et al., 1993, p. 315). This criterion was included as part of the design in order to ensure that all infants were starting at similar levels of responsiveness.

A pilot test of the experimental procedure was run with participants other than those who were to be in the actual study. Pilot tests are often used to discover problems and to fine-tune research methods before a study is conducted. Unlike the actual experimental procedure in which there was one observer, in this pilot test two observers independently recorded infant head turns. The goal was to determine the accuracy of observations. In the pilot test, the independent observers agreed 87 percent of the time. While there is no official single criterion for the acceptability level of this so-called interobserver reliability we think that 87 percent is high enough to inspire confidence in this aspect of the observations.

RESULTS

For the purposes of analysis, the individual trials were grouped into blocks of five trials each. The arithmetic mean of the babies' responses was calculated for trials one through five and that became the score for block one. The scores from trials 6 through 10 were averaged to make the score for block two, and so on. This is a procedure that is often used to simplify data for analysis or graphical depiction. On the first day, a significant decrease in responding was found over the six blocks of trials ($p < .0001$). At the end of these trials, following the 145-second break, infants showed a significant 72 percent recovery in response rate compared to the end of habituation ($p < .0001$). These data across the first day are shown in Figure 1.1.

The decrease, which is shown in Figure 1.1, is habituation: the fading of a response to a repeated stimulus. After a 145-second pause, there was, once again, strong responding. There is nothing surprising about the similarity of the change and no change groups at this point. They are effectively the same because the substitution in stimuli for the change group took place on the day following the collection of these data. Figure 1.1 displays only the data for turns toward the stimulus. When turns away were also considered, a more complete picture of behavior on the first day emerged. Figure 1.2 shows head turns toward and head turns away from the stimulus word on Day 1. These data are presented as a *difference score* in which the number of turns away has been subtracted from the number of turns toward. In Figure 1.2, positive scores reflect more turns toward the sound and the zero centerline indicates equal numbers of turns toward and away. The bars hanging below the zero line are cases where the turns away were more numerous than turns toward.

The difference scores for Day 1 found in Figure 1.2 show habituation as decreased turning toward the stimulus. In the fifth and sixth blocks of trials, a tendency for babies to turn away becomes evident. While we cannot know the cognitive state of the newborns, it might appear that they are developing an active aversion to hearing the stimulus word over and over. As in Figure 1.1, the recovery following a pause is clear.

When total head turns, toward plus away, were examined for Day 2, statistical analysis seeking differences between the groups found that the change group scored between the no change group and the age control group but was not consistently different from either.

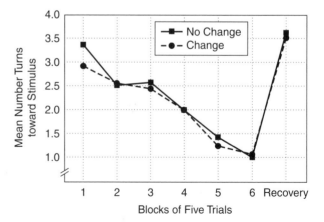

FIGURE 1.1   Infant Head Turns toward Stimuli on Day 1. Mean number of times infants turned toward the stimulus on Day 1, shown in blocks of trials consisting of five trials each.

Source: From Swain, I., Zelazo, P., & Clifton, R. (1993). Newborn infant's memory for speech sounds retained over 24 hours. *Developmental Psychology, 29,* 316.

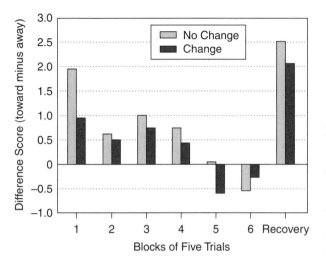

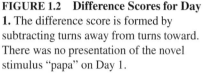

FIGURE 1.2   Difference Scores for Day 1. The difference score is formed by subtracting turns away from turns toward. There was no presentation of the novel stimulus "papa" on Day 1.

Source: From Swain, I., Zelazo, P., & Clifton, R. (1993). Newborn infant's memory for speech sounds retained over 24 hours. *Developmental Psychology, 29,* 318.

All three groups were quite similar. However, when turns toward and turns away were separated, different patterns of responding became evident. These are shown in Figure 1.3.

As in Figure 1.2, the data in Figure 1.3 are expressed as difference scores. You can see that as trials proceed, the no change group seems to be turning away from the stimulus more than the other groups. This even persists into the recovery phase. The change and age control groups both show increases in turning toward the stimulus during the recovery phase on Day 2, but the no change group does not. All groups showed additional responding to the novel stimulus *papa* at the end of testing.

DISCUSSION

The most important question addressed by this study was whether newborns could remember a word over a period of 24 hours. It appears from the results of this study that they can. The only systematic difference given to the change and the no change group was that one group was hearing a new word on the second day. In response, the increased turning away on the part of the no change group seemed to indicate that these infants knew that they were hearing the same old word. Although this may seem like a complicated procedure for a minor finding, the finding was not as insignificant as it may appear. If the results of this study are being correctly interpreted, newborns show the cognitive capacity to remember particular words for a day. This finding would be quite surprising to most people. In thinking about these results, it is important to remember that the participants were newborns. If you think back to the last time you saw a newborn, you may agree that for all their cuteness and cuddliness, from a cognitive standpoint newborns do not appear to be capable of learning new words.

You may have wondered what was found from observations of the behavior of the age control group in this study. If you make the comparison, age control data in Figure 1.3 appear to be quite similar to the Day 1 data of the other two groups (see Figure 1.2): Responding started strong, became habituated, then recovered after a rest period of 145

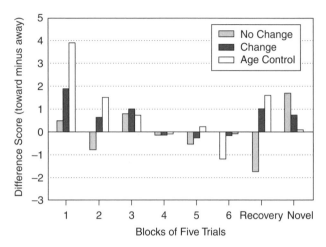

**FIGURE 1.3   Difference Scores for
Day 2.** The difference score is formed by
subtracting turns away from turns toward.

Source: From Swain, I., Zelazo, P., & Clifton,
R. (1993). Newborn infant's memory for speech
sounds retained over 24 hours. *Developmental Psychology, 29,* 318.

seconds. These data suggest that the differences seen in Day 2 in the other groups, particularly head turning away from the sound, are not a mere result of being a day older. On Day 2, change and no change group responses seem to be a result of remembering the stimulus word from the first day. If the age control group had shown a large tendency to turn away, then the case could be made that age, rather than specific previous experience, was responsible for this response. While there may seem to be little chance of this, development happens rapidly in the first days of life and for this reason age control groups strengthen experimental investigations of early development.

In the beginning of this chapter, we noted that Piaget did not anticipate the early appearance of cognitive competence as demonstrated in this study. Piaget did not do controlled experiments with participants randomly assigned to groups. In Piaget's early observations, his own children were the participants. His methods might best be described using the nontechnical term *demonstrations* (Piaget, 1954). Piaget rightly deserves to be considered a founder, if not the founder, of cognitive developmental psychology. Because he made specific statements about whether a child of a certain age could perform a particular behavior, his notions attracted attention from researchers. Some of his ideas have been shown to be incorrect and others have undergone modification. However badly his ideas may have fared in the face of newer research, we feel that Piaget deserves recognition for his early investigations of childhood thinking. Piaget's ideas, whether supported or not by contemporary research, have been the springboard for our current understanding. In contrast, the more vaguely worded early developmental ideas, such as those of Sigmund Freud and Erik Erikson, did not originate in systematic scientific observations and have been much less useful to current researchers.

It is our view that the so called *big theories* of development, in which one set of developmental stages is supposed to describe the behavior of all people, belong to an era that has passed. Most researchers now recognize that development is diverse and multidetermined. The studies in this book will illustrate the operation of many factors that influence the development of the individual.

CRITICAL THINKING TOOLKIT ITEMS

The term *experiment* means something very specific in science but may mean many things in the vernacular.

The experiment is the only scientific method that yields cause-and-effect conclusions.

Random assignment of experimental groups should eliminate systematic differences between groups, intending to leave only those that are created by an experimenter.

In most scientific studies, many variables are controlled so that they cannot account for the findings.

Carefully examine the operational definitions to be sure that you consider them to be adequate measures of the concept that is under study. This is a very important way to begin to think critically about a study. For example, if a study of intelligence used the ability to solve a single math problem as the operational definition of intelligence, it would be a weaker study than if it had used the outcome of a standardized IQ test as the operational definition.

Discovery of a confound is likely to be bad news. A goal of research design is to eliminate them.

REFERENCES

American Psychological Association. (1994). *Publication manual of the American Psychological Association* (4th ed.). Washington, DC: Author.

Apgar, V. A. (1953). A proposal for a new method of evaluation of the newborn infant. *Current Research in Anesthesia and Analgesia, 32,* 260–267.

DeCasper, A. J., & Fifer, W. P. (1980). Of human bonding: Newborns prefer their mothers' voices. *Science, 208,* 1174–1176.

Goodenough, F. L., & Tyler, L. E. (1959). *Developmental psychology: An introduction to the study of human behavior* (3rd ed.). New York: Appleton-Century-Crofts.

Granrud, C., Yonas, A., & Peterson, L. (1984). A comparison of monocular and binocular depth perception in 5 and 7 month old infants. *Journal of Experimental Child Psychology, 38,* 19–32.

Meltzoff, A. N., & Moore, M. K. (1994). Imitation and the representation of persons. *Infant Behavior and Development, 17,* 83–99.

Papalia, D. E., & Olds, S. W. (1992). *Human development* (5th ed., p. 115). New York: McGraw Hill.

Piaget, J. (1954). *The construction of reality in the child.* New York: Basic Books.

Spence, M. J., & DeCasper, A. J. (1987). Prenatal experience with low frequency maternal-voice sounds influence neonatal perception of maternal voice samples. *Infant Behavior and Development, 10,* 133–142.

Steiner, J. E. (1979). Human facial expression in response to taste and smell stimulation. In H. W. Reese & L. P. Lipsett (Eds.), *Advances in child development and behavior* (Vol. 13, pp. 257–295). New York: Academic.

Swain, I., Zelazo, P., & Clifton, R. (1993). Newborn infant's memory for speech sounds retained over 24 hours. *Developmental Psychology, 29,* 312–323.

Teller, D. Y., & Bornstein, M. H. (1987). Infant color vision. In P. Salapatek & L. B. Cohen (Eds.), *Handbook of infant perception* (Vol. 1, pp. 185–236). New York: Academic.

Walton, G. E., Bower, N. J. A., & Bower, T. G. R. (1992). Recognition of familiar faces by newborns. *Infant Behavior and Development, 15,* 265–269.

Zelazo, P. R., Weiss, M. J. S., & Tarquinio, N. (1991). Habituation and recovery of neonatal orienting to auditory stimuli. In M. J. S. Weiss & P. R. Zelazo (Eds.), *Newborn attention: Biological constraints and influence of experience* (pp. 120–141). Norwood, NJ: Ablex.

CHAPTER 2

DEEP ROOTS

As described in Chapter 1, the experiment is a very powerful research method. Unfortunately, some of the most interesting questions about human development cannot be addressed with this method because of the ethics or the practicality of assigning people to some types of experimental groups.

CORRELATIONS

The research method that is described in this chapter is called the *correlational study.* It is a nonexperimental scientific method that is frequently used in the study of development and behavior. A correlational approach assesses the magnitude of the relationship between two variables. Usually the variables are preexisting. The researcher measures these variables and then calculates the extent to which changes in one variable correspond to changes in the other. For example, there is probably a strong relationship between amount of time students spend studying and their grade point average (GPA). It would be possible to quantify this relationship by collecting some data. One might ask a number of college students to report their own level of each variable. Using the pair of numbers supplied by each individual, a correlation coefficient could be calculated for the entire data set.

Correlation coefficients, indicated by a lower case r, can range anywhere from $r = -1.00$ to $r = +1.00$. The correlation coefficient carries two pieces of information. Ignoring the sign, the absolute numerical value indicates the strength of the relationship between the variables. The nearer the correlation is to either end of the scale, the greater the magnitude of the relationship. A strong relationship means that if you know the value of one variable, you can make good predictions about what the value of the other variable will be. If you know how many hours students spend studying, you should be able to make some prediction about their GPA. You can make this prediction because the two variables are strongly correlated.

The negative or positive sign on the correlation coefficient indicates what is called the *direction* of the relationship. If the sign is positive, the relationship is direct. This means that the variables move in the same direction: If one increases, so does the other or if one decreases, so does the other. In contrast, if the sign is negative, the relationship is in-

Incorporating the research of J. A. DiPietro, D. M. Hodgson, K. A. Costigan, and T. R. B. Johnson, "Fetal Antecedents of Infant Temperament," 1996, *Child Development, 67,* pp. 2568–2583.

verse. The variables move in opposite directions: if one increases, the other decreases. The number of study hours and GPA are probably directly related. More study predicts higher GPA, or less study predicts lower GPA. Whether both are increasing or decreasing, in positive correlations the variables both move in the same direction. The number of cookies eaten and the number of cookies left in the cookie jar are examples of variables that are negatively correlated. For a real example from research, the rate of alcohol consumption in bars is negatively correlated with the tempo of the music: the faster the music plays, the slower the drinking (Schaefer, Sykes, Rowley, & Baek, 1988).

It is important to understand that both positive and negative correlations can be strong, and when this is the case, they enable us to make accurate predictions. The previous cookie jar example illustrated this point for negative correlations because the correlation is perfect, $r = -1.00$. If you know how many cookies were in the jar and know how many have been eaten, you can predict exactly how many are left. Sometimes people who are new to correlational thinking confuse negative correlations with weak correlations. This is a serious error. Weak correlations are found in the middle of the correlational range, closer to zero. They may be positive or negative, but if the number is low, the correlation is weak. For example, there is probably almost no correlation between hair color and intelligence. If you actually noted the hair color and IQ from a group of people and did the calculation, the resulting correlation coefficient, positive or negative, would be very close to zero.

It is common for psychological studies to produce very low correlations. There may be so many factors affecting any particular behavior that the correlation between any single factor and the behavior is likely to be weak. For example, Montgomery and Haemmerlie (1993) found that in a college student population, the correlation between drinking hard liquor and academic adjustment was $r = -.30$. Test yourself; you will know that you really understand strength and direction of correlations when you can make up examples in which you would expect strong positive and strong negative correlations, as well as a few in which the correlation approaches zero.

The interpretation of correlations requires critical thinking. How strong does a correlation have to be in order to permit important predictions to be made? One way to evaluate this is to square the correlation. The result indicates the percentage of the variation in one variable that is explained, or accounted for, by variation in the other variable. Let us imagine that the correlation between hours of study and GPA is .76, usually considered to be a high positive correlation. Multiplying .76 by itself shows us that 58 percent of the variation in GPA can be explained by variation in the number of hours studied ($.76 \times .76 = .58$). In other words, a little more than half of the ups and downs observed in GPA would be accounted for by ups and downs in study time. The rest of the GPA variation would be associated with other unknown factors.

Another way to evaluate a squared correlation is to think of it as being a rating on a scale from 0 to 100. The farther the square is away from 0 (or the closer that number is to 100), the more importance it carries. For mathematical reasons that are beyond the scope of our discussion, squaring a correlation gives a more accurate picture of the importance of the correlation than merely looking at the absolute value. If the value of a squared correlation is .07, the correlation has little power or importance. It is our value judgment that when the squares of correlations reach values somewhere around .30 they should begin to attract your attention, because knowing the score for one variable allows you to make some tentative prediction about the score for the other variable.

In psychology there are not many factors that, by themselves, account for large amounts of variation in behavior. This supports the notion that behavior does not have single causes; rather, it is multidetermined. While we have speculated that there might be a strong relationship between hours of study and GPA, it is probably nowhere near as high as the $r = .76$ in our example. Many factors in addition to hours of study are likely to affect GPA.

CORRELATIONS AND CAUSAL RELATIONSHIPS

Critical thinking is also required in the interpretation of the relationship between correlational outcomes and cause. If two variables are strongly correlated, it is tempting to conclude that one causes the other. This conclusion is commonly drawn by those who do not understand the nature of correlations. Strong correlations only show strong relationships. They are insufficient to permit causal conclusions. There is a fairly high correlation, $r = .58$, between the number of bars and the number of churches in American cities. If we were to jump to the causal conclusion that churches cause bars, it might seem that religion drives people to drink. It is more likely that there is a third factor causing both: city size. People go to church and people drink; larger cities have more bars and more churches (Schlinger & Poling, 1998). Strong correlations alone should not be taken as evidence of causal relationships between variables. The key word here is *alone*. Where strong correlations are found, one variable may actually cause the other but evidence beyond the correlation is required in order to demonstrate cause. An experiment would have to be done in order to confirm the causal link suggested by a correlation. Often it is not possible to meet all the strict requirements for an experiment; in these cases, while cause-and-effect relationships might be suspected, they cannot be confirmed.

In daily life, we often assume that strong correlations indicate cause and it might be difficult to function without this assumption. We assume that the strong relationship between crossing the street in front of moving cars and being hurt is causal. We do not have to test it by doing an experiment comparing a control group to people randomly assigned to cross a street in speeding traffic. This absurd example raises an important point. In daily life we might not need to apply strict criteria about correlation and cause to everything we see, hear, and do. However, within scientific domains, it is very important to make this distinction. Strong correlations should not be taken as evidence of cause. If you hear reports of study findings which assert that one variable causes another, either the study was a true experiment or the report is incautiously and incorrectly worded. As a critical thinker, you should recognize this. The first question you should ask when presented with study findings is "What was the research method used?" If the method was not an experiment, you should beware of cause-and-effect conclusions.

To put this in a contemporary context, tobacco companies can say that it has not been scientifically demonstrated that smoking causes lung cancer in human beings. There is an enormous amount of evidence that these two variables are related and some experiments with nonhuman animals have demonstrated causal links, but the experiment cannot be done on humans so the causal assertion cannot be confirmed, even though most researchers believe it exists.

In common with other scientific methods, correlations can be used to test hypotheses. The form of the hypothesis in a correlational study is usually the assertion that a relationship exists between two or more variables. When correlational designs are presented in the scientific research literature the authors sometimes refer to one of the variables in a correlation as an *independent variable* and the other as a *dependent variable.* In particular, statistical techniques use this terminology. Despite their wide usage, we believe that these terms should be reserved for the variables in an experiment. Only in an experiment are the independent variables really independent, that is, created by the experimenter. The variables in a correlational design are more accurately designated *subject variables* because they are chosen, not created or manipulated. Sex, age, IQ, GPA, socioeconomic status (SES), and marital status are examples of subject variables commonly investigated in developmental psychology. Some subject variables may also be called *antecedent* or *predictor* variables if they occur prior to other subject variables. The latest occurring subject variables may also be called *outcome* variables. Sometimes it is not possible to make the distinctions between predictors and outcomes because all variables occur at the same time.

If you were to do a study in which you were interested in the correlations between family income and children's IQ, you would be dealing with subject variables. You would measure both income and IQ for a group of people and then calculate the correlation coefficient. Imagine that you find a strong positive correlation: Higher family income is found to predict higher IQ. A little critical thinking will show you why it is important to understand the difference between a subject variable and an independent variable. Many other factors are closely associated with low income such as housing, neighborhood safety, family structure, parental education, parental occupation, quality of medical care, and quality of schooling. Income is not independent of these factors, as it would be if it were created and manipulated in an experiment. Finding a strong correlation between income and children's IQ does not isolate income as the cause of IQ differences. Any combination of the factors associated with poverty may be a component of IQ differences (Brooks-Gunn, Klebanov, & Duncan, 1996). Income may or may not be a cause; there is no way to tell when it is not an independent variable.

Contrast this situation with a study in which, for the independent variable, children from poverty were randomly assigned either to attend enriched day care or to be in a control group that did not receive day care. One of the measured outcomes was IQ. Children who attended day care subsequently developed higher IQs—the dependent variable (Campbell & Ramey, 1994). This study will be discussed in more detail in Chapter 20, "Making the Grade." Although this was a field experiment, it is reasonable to conclude that the independent variable was a cause of the subsequent IQ outcomes.

TEMPERAMENT

As a first example of correlational research, we have chosen a study of temperament. *Temperament* has become a technical term in developmental psychology referring to the individual differences in responding to the environment, particularly for infants and young children. These differences may include measures such as speed and magnitude of reaction to stimuli, emotional tone, activity level, vocalizations, and attention span.

Temperament has been shown to be quite stable across childhood. Kagan and Snidman (1991) reported that some 2-year-olds maintained a consistent temperament profile through at least age 8. While temperament is not the same as personality, it can be viewed as an early reactive style that subsequently becomes a component of a complex personality.

Temperament is not the result of any single underlying cause. Recently, considerable evidence has indicated that the biological makeup of the individual has a clear influence on temperament (Kagan, 1994). Differences in brain structures may be involved in temperament (Amaral, Price, Pitkanen, & Carmichael, 1992). As would be expected if there were a major biological component underlying temperament, specific biological characteristics have been found to associate with different temperaments. The presumption is that characteristics that usually occur together depend upon some of the same genes or biological systems that underlie temperament. For example, children who react more vigorously to unfamiliar stimuli, such as brightly colored toys or unusual smells, also have narrower faces in the second year of life (Arcus & Kagan, 1995). Temperament has also been linked to national origin, with more genetically homogenous populations showing less temperamental variability. Because these differences can be seen very early in life, biological components or causes are implicated (Kagan et al., 1994).

DiPietro, Hodgson, Costigan, and Johnson (1996) did a correlational study of the relationship between behavior of fetuses in the womb and the later temperament of these individuals as infants. They reasoned that the biological underpinnings of temperament ought to lead to detectable continuities in reactivity from the earliest possible measures, and so they undertook to measure fetal responsiveness and correlate it with measures of behavior in infancy. The overall hypothesis being tested was that fetal behavior would allow predictions to be made about temperament in infancy.

PARTICIPANTS

The participants in this study were 34 pregnant women, at least 20 years of age ($M = 28.4$ years). They (and their fetuses) volunteered to be in the study. None of the women were carrying more than one fetus. They were chosen based on low risk for problems concerning pregnancy. They had experienced no obvious problems with their pregnancies, did not smoke, and had graduated from high school ($M = 16.6$ years of education). Nineteen percent of the women were African American and the rest were Caucasian. Three of the women were dropped from the study when medical difficulties developed during pregnancy. All infants born to mothers continuing in the study were rated as being healthy at birth. Five minutes following birth, Apgar scores for babies in the study were 8 or higher. Slightly over half (55 percent) of the infants were girls.

FETAL HEART RATE AND MOVEMENT MEASURES

Fetal heart rate and other fetal movement was recorded at 20, 24, 28, 32, 36, and 38–39 weeks following conception using a fetal actocardiograph. This has been shown to produce accurate measures of heart rate as well as other movements when compared to movements observed on ultrasound recordings (Besinger & Johnson, 1989). The actocardiograph data were digitized and fed to a computer that stored the records. This equipment was able to generate measures of fetal heart rate and an additional measure: the variability in fetal heart rate. In addition to the digitized data, the computer also produced a graphic representation of bodily movement and heart rate that was scored by the researchers. The data from the actocardiograph operationally defined fetal movement and heart rate. At each visit, the participants experienced 50 minutes of fetal monitoring.

INFANT TEMPERAMENT MEASURES

Following birth, a standardized questionnaire, the Infant Characteristics Questionnaire (ICQ; Bates, Freeland, & Lounsbury, 1979) was used to assess infant temperament at 3 months of age and again at 6 months. This questionnaire was sent to the mothers in the mail. This instrument measured four temperamental characteristics:

1. *Fussy-Difficult:* tends to cry or be irritable without obvious reason such as hunger. Easily upset, difficult to soothe, changeable.
2. *Unadaptable:* does not react well to new situations or new people. Reacts badly to disruptions in life, such as a bath.
3. *Dullness:* lacks emotional tone or spontaneity. Low degree of activity.
4. *Unpredictable:* lacks regularity in daily habits or situations such as eating, sleeping, diapering, or being held.

Each mother was also asked to rate the overall activity of her infant on a scale from 1 to 7 in which higher numbers indicated more activity, to report how many times the infant woke up in the night, and to assess how much of the infant's diet consisted of breast milk.

RESULTS AND DISCUSSION

In order to assess stability of the fetal measures across time, each measure was correlated with the same measure taken at each of the six different fetal monitoring sessions between 20 weeks gestational age and 39 weeks gestational age. Table 2.1 displays the correlation coefficients, also called *intercorrelations,* between individual measures of fetal activity over different recording sessions.

Note that there is considerable variability among the correlations reported in Table 2.1. If you scan over them, however, you can probably see that the largest ones tend to occur among later measurement sessions and between sessions that are closely spaced in time. There is some evidence here for the dawning of stable activity patterns during the later part of the fetal period. High correlations mean that individual fetuses remained similar from one session to another. A high correlation would indicate that those who did not move much at one session did not move much at another and those who showed high movement at one session showed high movement at another session.

Table 2.2 shows measures of fetal heart rate as well as the variability found in heart rate. As with fetal activity shown in Table 2.1, the correlations in Table 2.2 differ extensively from one another, and range from $r = .03$ to $r = .60$. However, a considerable number

TABLE 2.1 Correlations between Measures of Fetal Activity

	Gestational Age (weeks)					
	20	**24**	**28**	**32**	**36**	**38–39**
GESTATIONAL AGE (WEEKS)						
20	—	.30	.27	.23	.05	.34
24	—	—	.11	.35	.26	.28
28	—	—	—	.55	.47	.16
32	—	—	—	—	.45	.48
36	—	—	—	—	—	.67
38–39	—	—	—	—	—	—

Note: The correlations are presented here in a table format that is very typical in the scientific literature. A little inspection will convince you that some cells are left empty because the data in them would be either pointless or redundant. For example, the first empty cell in the upper left corner would contain the correlation between activity at 20 weeks and activity at 20 weeks (pointless) and the empty cells below the diagonal would contain a mirror image of the data already displayed above (redundant).

Source: From DiPietro, J. A., Hodgson, D. M., Costigan, K. A., & Johnston, T. R. B. (1996). Fetal antecedents of infant temperament. *Child Development, 67,* 2572.

TABLE 2.2 Correlations between Measures of Fetal Heart Rate and Variability in Fetal Heart Rate

	Gestational Age (weeks)					
	20	**24**	**28**	**32**	**36**	**38–39**
GESTATIONAL AGE (WEEKS)						
20	—	.61	.56	.28	.26	.15
24	.58	—	.54	.43	.38	.16
28	.46	.53	—	.39	.56	.34
32	.24	.40	.60	—	.48	.25
36	.03	.30	.35	.43	—	.52
38–39	.61	.53	.55	.32	.48	—

Note: A common convention employed in this table is to use the cells below the diagonal that would otherwise be taken up by blanks replacing redundant data. These cells are used to plot another set of correlations as described in the title above the table. If you have no previous experience with tables containing correlational matrices, you should devote some time learning to read these tables because this kind of presentation is very common.

Source: From DiPietro, J. A., Hodgson, D. M., Costigan, K. A., & Johnston, T. R. B. (1996). Fetal antecedents of infant temperament. *Child Development, 67,* 2571.

of the correlations presented for both measures are quite large. These high correlations suggest that heart rate and heart rate variability show some stability in the fetal period.

The more interesting question was the extent to which fetal measures were related to the temperament of these individuals when they were 3 and 6 months old. Some variables showed no important relationship to any of the infant measures. Among these were the mother's age, the number of other children to whom she had given birth (called *parity*), infant birth weight, and infant sex.

The most consistently strong correlations were found between the measures fetal activity, periodicity, and infant temperament. In this study, *periodicity* was the number of times that a fetus changed from periods of activity to periods of inactivity during the monitoring session. *Fetal activity* was the total number of minutes that the fetus was moving during the session. These correlations are shown in Table 2.3. They are surprisingly high for behavioral science data; ordinarily correlations are quite small.

A number of correlations between other fetal measures and subsequent infant outcomes were large enough to be important, but no other fetal outcome approached the consistency found for activity level and periodicity. The data presented in Table 2.3 suggest that fetal activity level permits reasonably sound predictions to be made of a number of infant variables, with the exception of infant dullness.

Periodicity also permitted good predictions to be made in most cases because the correlations were so high. However, the relationships in this column were negative or inverse, so higher periodicity was associated with lower levels of infant measures. To choose one example, this meant that the more times a fetus changed from active to inactive, the less fussy and difficult it was as an infant. A number of the outcomes found in Table 2.3 might be in the expected direction but, ironically, unpredictability seemed to be an exception. Common sense might lead one to expect that frequent changes between activity and inactivity would be positively associated with infant unpredictability. However, the negative correlations indicate that the changeable fetuses were predictable infants.

TABLE 2.3   Fetal Activity Level and Periodicity Correlated with Various Infant Measures at 3 and 6 Months

	FETAL ACTIVITY LEVEL	FETAL PERIODICITY
INFANT MEASURE		
Fussy-Difficult 3 months	.52	−.36
Fussy-Difficult 6 months	.60	−.37
Unadaptability 3 months	.45	−.47
Unadaptability 6 months	.54	−.34
Dullness 3 months	.14*	−.50
Dullness 6 months	.27*	−.58
Unpredictability 3 months	.74	−.58
Unpredictability 6 months	.43	−.32
Activity level 3 months	.40	−.12*
Activity level 6 months	.37	−.02
Night waking 3 months	.42	−.58
Night waking 6 months	.34	−.32

*Indicates correlations too small to be considered significant based on statistical tests.

Source: From DiPietro, J. A., Hodgson, D. M., Costigan, K. A., & Johnston, T. R. B. (1996). Fetal antecedents of infant temperament. *Child Development, 67,* 2568–2583.

These data nicely illustrate the predictive power of both negative and positive correlations when they are strong. Squaring the correlations, we can see that over half of the variability in 3 month unpredictability was accounted for by fetal activity level ($.74 \times .74 = .54$) and about a third of infant dullness at 6 months is explained by fetal activity periodicity ($-.58 \times -.58 = .34$). While this may not seem like very much, the explanation of the remaining two thirds is probably spread over a very large number of much smaller factors. In much of behavioral science, a factor that predicts one third of the variability in behavior is a very large factor indeed.

The correlational data indicated that there were later temperamental differences between individuals who had been highly active fetuses and those who had been less active fetuses. DiPietro et al. (1996) noticed a particularly striking pattern of fetal activity in eight of the fetuses. This consisted of continuous periods, 3 minutes or longer, of very vigorous activity. In support of the correlational data, the mean scores for some infant temperament characteristics in babies who had been high-activity fetuses are compared to less active infants' scores in Figure 2.1. The data presented in Figure 2.1 serve as further confirmation that fetal activity is an important early indicator of infant temperament.

The elegant research described in this chapter contributes support for the notion that individual differences in human beings start well before birth. At least some measures of these differences showed stability across the end of the fetal period. Two measures of fetal activity, total activity and periodicity, also showed strong correlations with later measures of infant temperament. The stability and continuity that was found can be considered evidence for biological contributions to temperament, which are likely to be largely the result of genetics.

Probably no serious psychologist in the last 100 years has believed the naive proposition that temperament and personality have no genetic component. In the words of philosopher John Locke (1632–1704), this anti-genetics notion is sometimes called *tabula rasa,* meaning that the person has been born as a blank slate, with no biological predispositions. In psychology, *behaviorism* is the name given to less extreme versions of this view which, nevertheless, emphasize the influences of learning and experience rather than genetic factors. However, even the founder of behaviorism, John B. Watson (1924), grudgingly acknowledged that babies were born with some emotional tendencies, although he failed to

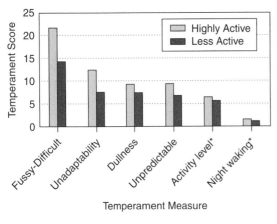

FIGURE 2.1   6-Month Temperament.
Comparison of infant temperament in babies who had been very active and less active fetuses.

*Indicates measures on which active and less active fetuses were not statistically significantly different.

Source: From DiPietro, J. A., Hodgson, D. M., Costigan, K. A., & Johnson, T. R. B. (1996). Fetal antecedents of infant temperament. *Child Development, 67,* 2568–2583.

appreciate the extent of individual differences in these characteristics. Current research in human development, such as the study reported in this chapter, consistently finds a variety of factors at work in shaping development. One of these, but only one, is innate biology.

CRITICAL THINKING TOOLKIT ITEMS

Correlations must be quite strong before they have much predictive power. If someone says, "There is a correlation between X and Y," they have said almost nothing of importance. Literally, this means only that the correlation is not zero. Low correlations, positive or negative, have little predictive power. As a rule of thumb, square the correlation to see what percent of variance it explains.

Strong correlations may be the result of cause-and-effect relationships. However, the mere existence of a strong correlation does not confirm anything about cause. An experiment is required in order to draw causal conclusions. In contrast, a very weak correlation probably indicates that there is not a causal relationship between variables because, by definition, it indicates that the variables are not related in any way.

Usually, the first question a critical thinker should ask about some supposed fact of human behavior is "What was the research method used to find this?" If it was not an experiment, cause-and-effect conclusions are unwarranted.

REFERENCES

Amaral, D. G., Price, J. L., Pitkanen, A., & Carmichael, S. T. (1992). Anatomical organization of the primate amygdaloid complex. In J. P. Aggleton (Ed.), *The amygdala* (pp. 1–66). New York: Wiley.

Arcus, D. M., & Kagan, J. (1995). Temperament and craniofacial variation in the first two years. *Child Development, 66,* 1529–1540.

Bates, J. E., Freeland, C. A., & Lounsbury, M. L. (1979). Measurement of infant difficultness. *Child Development, 50,* 794–803.

Besinger, R., & Johnson, T. R. B. (1989). Doppler recordings of fetal movement. *Obstetrics and Gynecology, 74,* 277–280.

Brooks-Gunn, J., Klebanov, P., & Duncan, G. (1996). Ethnic differences in children's intelligence test scores: Role of economic deprivation, home environment, and maternal characteristics. *Child Development, 67,* 396–408.

Campbell, F., & Ramey, C. (1994). Effects of early intervention in intellectual and academic achievement: A follow-up study of children from low-income families. *Child Development, 65,* 684–698.

DiPietro, J. A., Hodgson, D. M., Costigan, K. A., & Johnson, T. R. B. (1996). Fetal antecedents of infant temperament. *Child Development, 67,* 2568–2583.

Kagan, J. (1994). *Galen's prophecy.* New York: Basic.

Kagan, J., Arcus, D., Snidman, N., Feng, W., Hendler, J., & Greene, S. (1994). Reactivity in infants: A cross-national comparison. *Developmental Psychology, 30,* 342–345.

Kagan, J., & Snidman, N. (1991). Temperamental factors in human development. *American Psychologist, 46,* 856–862.

Montgomery, R., & Haemmerlie, F. (1993). Undergraduate adjustment to college drinking behavior and fraternity membership. *Psychological Reports, 73,* 801–802.

Schaefer, J., Sykes, R., Rowley, R., & Baek, S. (1988, November). *Slow country music and drinking.* Paper presented at the 87th annual meeting of the American Anthropological Association, Phoenix, AZ.

Schlinger, H. D., & Poling, A. (1998). *Introduction to scientific psychology.* New York: Plenum.

Watson, J. B. (1924). *Behaviorism.* Chicago: University of Chicago Press.

■ ■ ■ ■ ■

CHAPTER 3

DRINKING WITHOUT THINKING

Each of us began as a fertilized egg, called a *zygote*. In ordinary biological reproduction, shortly after fertilization, your zygote moved down one of your mother's fallopian tubes. By the sixth day after conception your zygote had become a group of cells. At about this time, you began to run out of the nutrients that were contained in your egg. You secreted an enzyme that ate a hole in your mother's uterine wall. Using the space thus created, you attached to your mother's circulatory system as a way of getting some nutrition from her. You did this by sending out tendrils that penetrated your mother's bloodstream. By about the 14th day you were fully attached to her, a process called *implantation.* One of your first projects was to secrete hormones and other substances that prevented menstrual periods, the shedding of the uterine lining to which you were attached. In addition, you used some chemical messages that kept your mother's immune system from reacting to you as a foreign object and rejecting you. Your first two weeks of life were a considerable challenge. As many as 30 percent of developing human organisms do not make it this far (Sadler, 1995).

The thin tendrils that attached you to your mother's bloodstream subsequently increased in size and changed shape, eventually becoming a disk-shaped structure called the *placenta.* As the original tendrils elongated, they became the umbilical cord, a long tube of blood vessels. This allowed you to remain attached to your mother's bloodstream and have some mobility within the uterus as you grew larger.

As a developing organism in your mother's uterus, your blood and your mother's were not directly connected; you did not share a bloodstream. In the placenta, your circulatory system was separated from your mother's bloodstream by a semi-permeable membrane that allowed specific substances, other than blood, to pass in one direction or the other. Nutrients and oxygen from your mother's bloodstream would pass across the membrane, leaving her blood behind, joining your bloodstream ready for your consumption. Waste products from your bloodstream would pass the other way across the membrane, leaving your blood behind. They would move into your mother's circulatory system for subsequent excretion to the outside world. Be nice to Mom—at one time you used her for a toilet.

Although the placenta acts like a filter, it is a somewhat imperfect filter. Sometimes harmful substances in the mother's blood can move across the placenta into the blood of the developing organism. These substances are called *teratogens* ("ta-**rah**-to-jens") and they

Incorporating the research of H.-C. Steinhausen, J. Willms, and H.-L. Spohr, "Correlates of Psychopathology and Intelligence in Children with Fetal Alcohol Syndrome," 1994, *Journal of Child Psychology and Psychiatry, 35,* pp. 323-331.

can damage developmental processes. The steps that occur in the prenatal development process are the result of millions of years of evolution and any deviation from this normal prenatal developmental pattern, such as exposure to foreign substances, may be deleterious in some way. There are many different types of teratogens. Most of them originate in the environment beyond the mother's body. These teratogens get into her system and pass to the offspring across the placenta. Environmental pollutants, maternal diseases, and drugs are three of the most important categories of teratogens.

Teratogenic environmental pollutants include herbicides containing dioxin. Agent Orange, which was used in Vietnam, and the industrial chemicals called PCBs are two other well-known examples. Both of these pollutants have been banned from use in the United States, but they have permeated the environment and are found in organisms such as fish. These teratogens are associated with birth defects so severe that miscarriage often results. Lead is another teratogenic pollutant. While it is no longer put in gasoline or paint, lead is still around. For example, old houses can have many layers of old lead paint. This can be a problem if a pregnant woman comes in contact with a powdery, chipped, or otherwise unstable paint surface.

Rubella, sometimes called German measles, is an example of a teratogenic disease. If a mother is infected before about week 11 of the pregnancy there is a high probability that the baby will be deaf, have heart defects, and suffer intellectual deficiencies. These complications are less likely to occur if the mother is infected a few weeks later. After 16 weeks, there is almost no chance of harm to the fetus from rubella (Miller, Cradock-Watson, & Pollock, 1982).

Rubella exposure illustrates a somewhat surprising point: Often the effects of a teratogen are only damaging if exposure occurs during a certain period of time. This is a common phenomenon among teratogens. The action of these agents is often quite specific, affecting particular organs or systems. A reason why time periods are so circumscribed is that the potential for damage to a particular system may be greatest when that system is being built. Once the basic components of the auditory system, for example, have been laid down, the system is less likely to be damaged by the presence of a teratogen. Imagine that a skyscraper is being built. If a poor-quality load of concrete becomes part of the building, it would have a much larger impact on the overall structure if it were put in the foundation than if it were to become part of the wall of a coffee lounge on the 83rd floor. This building analogy may not be as fanciful as it seems. It illustrates the two essential characteristics of teratogenic damage: The most damaging exposure is likely to be early and to occur in the development of foundational structures.

Other diseases can also have teratogenic effects. As a group, sexually transmitted diseases can be particularly serious. The syphilis spirochete can cross the placenta, moving from mother to fetus. If the mother is in an advanced stage of the disease, the infection can be lethal to the offspring. Not all teratogens act by crossing the placenta. In some cases, direct contact is the means of transmission. Infants born to mothers with herpes can contract the disease while moving through the birth canal. About half of these babies die (Subak-Sharpe, 1984). The incubation period for herpes can be as long as 21 days, so babies may develop symptoms such as hepatitis, pneumonia, blood clots, or brain damage in the weeks after they have left the hospital (Larson, 1987).

While we have been pointing out the failures of the placenta, it nevertheless frequently functions to protect the developing fetus from harmful substances in the mother's blood. It is a good, but not perfect, barrier for disease. It may not be successful at protecting the fetus from dangerous drugs. There are many drugs available to mothers now that were not around during the millions of years during which the placenta evolved. There is no particular reason why we should expect the placenta to recognize and exclude modern drugs. There has not been enough time for biological evolution to create a placenta that can discriminate among drugs that have appeared in the past few years.

A few of the drugs that are known teratogens are listed in Table 3.1. It should be apparent that the best advice for a woman who is planning to get pregnant is to avoid any and all substances that are suspected teratogens. A health care provider who is knowledgeable about drug effects should be consulted before a woman who may be pregnant takes any prescription or over-the-counter drugs. The importance of education about teratogens is highlighted by the time periods during which teratogens do the most damage. As noted earlier, this generally occurs quite early in the pregnancy and can even happen before the woman knows she is pregnant. For example, a woman who plans to stop taking a drug "when I get pregnant" is likely to take the drug during the first 4 to 6 weeks of pregnancy, when the fetal damage is done.

"Recreational" drugs are included in Table 3.1. While they are in no particular order, alcohol happens to be at the top. Many people do not understand that alcohol is a drug. The teratogenic effects of alcohol have been widely studied because, sadly, there are many cases of birth defects resulting from prenatal alcohol exposure. Collectively these effects are called fetal alcohol syndrome (FAS). This syndrome was first described in the late 1960s. A number of psychological and physiological characteristics are now considered to be symptoms of FAS. Children who have been prenatally exposed to alcohol may show symptoms of FAS, such as delayed motor or intellectual development. FAS may also produce facial abnormalities but is perhaps better known as a leading precursor of mental retardation (Jacobson & Jacobson, 1996). It may affect as many as 2 children per 1,000 births (Abel & Sokol, 1987) In this chapter we will look more closely at a piece of research by Steinhausen,

TABLE 3.1 Various Drugs That Can Act as Teratogens

ANTIBIOTICS	HORMONAL AGENTS	RECREATIONAL DRUGS	TRANQUILIZERS
Quinine, Quinidine	Androgens	Alcohol	Valium
Streptomycin	Diethylstilbestrol (DES)	Caffeine	Librium
Sulfonamides	Insulin	Nicotine	Meprobamate
Tetracyclines	Oral Contraceptives	Cocaine	Phenothiazines
		Marijuana	Thalidomide
		Methadone	

THERAPEUTIC DRUGS

Antihistamines (for sinus problems)	Accutane (acne treatment)
Dilantin (antiseizure drug)	Didrex (appetite suppressant)
Barbiturates (for sleep disorders)	
Aspirin	

Willms, and Spohr (1994). They conducted a study that identified correlates of FAS in long-term observations of a large group of children who had been diagnosed with FAS.

The methodology in this particular study is called a *cross-sectional research design.* This means that two age groups consisting of different children—in this case, preschool and school-age—were studied. If the same children had been studied at two different points in their life span, the study would have been considered longitudinal, not cross-sectional. Although the data presented here are cross-sectional, the children were also part of a larger longitudinal study and had been followed from 1977 to 1991.

PARTICIPANTS

The participants in this study were part of a group of 158 children who had been diagnosed with FAS. The children were referred for the study owing to the researchers' expertise in developmental disorders. Children joined the study at various ages from birth to 11.5 years old. Most of the children lived in Berlin, Germany.

PROCEDURE

A variety of different measures were taken on the children. These included medical and psychiatric assessments. The FAS diagnostic criteria included a confirmation of maternal alcohol abuse and

1. Prenatal or postnatal retardation of growth placing children in the bottom 10 percent of growth rate for normal children
2. Evidence of central nervous system (CNS) dysfunction such as lack of normal intellectual functioning
3. Two of the following three craniofacial (skull or face) abnormalities:
   a. Head circumference placing individual in bottom 3 percent of age group
   b. Microphthalmia or short palpebral fissures (abnormally small eyes)
   c. Flat filtrum (area above upper lip) or thin upper lip

ASSESSMENT OF IMPAIRMENT

Psychiatric impairment was assessed based on structured interviews designed for preschoolers (Richman & Graham, 1971) and school-age children (Rutter, Tizard, & Whitmore, 1970). These interviews were designed to allow the person conducting the assessment to diagnose and evaluate problem behavior. Psychopathology was rated for severity on 3- or 4-point scales. Each child was rated in this way for individual examples of psychopathology and, in addition, a total psychopathology score was derived by adding together the individual ratings. The psychopathologies that were rated are listed in Table 3.2.

Children were also given standardized intelligence tests. A standardized test is one in which average scores within a large population are known and individuals can be compared to these population averages. Obvious physical deformities, or morphological abnormalities,

TABLE 3.2   Pathologies Assessed in the Structured Interviews

Enuresis—lack of control over urination

Encopresis—lack of control over fecal elimination

Speech Disorders—including slurring and stuttering as well as abnormal expression of ideas

Eating Disorders—overeating or undereating

Sleep Disorders—insomnia or too much sleep

Stereotypies/Abnormal Habits—including repetitive behaviors without obvious function

Depression—depressed mood

Anxiety—fear of situations

Dependency Problems—for example, dependency on drugs or other substances

Relationship Problems—including problems with friendship or love

Conduct Disorders—including antisocial behavior such as aggression

Hyperkinetic Disorders—including inability to sit still

Note: The examples following each term are to help you understand what kind of behavior was assessed.

Source: From Steinhausen, H.-C., Willms, J., & Spohr, H.-L. (1994). Correlates of psychopathology and intelligence in children with fetal alcohol syndrome. *Journal of Child Psychology and Psychiatry, 35,* 323–331.

such as the craniofacial features mentioned previously, were assessed during a pediatric medical exam by one of the study authors.

RESULTS

The morphological characteristics of FAS turned out to be fairly good indicators of the extent of psychopathology. When children were divided into three groups based on severity of morphological damage, increasing severity was associated with increases in total psychopathology scores for both preschool children and school-age children. These data are shown in Figure 3.1. The differences associated with severity in Figure 3.1 were statistically significant for both preschoolers ($p = .03$) and school-age children ($p = .01$). The extent of each specific type of psychopathology at differing levels of morphological damage is shown in Figure 3.2.

There is a great deal of information in Figure 3.2. One of the things we want you to learn to do is to look at the graphs and tables in these chapters and to summarize the contents of them in a sentence or two. This necessarily involves looking beyond some of the individual findings and trying, instead, to see one or a few general descriptive trends. There is no way to arrive at summary statements of complex data that will satisfy everyone. One of the ways you might approach Figure 3.2 is to look along the columns trying to see if any one of the three levels of morphological damage appears to be consistently associated with higher or lower levels of specific pathologies. With a few exceptions, you can see that the severe group appears to score higher than the other two groups. Likewise, scan-

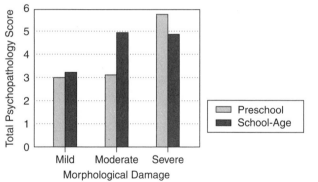

FIGURE 3.1   Morphological Damage and Psychopathology. Total psychopathology scores in preschool and school-age children with fetal alcohol syndrome shown by extent of observed morphological damage.

Source: From Steinhausen, H.-C., Willms, J., & Spohr, H.-L. (1994). Correlates of psychopathology and intelligence in children with fetal alcohol syndrom. *Journal of Child Psychology and Psychiatry, 35,* 325.

ning across for the low-scoring group, those children with the mild morphological damage seem to have lower pathology scores for most disorders. In order to judge the importance of the differences that you can see, it is helpful to know if these differences are statistically significant. The severe group scores were significantly different for enuresis ($p = .004$), encopresis ($p = .04$), speech disorders ($p = .007$), and depression ($p = .0001$).

Measured IQ also showed a relationship with the extent of morphological damage, as can be seen in Figure 3.3. The differences shown are significant ($p < .007$). The IQ scores of the children with severe morphological damage fall below 70, sufficient to classify them as having mild mental retardation. This would predict that they might be able to learn academic skills up to about a sixth-grade level. As adults they might be able to live independently if

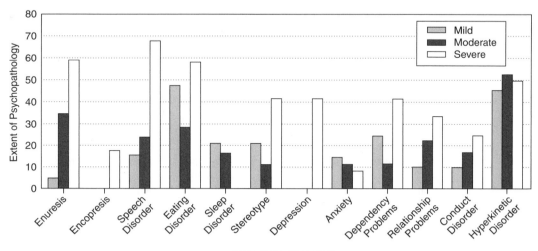

FIGURE 3.2   Morphology and Specific Psychopathology. Specific psychopathologies found in children with fetal alcohol syndrome, shown by extent of observed morphological damage.

Source: From Steinhausen, H.-C., Willms, J., & Spohr, H.-L. (1994). Correlates of psychopathology and intelligence in children with fetal alcohol syndrome. *Journal of Child Psychology and Psychiatry, 35,* 323–331.

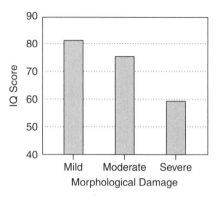

FIGURE 3.3   Morphology and IQ Score. Extent of morphological damage and IQ score in children with fetal alcohol syndrome.

given assistance with vocational and social skills. The IQ scores for the other two groups are above 70 but below 100 and might predict some vocational and academic limitations. Although there was no control group in this study, in a way, using an IQ score was a way of comparing these children to a non-FAS control group. In a large population of people, the average IQ score is 100. This large population could be considered the control group because although population IQs were not measured specifically for the purposes of this study they can be used as a comparison to evaluate the outcomes of FAS.

Although the data are not shown here, the preschoolers with the lowest IQ scores (equal to, or less than, 50) also had significantly higher frequencies for several psychopathologies: speech disorders ($p = .0006$), eating disorders ($p = .003$), depression ($p = .04$), dependency problems ($p = .001$) and hyperkinetic disorders ($p = .006$).

DISCUSSION

This study presented evidence of the long-term effects of FAS. The mothers of these children had abused alcohol during pregnancy, and the end result appears to have been morphological damage as well as considerable psychopathology in the children. Low IQ scores were also associated with morphological damage. Morphological damage seems to be a marker for other problems; knowing the extent of this damage in FAS permits cautious predictions to be made about levels of IQ and psychopathology.

From a methodological standpoint this study has a number of strengths and some weaknesses. We want you to acquire skills in the evaluation of assertions about behavior, particularly when those assertions are the result of research. This study included a fairly large number of participants with FAS. This is a strength because the results are less likely to be biased by a few unusual children who might not be typical of FAS cases. In large numbers, kids with FAS who are not typical for the disorder will contribute to results, but will not dramatically alter findings that are expressed as arithmetic means. Structured interviews are another strength. The interviews that were used to collect data on psychopathology followed specified standard procedures. If the interview content had been able to change at the whim of the person doing the assessment, there would be no consistency from child to child and no possibility of repeating the observations with different groups in the future.

This study can be criticized because it lacked control groups. While a control group might seem contrived in a study of this nature, it would provide a valuable baseline against which to measure the effects of FAS. It is difficult to judge the magnitude of the psycho-pathologic outcomes of FAS without reference to a group of non-FAS children who have been evaluated using the same structured interviews. As we noted, this was not a problem with the intelligence test part of the assessment.

The study can also be criticized because it appears that the researchers doing the assessments were aware of the hypothesis. As we noted in Chapter 1, it is good research procedure to try to ensure that individuals who are involved in collecting data from participants are unaware of the nature of the variables in the study. In this way researcher expectations, however subtle, cannot influence the results. In this study the presence of morphological abnormalities may have made it practically impossible to ensure unawareness in those doing the psychopathological assessments. Nevertheless, our confidence in the findings might increase if there had been some attempt to achieve this.

People who do not understand science are likely to think that scientific studies "prove" things. We will always use softer language in deference to the imperfections that are found in any study. Because no study is perfect, study findings do not warrant conclusions that are as absolute-sounding as the word *prove* might imply. Rather, scientists talk about the amount of confidence that may be placed in a study, based on perceived strengths and weaknesses. Except in the case of a serious confound, these weaknesses do not negate the findings of a study. The savvy person will weigh a study's strengths and weaknesses to make an informed decision about how much confidence to have in its findings. Confidence in study findings may be based on more than the structure of an individual study. Confidence may be boosted if the findings are consistent with findings of other studies that have investigated similar questions using different participants and procedures. In the case of this study, the findings are consistent with other studies of children with FAS (Streissgath, Bookstein, Sampson, & Barr, 1993).

The long-term effects of FAS were illustrated by the existence of psychopathologies in the school-age children. This illustrates a developmental phenomenon called a *sensitive period.* Older literature used the term *critical period* to describe the same thing. A sensitive period is a short period of time during which some kind of experience makes irreversible changes in the course of development. For this study, the early part of pregnancy is the "short period of time" in the definition; the "experience" is alcohol exposure; and the "changes" are the physiology that underlies the morphological damage and psychopathology.

Teratogens do not have to be administered in massive doses in order to have serious effects. Although the mothers in the study by Steinhausen et al. (1994) were all abusers of alcohol, lower amounts of alcohol consumption have also been implicated. Moderate social drinking such as one glass of wine or beer a day can result in symptoms associated with FAS (Jacobson & Jacobson, 1996). The danger of teratogenic alcohol for the woman who is unaware that she has become pregnant should be obvious. The use of alcohol can lead to serious developmental damage.

Older theories about human psychological development postulated many critical periods. For example, Freud believed that the experiences of the first five years—the time when boys fall in love with their mothers and fear penile-related retribution from their fathers—produced irreversible changes in the personality of the boys. This nonsensical assertion cannot be evaluated by scientific research because the postulated happenings occur unconsciously and are not subject to observation, manipulation, or both. Critics of our position may say something such as "Freud's ideas cannot be falsified, or shown to be incorrect, so they may be correct" (for a version of this, see Horgan, 1996, p. 111). We believe that this particular defense of any notion, including those of Freud, is absurd. There are many ideas that might be treated in this manner, but it is unreasonable to go through life acting as if all events that cannot be shown to be incorrect should be considered to be correct. A giant asteroid, which no astronomer has noticed, is going to strike the earth within the next hour, resulting in the total destruction of the planet. As phrased, this cannot be demonstrated to be incorrect, but you would probably not want to consider it to be correct. If you did, we doubt that you would bother finishing this article. Would you spend your last half hour on Earth studying psychology?

CRITICAL THINKING TOOLKIT ITEMS

Check to ensure that the researchers who have direct contact with participants are, whenever possible, unaware of hypotheses or group assignment.

Avoid absolutist language, such as saying that a study has "proved" something, because all studies have practical limitations or other weaknesses.

Consider the weight of evidence—such as the findings of similar studies—when forming an opinion about confidence in the findings of a particular study.

REFERENCES

Abel, E. L., & Sokol, R. J. (1987). Incidence of fetal alcohol syndrome and economic impact of FAS-related anomalies. *Drug and Alcohol Dependency, 19,* 51–70.

American Psychological Association. (1994). *Publication manual of the American Psychological Association* (4th ed.). Washington, DC: Author.

Horgan, J. (1996, December). Why Freud isn't dead. *Scientific American, 275,* 106–111.

Jacobson, J. L., & Jacobson, S. W. (1996). Prospective longitudinal assessment of developmental neurotoxicity. *Environment Health Perspectives, 104,* 275–283.

Larson, E. (1987). Trends in neonatal infections. *Journal of Obstetrical Gynecological and Neonatal Nursing, 16,* 404–409.

Miller, E., Cradock-Watson, J. E., & Pollock, T. M. (1982, October). Consequences of confirmed maternal rubella and successive stages of pregnancy. *Lancet, 2* (8302), 781–784.

Richman, N., & Graham, P. J. (1971). A behavioral screening questionnaire for use with three-year-old children—Preliminary findings. *Journal of Child Psychology and Psychiatry, 12,* 5–33.

Rutter, M., Tizard, J., & Whitmore, K. (1970). *Education health and behaviour.* London: Longman.

Sadler, T. W. (1995). *Langman's medical embryology* (7th ed.). Baltimore: Williams & Wilkins.

Steinhausen, H. -C., Willms, J., & Spohr, H. -L. (1994). Correlates of psychopathology and intelligence in children with fetal alcohol syndrome. *Journal of Child Psychology and Psychiatry, 35,* 323–331.

Streissgath, A. P., Bookstein, F. L., Sampson, P. D., & Barr, H. M. (1993). *The enduring effects of prenatal alcohol exposure on child development, birth through seven years: A partial least-squares solution.* Ann Arbor: University of Michigan Press.

Subak-Sharpe, G. J. (Ed.). (1984). Genital herpes. *The physician's manual for patients* (pp. 370–372). New York: Times Books.

Vorhees, C. V., & Mallnow, E. (1987). Behavioral teratogenesis: Long-term influences on behavior from early exposure to environmental agents. In J. D. Osofosky (Ed.), *Handbook of infant development* (2nd ed., pp. 913–971). New York: Wiley.

■ ■ ■ ■ ■

CHAPTER 4

THE NOSE KNOWS

We are sure that you have heard someone say that some people and certain animals possess a "maternal instinct." It is not clear what is meant by this phrase, especially when human beings are concerned. One definition of this phenomenon describes a supposedly unlearned set of responses possessed by all mothers as part of their genetic endowments (Bowlby, 1973). These instinctual responses, such as bonding to the infant, are popularly thought to appear when a mother sees an infant, usually her own biological offspring. Popular culture seems to suggest an almost magical bond between mothers and their babies. This bond is supposed to be instantaneous and automatic, with deep and mysterious causes. In contrast, psychological research has found many prosaic factors that are involved in attachment between mothers and infants.

In a famous series of studies on monkeys, Harry Harlow (1958) demonstrated that an infant's love for its mother depended upon the availability of contact comfort—that warm, snugly feeling an infant gets when being held. Harlow gave infant monkeys a choice between spending time on a model mother made of cold, hard wire that fed them with a bottle or a mother made of soft, cuddly cloth, that did not feed the infants. The infants bonded to the cloth mothers and went to the wire mothers only when they were hungry. Harlow's work could be considered a negation of Freud's assertion that attachment between child and mother happens because mothers satisfy their baby's need for oral gratification through sucking. As with most of Freud's ideas, this one is easily called into question by any scientifically oriented critical thinker who investigates the research methods used by Freud to collect the so-called *data*.

Bonding is not merely a matter of an infant becoming attached to a caregiver; it also includes the caregiver, parent or otherwise, becoming attached to the baby. A few parent variables that have been shown to make a difference in attachment are the extent to which the parental style is controlling (Mangelsdorf, Gunnar, Kestenbaum, Lang, & Andreas, 1990); the parent's social relationships with other adults (Levitt, Weber, & Clark, 1986); and the sensitiveness of parental response to the infant (Belsky, Gilstrap, & Rovine, 1984).

It has been known for a long time that odor recognition between mothers and offspring is an important part of bonding in nonhuman animals (Porter, Cernoch, & Balogh, 1985). Based on this evidence it might seem reasonable to think that smell would play an important role in early bonding between human mothers and their infants. Do you think

Incorporating the research of A. Fleming, C. Corter, M. Surbey, P. Franks, & M. Steiner, "Postpartum Factors Related to Mother's Recognition of Newborn Infant Odours," 1995, *Journal of Reproductive and Infant Psychology, 13,* pp. 197–210.

your mother would recognize you by your smell? Are we like other animals in that regard? Fleming, Corter, Surbey, Franks, and Steiner (1995) investigated the ability of new mothers to recognize their infants by smell.

PARTICIPANTS

The participants in the research reported by Fleming et al. (1995) were women who had become new mothers within the previous 5 days. These mothers were contacted in the hospital where their babies were born. They were primarily Caucasian and of middle to upper middle socioeconomic status (SES). They were married and ranged in age from 20 to 39 (*M* = 29) They had no known history of psychiatric or gynecological problems. Their babies were born in full-term vaginal deliveries.

The women were approached on the first day following birth and asked if they would be willing to take part in a study involving parental responses to odorants, including those from infant, adult, and synthetic origins. Parents who agreed were asked to provide samples of body odors from their infants by means of supplying a T-shirt which had been worn by their baby for 8 to 10 hours on the first, second, or third day of life.

The control group participants were recruited from introductory psychology classes. The criteria for selection were the same as for the groups of mothers, except that the students did not have children. They were primarily unmarried and ranged in age from 18 to 42 (*M* = 24).

QUESTIONNAIRES

Mothers were given questionnaires that asked about demographics, their experiences in giving birth, the amount of time they had spent with their infant, and their feelings about the new baby. The questionnaires had been used in an earlier study by Fleming, Ruble, Flett, and Shaul (1988) in which the ability of the questions to measure maternal characteristics was under investigation. Sometimes psychology questionnaires are called *soft measures* because they are not direct observations of behavior. It is well known that people's recollections about the past may not be accurate (Neisser & Harsch, 1992). The outcomes measured for the mothers, such as feelings about the new baby, were operationally defined as questionnaire responses.

The field of psychometrics involves the study of the construction of psychological tests, including questionnaires, and other psychological scales. These instruments can be more accurate if they are carefully constructed. While *soft measure* may seem a somewhat pejorative term for them, you should be aware that not all tests, questionnaires, or scales necessarily yield poor-quality data. If you are trying to make a decision about the quality of a soft measure, you should seek information about the psychometric qualities of reliability and validity.

RELIABILITY AND VALIDITY

In a discussion of agreement between observers, Chapter 1 introduced the concept of reliability in the form of interobserver reliability. In a more general sense, reliability means that a measure is repeatable and the same outcome will be found when people are retested with the same instrument. A reliable questionnaire given to mothers asking about their first birth experience should produce the same results if given immediately following birth and one week later. This measurement characteristic is often mentioned along with another one, validity. Validity refers to the accuracy of the measurement. A test, questionnaire, or scale is valid if it measures what it is supposed to measure. Often if a measure is valid, it is also reliable. However, a valid measure cannot be reliable if the characteristic being measured changes rapidly. For example, in a carefully conducted longitudinal study of the academic outcomes associated with nutritional supplements in Guatemala, Gorman and Pollitt (1996, p. 316) said that they had "no reliable measure of family size." This was not because it was impossible to record the sizes of families over the years. Instead it was because the sizes of families kept changing over time. In this case a valid measure was not reliable. Even professionals working in psychology sometimes confuse these terms, saying "reliable" when they mean "valid." Reliability and validity are different concepts that sometimes overlap and we would like you to aim for precision when using them.

If you want to critically evaluate research that has used a test, questionnaire, or scale to measure some characteristic, you may be able to find evidence for reliability, validity, or both. This information might be found within the study itself or in journal articles that are referenced in the article. If the measure is a published instrument, information about these characteristics may be found in volumes that consist wholly of reviews of psychological measures, such as *Tests* (Maddox, 1997) or *Tests in Print IV* (Murphy, Conoley, & Impara, 1994).

BEHAVIOR OBSERVATIONS

The study by Fleming et al. (1995) was unusual in the number of different research methods used to address the main question. In addition to the questionnaire soft measures, Fleming et al. (1995) also employed what we will call a *hard measure,* that is, a direct observation of behavior. In this study, new mothers were observed feeding their babies during a single 10-minute period. A researcher entered the behavior observations directly into a laptop computer. A typical way to approach this type of data collection is to use a form with pre-constructed categories for behavior. The form should be designed to be convenient to use. As each behavior happens, the observer enters it into the data record by marking the appropriate place on the form displayed by the computer. Usually, the computer is able to keep track of a time scale as well, recording when each behavior happens. The categories that were recorded in the Fleming et al. study included such things as looking at the baby's face, affectionate contact (such as stroking or hugging, talking or singing to the baby), and caregiving such as burping or arranging covers. The behaviors listed above for this study were operationally defined by the procedure of observing and entering observations into the categories specified in the computer. You will remember from Chapter 1 that an operational definition describes variables in terms of the way they are measured.

To examine interobserver reliability for the behavior-recording scheme, two independent observers watched 6 to 10 videotapes of nursing mothers. In a pilot test, different observers agreed between 70 percent and 100 percent of the time (Fleming, Steiner & Anderson, 1987; Fleming et al., 1988)

Study 1 Procedures

Compared to other stimuli such as sound or light, odors are difficult to collect and dispense. In order to achieve reliable amounts of participant exposure to infant body odors, careful procedures were followed. Infants were clothed in 100 percent cotton T-shirts for one of their first three days of life. At all times, the babies wore infant hospital gowns over the T-shirts. This was done to try to minimize other odors on the T-shirts. The 23 mothers who participated in Study 1 were asked not to use substances on themselves or their infants that would add smells, such as deodorant, perfumes, or perfumed products. They were instructed to use only the hospital soap on themselves and their babies.

When the T-shirt containing the baby's odor was removed from the infant, it was placed in a 250-ml glass jar and frozen at −30°C until it was to be used for testing. An hour before the test, the shirts were removed from the freezer and allowed to return to room temperature. For presentation to the mothers, shirts were placed in open plastic bags within cardboard buckets of the type that are used for dispensing ice cream.

Study 1 centered on a recognition task in which mothers were given two of the buckets containing T-shirts. All of the participants in Study 1 were new mothers: there was no control group per se. Instead, each mother served as her own control because she was exposed to the odor of both her own infant's T-shirt and the T-shirt of another infant. The buckets were presented in a randomized order and each was presented three times. Mothers were allowed as much time as they wanted to sniff each bucket and to make a judgment as to whether the T-shirt was from their own infant or another infant.

Study 2 Procedures

Study 2 used 62 mothers meeting the same criteria as Study 1. However, this time their performance was compared to the control participants from introductory psychology classes. These control participants consisted of 38 males and 40 females. The odor recognition task was different than in Study 1. In Study 2, participants were presented with three different stimulus odors: infant T-shirts, adult sweat, and scented lotion.

The infant T-shirts were collected and frozen as in Study 1. In addition, human sweat was collected from male and female volunteer donors. These donors were instructed not to shave their armpits or use deodorants for a week before the sweat odors were collected. They were asked to bathe with a nonscented soap. On the day that odors were collected, they wore 10 cm × 10 cm cotton pads taped to their clothing in the vicinity of their armpits. The pads were worn for 8 to 10 hours during a normal day. At the end of this time, the pads were placed into 100-ml glass jars and frozen until they were required for the study.

The scented lotions which were used as part of this study were aloe cream, Nivea cream, and Keri cream. An hour before testing, these lotions were put on cotton swabs and placed in sterilized, freshly washed, plastic squeeze bottles with narrow spouts. For the purposes of testing, the sweat samples and the T-shirts were defrosted and also placed in squeeze bottles. In the test situations, participants were told to aim the spout of the bottle at the top lip under the center of the nose and "to squeeze gently, producing a steady stream of odorized air" (Fleming et al., 1995).

Participants received three series of odor exposure tests, one for each type of stimulus: infant T-shirt, human sweat, and lotion. The procedure was a preexposure recognition task. Participants were exposed for a period of 10 seconds to one odor from one of the three stimulus types, for example, Nivea cream. This was followed by a 30-second interval and then another 10-second exposure to the same odor. The odor, in this example Nivea cream, was designated the *target odor*. Some participants waited 30 seconds and some waited 180 seconds for the study to continue. Following this interval, participants were given three recognition tests of 5-second duration separated by 30-second intervals. Continuing the example of the lotion scent, these recognition tests presented each odor once: Nivea, Aloe, and Keri. The order of the stimuli in the recognition tests was randomized. The task of the participants was to recognize which of the three odors in each short recognition test was the target odor to which they had been preexposed. For this part of the study, the infant T-shirts that were used were from infants who were all unfamiliar to the mothers.

Forty of the mothers in Study 2 were given an additional test. First, their own or another infant's T-shirt was presented as the target odor. This was followed 30 seconds later by the presentation of three odors (own infant and two other infants) as a recognition task. Half of the mothers had this task before the lotion-sweat-T-shirt recognition trials and half had it afterwards.

Participants were not told what any target stimulus was and they were not told if they had been correct in odor recognition. Instructions were presented by a tape recorder in order to ensure that each participant heard the same thing. Bottles were numbered for presentation by the experimenter. The participants' scores were the number of correctly recognized target odors.

RESULTS

In Study 1, the spontaneous recognition task, the mothers demonstrated that they were able to identify their own infant's T-shirt in the two-bucket task. In random presentation of infant T-shirts, they correctly identified their own infant's shirt. Combining all trials, mothers chose correctly 82.6 percent of the time.

Study 2 was designed to see if mothers and the control group could recognize odors to which they had been preexposed. If we believed that mothers have a special or heightened ability to recognize the smell of babies, we might have suspected that mothers would be better at recognition of infant T-shirt odors. When tested with T-shirts that did not belong to their own infant, they were as good as people who were not mothers at recognizing the scent of an unfamiliar infant. These data are found in Figure 4.1. Although there might appear from Figure 4.1 to be some differences, there were no significant differences seen between the performances of mothers, non-mother females, and males. The performance of all three types of participants was similar for all three types of odor (sweat, lotion, T-shirt).

Remember that the data in Figure 4.1 were from mothers who were exposed to unfamiliar infant T-shirts. As you can see, changing the presentation interval from 30 seconds to 3 minutes did not make much difference in the pattern of the outcomes. When there are

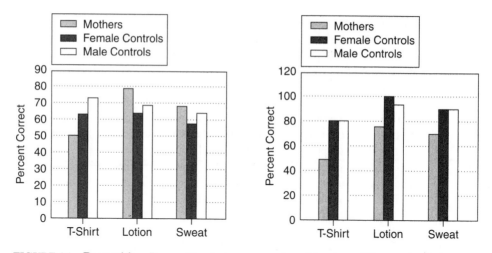

FIGURE 4.1   Recognition. Recognition tests were conducted for three different stimulus categories with a 30-second (left) or 3-minute (right) interval between presentation of the target and the test stimuli. Infant T-shirts were unfamiliar to all participants in the comparisons shown here.

Source: From Fleming, A., Corter, C., Surbey, M., Franks, P., & Steiner, M. (1995). Postpartum factors related to mother's recognition of newborn infant odours. *Journal of Reproductive and Infant Psychology, 13,* 204.

three choices the chance level for success is 33 percent. All of the participants—mothers and others—achieved recognition scores that significantly exceeded the chance level. Significance levels ranged from $p < .04$ to $p < .0001$.

In the three-choice trial in which mothers were preexposed either to their own infant's T-shirt or the T-shirt of another infant, the mothers could recognize their own infant's shirt but they were not better at recognizing their own infant's shirt compared to that of another infant. The data for this are shown in Figure 4.2.

Data from these mothers who had taken part in Study 2 were divided into three groups based on their recognition performance for infant odors.

1. *Consistently Accurate:* Those who were correct in their identification of infant odor (own infant and other) on all three trials (25 percent of the mothers).

FIGURE 4.2   New Mother's Recognition Performance. Recognition performance of new mothers when the preexposure target stimulus was either their own infant's T-shirt or that of an unfamiliar infant.

Source: From Fleming, A., Corter, C., Surbey, M., Franks, P., & Steiner, M. (1995). Postpartum factors related to mother's recognition of newborn infant odours. *Journal of Reproductive and Infant Psychology, 13,* 204.

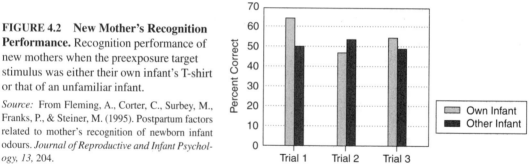

2. *Consistently Inaccurate:* Those who were incorrect about infant odors on all three trials (17 percent of mothers).
3. *Inconsistent:* Those who were correct some of the time (57 percent of mothers).

Mothers in these three groups were compared on several background measures derived from questionnaires in the study. Mothers who consistently correctly recognized their own infant's T-shirt had started nursing the baby more quickly following birth than other mothers ($p < .01$). They also spent more time in contact with their infant during the first 12 hours following birth ($p < .05$). These data are shown in Figure 4.3. There were no significant differences between the three groups of mothers when they were trying to recognize the T-shirt odors of unfamiliar infants.

The attitudes of the mothers also had a relationship to their recognition of preexposed infant odors. The consistently inaccurate recognition group had more negative feelings about children ($p <. 05$). The consistently inaccurate women also had less experience with newborns prior to having their own baby ($p < .01$). No significant differences were found among groups in the quantity of routine caregiving that infants received from their mothers.

During the naturalistic observations, the amounts of time the mothers spent in close proximity to the infant and in affectionate interaction with the infant were recorded. These are reported in Figure 4.4. In spite of the variability in the data presented in Figure 4.4, you can see that the consistently accurate group of mothers had more nasal proximity. This difference was statistically significant at the $p < .01$ level. It might look as if there were more affectionate behavior in this group than the inconsistent group, but the difference between consistent and inconsistent groups was not significant ($p < .08$). The consistently inaccurate group is not shown in Figure 4.4 because there was no obvious trend in the data for that group.

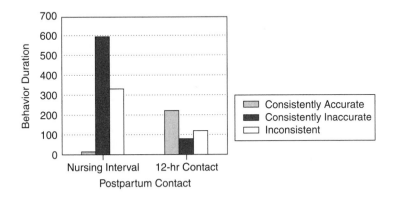

FIGURE 4.3   Proximity Measures for Mother Recognition Groups.
Time interval (in minutes) between birth and first nursing and amount of time spent with infant in first 12 hours following birth for mothers who always recognized their own infant's scent (consistently accurate), mothers who never recognized their infant's scent (consistently inaccurate), and mothers who sometimes recognized their infant's scent (inconsistent).

Source: From Fleming, A., Corter, C., Surbey, M., Franks, P., & Steiner, M. (1995). Postpartum factors related to mother's recognition of newborn infant odours. *Journal of Reproductive and Infant Psychology, 13,* 205.

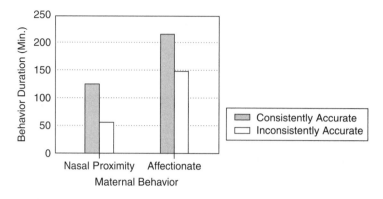

FIGURE 4.4 Naturalistic Observations. Results from the naturalistic observation include data on proximity and affection from mothers who were consistent and mothers who were inconsistent in recognizing their own infant's T-shirt by smell.

Source: From Fleming, A., Corter, C., Surbey, M., Franks, P., & Steiner, M. (1995). Postpartum factors related to mother's recognition of newborn infant odours. *Journal of Reproductive and Infant Psychology, 13,* 206.

DISCUSSION

As we will often see in studies, the outcomes here are not as straightforward as we would like them to be. For example, the outcomes of this study would be easier to recount to a friend if all mothers were better at recognizing the smell of their own infant's T-shirts compared to those of other infants, or if all mothers who could recognize their own infant's shirts were more experienced mothers on each variable measured.

One reason why findings in psychology are rarely as clear-cut as this is that there is enormous variability within populations of organisms, human and otherwise. In the typical psychology study, people are divided into a few groups based on some difference among them. In an experiment the difference is created by the researcher, as we saw in Chapter 1 where newborns were exposed to different sounds manipulated by the experimenters. In other types of studies, the differences that result in assignment to groups are preexisting; they are not created by a researcher. For example, some studies of teratogen exposure may compare babies who were exposed to a teratogen with babies who were not exposed. Babies were not randomly assigned to receive these treatments from experimenters; instead, they received them before the research began.

It is unlikely that the differences between groups of people in studies, whether created or preexisting, are the only differences among participants. Researchers try to identify and control or randomize systematic differences between groups, but group members will still not be the same in every way excepting the characteristic being studied. While unknown or uncontrolled differences among participants may not make a systematic difference between groups, they will contribute to the variability within each group that may act to mask or obscure whatever systematic differences are there.

If you think about the thousands of differences which might exist within a group of new mothers, it may even begin to seem surprising that anything systematic is found when they are sorted into groups based merely on ability to recognize infant T-shirt odors. A careful approach is required to find relationships among groups of people. The best means yet devised for doing this is science. People who do not understand psychological science may tend to denigrate the importance of findings that are not all-or-none—for example, all mothers do this; all infants are like that. To expect all-or-none outcomes is to show an ignorance of the diversity that exists among human beings.

Understanding that study results will contain some unexplained and uncontrolled variability, how can we summarize what was learned from the work of Fleming et al. in this study? There appeared to be nothing mystical or surprising about the ability of mothers to recognize odors of any sort, including the odors of infants. Mothers performed well in Study 1 when they had to choose their infant's scent. However, in the Study 2 task where matching to a target stimulus was required, all participants did well. Mothers were not superior to non-mother females or males. Perhaps surprisingly, mothers were not better than others at matching the target scent of their own infants compared to the scent of other infants as shown in Figure 4.2. One reason for this may have been that mothers were quite good at recognizing any odor.

However, some mothers were better than others at recognizing the smell of their own infants. Here, again, there was no need to resort to any hypothesis of instinctively heightened sensory abilities. A few reasons why some mothers were better at odor recognition of their own infants were suggested by rearranging mothers into groups that were consistently accurate, consistently inaccurate, and inconsistent at recognizing their own infant's T-shirt. Mothers who were consistently accurate had experienced a shorter interval between birth and the start of nursing and had more contact with their infants in the first 12 hours following birth. More contact with the infant in the first 12 hours might have provided more experience with the odor of the infant. Nursing might have facilitated odor recognition because of the proximity of the infant to the mother's nose during this activity. When mothers who were consistently accurate at recognizing their own infant's odor were compared with those who were inconsistently accurate, the consistently accurate mothers had been observed to spend more time in close proximity to the infants. This would give them more opportunity to learn the smell of their offspring.

Part of the explanation for the recognition performance of these mothers may be what has been called *phenotype matching* (Porter et al., 1985) in which mothers recognize offspring through cues that may include matching the infant's odor to their own odor. Even if this were operating, it may not be a particularly powerful effect because, as shown in Figure 4.1, they were good at recognizing an infant target odor even if the infant was not their own. In any event, there was no evidence in this study for a maternal instinct that distinguished mothers from other people in terms of their ability to detect their own offspring through smell.

OBSERVING THE OBSERVERS

While you were reading the descriptions of the researchers sitting in the hospital rooms entering behavior observations into a computer, you may have asked yourself how likely it is that the presence of the observer changed the behavior under observation. This can be an issue except in the most unobtrusive observations, when the observer is taking care to be hidden. Lab studies in psychology can be criticized for being too artificial. If you imagine a continuum where a laboratory study is at one end and a naturalistic observation in a real setting is at the other end, it is difficult to imagine any study at or between these extremes that would be above criticism. Understanding this situation is important for your critical thinking skills. Any study can be criticized for the extent of its artificiality but this may not always be a very important criticism. Because the artificiality criticism can apply to all studies, one response to it would be to throw up our hands and say that all science is bogus. We believe that while all scientific studies have flaws, science is, nevertheless, the best method yet devised for finding out how the world works. It is better than common sense, it is better than informal anecdotal observations, it is better than asking your grandmother, it is better than uncritically accepting the opinion of some so-called expert ("You are not going to pay a lot for this muffler!").

Where does this leave us? Some criticisms of studies are more important than others. We want you to learn to search for problems such as confounds, which seem to offer explanations for the outcomes of a study that were unanticipated by the authors. That search may lead to the most important kind of criticism of a study. We started this discussion with the issue of whether an observer would influence the behavior of a new mother with her baby. Of course this could happen. We would be far more concerned if there were some reason to think that observer presence was a confound: that it was acting differentially on mothers in such a way that it was responsible for differences between groups in outcome measures. In our opinion, there is no particular reason to think outcomes were differentially affected by observer presence. However, observer presence may have affected the behaviors of the mothers. At least for the observation of mothers and newborns, we cannot imagine a way to completely overcome this, a way to observe with no observer. The observer could be farther away or could be watching a video of the mother, but the mother would still be aware of observations. Ethics in scientific psychology forbid procedures such as using a secret hidden video camera to watch a new mother in her room without her permission.

Do we have a little less overall confidence in this study because the observers might have affected the behaviors of the mothers? Yes. Is this a serious problem that undermines any credibility the study might have? No. Does this make us throw up our hands claiming that any outcomes of this study are misleading? No. Does this undermine our contention that science is the best method yet devised for finding out about behavior? No. Does this convince us that psychology cannot be scientific because too many unknown factors influence behavior? No. In summary, we want you to be critical, but we want your criticisms to display your education, not your ignorance.

CRITICAL THINKING TOOLKIT ITEMS

Seek evidence of reliability and validity for soft measures.

Seek evidence for interobserver reliability for behavioral observations.

Sort potential criticisms into two initial categories: confounds and other problems. For example, observers may influence the behaviors being observed. That is one level of criticism of the observational method. If, however, you can argue that the presence of the observer influenced the behavior in one research group more than in another, you have a more important criticism: a potential confound.

REFERENCES

Belsky, J., Gilstrap, B., & Rovine, M. (1984). The Pennsylvania Infant and Family Development Project, I: Stability and change in mother-infant and father-infant interaction in a family setting. *Child Development, 59,* 692–705.

Bowlby, J. (1973). *Separation and loss: Vol 1. Attachment.* New York: Basic.

Fleming, A., Corter, C., Surbey, M., Franks, P., & Steiner, M. (1995). Postpartum factors related to mother's recognition of newborn infant odours. *Journal of Reproductive and Infant Psychology, 13,* 197–210.

Fleming, A. S., Ruble, D. N., Flett, G. L., & Shaul, D. (1988). Postpartum adjustment in first-time mothers: Relations between mood, maternal attitudes, and mother-infant interactions. *Developmental Psychology, 24,* 77–81.

Fleming, A. S., Steiner, M., & Anderson, V. (1987). Hormonal and attitudinal correlates of maternal behavior during the early postpartum period. *Journal of Reproductive and Infant Psychology, 5,* 193–205.

Gorman, K., & Pollitt, E. (1996). Does schooling buffer the effects of early risk? *Child Development, 67,* 314–326.

Harlow, H. (1958). The nature of love. *American Psychologist, 13,* 673–685.

Levitt, M. J., Weber, R. A., & Clark, M. C. (1986). Social network relationships as sources of maternal support and well-being. *Developmental Psychology, 22,* 310–316.

Maddox, T. (1997). *Tests: A comprehensive reference for assessments in psychology, education, and business* (4th ed.). Austin, TX: Pro-Ed.

Mangelsdorf, S., Gunnar, M., Kestenbaum, R., Lang, S., & Andreas, D. (1990). Infant proneness-to-distress, temperament, maternal personality, and mother-infant attachment: Associations and goodness of fit. *Child Development, 61,* 820–831.

Murphy, L. L., Conoley, J. C., & Impara, J. C. (1994). *Tests in print IV: An index to tests, test reviews, and the literature on specific tests.* Lincoln, NB: Buros Institute of Mental Measurements.

Neisser, U., & Harsch, N. (1992). Phantom flashbulbs: False recollections of hearing the news about *Challenger.* In E. Winograd & U. Neisser (Eds.), *Affect and accuracy in recall: Studies of "flashbulb" memories* (pp. 9–31). New York: Cambridge University Press.

Porter, R. H., Cernoch, J. M., & Balogh, R. D. (1985). Odor signatures and kin recognition. *Physiology and Behavior, 34,* 445–448.

CHAPTER 5

GIMME THE BALL

Clever research methodology has been responsible for much of the progress that has been made in the investigation of Jean Piaget's notions about cognitive development. Part of the fun of psychological science is to find valid ways to test predictions about behavior. Often the primary challenge is to design apparatus and procedures that successfully eliminate potential confounds. Sessions in which professionals discuss research methods are lively and inventive, with ideas flying in all directions. These meetings sometimes seem to have more the flavor of creative arts than science, when passion for good science blends with good humor in the search for an elegant design. The team member who wakes up in the middle of the night with a better design to test hypotheses or a better way to eliminate confounds is likely to wake the others and start the discussion rolling again. We do not know if this is the kind of atmosphere experienced by all the authors of the studies discussed in this book, but we can be sure that many of them have had similarly invigorating experiences. We mention this point because we want you to understand that scientific psychologists are often intelligent, witty, and fun people, who have been brought to science by their interest in meeting the challenges inherent in the investigation of behavior. If you are interested in knowing more, Merrens and Brannigan (1996) present a number of autobiographical accounts regarding the personal lives and research of a number of important developmental psychologists.

We have noted in other chapters that we are suspicious of traditional theories that attempt to describe the development of all individuals using a single set of stages. However, there are other reasons for wondering about the validity of these notions, reasons that go beyond their claims to universality. In some cases, the kind of data that we would consider worthy of the label "scientific" are not available to support these stage theories. The ideas of Freud and Erik Erikson fall into this category because they were primarily based on the authors' own highly subjective experiences and opinions. Furthermore, the observations they made were so unsystematic that the descriptions of development they formulated may not be any more valid than untested ideas anyone might advance regarding the development of behavior.

As we noted in Chapter 1, the developmental stages proposed by Jean Piaget were based on observations of his own children. One of his observations involved a cognitive skill called *object permanence*. Object permanence is the ability to understand that objects

Incorporating the research of N. Goubet, & R. K. Clifton, "Object and Event Representation in 6½-Month-Old Infants," 1998, *Developmental Psychology, 34,* pp. 63–76.

continue to exist even when they are out of sight. One of Piaget's lasting contributions to developmental psychology is the recognition that children think differently than adults. Object permanence, or the lack thereof, is one example of the disparity between child and adult thought processes. You have to admit, if you think things cease to exist simply because they are no longer in sight, you are approaching the world very differently than most adults. It might be nice to think that the dirty dishes in your sink cease to exist merely because they are out of sight, but, unfortunately, they still reside there in the same crusted-over state they have been in for the past two weeks.

Piaget (1954) reported a test of object permanence with his 9-month-old daughter Lucienne:

> I offer Lucienne a celluloid [plastic] goose which she has never seen before; she grasps it at once and examines it all over. I place the goose beside her and cover it [with a blanket] before her eyes, sometimes completely.... When the goose disappears completely, Lucienne immediately stops searching even when she is on the point of grasping it. (pp. 29–30)

His operational definition of object permanence was a search for the missing goose by Lucienne.

This is a good example of one of the small demonstrations that formed the basis for Piaget's understanding of child cognitive development. Because the descriptions of behavior and the ages of the children were very specific, other researchers have been able to assess the conclusions of the Piagetian anecdotes with more powerful research methods. Renee Baillargeon (pronounced "**bay**-ar-jon"; 1994) assessed object permanence with an approach she called the *violation-of-expectation method.*

THE CARROT OBJECT PERMANENCE EXPERIMENT

In one version of this method (Baillargeon & DeVos, 1991), a control group of infants was alternately shown a short carrot and a long carrot, which were slid along a track that moved them behind a screen and then out the other side. The screen was large enough so that during the time in which the carrots were behind the screen they could not be seen at all, as shown in the top half of Figure 5.1.

The carrots moved across in one trial after another until criteria for habituation were achieved. Once the children were habituated to the carrots moving behind the screen, the situation was changed. In the new situation, the carrots passed behind a different screen, one that had a notch cut out of it, as shown at the bottom of Figure 5.1. What followed is called, in the developmental psychology literature, the *possible event* and the *impossible event.* In the possible event, the short carrot was moved behind the screen and out the other side. Because the short carrot was so short, it could not be seen during the time that it was behind the screen. For the impossible event, the tall carrot was moved behind the screen and did not reappear in any way until it moved out the other side. This was "impossible" because the notch in the screen was so deep that the tall carrot should have been visible while it was passing behind the notched part of the card. It was not visible in the notch, yet it eventually appeared at the other side of the screen, moving along as if nothing special

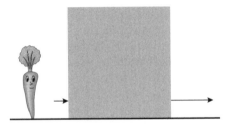

Short Carrot Event

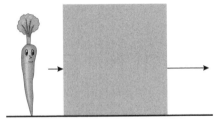

Tall Carrot Event

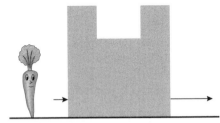

Possible Event   Impossible Event

FIGURE 5.1   Diagram of tall and short carrot habituation events (top) and possible and impossible carrot events (bottom).

From "Object Permanence in Young Infants: Further Evidence," by R. Baillargeon, and J. DeVos, 1991, *Child Development, 62,* p. 1230. Used by permission.

had happened. Special effects in the movies have trained us to believe that no visual event is impossible, but the strange case of the disappearing tall carrot should be surprising to a baby if it occurs after the development of object permanence.

The infants were given three pairs of these tests with the notched card, alternating between possible (the short carrot) and impossible (tall carrot) events. You should be able to figure out why this would be a test of object permanence. If children watching the impossible event in some way show that this surprises them, one might be able to conclude that they believe the carrot continues to exist even though it is behind the screen. They show surprise because they wonder, as we might, how the carrot managed to move past the notch without being seen. In contrast, if the children do not have object permanence, if they think objects cease to exist when not being watched, there would be no reason for them to show any particular surprise when a carrot disappears and reappears. You might make the argument that a disappearing-reappearing carrot is a surprising event in itself and that even children without object permanence would show surprise as the carrots come and go. This is the reason why the short carrot was also run past the notched screen. If a child did not have object permanence, the reaction to long and short carrots should be the same—carrots here and there, coming and going. However, if the child has object permanence, then the reaction to the possible and impossible events should be different. The impossible event involving the long carrot should be a surprise. The short carrot possible event, which does not contradict object permanence, should be less interesting, and maybe even boring. Baillargeon and DeVos found that babies looked longer at the impossible event, suggesting that they had object permanence; they knew that the carrot should have continued to exist even when out of sight.

In the passage from Piaget quoted earlier, his 9-month-old daughter did not seem to have object permanence, yet using sophisticated methods, Baillargeon and DeVos (1991) found it in children as young as 3½ months. It is not clear to us why many standard textbooks have chosen to play down instances where the work of Piaget has been scientifically evaluated and shown to be wrong. We would not expect an astronomy text to present pages of detail about the geocentric view that the Earth is the center of the universe and then, in an aside, note that this has been shown to be wrong.

About now you may be asking yourself who cares about object permanence anyway, and why is it so important. There are at least two reasons. One is that it illustrates a difference between the way children and adults think about the world. Piaget thought that this took almost a year to develop. As new research pushes the timetables earlier and earlier, we might begin to wonder if perhaps children are born with a version of object permanence that is as yet undetected because of inadequate research strategies. We do not offer this as a completely serious proposition, but it does seem that new research has repeatedly found earlier competencies. If children think differently about the world for a only very short period of time, the importance of the distinction between child and adult thought is eroded. A second reason why object permanence is important is that without this skill, rational understanding of the world is impossible. We find it comforting that new research suggests an earlier onset of object permanence. There is enough irrationality in the world without assuming that all children are necessarily sentenced to long periods of this version of cognitive immaturity.

For Piaget and subsequent researchers interested in infant cognition, a central question concerns what can be represented in the mind of a small child. In exploring this domain, you must understand that cognitive/developmental researchers use the word *representation* in a specialized manner. We think a good way to understand the cognitive psychologist's use of the term *representation* is to hyphenate it as *re-presentation,* meaning, literally, to present again. The notion here is that children experience objects and events in the world and need to present the objects and events to themselves again, in their minds, in order to be able to think about the world. In the case of Piaget's daughter's inability to find the toy under the blanket, Piaget thought that she could not "re-present" an image of the toy goose in her mind. Piaget thought her mind was physiologically too immature to accomplish this task. In contrast, the work of Baillargeon and DeVos' suggested that even small children can represent missing objects in their minds. This opened the question of why 9-month-old infants have difficulty with Piaget's cover-the-attractive-object task. If they can represent the missing object in their minds, why do they not search for it?

At least two reasons for this are possible. Children may lack the motor abilities, such as reaching and grasping, to execute the search. A second possibility is that they lack the cognitive ability to correctly sequence these movements into an effective search. The work of Goubet and Clifton (1998) sought to investigate these alternatives. A basic hypothesis was that if children have object permanence, they should reach for known objects in a dark room. Goubet's and Clifton's work is an outstanding example of ingenious research design. Their study was reported as two experiments. After the initial data were collected, some unanticipated problems appeared in the ability of the procedure to rule out rival hypotheses. The second experiment was designed to answer these problems and it is the one we describe here.

Baillargeon's and DeVos's demonstration, and others like it, used visual attention as the measure of object permanence. Goubet and Clifton (1998) pointed out that visual attention removes the motor component, making the tested behavior unlike Piaget's demonstration in which an attractive toy was hidden. In Piaget's example the child must not only possess object permanence, but must also be able to plan a search for the hidden toy and be able to put the motor responses—the reaching body movements—together in the correct order to achieve the goal of toy retrieval. In contrast, the violation-of-expectation method required the cognitive skill known as object permanence without the planning and execution of a search that were embedded in Piaget's task.

PARTICIPANTS

The participants in this study started as a group of 40 infants. Seven of them had to be eliminated from the study because of fussiness and one was dropped because he became too old to meet the age criterion for the study. The 32 remaining infants were randomly assigned to one of two research groups. The group called the *side-experienced* group consisted of eleven females and five males; the group designated *midline-experienced* was made up of nine females and seven males. Though it might have been better to have equal gender representation in the groups, random assignment did not produce this outcome. The infants ranged in age from 26 to 30 weeks old. The mean age for side-experienced infants was 27.5 weeks, and for midline-experienced it was 27.9 weeks; in other words, these children were about 5½ months old. The infants were located using newspaper birth announcements; their families were first contacted by a letter and subsequently by phone. The babies had been full-term at delivery and showed no signs of ill health.

APPARATUS

We began this chapter by talking about clever research design. In our view, the apparatus in this study was part of a particularly creative approach to the study of object permanence. One version of the apparatus is shown in Figure 5.2.

The apparatus consisted of a square wooden vertical shaft, 11 cm × 9 cm, which was 61 cm long, and had a clear Plexiglas panel at the front. Wooden knobs were attached to the left and right walls of this shaft. When a small yellow plastic ball was dropped down this shaft, it ricocheted off these knobs creating an interesting sound as it fell. Three wooden chutes (7.5 cm × 5.5 cm × 49 cm long), rather like rain gutters, were built to be attached to the end of the vertical shaft. Two of them were designed so that they could be simultaneously attached to the vertical shaft, flaring out to the right and the left of a seated participant. The third chute (not shown in Figure 5.2) was designed to be used with the other group of participants and to run directly from the bottom of the shaft to the midline of the participant's body. The chutes sloped downward from the end of the shaft to the participant's seat so that the ball would roll to the participant and be within reach when it stopped. The top two thirds of each chute also had wooden knobs attached to it so that the ball would

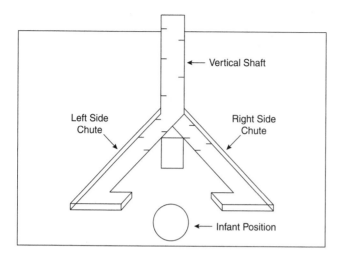

← Vertical Shaft

Left Side
Chute

Right Side
Chute

← Infant Position

**FIGURE 5.2   Diagram of
Apparatus with Side Arms
in Place.**

Source: Modified from "Object and Event
Representation in 6½-Month-Old Infants,"
N. Goubet, and R. K. Clifton, 1998, *Developmental Psychology, 34,* 71. Copyright ©
American Psychological Association. Reprinted with permission.

continue to make noise as it started to roll down the chutes toward the participants. The remaining area of each chute, the end nearest the participant, was padded with felt, so that the ball would roll silently during its final approach to the participant. The left and right chutes each turned back toward the participant's midline at their ends in order to bring the ball within easy reach. The apparatus with the right- and left-angled chutes in place is shown in Figure 5.2.

The midline chute, not shown in Figure 5.2, could be attached to the center of the apparatus when required. When the midline chute was in place, the two side chutes shown in Figure 5.2 were covered in black cloth. An infrared video camera was placed above and slightly behind the infant. This permitted observations to be made in the dark because it was able to image the participants using their body heat, rather than visible light. A video monitor was placed under the table to produce white noise, the noise a TV makes when it is not tuned to a real channel. This white noise was not very loud (51.5 dB) but could mask any slight noises that the ball might make while rolling in the padded sections of the channels.

PROCEDURE

Research sessions were conducted in a sound-deadened chamber designed to eliminate echoes. The chamber was connected to another room where the video equipment was located. The infants were seated on a parent's lap during the session. The parents wore opaque glasses to prevent them from seeing what was happening during trials and thereby influencing the performance of the baby. Parents also wore headphones that played a cocktail of masking sounds consisting of the sound of a ball rolling down the apparatus at midline and a rattle being shaken. This prevented the parent from knowing when and where the real ball was rolling.

Two experimenters conducted each session. One of them was in the chamber with the parent, infant, and ball-rolling apparatus. She presented the stimuli and controlled the lights. The second experimenter was in another room and was responsible for timing the trials and videotaping behavior. The first experimenter wore headphones through which she could receive instructions from the second experimenter.

The entire apparatus was covered by a curtain between trials. At the beginning of a trial, the curtain was opened and the plastic ball was tapped on the top of the vertical shaft in order to draw the infant's attention. When the infant looked at the ball, it was dropped down the shaft, and fell, hitting the pegs.

TRAINING TRIALS

The side-experienced group was given six practice trials in the light. On three trials the ball was sent to the left arm and on three it went to the right, in random order. The midline-experienced group received six training trials in the light during which the ball clattered down the vertical shaft then rolled down the single midline chute directly at the infant. These midline-experienced infants never saw the right and left side chutes because the chutes were covered with cloth during training. Both groups were given 15 seconds to pick up the ball after it finished rolling down a chute. If they did not, they were handed the ball and allowed to play with it for a few minutes. Then the curtain was closed and, after a few seconds, another trial was presented.

TEST TRIALS

To test object permanence, both the midline- and side-experienced groups received eight trials in complete darkness with the ball rolling down the right or left side path, with right and left order randomized, but with no more than two similar trials in a row. If the child did not reach and grasp the ball on these test trials, the ball was removed and the curtain was closed before the lights were turned on. During test trials for the midline-experienced group, the cloth covering the side arms was removed to make these arms available for use. Also during tests, the midline chute was removed and taken away. Remember, the midline-experienced group never saw the side arms of the apparatus. These side chutes had been covered with cloth during the training trials and during the test trials they were always out of sight because the lights were off whenever the curtain was open.

DATA COLLECTION

The videotapes were analyzed one frame at a time. This is a standard procedure when there is a need to measure and count small aspects of behavior. In essence, the videotape consisted of 33 still pictures taken during each second of recording. Many aspects of the behavior of the infant were analyzed including the time until the infant's hand made contact with any part of the apparatus; the hand that was used for this first contact; locations of all contacts between an infant's hand and any part of the apparatus; and the duration of search.

For the purpose of data analysis, the area around the apparatus that centered on the infant was divided into two imaginary halves. Called *hemifields,* these areas corresponded to the right and left of the apparatus from the perspective of the infant. As shown in Figure 5.3, each hemifield was divided into three subsections: sound, silent, and target.

In the sound sections the ball continued to make noise by hitting the pins; in the silent section it rolled quietly on the felt lining; and in the target section it could be reached. The hemifields and subfields were introduced over the video screen only as part of scoring the videotapes. They were not visible to the participants. A few trials had to be discarded because infants fussed or because their hands could not be seen. In total 98 of 128 side-experienced trials produced usable data, as did 115 out of 128 for the midline group. A reliability check was done on the scoring of the videotapes. Over half the tapes were scored by two scorers and agreements on specific aspects of coded behavior ranged from 87 percent to 99 percent.

RESULTS AND DISCUSSION

Infants readily reached for the ball in the light training trials and in the dark trials as can be seen in Table 5.1. In a few ways the two groups were similar. In the dark trials both groups of infants usually waited a few seconds after the ball had stopped rolling before they reached out (side-experienced, $M = 4.12$; midline-experienced, $M = 4.34$). Infants started to reach before the ball rolled into the silent area (defined in Figure 5.3) on only 5 out of 197 total dark trials. The tendency of infants in both side-experienced and midline-experienced groups was to perform two or three reaches per trial (side-experienced, $M = 2.79$; midline-experienced, $M = 2.49$). Both groups spent about the same amount of time searching for the ball once a hand was in contact with the apparatus (side-experienced, $M = 8.12$ sec.; midline-experienced, $M = 7.68$ sec.).

In the dark, when the ball rolled to the left, there was no significant difference between the groups in their tendency to reach to the left. However, when the ball rolled to the

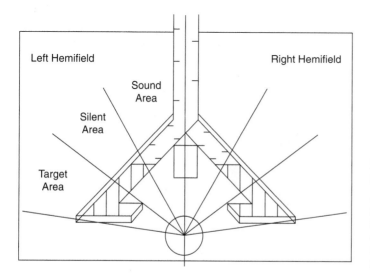

FIGURE 5.3   Apparatus with Scoring Areas Shown.

Source: From "Object and Event Representation in 6½-Month-Old Infants," by N. Goubet and R. K. Clifton, 1998, *Developmental Psychology, 34,* 71. Copyright © American Psychological Association. Reprinted with permission.

TABLE 5.1   Percentage of Reaching for Both Groups in Dark and Light Trials

	LIGHT TRIALS	TOTAL DARK TRIALS	RIGHT DARK TRIALS	LEFT DARK TRIALS
GROUP				
Midline-experienced	95%	86%	84%	88%
Side-experienced	99%	84%	83%	85%

Source: From Goubet, N., & Clifton, R. K. (1998). Object and event representation in 6 ½ month-old infants. *Developmental Psychology, 34,* 63–76.

right, the midline group was significantly more likely to reach to the left ($p < .001$) when all first contacts with the apparatus were considered. Despite random assignment to groups, it appeared that the midline group contained a high number of left-reachers. It is difficult to imagine that the experience with the midline chute would somehow have predisposed these babies to reach to the left. Random assignment is supposed to result in groups that are not different in preexisting behavior. However, because the assignment is random, rather than selected in some other way, occasionally groups will be different. Similarly, if you toss five coins, the number of heads and tails will be random. It is unlikely, but not impossible, that on the first toss all five will come up heads. It is much more likely that you will get a mix of heads and tails among your coins but occasionally random processes will produce outcomes that, superficially, do not appear to conform to simple expectations of randomness.

Although there were behavioral similarities between groups, there were also some differences in dependent measures. The authors separately reported the results of the first dark trial in which the ball went to the left and the first dark trial in which the ball went to the right. This was done because there was minimal opportunity in these early trials for the infants to learn responses or for reinforcement on one side to build a tendency to reach to that side. Figure 5.4 shows the average percentage of time that the side and midline groups were correct in their first contact with the ball, broken down by the area in which the reach occurred (see Figure 5.3 for definitions of these areas).

FIGURE 5.4   Correct First Contacts. Correct first contacts in each area of the apparatus for the first two dark trials.

Source: From Goubet, N., & Clifton, R. K. (1998). Object and event representation in 6½ month-old infants. *Developmental Psychology, 34,* 63–76.

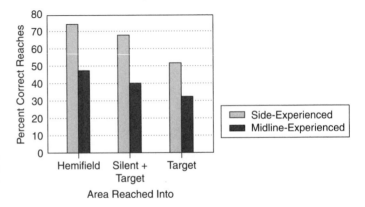

Because there are two trials depicted in this figure, if an individual infant was correct on one trial, their score would be 50 percent; if correct on both, their score would be 100 percent. It was found that the side-experienced group was more likely than expected by chance to reach into the correct hemifield ($p < .01$) and was also more likely than expected by chance to reach into the correct space when target and silent areas were combined ($p < .03$). When reaches confined to the target area were considered alone, the difference was not statistically significant ($p < .096$), although the trend was in the same direction.

When all dark trials were considered, the pattern was similar to that for the first two reaches. These data are shown in Figure 5.5. The difference between groups for correct hemifield (left or right) was statistically significant ($p < .02$) but the other two differences were not. The statistical test for differences between the two groups for reaching within the correct silent and the correct target areas produced a significance level of $p < .057$. Technically, this result is not significant because it does not satisfy the generally accepted cut-off for significance of $p < .05$ or smaller. The researchers say that "this difference held marginally" as a way of pointing out that it did not quite meet usually accepted criterion (p. 74).

A strict conservative interpretation of this result is that it was not significant. On the other hand, it pays to remind ourselves what statistical significance means. As you know from reading Chapter 1, this finding means the probability is 5.7 times out of 100 that this difference was the result of chance factors, rather than the side or midline experience manipulated by the experimenters. Even though it exceeds the canonical $p < .05$ level, many people would say that these findings were not likely to have been the result of chance. The problem is, of course, where *do* we draw the line if we begin to hedge beyond accepted levels? There is no simple answer to this question, but this situation does present us with an opportunity for critical thinking. If this difference had produced a probability level of $p < .20$, where chance could account for the results one time in five, we would probably not agree that differences held "marginally." Aside from the word *nonsignificant* there is no absolute standard for assessing probability levels that only slightly exceed .05. The things we consider when making an assessment of significance are: (1) the importance of the phenomenon under study; and (2) the other evidence that is available.

If the differences were the outcomes of a drug trial in which a new drug might be suspected of helping some people and killing other people, we would want to be very

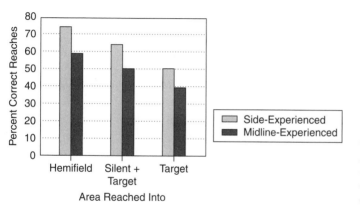

FIGURE 5.5   Correct First Contacts. Correct first contacts in each area of the apparatus for all dark trials.

Source: From Goubet, N., & Clifton, R. K. (1998). Object and event representation in 6½ month-old infants. *Developmental Psychology, 34,* 63–76.

sure that the differences found were not the result of chance. We would feel the same if the differences under examination were outcomes of strength tests used in concrete for highway bridges. We would hold to a very conservative interpretation of probability levels in such cases. As the findings move further from life-and-death situations, we might be more willing to assign some meaning other than strict statistical significance to so-called marginal findings. In the case of these results, we also have other evidence that points in the same direction, specifically the data for the first two dark trials, which is found in Figure 5.4. That may also convince us to give some weight to marginal findings. Ultimately, you have to decide for yourself how much confidence you have in these findings.

CONCLUSIONS

Whatever the interpretation of marginal differences in this research, Goubet and Clifton showed that previous experience played a role in accuracy of searching in the dark. The infants understood what was happening in the dark and were able to reach for a ball that they could not see. The midline group did less well because with no light experience of apparatus side arms, the dark trials may have been puzzling. Midline- and side-experienced groups both reached out in the dark. Whatever small differences may have existed between groups, an overview indicates that the infants responded to the unseen ball. These are important findings because they indicate the complexity of events abstractly represented by infants who are 27 weeks old. The evidence was compelling that this representation included object permanence.

The dark-reaching task was quite similar to Piaget's original task, certainly more so than the visual attention-dependent measure in other recent studies of object permanence. The findings question the conclusion that Piaget's child could not retrieve objects because the reaching was too complex for her. The possibility continues to exist that the difficulty of planning a search for an object under a blanket accounts for some of the poor performance. At the least, Goubet and Clifton's work is additional evidence that Piaget's timetable for the appearance of object permanence was incorrect. In a larger sense, it may cast doubt on Piaget's depiction of the limited mental abilities of the infant.

CRITICAL THINKING TOOLKIT ITEMS

Statistically nonsignificant findings may be given some weight if the importance of the phenomenon under study and other evidence available are carefully considered. Giving these findings some consideration is not the same as statistical significance, however.

Random assignment will not always produce equal distributions of particular characteristics across groups. Particularly in small groups, measures should be taken following random assignment to try to ensure that some confounding variable does not still exist.

REFERENCES

Baillargeon, R. (1994). How do infants learn about the physical world? *Current Directions in Psychological Science, 3,* 133–140.

Baillargeon, R., & DeVos, J. (1991). Object permanence in young infants: Further evidence. *Child Development, 62,* 1227–1246.

Goubet, N., & Clifton, R. K. (1998). Object and event representation in 6½-month-old infants. *Developmental Psychology, 34,* 63–76.

Merrens, M., & Brannigan, G. (1996). *The developmental psychologists. Research adventures across the lifespan.* New York: McGraw-Hill.

Piaget, J. (1954). The development of object concept. *The construction of reality in the child* (pp. 1–96). New York: Basic.

CHAPTER 6

ATTACHMENT IN SEPARATION

THE QUASI-EXPERIMENT

The research that is central to this chapter is an example of a research design called a *quasi-experiment*. Literally this means a method that resembles an experiment but falls short in some way. The term *quasi-experiment* is used broadly to indicate a large variety of designs. We will focus on the lack of random assignment to groups as the defining characteristic of the quasi-experiment. There are many situations in which random assignment is not possible. People cannot be randomly assigned to groups based on characteristics such as sex, ethnicity, or income. Studies that investigate such characteristics as subject variables cannot be experiments. Sometimes ethics or practicality prevents researchers from randomly assigning participants to groups that will experience adversity. For example, groups in which the important variable is a particular disease, a stressful life situation, or a natural disaster would have to be studied in some way that does not require random assignment (Cook & Campbell, 1979). Quasi-experiments can be viewed as falling somewhere between true experiments and nonexperimental methods—such as surveys and case studies—in terms of the robustness of the conclusions that can be drawn.

You will recognize by now that the quasi-experiment forfeits the ability to demonstrate cause-and-effect relationships. This is because in a quasi-experiment people are assigned to groups based on preexisting characteristics, for example, poverty or sex. This creates an inherent potential confound because as we discussed in Chapter 2, many characteristics strongly correlate with subject variables such as these. A quasi-experiment will be unable to separate these influences because people are not randomly assigned to groups in which the variable is manipulated. It is important for you to discriminate between random selection of participants and random assignment. Participants in a quasi-experiment might be randomly selected but they will not be randomly assigned to groups. We might randomly select a number of students from a college to participate in a study of age and writing skills. Because the groups in this study will be defined by age, the study cannot be a true experiment. In order to discriminate between an experiment and a quasi-experiment, ask yourself how people were assigned to groups. If the participants

Incorporating the research of C. Kier, and C. Lewis, "Infant-Mother Attachment in Separated and Married Families," 1997, *Journal of Divorce and Remarriage, 26,* pp. 185–194.

were not assigned randomly to groups, the study is not likely to be an experiment. A significant exception is where the experiment is a within-subjects design. In this case, each participant serves as his or her own control and it is meaningless to speak of random assignment.

Even though the control of random assignment is lost, quasi-experiments generally feature more control than nonexperimental methods. One reason for this is that there is usually some control over the antecedent subject variable. For example, in a study of sex differences on puzzle solving among college students, women might be randomly selected for inclusion in the study and compared to men who have been randomly selected. The random selection of participants found in a quasi-experiment eliminates some potential confounds that might otherwise appear, but this selection does not have the integrity of an experiment where people are also randomly assigned to groups. However, the random selection of participants as a way of recruitment in a quasi-experiment would be better than using a survey design, where participants are self-selected by deciding to return a questionnaire. If carefully designed and conducted, the true experiment is preferable to the quasi-experiment; however, many interesting and important variables within developmental psychology cannot be studied with true experiments.

If you are going to think critically about a study with a quasi-experimental design, you should question the extent to which the potential confound embedded in nonrandom group assignment is likely to account for the results. This involves a judgment, as does all evaluation of research. Armchair speculation or philosophy, the process of merely sitting and thinking, may not be sufficient to identify confounds that may account for results in quasi-experiments. A library or electronic search of the research literature in psychology may indicate the extent to which suspected confounding variables are correlated with variables used for group assignment. Where correlations are strong, the potential for confounding is high. For example, much has been written about the relationship between birth order and various personality characteristics, but there is also an inverse relationship between family size and socioeconomic status (SES). In this case, SES may account for some of the effects claimed for birth order (Ernst & Angst, 1983).

ATTACHMENT

Developmental researchers have long been interested in the attachment that occurs between parents and infants. Freud (1940) had some ideas about this but, as usual, they were an arcane tangle of reified constructs that would be thoroughly comic if they were not taken seriously by so many nonscientists. Eric Erikson (1963) contributed his usual brand of armchair philosophy, agreeing with Freud that attachment was the foundation of all other social relationships. As part of your critical thinking about assertions concerning behavior, you should be leery of sources that use words such as *Freud believed, Freud theorized, Freud noted,* or *Freud said.* None of these should be taken to indicate that Freud did anything beyond putting pen to paper and writing his opinion. The only empirical roots of his beliefs about childhood were retrospective case studies. No serious scientist would consider his conclusions to be in a league with those from accepted scientific methodology. Appropriate caution leads careful scientific writers to use some of the same tentative language that might be used to describe mere speculation. It is very important that you question the methodology underlying assertions about behavior.

In the past 20 years, a number of studies have identified factors associated with the quality of attachment. The most important influence seems to be the quality of interaction between babies and parents (van Ijzendoorn, Goldberg, Kroonenberg, & Frankel, 1992). Secure attachment has been widely associated with a style of parenting called *sensitive care*. This refers to caregiving that is consistent and responsive. The infant gets an early role in the determination of events, such as when feeding will begin and at what pace it will proceed. The baby is not ignored when it signals a genuine need. In contrast, insecure attachment, sometimes called *anxious attachment,* is associated with parenting that is rejecting, interfering, or inconstant. Mothers in this kind of relationship are likely either to overestimate or underestimate their baby's needs. In failing to match their behavior to the baby's needs, mothers can be cold, irritable, provide only perfunctory care, or might even be abusive.

Attachment Outcomes

A number of outcomes have been found to be associated with attachment type when securely and insecurely attached children are followed over extended periods of time. After age 1, infants who were securely attached become toddlers who are more cooperative. They are more likely to heed parental prohibitions such as "Don't touch that" and to explore new activities with the parent. By age 5, they adapt better to unpredicted changes in the routine of preschool (Arend, Gove, & Stroufe, 1979). In a longitudinal study, 12-year-old adolescents who had been securely attached as infants had better social skills, closer friendships, and more competence in dealing with peers when observed in a day camp setting (Shulman, Elicker, & Sroufe, 1994).

While findings such as these are impressive, secure attachment does not always predict more favorable developmental outcomes (Belsky & Cassidy, 1994). One of the reasons for this is that the paradigm of the sensitive period, described in Chapter 3, does not seem to apply to attachment. You will remember that the criterion for a sensitive period is early experience that has an irreversible effect. Early attachment style and its benefits have not been shown to be irreversible. It is not good enough merely to create secure attachment in early childhood. Attachment styles can change as family and social circumstances change (Feiring, Fox, Jaskir, & Lewis, 1987). Attachment is an ongoing process and the adjustment of children beyond infancy depends upon a continuity of care.

Continuity in family life, and perhaps of care, may be disrupted by events such as job loss, illness, or divorce. British psychologists Kier and Lewis (1997) conducted a quasi-experiment to assess the extent to which marital separation and divorce influence the attachment behaviors of small children. Their intent was to test two mutually exclusive hypotheses. One of these, the *early adversity* hypothesis, suggests that infants are affected by stressful life events such as the breakup of a parental relationship. The effect of this adversity is to disrupt the pattern of secure attachment to the mother. The rival hypothesis, called the *protective* hypothesis, suggests that infants are unlikely to be affected by stressors in early life because the immaturity of their cognitive systems protects them from these events. In the simplest terms, this is the idea that they are too young to know what is going on.

PARTICIPANTS

The participants were 76 infants and their mothers. Half of the mothers had been separated from the fathers of the children and half were still living with the father of the child. They were recruited as volunteers through contacts with social services workers, play groups, parenting groups, media, law courts, and nomination by other participants. They were largely second-borns and came from the middle of the SES spectrum (C. Lewis, personal communication, January 6, 1999). Other characteristics of the participants are shown in Table 6.1.

ASSESSING ATTACHMENT

The attachment of infants was assessed using a method called the *strange situation,* originated by Canadian clinical psychologist Mary Ainsworth. This has become the accepted method for the measurement of attachment behavior. It is so standard in developmental psychology that research reports tend merely to label it the strange situation, make reference to Ainsworth's book (Ainsworth, Blehar, Waters, & Wall, 1978), and otherwise eschew detailed descriptions of methodology. The strange situation exposes an infant to the mother, an unfamiliar caregiver, and a variety of attractive toys in an eight-step procedure. Generally the strange situation is conducted in a small laboratory room where the following episodes take place:

1. The mother and baby are present in a small room with an observer. The observer orients the mother and baby to the room and its contents for about 30 seconds and then leaves.
2. The mother and baby are left alone in the room for about 3 minutes. The baby explores while the mother watches. If the baby does not start to play with toys after 2 minutes, the mother encourages this activity.

TABLE 6.1   Participant Characteristics

	PARENTS SEPARATED GROUP*	PARENTS TOGETHER GROUP
Mothers separated from fathers (months)	13.13	0
Total time since start of relationship (years)	6.3	7.64
Total time in intact relationship (years)	4.96	7.64
Age of infant (months)	21.82	20.08
Number of male infants in group	15	15
Number of female infants in group	23	23

*Two of the children in the separated group were from the same family.

Source: From Kier, C., & Lewis, C. (1997). Infant-mother attachment in separated and married families. *Journal of Divorce and Remarriage, 26,* 188.

3. The stranger enters the room and is silent for a minute, after which the stranger converses with the mother for a minute. After 3 minutes, the mother quietly leaves the room.

4. The baby is left alone with the stranger for 3 minutes. This time is cut short if the baby becomes very distressed. The stranger interacts appropriately with the baby.

5. The stranger leaves as the mother returns, greeting and comforting the baby. The mother tries to re-engage the baby in play, if necessary. The mother stays for 3 minutes, or longer if more time is required for play to start. The mother then leaves saying "bye, bye."

6. The baby is left alone to play for 3 minutes. The time may be cut short if the baby is unduly distressed.

7. The stranger returns and again gears her behavior to that of the baby for 3 minutes.

8. The mother enters, greets, and holds her baby while the stranger quietly leaves. This episode lasts an additional 3 minutes.

Typically, the strange situation is videotaped so that behavior observations can be carefully quantified by several observers. One of the ways that behavior in the strange situation is quantified is by using a scoring system called the *Attachment Q-Sort* (Waters & Deane, 1985). As you may know from other psychology courses, the Q-sort is a common method of turning behavioral observations into numerical data. In a Q-sort, an observer is given a pile of cards containing descriptions of behavior. An observer watches the behavior and sorts the descriptive cards into several numbered piles ranging from, for example, 1—least characteristic to 5—most characteristic, with three piles in between. If a card is put in the first pile, it is given a score of 1, as a way of converting the card behavior descriptions to numerical data. Numerical data has the advantage over qualitative descriptions in that it can be averaged to describe groups. Imagine that the behavior "clings to mother" has been scored 1 for a particular child. This numerical scoring system enables a comparison between this child and other groups of children. If the average for a large group is 3.6, then it is possible to see that a child who scores 5 clings more than average. A statistical analysis can determine the likelihood that this is a significant difference.

MOTHER AND INFANT ATTACHMENT BEHAVIORS

Ainsworth et al. (1978) initially identified three different patterns of attachment that might be observed in the strange situation. A fourth group was added subsequent to the research of Ainsworth et al. (1978).

Group A—Avoidant Attachment

Mother is unavailable and rejecting. These mothers have only infrequent body contact with the infant and are irritable or angry in some of the interactions that take place. At times these mothers may be intrusive and even overstimulating. They may try to play with a baby who is falling asleep.

Baby avoids mother in reunion episodes of strange situation. If the baby greets the mother, the greeting is low intensity and mixed with avoidance actions such as turning away or moving away. Baby does not seek interaction with the mother during reunions. The baby shows little active resistance to interaction with the mother, instead exhibiting casual disregard. The baby treats stranger the same way. The baby is unemotional and is not much distressed when mother is gone. The baby may be distressed when left completely alone, but return of the stranger or mother alleviates fussing.

Group B—Secure Attachment

Mother is soothing and warm. The mother holds her infant carefully and tenderly. Although she likes to hold her baby, she also serves as a secure base for exploration. She interprets her baby's signals accurately and interacts with her baby. She responds more quickly to the baby's cries.

Baby wants and actively seeks contact with mother. He responds strongly to reunion with the mother. Baby shows more interest in having contact with mother than with stranger. During separation, the baby is distressed by absence of the mother, not merely because of being left alone. The baby may be somewhat comforted by the stranger but clearly wants the mother. After return of mother, the baby settles to play.

Group C—Ambivalent Attachment

Mother has an inconsistently available parenting style in which the baby's needs only elicit a response some of the time. These parents display little affection for and are awkward in their handling of the child (Cassidy & Berlin, 1994). The mothers are not intensively involved in giving care but, when the baby tries to explore, the mother will interfere, returning the baby's attention to herself.

Baby obviously resists contact, particularly in the second reunion with the mother during the last episode of observations. The baby may seem angry or passive. Nevertheless, the baby seeks proximity and contact with mother at times. The baby may alternately resist and seek contact. The baby fails to return to exploration after reunion with mother, but rather focuses on the parent and cries.

Group D—Disorganized Attachment

Mother is neglectful or even abusive. Depressed mothers may also show the mixed patterns of behavior associated with insecure-disorganized attachment, which include closeness and sad-appearing avoidance (Lyons-Ruth, Connell, Grunebaum, & Botein, 1990).

Baby displays disoriented behaviors in the presence of the mother such as freezing with a trance-like expression or falling face down on the floor and continuing to lay there. The baby may cry when the mother is gone and then run away from her when she returns. The baby may cling to the mother while, at the same time, leaning away. In one study, 82 percent of babies who had been mistreated had developed this style of attachment compared to approximately 20 percent of children who were not obviously mistreated (Carlson, Cicchetti, Barnett, & Braunwald, 1989).

Crittenden (1985) found that infants who had been abused were not classifiable in strange situations using one of the first three groups (A, B, or C). Subsequent analysis of videotapes showed that even among low-risk infants who had not been neglected or abused, 15 percent to 25 percent could be assigned to Group D. This included many who, in the past, would have been assigned to Groups A or C (Main & Solomon, 1990).

Kier and Lewis (1997) used several women to play the part of the stranger in the strange situation. All of these women were unaware of the hypothesis. The researchers used a trained coder to score the videotapes of the strange situation and, based on the coding, to assign mother-infant pairs to one of the four groups. This coder was unaware of the aims of the study and, therefore, could not introduce any unintended bias into the procedure or the ratings.

RESULTS AND DISCUSSION

The percent of children found to belong to each attachment group is shown in Figure 6.1. The percentages that are shown in this figure roughly conform to the findings of other researchers who have studied attachment. Working with a normal population of babies and mothers, Ainsworth et al. (1978) found that about 22 percent of infants were Group A (avoidant), 66 percent were Group B (secure), and 12 percent were Group C (ambivalent). Estimates vary more for Group D. In the past it is likely that some Group D individuals had been assigned to Group B. Main and Solomon (1990) coded 200 previously unclassifiable videotapes and found that about 20 percent might fall into Group D. Kier and Lewis conducted their study in Great Britain whereas Main and Solomon (1990) studied children who lived in the San Francisco Bay area. Cultural differences in child rearing may certainly affect behavior in the strange situation. In some cultures secure attachment is more common than in others (van Ijzendoorn & Kroonenberg, 1988).

Kier and Lewis (1997) did not perform a statistical analysis on the data shown in Figure 6.1 because they felt that the numbers of participants in each group were too small to show effects that might have existed. Statistical tests tend to be very sensitive to the number of cases in a data set and statistically significant differences are difficult to achieve when the number of data points is small. In order to perform some analysis, Kier and Lewis

FIGURE 6.1   Percent of Children by Attachment Type. Attachment styles of children whose parents were separated or together.

Source: From Kier, C., & Lewis, C. (1997). Infant-mother attachment in separated and married families. *Journal of Divorce and Remarriage, 26,* 185–194.

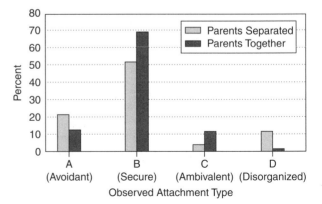

combined the data for avoidant, ambivalent, and disorganized together into one larger group that they labeled *anxious*. As part of your critical thinking, you should be careful to evaluate after-the-fact recombinations of groups in research studies. There is no widely accepted rule to which you can turn in order to decide if this is warranted; you will have to make your own judgment. At one extreme, you can imagine that it would be possible to merely throw the data from groups of participants together haphazardly, until differences between groups showed statistical significance. Clearly, this is unacceptable because there is no logic behind the combination of groups and the groups may no longer provide a meaningful test of the hypothesis in the study.

In the Kier and Lewis study, however, there was a clear logic to the recombination: The three groups being combined all represented children who were not securely attached. The research literature in the area of attachment often lumps all insecurely attached children into one group for analysis or discussion. The comparison between these three groups combined and Group B is a comparison between securely attached children and children who are not securely attached, regardless of the specific manifestation of insecure attachment. Data for this comparison are found in Figure 6.2.

A statistical analysis of the data in Figure 6.2 indicated that there was no significant difference in attachment style as a result of being in a family that was separated or together. While it might appear that secure attachment was more common in families where the father was in residence, this was not demonstrated statistically.

The results shown in Figure 6.1 suggested that neither the separated nor the together groups were different in attachment from expected norms in a large population. Analysis of the data presented in Figure 6.2 suggested that separation or lack of separation in infancy did not associate with differences in attachment between mother and infant. Kier and Lewis (1997) believed that this lack of differences supported the protection hypothesis. The attachment style of infants did not seem to be affected by the separation of father and mother. There may, of course, be other components of this outcome. Because this was a quasi-experiment, we would not be able to say that the subject variable of separation caused anything even if a difference had been found. It is possible that the findings were the result of separated mothers putting extra attention into the relationship with their child once the relationship with the father broke up. Contrary to some popular beliefs, separated or divorced mothers have not always been found to be different than married mothers. Wynn and

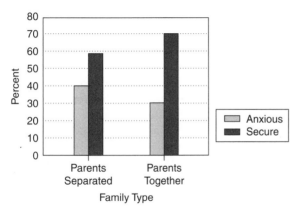

FIGURE 6.2 Anxious and Secure Attachment. Percentage of children who were anxious and secure in attachment to mothers who were separated or living together with the fathers of the children.

Source: From Kier, C., & Lewis, C. (1997). Infant-mother attachment in separated and married families. *Journal of Divorce and Remarriage, 26,* 185–194.

Bowering (1990) found that mothers without partners were similar to married mothers in their basic homemaking practices.

Kier and Lewis (1997) tentatively concluded that their results had supported the protective hypothesis. Although new research, some of which has been discussed earlier in this book, has generally found that infants are more competent than previously expected, they do have some limits to their cognitive abilities. This was suggested by the protective hypothesis. The protective hypothesis presents the notion of immaturity in a way that may be new to you: It posits that immaturity may be adaptive and may have some function or value to the individual. This is echoed by Bjorkland and Green (1992), who reviewed the literature and concluded that cognitive and motor immaturity might not be a mere deficit, but, rather, might ultimately have survival value for the individual. A toddler who cannot run fast is not able to suddenly run into the path of a car; the child is protected by its motor immaturity.

Kier and Lewis (1997) presented an interesting study, but they were careful to point out that there may be a variety of explanations for the findings. In order to be critical in your evaluation of study findings, it is important not to overgeneralize. To be specific about this study, no significant differences were found in attachment when operationally defined by behavior in the strange situation. No one who thinks critically would take the findings of this study and conclude, for example, that divorce has no effect on children. Indeed, there is much literature to the contrary (e.g., see Allison & Furstenberg, 1989; or Peretti & di-Vitorrio, 1993). The research on effects of divorce has tended to focus on older children and on personality variables that reach far beyond maternal attachment.

It is possible that Kier and Lewis (1997) did not find differences because problems appear as a *sleeper effect,* in which early stress smolders away only to later kindle a number of personality problems. The research support for this kind of effect is scant, maybe in part because it is so difficult to study. However, Ghodsian, Zajicek, and Wolkind (1984) found a relationship between maternal depression when children were 14 months old and behavior problems when the same children were 42 months old. This looked like a sleeper effect because the children who showed no behavior problems at 14 months eventually did have problems at 42 months even if their mothers had recovered from depression by that time. A more typical scenario than the sleeper effect is that following divorce, problems between the parents get worse even though the parents are no longer together (Hetherington, Cox, & Cox, 1982).

At the very least, the study by Kier and Lewis (1997) demonstrated that divorce does not necessarily have to lead to disruptions in early attachment. This study is a bit unusual because the findings reported showed no significant differences. This kind of outcome is sometimes called a *negative result* in scientific parlance. Usually, if a study does not find significant differences, it does not get published. Negative results are sometimes considered to be worthless. For technical reasons, finding no difference does not mean that the groups were the same or identical. Indeed, you can see from the data in Figures 6.1 and 6.2 that these groups were not the same. In strict scientific methodology, hypotheses usually propose that specific significant differences will be found, and failing to find these differences leaves an uninterpretable result. However, in the real world, finding no significant difference can be interesting and important, as this study illustrates.

CRITICAL THINKING TOOLKIT ITEMS

When evaluating quasi-experiments, assess the likelihood that variables other than those named in assignment to groups are important in determining the outcome measures. This will be a judgment call and may involve searching some additional literature concerning the effects of variables that are strongly correlated with those used in quasi-experimental group assignment.

New combinations of research groups after data collection is finished should have some clear underlying logic. Otherwise, we are tempted to think that it has been done in a haphazard way designed only to achieve statistical significance in otherwise non-significant findings.

Be cautious about assertions that rest on the statements of people who are believed to be great authorities. You should ask what they did in order to come to their conclusions. If their methods are weak, their ideas may be worth little.

REFERENCES

Ainsworth, M. D. S., Blehar, M. C., Waters, E., & Wall, S. (1978). *A psychological study of the strange situation.* Hillsdale, NJ: Erlbaum.

Allison, P. D., & Furstenberg, F. F. (1989). How marital dissolution affects children: Variations by age and sex. *Developmental Psychology, 25,* 540–549.

Arend, R., Gove, F., & Stroufe, L. (1979). Continuity of individual adaptation from infancy to kindergarten: A predictive study of ego-resiliency and curiosity in preschoolers. *Child Development, 50,* 950–959.

Belsky, J., & Cassidy, J. (1994). Attachment: Theory and evidence. In M. Rutter & D. Hay (Eds.), *Development through life* (pp. 373–402). Oxford: Blackwell.

Bjorkland, D., & Green, B. L. (1992). The adaptive nature of cognitive immaturity. *American Psychologist, 47,* 46–54.

Carlson, V., Cicchetti, D., Barnett, D., & Braunwald, K. (1989). Disorganized/disoriented attachment relationships in maltreated infants. *Developmental Psychology, 25,* 525–531.

Cassidy, J., & Berlin, L. J. (1994). The insecure/ambivalent pattern of attachment: Theory and research. *Child Development, 65,* 971–991.

Cook, T. D., & Campbell, D. T. (1979). *Quasi-experimentation: Design & analysis issues for field settings.* Boston: Houghton Mifflin.

Crittenden, P. A. (1985). Maltreated infants: Vulnerability and resilience. *Journal of Child Psychology and Psychiatry, 26,* 85–96.

Erikson, E. H. (1963). *Childhood and society.* New York: Norton.

Ernst, C., & Angst, J. (1983). *Birth order: Its influence on personality.* New York: Springer.

Feiring, C., Fox, N. A., Jaskir, J., & Lewis, M. (1987). The relation between social support, infant risk status, and mother-infant interactions. *Developmental Psychology, 23,* 400–405.

Freud, S. (1940). An outline of psychoanalysis. In J. Stratchey (Ed. and Trans.), *The standard edition of the complete psychological works of Sigmund Freud:* Vol. XXIII. (pp. 141–208). London: Hogarth.

Ghodsian, M., Zajicek, E., & Wolkind, S. (1984). A longitudinal study of maternal depression and child behavior problems. *Journal of Child Psychology and Psychiatry, 25,* 91–109.

Hetherington, E. M., Cox, M., & Cox, R. (1982). Effects of divorce on parents and children. In M. E. Lamb (Ed.), *Nontraditional families: Parenting and child development* (pp. 233-288). Hillsdale, NJ: Erlbaum.

Kier, C., & Lewis, C. (1997). Infant-mother attachment in separated and married families. *Journal of Divorce and Remarriage, 26,* 185–194.

Lyons-Ruth, K., Connell, D. B., Grunebaum, H. U., & Botein, S. (1990). Infants at social risk: Maternal depression and family support services as mediators of infant development and security of attachment. *Child Development, 61,* 85–98.

Main, M., & Solomon, J. (1990). Procedures for identifying infants as disorganized/disoriented during the Ainsworth strange situation. In M. T. Greenberg, D. Cicchetti, & E. M. Cummings (Eds.), *Attachment in the preschool years* (pp. 121–160). Chicago: University of Chicago Press.

Peretti, P. O., & di-Vitorrio, A. (1993). Effect of loss of father through divorce on the personality of the preschool child. *Journal of Social Behavior and Personality, 21,* 33–38.

Shulman, S., Elicker, J., & Sroufe, L. A. (1994). Stages of friendship growth in preadolescence as related to attachment history. *Journal of Social & Personal Relationships, 11,* 341–361.

van Ijzendoorn, M. H., Goldberg, S., Kroonenberg, P. M., & Frankel, O. J. (1992). The relative effects of maternal and child problems on the quality of attachment: A meta-analysis of attachment in clinical samples. *Child Development, 63,* 840–858.

van Ijzendoorn, M. H., & Kroonenberg, P. M. (1988). Cross-cultural patterns of attachment: A meta-analysis of the strange situation. *Child Development, 59,* 147–156.

Waters, E., & Deane, K. E. (1985). Defining and assessing individual differences in attachment relationships: Q-methodology and the organization for behavior in infancy and early childhood. In I. Bretherton & E. Waters (Eds.), *Growing points of attachment theory and research. Monographs of the Society for Research in Child Development, 50* (1–2, Serial No. 209).

Wynn, R. L., & Bowering, J. (1990). Homemaking practices and evening meals in married and separated families with young children. *Journal of Divorce & Remarriage, 14,* 107–123.

CHAPTER 7

A FAMILY AFFAIR

In the previous chapters we have highlighted various research methods while, at the same time, we have tried to introduce some of the knowledge about human development that has been produced using these methods. So far, we have not placed much emphasis on any particular formal theory, except for a brief discussion of Piagetian theory in Chapter 5. While the word *theory* can be used in a number of different ways, we consider a theory to be an idea that organizes and explains the observations and other findings in specific studies (Cozby, 2001). The development of object permanence in a child can be seen as an example of the correctness of Piaget's theory that the thinking of a small child becomes more abstract as the child gets older. Even though a number of researchers have questioned Piaget's findings about the timing of skills such as object permanence, nevertheless, the central idea of children's thinking progressing to adult-like rationality has been widely supported. In addition to organizing findings, a theory might also generate new knowledge. Because Piaget made such specific predictions about behavior, his theory has been a hot topic for researchers. You can see this from other examples of research presented in this book.

In past chapters, we may have seemed a bit harsh in our dismissal of theories that, for practical purposes, cannot be falsified. We do not want this book to be atheoretical; there are many theories discussed in this book. Right now some of the theories discussed have more support and some have less. We have tried, however, to avoid wasting your time with theories that are so vaguely worded as to be untestable.

To begin this chapter, we are going to discuss a viewpoint, which might also be considered a theory or group of theories, called *ecological psychology*. In one form or another, ecological psychology has been around for quite a while. One contemporary branch of it is called *family systems theory*. The notions that might be collected under the heading ecological psychology stress the roles of multiple people and contexts in the development of an individual.

ECOLOGICAL PSYCHOLOGY

Minuchin (1988) was probably being slightly sarcastic when she called research that was restricted to the interactions between a mother and a child "the hardiest perennial in the

Incorporating the research of L. J. Horwood, and D. M. Fergusson, "A Longitudinal Study of Maternal Labour Force Participation and Child Academic Achievement," 1999, *Journal of Child Psychology and Psychiatry, 40,* pp. 1013–1024.

developmental field." She is probably correct that the *dyad,* or two-person group, has been studied more than anything else in human development. Most available research designs and statistical analyses are compatible with these kinds of studies. In an important early review, Bronfenbrenner (1979) argued that research should look beyond the dyad to the contexts or surroundings in which dyads are located. For example, we know that a great deal of behavior change can take place through the process called *social learning,* or *imitation.* A child sees someone do something and sometimes that child can immediately perform this behavior, even though the child had never seen it before. Other times a child can be repeatedly shown the same behavior and still be unable to perform it. As long as the child is biologically capable of the behavior, explanations need to be found for why some behaviors are learned so quickly while others are resisted.

Based on the available research, Bronfenbrenner (1979) described four propositions that establish conditions in which behavior is likely to change or develop. Research conducted since these propositions were formulated has supported Bronfenbrenner's contentions. Here are the four propositions, quoted from Bronfenbrenner:

> *Proposition 1.* A primary developmental context is one in which the child can observe and engage in ongoing patterns of progressively more complex activity jointly with or under the guidance of persons who possess knowledge and skill not yet acquired by the child and with whom the child has developed a positive emotional regard. (p. 845)
>
> *Proposition 2.* A secondary developmental context is one in which the child is given opportunity, resources, and encouragement to engage in the activities he or she has learned in primary developmental contexts, but now without the active involvement or direct guidance of another person possessing knowledge and skill beyond the levels acquired by the child. (p. 845)
>
> *Proposition 3.* The developmental potential of a setting depends upon the extent to which third parties present in the setting support or undermine the activities of those actively engaged in interaction with the child. (p. 847)
>
> *Proposition 4.* The developmental potential of a setting is increased as a function of the number of supportive links between that setting and other contexts involving the child or persons responsible for his or her care. Such interconnections may take the form of shared activities, two-way communication, and information provided in each setting about the others. (p. 848)

If all four propositions are met, development is quite likely to happen. These propositions are really quite easy to learn if the language is simplified a bit. Proposition 1 is really another name for teaching: a one-on-one interaction with a more skilled person where there is positive emotional regard. Proposition 2 merely adds that learning takes place when the individual can practice new skills alone. Proposition 3 says that others in the immediate setting should support the learning effort and Proposition 4 says that other contexts such as home, school, recreation sites, and peer groups should also support the learning.

While Bronfenbrenner phrased the propositions in terms of child development, they probably do not have age boundaries. Imagine, for example, trying to teach an elderly grandfather how to use e-mail. First you would have the one-on-one instruction, then you would leave him alone to practice. Probably most of us remember the feeling of being left alone to try to remember how to perform some computer routine for the first time. It can be frustrating, but it can also be a very good learning experience. Proposition 3 suggests that it would be important for the e-mailing grandpa to be supported by others in the setting. This might mean that others around the house would share his excitement at his first successful attempts and encourage him to continue to try in the face of failure. Lastly, Proposition 4 could be achieved if settings beyond the home also supported his learning. For example, Proposition 4 would be met if he were successful in sending some e-mails for his peers at the local senior citizen center. Note that in three of the four propositions we have moved beyond the initial teaching dyad and we have proposed that the grandfather's learning is a result of interactions with other people in other settings. This type of emphasis is typical of ecological psychology.

In contrast, it is more usual that developmental research identifies one or two variables and attempts to describe the role played by these variables in development. For example, in Chapter 6, children from homes where parents were separated were compared to children from homes where parents were together. The outcome measured in this quasi-experiment was attachment to the mother. Of course, the authors of that study realized that many factors affect attachment but for practical reasons they identified one and investigated it. As you will recall, there were no particularly striking differences in attachment between the two groups of children in this study (Kier & Lewis, 1997). As often happens, this research creates more questions than it answers. Perhaps, as Kier and Lewis proposed, the children were too immature to know what was going on and were not affected by separation of parents. That could have been one factor. In addition, perhaps the separated mothers spent far more time with their children because they were aware that there was only one parent available most of the time. Maybe friends, neighbors, and relatives flocked around to help, so that the children with separated parents received considerable social stimulation in spite of the separation. Perhaps all of these things were going on at once. A different kind of approach would be required in order to take account of these events. This different approach would be consistent with the principles of ecological psychology.

THE SOCIOLOGY OF SCIENCE

By now you might be asking yourself why not simply investigate all these influences at once and find out what really is going on? If you continue to read this book carefully, you will probably find yourself asking this question repeatedly. The operative word in the question is *simply*. Investigating all the influences that might impinge on a behavior is never going to be simple. Even if all influences cannot be investigated, you will sometimes wonder why at least a few more were not included. We think the most likely answer to this question is that there are always practical constraints. One of these practical constraints is financial: Thorough research is very expensive. Expense does not only refer to money itself. For most researchers money and time are the same resource. If more time is going to be spent carefully investigating additional variables, this will generally cost more money.

Another set of practical constraints concerns the sociology of science in academic institutions. Most psychological research is conducted in association with colleges or universities. The realities are that these institutions take account of the publication record of a scientist in making decisions about hiring, promotion, salary, and tenure. Some level of publication in established journals is a required activity for faculty in the sciences at most academic institutions. This feature of academic life means that it is often unwise for a researcher to embark on a very time-consuming piece of research that does not lead to timely publication. We do not want you to think that, as a result, research is merely cranked out as quickly as possible in order to build a list of publications. Responsible scientists do not operate this way. However, the requirements of a job may mean that scientists have to place limits on the scope of single pieces of research in order to retain their position in the academic environment. Even if individual research studies are quite narrow in focus, they may nevertheless be valid tests of specific hypotheses. In addition, most scientists have faith that interesting small studies will attract follow-up research which replicates the original while adding a new variable or two. No matter how small a research study might be, it can still provide a piece of the overall human development puzzle if it is carefully designed.

THE ECOLOGY OF MATERNAL EMPLOYMENT

Children get exposed to a variety of skilled persons and multiple development contexts through being placed in different child-care settings when the primary family caregiver returns to work. Most women no longer drop out of the workforce to raise children. Rather, they return to work before children are grown (Piotrkowski, Rapoport, & Rapoport, 1987). In the past, women were likely to feel pressure from others if they decided to return to work when their children were small. It was not unusual for these mothers to feel guilty, thinking that their children were going to be disadvantaged by not having a full-time mom at home. More recently, this has changed as many more mothers find themselves back at work, even when children are very small. According to 2000 Federal Bureau of Labor Statistics (http://www.bls.gov/), almost 54 percent of women who have infants less than a year old are working. As you might expect, a search for Internet information about working mothers will turn up everything from summaries of research studies to chat rooms full of advice from experienced people.

The approach of ecological psychology includes people other than mothers in child-rearing settings. There have been a number of recent studies on the roles of fathers. It seems as if the presence and activities of the father can buffer effects of mother absence owing to work. Among school-age children, if the father is more involved with the children, they tend to do better on academic indicators and have better social skills (Gottfried, Bathurst, & Gottfried, 1994). It has also been found that fathers are likely to be more involved with children when the mother works (Bryant & Zick, 1996). This shows that fathering cannot be understood merely by studying the father-child dyad. Instead, at least the triad of mother, father, and child must be understood in order to explain paternal investment of time and attention.

Older studies of the children of working mothers suggested that these children exhibited a variety of cognitive and behavioral problems. It is now generally recognized that the data from these studies suffered from several serious flaws. This is an area of investigation in which older studies may not answer current questions simply because the social circumstances have changed so much in recent years. Older studies may have been accurate at the time they were done but have little to say about the situation today. In some cases, conclusions of past studies were based largely on the experience of low-income women. This means that low socioeconomic status (SES)—and all the circumstances that correlate with it—could be confounded with maternal employment in having effects on the child. The description of a confound presented in the first chapter of this book is phrased to refer to experiments. However, we might also speak of a confound in a nonexperimental situation such as this where older studies did not adequately take account of SES.

Recently, analysis of data from a large and representative study of about 12,600 women and their children—the National Longitudinal Survey of Youth (NLSY)—found only a few effects of maternal employment on child outcomes. The children of mothers who went back to work sooner scored slightly lower on verbal achievement and were slightly less likely to be obedient or to comply with others. These differences were small and short-lived. The working hours of fathers were not associated with any significant effects in the NLSY (Harvey, 1999).

Probably maternal employment should no longer be viewed as negatively affecting a child. Employed mothers tend to spend considerable time with their children when they are home, having them nearby when doing chores rather than keeping them out of the way (Bryant & Zick, 1996). Employed mothers may gain considerable esteem and satisfaction from work and the more satisfied a mother is with work, the more likely she is to be a good parent (Parke & Buriel, 1998; Demo, 1992). It is also possible that the weak relationships that have been found between mother's work and child outcomes are a result of factors other than the work. It is not possible to do true experiments to compare working and non-working mothers. They must be studied using some kind of quasi-experimental approach. As a result, the direction or nature of cause and effect cannot be determined. It might be, for example, that the weak but negative outcomes associated with maternal employment are a result of some mothers choosing to go back to work because they are less interested in their children. This group might not be very good mothers regardless of whether they work. If they also happen to experience unsatisfactory child outcomes, it may be nothing to do with their work.

In the past, some gender differences have been found in the extent to which children were affected by maternal employment. Boys have been shown to be more likely to receive low teacher ratings of grades and school work habits when mothers work. In contrast, girls do the same or better under these circumstances (Goldberg, Greenberger, & Nagel, 1996). In a study of adolescents, Richardson, Radziszewska, Dent, and Flay (1993) found that the children who were unsupervised because parents were at work were more likely to use drugs, to exhibit poor academic achievement, and to be depressed. This effect was most pronounced on girls and was mediated if parents at least knew where their children were at any given time.

Clarke-Stewart (1993) reviewed a large number of studies of day care. It is likely that many of these are, in effect, studies of working mothers. In a very large study including 1,300 families, it was found that mothers were less sensitive to their children if the children were in day care, starting at 6 months of age. The children were found to be less affectionate toward their mothers. However, it is important to understand that the relationships were quite weak and, therefore, may not be very important in real life (National Institute of Child Health and Human Development Early Child Care Network, 1997). Other research has concluded that there seems to be no reason why children in day care should not form close relationships with parents (Lamb, 1998). Not surprisingly, the research suggested that children were likely to develop in positive ways when the day care context was high quality (Parke & Buriel, 1998).

While the main study to be discussed in this chapter is not a clear example of ecological psychology per se, it is in the same spirit because it considers the effects of multiple settings on development. Horwood and Fergusson (1999) conducted a careful study of the effects of maternal employment on child academic measures. This study began at the birth of the child participants, yet most of the data in this particular study were collected when the children were school-age. For many families the issue of the working mother appears early in the child's life, within the first year following the birth of a baby. It is for this reason that we decided to place this material adjacent to other chapters on early childhood.

PARTICIPANTS

The participants were part of an extensive longitudinal study—the Christchurch Health and Development Study (CHDS)—that was conducted in New Zealand. Rather than do any selecting, random or otherwise, this study started with almost all the children who were born in Christchurch, New Zealand, during a particular four-month interval in the year 1977. Christchurch is a large, modern city. Initially there were 1,265 children in the study, including 635 males and 630 females. Because of the sampling criteria, the children were almost certainly quite representative of the population of urban New Zealand. The mean age of the mothers was in the mid-20s and between a quarter and a third of the families were low SES. Less than a quarter of the children lived in single-parent families. For the data discussed in this chapter, the birth cohort of 1,265 was reduced by events such as families leaving the area, refusal to continue in the study, and death. We will discuss findings from different times across the study; the group of participants contributing to these data ranged from 725 to 1,032, depending on the age of the children and the particular measure. Horwood and Fergusson (1999) present a lengthy discussion and considerable evidence to attest that the participants remaining in the study were sufficiently similar to the original sample so that bias was not introduced as a result of attrition.

MEASURES

The measures taken in this study were very numerous and extended over the early part of the lives of the children. Overall, the children were studied from birth until they were 18 years old. After data collection at birth, there was a 4-month follow-up and then data were collected again at yearly intervals until the children were 16 years old. Additional data were collected again at age 18. The mothers were interviewed to collect demographic information such as full- or part-time maternal employment, hours per week worked, and number of years worked. Mothers also reported things such as their age, educational background, and SES. The child's birth order, the number of parents in the home, and family size were also reported. The mother's emotional responsiveness to the child was observed and recorded using a subscale of the Home Observation of Measurement of the Environment (HOME) Inventory (Bradley & Caldwell, 1977). The children's teachers did assessments of the children, and the children were evaluated using measurement instruments including standardized academic tests. The researchers also recorded the receipt of school certificates that indicated a mastery of different subject matter at a level expected for entry into a university. Some other official records were accessed for additional information.

RESULTS

For the purposes of assessing the effects of maternal employment, academic achievement scores were sorted into one of four groups reflecting the number of hours the mother worked each week: 0, 1 to 19, 20 to 29, and 40 plus. The results for the standardized tests of reading comprehension at age 10, mathematics at age 11, and overall scholastic abilities at age 13 are presented in Figure 7.1. We selected these from a table of scores because they are quite typical of the main findings.

The scores presented in Figure 7.1 were all scaled to have a mean of 100 to facilitate comparison. It is interesting that there was not much real difference between the scores. Statistical analysis indicates that for each test, the mothers who did not work at all had children with lower scores. Beyond that, the statistical analysis showed no clear trend for increased test scores to be associated with longer maternal presence in the workplace. Additional analysis of the data indicated that the test scores of boys and girls were similarly affected by maternal work—there were no gender differences.

Figure 7.2 shows a few of the other variables compared to maternal hours worked per week. For the purposes of this chapter, we have chosen a few of the variables to illustrate

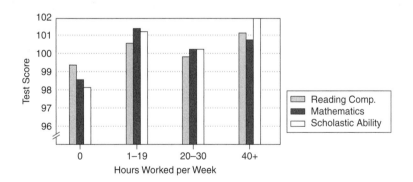

FIGURE 7.1   Maternal Employment and Child Academic Performance.
Children's test scores in reading comprehension (at 10 years old),
mathematics (at 11 years old), and scholastic ability (at 13 years old) by
numbers of hours the mothers worked per week.

Source: From Horwood, L. J. & Fergusson, D. M. (1999). A longitudinal study of maternal labour force participation and child academic achievement. *Journal of Child Psychology and Psychiatry, 40,* 1017.

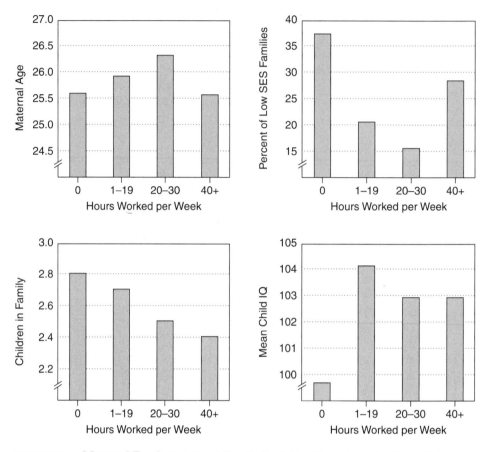

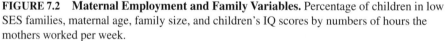

FIGURE 7.2   **Maternal Employment and Family Variables.** Percentage of children in low SES families, maternal age, family size, and children's IQ scores by numbers of hours the mothers worked per week.

Source: From Horwood, L. J., & Fergusson, D. M. (1999). A longitudinal study of maternal labour force participation and child academic achievement. *Journal of Child Psychology and Psychiatry, 40,* 1019.

the general finding of this study that the mothers who did not work at all had the most disadvantaged family and social situation. Statistical analysis showed that they were younger, less educated, lower SES, more likely to be single parents, more likely to have larger families, and to have children who tested lower on IQ tests. As in the data for academic outcomes, shown in Figure 7.1, except for the number of children in the families, there was no linear change across increasing time spent at work.

In summary, there was a weak but significant finding that the outcomes for nonworking mothers were worse than the outcomes for working mothers. Because of the very extensive data collected in this impressive study it was possible to do additional analyses to investigate the role of other factors on these outcomes. Using a complex statistical analysis, it was possible to discover the impact of other variables on the weak relationship already described. It was found that the variables of maternal education, SES, child birth order, maternal emotional responsiveness, and child IQ all had an impact. Once the effects of these variables were included statistically, no further explanation was required for the relationship between maternal employment and child academic outcomes.

Horwood and Fergusson (1999) recorded extent of maternal employment in a number of different ways including full- or part-time employment and the age of the child at the time when the mother joined the workforce. In an analysis that considered a number of different definitions of maternal work, the findings above were replicated. After allowance was made for the effects of maternal education, SES, child birth order, maternal emotional responsiveness, and child IQ, no relationship remained between maternal employment and child academic outcomes.

Discussion

One of the small surprises is that the data assembled here suggest that, if anything, the children who showed disadvantage were those who had nonworking mothers. It is important to understand that this was probably not a direct effect of work or lack thereof because the consideration of other variables eliminated the differences between working and nonworking mothers. It is also interesting that there was no difference in child outcome found when a little maternal work was compared to a lot of work. Those who would suggest that working mothers are necessarily doing something bad to their children are likely to be wrong. As Horwood and Fergusson (1999) noted, "concerns in this area have been driven more by political and ideological debates…than by evidence-based analyses" (p. 1021).

There is no evidence here that working mothers harm their children with respect to academic outcomes. Returning to the ideas of Bronfenbrenner described earlier in this chapter, there is no reason why having a working mother should prevent a child from receiving the ideal set of developmental contexts described in Brofenbrenner's four propositions. If we imagine that the child of a working mother is placed in day care, research has suggested that the most important question concerns the quality of the day care. Day care can be cursory and business-like or nurturing, warm, and supportive. It is interesting that in our society we often say "day care," suggesting that we are taking care of the day, rather than "child care," which emphasizes the best possible care of the child. An earlier chapter suggested that continuity of sensitive care may be the single most important variable in attaining favorable child outcomes. The research presented here does not contradict this contention. It was further noted that good developmental outcomes result from a continuity of care. This may be achieved in spite of a variety of caregivers and caregiving contexts, as long as the people and settings provide a safe, stimulating, and responsive environment.

CRITICAL THINKING TOOLKIT ITEMS

Behavior is determined by many different components, both historical and current. Practical limitations may mean that only few variables can be investigated in a single study.

Although not the ideal situation, small studies can often make important contributions to knowledge as long as the methodology is sound.

REFERENCES

Beitel, A. H., & Parke, R. D. (1998). Paternal involvement in infancy: The role of maternal and paternal attitudes. *Journal of Family Psychology, 12,* 268–288.

Bradley, R. H., & Caldwell, B. M. (1977). Home observation for measurement of the environment: A validation study of screen efficiency. *American Journal of Mental Deficiency, 81,* 417–424.

Bryant, W. K., & Zick, C. D. (1996). An examination of parent-child shared time. *Journal of Marriage and the Family, 58,* 227–238.

Bronfenbrenner, U. (1979). Contexts of child rearing: Problems and prospects. *American Psychologist, 34,* 844–850.

Clarke-Stewart, K. A. (1993). *Daycare* (rev. ed.). Cambridge, MA: Harvard University Press.

Cozby, P. C. (2001). *Methods in behavioral research.* Mountain View, CA: Mayfield.

Demo, D. H. (1992). Parent-child relations: Assessing recent changes. *Journal of Marriage and the Family, 54,* 104–117.

Harvey, E. (1999). Short-term and long-term effects of early parental employment on children of the National Longitudinal Survey of Youth. *Developmental Psychology, 35,* 445–459.

Horwood, L. J., & Fergusson, D. M. (1999). A longitudinal study of maternal labour force participation and child academic achievement. *Journal of Psychology and Psychiatry, 40,* 1013–1024.

Goldberg, W. A., Greenberger, E., & Nagel, S. K. (1996). Employment and achievement: Mothers' work involvement in relation to children's achievement behaviors and mothers' parenting behaviors. *Child Development, 67,* 1512–1527.

Gottfried, A. E., Bathurst, K., & Gottfried, A. W. (1994). Role of maternal and dual-earner employment status in children's development: A longitudinal study from infancy through early adolescence. In A. E. Gottfried, & A. W. Gottfried, (Eds.), *Redefining families: Implications for children's development* (pp. 55–97). New York: Plenum.

Kier, C., & Lewis, C. (1997). Infant-mother attachment in separated and married families. *Journal of Divorce and Remarriage, 26,* 185–194.

Lamb, M. E. (1998). Nonparental child care: context, quality, correlates, and consequences. In W. Damon (Ed.), *Handbook of Child Psychology:* Vol. 4. (5th ed., pp. 73–133). New York: Wiley.

Minuchin, P. (1988). Relationships within the family: A systems perspective on development. In R. A. Hinde, and J. Stevenson-Hinde (Eds.), *Relationships within families: Mutual influences* (pp. 7–26). Oxford: Clarendon.

National Institute of Child Health and Human Development Early Child Care Network. (1997). The effects of infant child care on infant-mother attachment security: Results of the NICHD study of early child care. *Child Development, 68,* 860–879.

Parke, R. D., & Buriel, R. (1998). Socialization in the family: Ethnic and ecological perspectives. In W. Damon (Ed.), *Handbook of child psychology: Vol. 3* (pp. 463–552). New York: Wiley.

Piotrkowski, C. S., Rapoport, R. N., & Rapoport, R. (1987). Families and work. In M. B. Sussman, & S. K. Steinmetz, (Eds.), *Handbook of Marriage and the Family* (pp. 251–284), New York: Plenum.

Richardson, J. L., Radziszewska, B., Dent, C. W., & Flay, B. R. (1993). Relationship between after-school care of adolescents and substance use, risk-taking, depressed mood, and academic achievement. *Pediatrics, 92,* 32–38.

CHAPTER 8

PLEASE PASS THE VEGETABLES

Developmental psychologist Jean Piaget proposed a detailed theory of cognitive development in which children pass through several discrete stages as they begin to think more like adults. Basically, Piaget's theory maintained that, across childhood, the thought processes of children change along two major dimensions: from concrete to abstract and from egocentric to being able to consider the views of others. In regard to the first dimension, the development of object permanence is a good example of how children begin to think in an abstract manner. You will recall from Chapter 5 that object permanence occurs relatively early in the life span. The realization that objects continue to exist when they are out of sight requires going beyond the observed reality of the missing object. Features of the object must be abstracted and represented in the mind as part of the understanding that objects are permanent.

The second major dimension along which change progresses in the Piagetian view of cognitive development involves the reduction of egocentricity. It is important to understand the restricted sense in which the concept of egocentricity is used by researchers interested in cognitive development. Unlike the vernacular meanings of *egocentricity,* which may include concepts such as selfishness, within Piagetian thought this term means "unable to take the views of others." Piagetians interpret egocentricity, literally, as the person at the center of his or her own world, unable to see the worlds of others. According to this interpretation, egocentricity may be used to label either a person's inability to see physical things as others see them or a person's unawareness that others may have different feelings, thoughts, or beliefs than one's own.

Piaget and Inhelder (1956) constructed a demonstration of the first of these types of egocentricity, the inability to see other people's viewpoints of physical things. Called the three-mountain problem, in this demonstration, a child was seated at a table in front of three papier-mâché mountains (see Figure 8.1). There were other chairs positioned around the table and the child was asked to identify what the three mountains would look like to a doll sitting at another position. Most typically the child was asked to identify this other viewpoint by: (1) drawing a picture of the mountains as they would be seen from a different chair; (2) identifying a picture of the mountains as seen from another position; or (3) choosing a three-dimensional model of another viewpoint. Piaget found that children

Incorporating the research of B. Repacholi, and A. Gopnik, "Early Reasoning about Desires: Evidence from 14- and 18-Month-Olds," 1997, *Developmental Psychology, 33,* pp. 12–21.

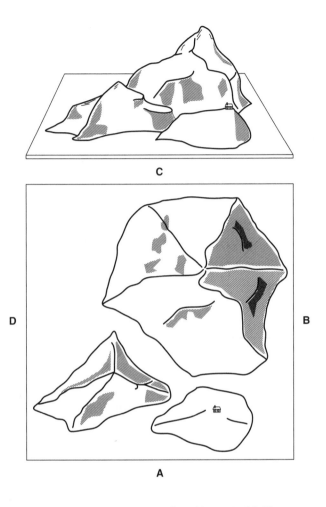

FIGURE 8.1   Piaget's Three-Mountain Problem. At the top is the table with the three dimensional mountains. At the bottom, four positions around the table are shown looking from above the table. Children were tested to see if they could determine how the mountains might look from the positions (B, C, & D) other than the one they occupied (A).

Source: From Piaget, J., & Inhelder, B. (1956). *The Child's Conception of Space* (p. 211). New York: Norton.

could not typically perform this task correctly until they were 9 or 10 years old. However, this is not particularly surprising because this task represents a considerable cognitive challenge. Borke (1975) replicated Piaget's work with a couple of changes. Where Piaget's mountains had been quite featureless, Borke added more details to the mountains, such as houses and trees. In addition, Borke gave the children a small model of the main mountain display that could be rotated until the correct view was selected. This was believed to be an easier task than having to compare three different models or pictures. With these modifications, Borke found that children as young as 3 years old were able to correctly identify the mountain scene as it would be seen from different perspectives.

While the three-mountain problem is an example of how children can understand the views of others in relation to the physical environment, it does not tell us much about the ability of children to understand internal states: beliefs, thoughts, or feelings. By the time children are 18 months old they are beginning to talk about feeling states (Wellman & Bartsch, 1994). Before 18 months, infants show some primitive evidence that they understand other's emotions. Hornik, Risenhoover, and Gunnar (1987) found that from 9 to 12 months infants begin to attend to their mother's facial expressions, presumably to help them understand what to do in unfamiliar situations, such as being presented with a novel toy. This behavior, called *social referencing,* suggests that the infant is beginning to understand that others have internal states that may differ from their own. Knowledge of these states may benefit infants and mechanisms for detecting these states may have evolved due to their obvious survival value. Recognizing that a parent is frightened might keep an infant from serious harm. Imagine the look on a parent's face as an infant reaches out to pick up a sharp piece of broken glass or to touch a hot stove.

Repacholi and Gopnik (1997) designed a study to test young infants' abilities to understand and to acknowledge the desires of another person, in this case, the desires of a stranger. This skill is essential to social functioning because the actions of others are often motivated by wants and these actions are not understandable without the interpretation of verbal and nonverbal indications of desire. If the desires of others are interpreted egocentrically by a child, that child is likely to face difficulty in social situations. While this is not the same kind of egocentricity that Piaget demonstrated with the three-mountain problem, it is certainly a kind of egocentricity. A nonegocentric appreciation of other's desires is probably more central to most interpersonal situations than a nonegocentric appreciation of physical visual perspectives. For this reason, we believe that research about desires may be considered more important than Piaget's original demonstrations.

PARTICIPANTS

Participants were 180 healthy infants who were either 14 or 18 months old at the time of the study (range = 13.8 to 18.9 months). The parents of the participants had volunteered and consented to their infants' involvement in a research study conducted by the Institute of Human Development, University of California, Berkeley. Most of the infants came from white middle-class families and were currently living with both parents. Twenty-one infants had to be dropped from the study owing to reasons such as fussiness, failure to complete research tasks, drowsiness, crying, or parental interference. The final sample was composed of 159 infants. There were approximately equal numbers of boys and girls in each of the two age groups.

DESIGN AND PROCEDURE

Individual pairs of parents and infants were brought into a small laboratory room. Most of the infants were placed in a high chair adjacent to a small table during the testing procedure while parents sat behind the infants. Parents were given a magazine to read in order to discourage parent-child interaction. A few infants (6 percent) who refused to sit in the high chair sat on their parent's lap. Parents were asked not to attend to their infants during the testing procedure. The method used by the researchers to examine the infants' ability to interpret the desires of others consisted of a nonverbal decision task that involved presenting two dissimilar foods. The two foods presented to the infants were Pepperidge Farm Goldfish crackers and raw broccoli florets. The food items were placed in separate bowls on a tray. Before the testing procedure the infants were allowed 45 seconds to taste each of the foods and a baseline measure was obtained for each child's initial food preference.

These two foods were chosen because it was assumed that infants would recognize these foods and because the two foods taste considerably different. It was believed that the infants would strongly prefer the taste of the crackers and dislike the broccoli. This was largely correct—93 percent of the participants showed a clear preference for the crackers.

During the testing procedure the tray with the food bowls was placed in front of the examiner who sat across the table from the infant. The examiner tasted both foods and responded with a positive emotional display toward one of the foods and a negative emotional display toward the other. The food-request procedure involved two separate preference groups: *matched* and *mismatched.* The matched condition was designed to be congruent with the child's preference for a particular food item. For example, if the infant demonstrated the typical preference for the Goldfish crackers, the examiner in the matched condition indicated a positive response (happiness) after tasting the crackers and a negative response (disgust) after tasting the broccoli. In contrast, the mismatched condition was designed to be the converse of the child's food preference. In this condition, the examiner displayed a positive response after tasting the food that was not preferred by the child and a negative response to the food the child liked.

The emotional states of happiness and disgust expressed by the examiner were based on the descriptions of facial expressions presented by Ekman and Friesen (1975). The vocalizations "mmm" and "eww" were used to convey these two emotional states. For instance, in the matched condition for a child who liked Goldfish crackers, the examiner would taste the crackers and respond, "mmm...crackers...mmm." Similarly, the examiner in this matched condition, after eating the broccoli might say, "eww...broccoli...eww." Equal numbers of male and female infants were randomly assigned to either the matched or the mismatched group.

After enacting the appropriate emotional display, the examiner requested some more food from the child and moved the tray with the two food bowls in the child's direction. At the same time, she reached out her hand toward the child with her palm turned upright. The food-request procedure was performed in this manner to ensure that the child could not reach for a food bowl before the examiner was able to indicate her emotional response. In making the request, the examiner simply said, "Can you give me some?" No reference was made to which food she wanted, hence, each child had to make a decision about which food to offer based on the examiner's previous emotional display.

The examiner withdrew her hand if she was not initially offered any food. Thereafter the examiner made additional requests. Requests were made only from participants who did not have any food in their hands or mouths and were not reaching for either bowl. This was done to ensure that the infant participants would not think that the request was in response to the food they had in their possession or the food they currently tasted. The presentation of the bowls was counterbalanced so that one kind of food would not always be presented on the same side of the participant at the beginning of the testing procedure.

The researchers hypothesized that the infants would respond egocentrically and offer the food they themselves preferred, regardless of whether the examiner indicated a positive or negative reaction to that food. This type of detached responding was supported by past research which found that young infants who preferred distinct and familiar toys did not pay attention to accompanying emotional reactions from adults (Gunnar & Stone, 1984). In Repacholi and Gopnik's study, infants were considered to have behaved nonegocentrically if they gave a food they disliked to the examiner based on her demonstrated preference for that food. Doing this would be responding to the desires of another person in contrast to the infant's own preference. The extent of this behavior operationally defined egocentricity.

Following the experience with the examiner, each child was permitted to taste the food again to determine if his or her food preference had changed as a result of the examiner's emotional display. All participants were videotaped throughout the session. Videotapes were later analyzed for content by coders who were unaware of the participants' research condition—matched or unmatched.

QUESTIONNAIRE MEASURES

Two questionnaires were mailed to the parents of the participants prior to the study. The first questionnaire was the Internal State Language Questionnaire designed to assess the infant's knowledge of words that represent internal states. These are words generally known by young infants between 18 and 24 months of age (Bretherton & Beeghly, 1982). Examples of these words were given so parents could record whether their child used any of the words and, if so, in what context. Two additional questions examined if infants understood how to give objects in response to a verbal request or to a nonverbal gesture such as an outreached upturned hand. The data obtained indicated that four of the 14-month-olds did not understand how to give an object in response to a verbal request, while only one of the participants did not understand how to give an object in response to a nonverbal gesture. Parents reported that all of the 18-month-olds understood both verbal and nonverbal requests to give objects.

The second questionnaire was an altered version (Buss & Plomin, 1984) of the Colorado Childhood Temperament Inventory or CCTI (Rowe & Plomin, 1977). This is what might be considered a test of child temperament or, stretching a point, a type of early personality test. You will remember the description of temperament from Chapter 2. This questionnaire was included to test whether personality differences, especially sociability differences, had any effect on the way a child understood the desires of another person.

RESULTS

Not all of the participants responded to the examiner's initial or subsequent requests for food. The levels of compliance and noncompliance to the examiner's requests are presented in Figure 8.2.

There was a significant difference in overall noncompliance based on the participant's age grouping, with 14-month-olds complying less with the examiner's requests for food than their 18-month-old counterparts ($p < .001$). Furthermore, there was a significant difference between the matched and mismatched conditions of the 14-month-olds based on their willingness to comply with the examiner's request for food ($p < .01$). For 18-month-olds, no significant differences were obtained based on preference group; matched and mismatched did not differ in their compliance with requests. Figure 8.2 seems to confirm that 14-month-olds were less adept in the ability to comply with this simple request for food. While graphically presented material can be compelling, it is important to be a critical thinker when trying to interpret graphs and tables. Compliance differences seem large when 14-month-olds are compared to 18-month-olds in Figure 8.2, but the critical thinker

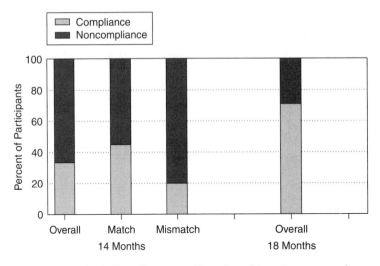
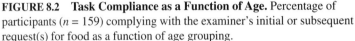

FIGURE 8.2   Task Compliance as a Function of Age. Percentage of participants ($n = 159$) complying with the examiner's initial or subsequent request(s) for food as a function of age grouping.

Source: From Repacholi, B., & Gopnik, A. (1997). Early reasoning about desires: Evidence from 14- and 18-months-olds. *Developmental Psychology, 33,* 12–21.

will also look to see what is being scaled and how the *y*-axis is arranged. Additionally, it is important to consult the text that accompanies graphs to see if differences were statistically significant. Sometimes this information will be supplied in a graph or table, and sometimes not. If it is not, you should dig it out.

Figure 8.3 shows the percentage of participants responding to the examiner's request for food across both age groups in both the matched and mismatched conditions. The 14-month-old infants overwhelmingly responded by giving the examiner crackers ($p < .01$),

FIGURE 8.3   Type of Food Given to Examiner as a Function of Age and Performance Group Assignment.

Source: From Repacholi, B., & Gopnik, A. (1997). Early reasoning about desires: Evidence from 14- and 18-months-olds. *Developmental Psychology, 33,* 12–21.

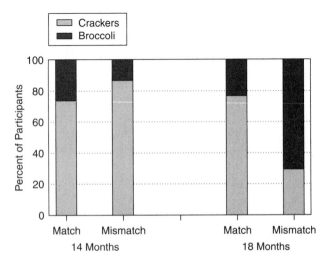

regardless of the preference that had been displayed. With their tendency to give crackers, 14-month-olds in the mismatched group made more mistakes ($p = .009$) because the correct response would have been to give broccoli.

As you can see from Figure 8.3, about the same percentage of participants in the matched conditions offered the examiner the correct food regardless of their age (14 months, 72 percent; 18 months, 76 percent). Among the 18-month-olds, however, group assignment (matched or mismatched) was not significantly related to whether the infants correctly offered the examiner the desired food. The 18-month-olds offered broccoli to the examiner in the mismatched condition significantly more often than did 14-month-olds ($p < .01$). The 14-month-olds typically responded egocentrically in this condition by offering the examiner crackers. A few of the participants engaged in teasing behavior in which they would present one of the food items to the examiner and then pull it away from her. The 14-months-olds were more likely to engage in this type of behavior than were the 18-month-olds (35 percent vs. 11 percent), however, the 18-month-olds who did this ($n = 6$) only teased the examiner with the food she desired. This was another indication that the 18-month-olds understood the desires of the examiner. In contrast, among the 14-month-olds who teased the examiner ($n = 9$), two of the participants teased her with the food item she did not desire.

Among the 18-month-old age group, correct responses to the examiner's desires were significantly related to the age of the participant: Older participants appeared more likely to offer the desired food. To further explore this effect, the researchers separated the 18-month-old participants into two groups, using the median age as the dividing point. The median is the middle score in a distribution of scores. By definition, 50 percent of the scores are above the median and 50 percent are below it. The median age was 18.27 months old in this group. In the median split that created two groups, the younger participants were between 18 and 18.27 months old and older participants were older than 18.27 months. The researchers examined the data on this new division of participants for ability to interpret the examiner's desires. The results are presented in Figure 8.4.

As you can see from examining Figure 8.4, there appear to be no significant differences between the age groups in their ability to offer the correct response (i.e., offer crackers) to the

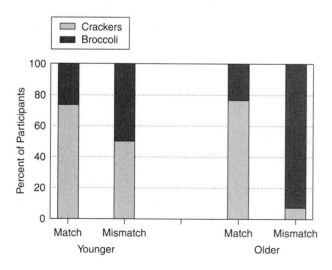

FIGURE 8.4   Type of Food Given to Examiner as a Function of Median Split of 18-Month-Olds and Preference Group.

*Younger, < 18.27 months, and older ≥ 18.27 months.

Source: From Repacholi, B., & Gopnik, A. (1997). Early reasoning about desires: Evidence from 14- and 18-months-olds. *Developmental Psychology, 33,* 12–21.

examiner in the matched condition. However, the younger 18-month-olds were significantly more likely to make an incorrect response (i.e., offer crackers) to the examiner in the mismatched condition ($p = .03$). Also, the difference in food offered for the younger 18-month-olds, that is, whether they offered crackers or broccoli in the mismatched condition, did not exceed chance. They could have been ignoring the examiner's expression and taking a guess about which food to give. Unlike the 14-month-olds, the younger 18-month-olds did not as frequently make a wrong response in the mismatched condition. They were intermediate in age and in errors between the original 14-month-old group and the older 18-month-old group. This can be seen when mismatch errors for 14-month-olds and both groups of 18-month-olds are plotted on the same set of axes. This has been done in Figure 8.5.

The bars depicting crackers in Figure 8.5 show errors made owing to egocentricity. Because all of these are mismatch groups, the children were being asked to understand that the examiner did not share the child's own food preference for crackers. Broccoli is the correct and nonegocentric response and it can be seen to increase dramatically between 14 months and 18.27 months of age.

Repacholi and Gopnik compared the performance of participants using the questionnaire measures that assessed infant temperament and the number of words possessed which referred to internal states. There were no statistically significant differences that related to infant temperament. With respect to knowledge of words denoting internal states, unsurprisingly, the 18-month-olds were found to have more of these words than the 14-month-olds ($M = 3.92$ at 18 months; $M = 1.42$ at 14 months; $p < .001$). For the 18-month-old infants, internal state words did not show any relationship to compliance with food requests or with correct choices of food given. However, 14-month-olds who used at least one word denoting positive emotion were more likely to comply with the request for food.

DISCUSSION

As a scientific thinker, you should be able to look critically at a finding such as the one presented here. Once you are familiar with the entire study, you will need to ask yourself

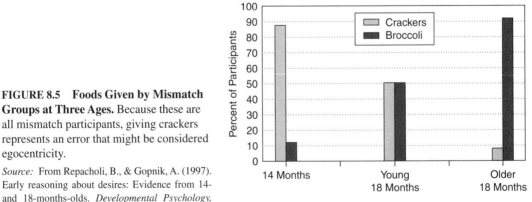

FIGURE 8.5   Foods Given by Mismatch Groups at Three Ages. Because these are all mismatch participants, giving crackers represents an error that might be considered egocentricity.

Source: From Repacholi, B., & Gopnik, A. (1997). Early reasoning about desires: Evidence from 14- and 18-months-olds. *Developmental Psychology, 33,* 12–21.

if there was any way the 14-month-olds' lack of compliance, shown in Figure 8.2, could have accounted for the outcomes measured in this research? In other words, can this be a confound? If you were to think this to be at all likely, you might adjust your confidence in the findings accordingly. Authors of scientific articles give you this information in order to help you think critically about their work.

You should also ask yourself what other factors may have contributed to this particular result? For instance, is it important that the infants had never had any contact with the examiner prior to their testing? Recall that the infants were placed in a situation where they had to respond to the requests of a complete stranger, while their parents ignored them. This might be a more challenging task for younger infants than older infants. Stranger anxiety, the fear of strange people, is supposed to be fully developed by 14 months and it can still be seen in 18-month-olds (Berger, 1998). If you were a researcher conducting this study, you might want to consider this an issue. While we have no particular reason to think it was responsible for the results in this study, we want you to be able to consider such questions and to make sound evaluations of research based on your evaluation of findings and methodology.

Based on the data obtained from the 14- and 18-month-old infants, the 18-month-olds were more successful in offering the examiner the food she desired regardless of whether they were in the matched or mismatched condition. The 14-month-olds were more likely to respond egocentrically and offer the food they themselves preferred regardless of the examiner's desires. We believe this was a very well-constructed study but you should keep in mind that no study could possibly eliminate every single rival explanation for the results. The authors have made a strong case for a response difference in younger children compared to older children. It seems likely to us that egocentricity differences are a reasonable explanation of the results. If this interpretation is correct, then this study seems to have shown a noticeable decrease in egocentricity between 14 and 18 months of age. This might be viewed as being inconsistent with Piagetian expectations because Piaget (1924) believed that there would be substantial egocentricity until at least age 4 or 5.

The kinds of tasks used by Piaget, such as the three-mountain problem, were so complex that they were seemingly impossible for small children. Children could not do these tasks, so the children appeared to be egocentric. New research methods, focusing on ecologically valid tasks such as giving a food object to an adult, have suggested that some egocentricity might fade quite early in life.

The important outcome in this study was quasi-experimental because children cannot be randomly assigned to age groups. You will remember that while a true experiment can yield cause-and-effect conclusions, a quasi-experiment cannot. A number of characteristics including, but not limited to, egocentricity that make 14-month-olds different from 18-month-olds could have been responsible for the results. Perhaps the 14-month-old infants did not understand that they were supposed to respond to the examiner's emotional state by giving her the food she seemed to prefer. It is also possible that the 14-month-old infants may have been more influenced than older children by the examiner's negative emotional display. Indeed, the authors state: "…the infants appeared to be intrigued by the disgust expression; they did not react to it negatively but rather with laughter and increased attention" (Repacholi & Gopnik, 1997, p. 17). Future studies could be specifically designed to investigate these factors. In a quasi-experiment there will always be multiple factors that might be responsible for outcomes. You will be able to appreciate this if you think about all the ways that two age groups of children might be different.

A true experiment with random assignment to groups and the introduction of a manipulated independent variable is the way to isolate cause and effect. However desirable it might be to do a true experiment, age cannot be a true independent variable in the sense that we discussed in Chapter 1. This is a limitation of research and one that we must live with, like it or not.

CRITICAL THINKING TOOLKIT ITEMS

When viewing graphically presented material there are several questions you should ask in order to critically evaluate the data. The answers will not always be readily available in accompanying material, although they should be if the data are presented in a scientific journal article. Figure 8.6 is a sample graph with fictitious data and some questions about it.

1. What is being scaled on the *y* axis? If these are IQ scores you know that the population mean is 100. If they are not IQ scores, what are they? This could be some kind of transformation of scores such as the percentile rank on an intelligence test. If that were so, then 100 would be the highest possible, not the mean. In other words, what is the operational definition of intelligence?
2. What is being scaled on the *x* axis? We gave you verbal labels and that has made the data quite difficult to interpret. For example, "high" might be an annual income of $50,000 and up or it might be $100,000 and up.
3. How large is the effect? This is where the knowledge of the *y* axis becomes useful. If these are IQ scores, the differences are quite small.
4. Which of the differences are statistically significant? These differences have been made to appear quite large by truncating the *y* axis. Their visual appearance is irrelevant because it can be so misleading. Truncated axes should have some sort of break line, but they do not always do so.

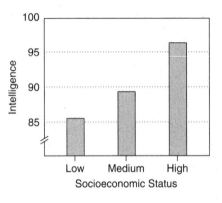

FIGURE 8.6   Intelligence as a Function of SES.

REFERENCES

Berger, K. S. (1998). *The developing person through the life span* (4th ed.). New York: Worth.

Borke, H. (1975). Piaget's mountains revisited: Changes in the egocentric landscape. *Developmental Psychology, 11,* 240–243.

Bretherton, I., & Beeghly, M. (1982). Talking about internal states: The acquisition of and explicit theory of mind. *Developmental Psychology, 18,* 906–921.

Buss, A. H., & Plomin, R. (1984). *Temperament: Early developing personality traits.* Hillsdale, NJ: Erlbaum.

Ekman, P., & Friesen, W. (1975). *Unmasking the face: A guide to recognizing emotions from facial cues.* Englewood Cliffs, NJ: Prentice-Hall.

Gunnar, M. R., & Stone, C. (1984). The effects of positive maternal affect on infant response to pleasant, ambiguous, and fear-provoking toys. *Child Development, 55,* 1231–1236.

Hornik, R., Risenhoover, N., & Gunnar, M. (1987). The effects of maternal positive, neutral, and negative affective communication on infant responses to new toys. *Child Development, 58,* 937–944.

Piaget, J., & Inhelder, B. (1956). *The child's conception of space.* New York: Norton.

Repacholi, B., & Gopnik, A. (1997). Early reasoning about desires: Evidence from 14- and 18-month-olds. *Developmental Psychology, 33,* 12–21.

Rowe, D. C., & Plomin, R. (1977). Temperament in early childhood. *Journal of Personality Assessment, 41,* 150–156.

Wellman, H. M., & Bartsch, K. (1994). Before belief: Children's early psychological theory. In C. Lewis & P. Mitchell (Eds.), *Children's early understanding of mind: Origins and development* (pp. 331–354). Hillsdale, NJ: Erlbaum.

CHAPTER 9

SPARE THE ROD

Aggression in childhood has been a topic of psychological research for many years. Several viewpoints, or models, regarding the origin of aggression have resulted from this investigative effort. These models are not mutually exclusive; that is, you do not have to choose one of them as the answer to questions about where aggression originates. As with most other behaviors, aggression is multidetermined: It has many sources. While alternative models concerning the development of aggression highlight different factors, it is generally agreed that numerous influences operate to shape aggressive behavior. Biological factors have been shown to be prominent among these.

THE BIOLOGY OF AGGRESSION

Two lines of evidence have instantiated the role of biology in aggression: research about hormones and the study of temperament. Many studies of aggression conducted in different settings with children of different ages have suggested that boys are more aggressive than girls. It would be easy to interpret this as social learning; certainly, there are many aggressive males to be imitated on television, in movies, and in real life. However, there is also evidence that male hormones play a role. A study of 17-year-old males in Sweden found that those who had higher blood testosterone levels were more likely to respond aggressively to provocation (Olweus, Mattson, Schalling, & Low, 1988). This is a quasi-experimental outcome, so it is important to be cautious about drawing cause-and-effect conclusions, because either of these might cause the other. Nevertheless, this finding argues for inclusion of biological components among the reasons for aggression.

As you will remember from Chapter 2, *temperament* is the name given to differences in reactivity that can be observed among newborn infants. It is believed that temperament has a significant genetic component. Some of the evidence for this came from temperamental differences found when samples from different countries were compared (Kagan et al., 1994). Additional evidence has shown that temperamental differences are apparent so early

Incorporating the research of Z. Strassberg, K. A. Dodge, G. S. Pettit, and J. E. Bates, "Spanking in the Home and Children's Subsequent Aggression toward Kindergarten Peers," 1994, *Development and Psychopathology, 6,* pp. 445–461.

in life that they are unlikely to be influenced much by social learning. Eisenberg, Fabes, Nyman, Bernzweig, and Pinuelas (1994) studied temperamental precursors of aggression. They found that temperamentally difficult kids at 6 months old were likely to show uncooperative behavior when they were 3 years old. These children were shown to be in conflict with their mothers, to get into trouble for their actions, and to be difficult to control. This can be used as additional evidence for a biological role in aggression because the "difficult" antecedent behavior was observed so early in life.

LEARNING AND AGGRESSION

Another model for the origin of aggression focuses on imitation of behavior, particularly aggressive behavior depicted on television. Hundreds of studies in this area have suggested that aggressive acts can be learned through television watching (Smith & Donnerstein, 1998; Gerbner, Gross, Morgan, & Signorielli, 1994). Longitudinal studies have shown that the effects of watching violent television can be long lasting. For example, the amount of television violence watched when children were 8 years old allowed predictions to be made about aggression at age 19 and criminal activity at age 30 (Eron, 1987; Huesmann, Eron, Lefkowitz, & Walder, 1984).

While television has clearly been implicated as a component of aggressive behavior, there are a few contrary indications. In one interesting study, aggression was measured before and after television was introduced to the remote island of St. Helena in the South Atlantic in the mid-1990s. Analysis of before and after tapes of children playing on playgrounds showed no difference in behavior as a result of the influence of television. This within-subjects comparison depended upon the rare circumstance of finding a population of children who had not initially been exposed to television. Although interesting, this island is so isolated that we would be cautious in generalizing its situation to the rest of the developed world.

For a number of years, research has suggested that physical punishment by parents may be one component of undesirable childhood aggression. It is well known that children can learn aggressive behavior through imitation (Bandura, 1991). In this model, childhood aggression is believed to originate from the physical punishment itself. It is thought that children learn to adopt aggressive solutions to interpersonal difficulties because they have experienced aggression from their parents.

The adage "spare the rod and spoil the child" suggested that failure to use physical discipline on children was the same as making no effort to shape the child's behavior. Yet, there are other ways to control child behavior besides physical discipline. One of the most common alternatives involves using so-called negative punishment rather than positive punishment, the category into which aggressive discipline falls. Technically, punishment is a consequence that reduces the frequency of a behavior. In positive punishment, a stimulus is added to the situation immediately following the behavior. That stimulus is usually something painful and aversive, such as a spanking. Conversely, in negative punishment, a stimulus is removed in order to reduce the frequency of behavior. The most common name for negative punishment of small children is time out. Originally this was called "time out from reward," reminding us that rewards are removed. Accordingly, a time out paradigm might involve a child spending time away from some source of reward, for example, social interaction. Ideally, this might mean that the child is placed in a featureless room which is not frightening or harmful, but which contains no sources of reward. Removal of privileges is another example of negative punishment. Note that the psychological uses of the words *negative* and *positive* in delineating punishments or rewards do not carry any connotation of good or bad. In this technical usage, they merely indicate that a stimulus has been removed or added.

Parents probably use positive physical punishment because it seems to work quickly. Punished behavior ceases, at least for the time being. However, the supposed benefits of positive punishment are likely to be short-term. In addition to this difficulty, punishment is likely to be effective only if undesirable behavior is consistently and immediately punished. Psychologist Gerald Patterson conducted well-known research through the Social Learning Center in Eugene, Oregon. This center has been a world leader in research about the origins of aggressive behavior. Patterson (1995) reported that the families who use punishment inconsistently and erratically, and who do not use rewards to promote prosocial behavior, are likely to have aggressive children.

EXTERNAL VALIDITY

Studies of aggression have been undertaken in lab and field settings. Well-constructed field studies are likely to have a better claim to what is called *external validity*. External validity is the extent to which the results of a study can be generalized to situations beyond those which were characteristic of the study itself. Usually this means that the results of a study are believed to apply to real-world settings. If the results of a lab study only applied to freshman students in a small white room at a certain state university on Thursday, March 17th, they would have no external validity. The study itself would probably be of little use if its findings could not be generalized to other people in other places. A good way to apply critical thinking to the evaluation of a study is to ask yourself about the extent of external validity. *Internal validity* is a related concept for critical thinking, but it refers to the extent to which a study adequately tests its hypothesis. Internal validity may be low owing to weaknesses in the research methodology. A confound would be a classic example of a threat to internal validity. An invalid scale used to measure an outcome would be another threat to internal validity. For two examples that are more subtle, you might question internal validity if a psychological test was used on a group that did not resemble the standardization population for the test, or if within-subjects experimental treatments were inadequately counterbalanced.

A very highly controlled lab study may have very high internal validity but low external validity. Strassberg, Dodge, Pettit, and Bates (1994) did a study that investigated the relationship between physical punishment and aggressive behavior in children. It was a longitudinal study in which the outcomes were measured in field settings, increasing external validity.

PARTICIPANTS

The sample of participants for the study came from kindergarten preregistrations in Nashville and Knoxville, Tennessee, and Bloomington, Indiana. The participants included 273 children who were going to begin kindergarten within the year. Their mothers also participated, and when possible, their fathers participated as well. The gender and ethnicity mix for the three cities is shown in Table 9.1.

As can be seen, the gender breakdown of child participants at each of the three sites was roughly equal and the sample included some ethnic diversity in that about 18 percent of the participants were African American. The families were from a wide range of socioeconomic status (SES) levels. SES was derived from self-reported parental education and occupational information.

PROCEDURE

The researchers explained the research to the parents at a kindergarten preregistration and took the names of parents who were willing to be contacted further about the study. Willing potential participants were given more information about the study in a follow-up phone call. About 70 percent of the families agreed to participate. They were paid $20 to take part in the study.

Because this was not an experiment, there were no independent variables or dependent variables. This was, instead, a correlational study. A number of measurements were made and then relationships were sought between those measures and some subsequent outcomes. As you will remember from Chapter 2, correlational data do not allow us to conclude that strongly related measures are causally linked, although this may in fact be the case. Even high correlations do not permit a determination to be made about causal relationships. If some variables in a correlational study occur ahead of the others in time, those occurring first may be called *antecedent variables* or *predictors*. The antecedent variables in the study by Strassberg et al. (1994) were sex of child, sex of parent, SES, and parental disciplinary behavior.

SES was operationally defined using the Hollingshead four-factor classification scheme. The Hollingshead scheme numerically rates occupation type and years of education. These scores are multiplied by a measure of marital status. Gender is also considered. The result is a social status score that can vary from 8, for the lowest SES, to 66 for the

TABLE 9.1   Gender and Ethnic Mix of Child Participants

	Girls		*Boys*	
	AFRICAN AMERICAN	CAUCASIAN	AFRICAN AMERICAN	CAUCASIAN
Nashville	17	31	20	30
Knoxville	3	46	9	43
Bloomington	0	32	0	39

Note: There were three other children in the study who did not fit into these ethnic categories. One was from Nashville and two were from Knoxville.

Source: From Strassberg, Z., Dodge, K. A., Pettit, G. S., & Bates, J. E. (1994). Spanking in the home and children's subsequent aggression toward kindergarten peers. *Development and Psychopathology, 6,* 448.

highest SES. The Hollingshead scheme correlates highly with other methods of measuring SES (Gottfried, 1985).

The discipline practices of the parent were operationally defined by outcomes from the Conflict Tactics Scale, or CTS (Straus, 1979, 1987). This scale measures 14 different behaviors used to discipline children, ranging from discussion with the child to exercising serious physical violence. The CTS is a written questionnaire that was filled out by parents. A mathematical conversion of the data was used by Strassberg, et al. (1994) so that the disciplinary behavior frequency could be expressed in terms of the number of times per week a particular form of discipline was used. The reported outcome scores ranged from 0, never used in a week, to 6, used almost every day. Only the CTS items that measured physical punishment were used as outcome measures in this study. These items were separated into two categories: spanking and violence. *Spanking* was defined as spanking on the buttocks with a hand or with some other object. *Violence* was hitting with a closed hand or fist, hitting with another object, or beating up the child. Spanking occurred in a controlled and planned manner, whereas violence was defined as impulsive and spontaneous.

If you are surprised that researchers would give a questionnaire asking parents if they beat their children, so were we. The researchers discussed the ethical issue of whether they were obliged to notify the appropriate social services agency concerning parents who used severe punishment. At least in Tennessee, where most of the data were collected, the law requires reporting of "known or observed recent injury" to a child (Strassberg et al., 1994) but not the description of parental acts. In other words, the researchers were not required to notify authorities based on parents' responses to questions in the study. They would have been required to do so if they had seen children with injuries. Even so, the researchers decided to report six of the families to authorities for further investigation based on the parental descriptions of disciplinary practices. As an additional approach to the ethical issue, all parents participating in the study were made aware that social services help with family problems was available to them if they wanted it.

MEASURING AGGRESSION

About 6 months after the data from interviews and questionnaires were collected from parents, the children were observed and recordings were made of aggression directed toward peers. Trained observers watched the participant children, focusing on one at a time, while the children interacted with peers on a playground and in a classroom. Three types of aggression were recorded:

1. *Bullying:* an attack on another child, which was not provoked by the child who was attacked.
2. *Reactive Aggression:* an aggressive response to intentional or accidental behavior of another child.
3. *Instrumental Aggression:* aggression to obtain a toy or other object. The purpose of this aggression was to obtain a goal, not necessarily to hurt a person.

Children were observed for a total of 12 observation periods, each of which was 5 minutes long. The observations took place on six or more days over several weeks. The observers recorded the occurrence of bullying, reactive aggression, and instrumental aggression within each 10-second interval of a 5-minute observation period. Scores were calculated as the frequency of a particular type of aggression per hour. The aggression subtype scores were also summed to produce a total aggression score.

An additional observer scored 130 randomly selected 5-minute observation sessions at the same time in order to assess interobserver reliability. For total aggressive acts, the interrater agreement was 96 percent. Agreement was a bit less for the three different kinds of aggression but it was nevertheless high, ranging from 87 percent to 93 percent.

RESULTS

Male children were more likely to be aggressive than females (all $p < .02$) on each type of aggression and in total aggressive behavior, as is shown in Figure 9.1. The finding that males are more aggressive than females is one of the most frequently substantiated outcomes in the literature of developmental psychology (Loeber & Hay, 1993).

A total of 169 of the homes consisted of two parents and 104 were mother-only single-parent homes. The aggression scores from observation of children were not significantly correlated with the presence or absence of a father in the home.

The three individual subtypes of aggression as well as total aggression observed in participant children were all significantly negatively correlated with SES. The numerical value of these correlations was quite low, however, ranging from $r = .15$ to $r = .24$. Although these were statistically significant ($p < .02$), this only indicated that they were significantly different from no relationship, or $r = 0$. Even though they were significant, the correlations were so low that they did not have much predictive power: Knowing the value of one does not allow you to say much about what the value of the other is likely to be. In other words, if we tell you that a child has been observed to be aggressive, that does not allow you to make any confident predictions about the SES of that child. You can see this for yourself if you square the correlations described in Chapter 2.

There were some SES differences in punishment use. These are shown in Figure 9.2. The group of mothers who used violent discipline shown in Figure 9.2 was of significantly

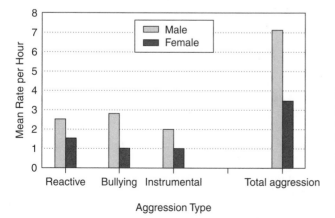

FIGURE 9.1   Mean Rates of Aggression per Hour. Mean rates of different kinds of aggression observed in male and female children.

Source: From Strassberg, Z., Dodge, K. A., Pettit, G. S., & Bates, J. E. (1994). Spanking in the home and children's subsequent aggression toward kindergarten peers. *Development and Psychopathology, 6,* 445–461.

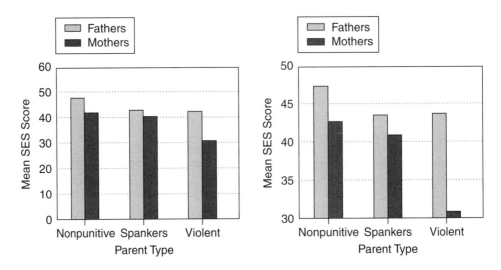

FIGURE 9.2 SES and Punishment. The left- and right-hand graphs contain the same data. In order to help you develop critical thinking skills, we have replotted the data on the right hand graph with a truncated *y* axis from which a small section has been selected and stretched. While there are some differences, these appear to be much larger on the right-hand graph. Graphs such as the one on the right should have some kind of break line in the *y* axis—missing here—to indicate that part of the axis had been clipped off, possibly exaggerating the appearance of the data.

Source: From Strassberg, Z., Dodge, K. A., Pettit, G. S., & Bates, J. E. (1994). Spanking in the home and children's subsequent aggression toward kindergarten peers. *Development and Psychopathology, 6,* 445–461.

lower SES than the nonpunitive mothers or the spankers ($p < .001$). The statistical test applied to the fathers showed no significant differences but Strassberg, et al. (1994) noted a "marginal trend" for nonpunitive fathers to be higher SES than violent and spanking fathers ($p < .15$). The interpretation of marginal trends is up to you, as we discussed in Chapter 5. In order to interpret these data, it is important to remember that Hollingshead SES outcomes are scored between 8 and 66. While the mothers' scores cannot be interpreted in terms of a single dimension, such as income dollars, you should notice that the difference found for mothers represents about 25 percent of the possible SES range with this instrument. This is substantial and probably reflects some real lifestyle differences associated with SES.

The main question addressed by this study was whether parental punishment practices had a relationship to subsequent aggression in children. This question was addressed separately for mothers and fathers. The most clear-cut results came from associations between the type of punishment used by the mothers and aggressive acts of the children. It is possible that punishment from the mothers had more pervasive effects than fathers because mothers typically do more child care. For maternal punishment, spanked children were more aggressive ($M = 4.62$) overall than children whose mothers did not use spanking or violence ($M = 2.24$). This 106 percent difference was statistically significant ($p < .05$). Children whose mothers used violent punishment were aggressive more frequently than children who were spanked (violent $M = 8.54$, spanked $M = 4.62$). This was a significant 85 percent increase ($p < .02$). In the subcategories of aggression, children who received violent punishment from mothers were more likely to be reactive in aggression and to bully others than children who were spanked by mothers (both $p < .03$). No difference was found for instrumental aggression across different punishment types.

There were significant correlations between violence as a maternal style and the different types of aggressive behavior. While these correlations were not large, ranging from $r = .21$ to $r = .25$, they were all statistically significant ($p < .001$). For spanking, an additional analysis showed that while there was a positive correlation between whether spanking occurred and observed aggressive behavior, surprisingly this was not found to vary with frequency of spanking. In other words, the occurrence—or not—of spanking mattered, but how often it happened did not. The frequency is not significant, but spanking is significant. In contrast, for maternal violence, both whether violence happened as well as how often it happened mattered.

Boys who were spanked by their fathers showed more overall aggression ($M = 5.4$) than boys with fathers who did not use any aggressive punishment ($M = 1.63, p < .01$). This relationship did not hold for punishment by fathers directed at girl children. Spanked boys also bullied others more frequently than boys whose fathers used no aggressive punishment ($M = 1.5$; $M = 0.0, p < .02$).

Strassberg et al. (1994) noted that children who were violently punished by fathers "aggressed marginally more frequently (by 40%)" (p. 454) than children who were spanked by fathers ($p < .10$). The violently punished children bullied others "marginally more frequently" (p. 454) than did children who were spanked ($p < .10$).

Paternal violence had low but significant correlations with reactive and bullying aggression. As was seen with the mothers, there was a positive correlation between ever having been spanked and aggression but no correlation between *the amount of spanking* and aggression.

Some of the families in this study were two-parent families and Strassberg et al. (1994) wondered to what extent similar or different punishment practices of the two parents in a home had an effect on observed aggression in their children. As mentioned in Chapter 6, when a study population gets broken down into small categories, its statistical power is lost. When numbers of participants are small, it is very difficult to find statistically significant differences, even though the observed differences are quite large. The mathematics of the calculations of most statistical tests take the number of participants into account and tend to find no differences when there are few participants. In this case, looking at two-parent families required removing all the single-parent families from consideration, drastically reducing the number of participants available for analysis. Mean total aggression scores by parental type are presented in Table 9.2.

Note the small numbers of children who end up in each cell of Table 9.2. Strassberg et al. (1994) pointed out the impossibility of doing statistical tests on these data, stating that the data were presented for "qualitative inspection." The data presented here are interesting to look at, and we encourage you to try to tell a story consistent with the data. Putting the numbers into a story will help you to remember their apparent relationships to each other. An example of a story someone might tell after examining Table 9.2 would be that when a child had two violently punishing parents, he or she displayed high levels of aggression. While interpreting these kinds of data or, in our terms, telling stories it is important to

TABLE 9.2   **Mean Total Child Aggression Scores**

Mother Type	Father Type		
	NONUSE	SPANKING	VIOLENT
Nonuse	0.20	5.00	no cases
	$n = 5$	$n = 5$	$n = 0$
Spanking	4.48	4.34	4.50
	$n = 13$	$n = 93$	$n = 6$
Violence	2.89	5.49	6.86
	$n = 1$	$n = 19$	$n = 7$

Note: These have been cross-tabulated by mother and father aggression types. The designation *n* indicates the number of children in each cell of the table. Cross-tabulation means that a given cell contains the data for children whose mothers reported the type of aggression shown along the side and whose fathers reported the type of aggression shown along the top. For example, children whose mothers and fathers did not use aggression (nonuse) have an aggression score of .20. If the father spanked and the mother did not use aggression, the children score 5.00, and so on.

Source: From Strassberg, Z., Dodge, K. A., Pettit, G. S., & Bates, J. E. (1994). Spanking in the home and children's subsequent aggression toward kindergarten peers. *Development and Psychopathology, 6,* 455.

remember that the story is just that: a story. The data may suggest this particular story, but the evidence is not very robust. By this we mean that we cannot put much confidence in it. Without the statistical backing that would come from a larger number of cases, acceptance of this story must remain quite tentative. Caution in phrasing is one of the features that distinguish people who understand science from people who do not. People who do not understand the workings of science are more likely to state outcomes in absolute terms with no reference to the robustness of the data. Taking account of our brief diatribe, you should have a careful look at Table 9.2 and construct a cautious story or two in order to summarize the data for yourself.

DISCUSSION AND CONCLUSIONS

Aside from the main findings, probably the most interesting indications from this study were the high total frequencies of physical punishment and of aggression that were reported. Boys were observed to have a total mean aggression rate of more than seven incidents per hour. Girls were also substantially aggressive at half this level. From Table 9.2 it can be seen that among the two-parent families, 33 of the children, or 22 percent, experienced at least one violent parent. Seven of them had two violent parents. It pays to remember that this violence was directed at prekindergarten children. If we consider that parents might be more likely to underreport than overreport this behavior, the actual levels may even be higher than were shown here.

Another important finding was that the frequency of spanking did not seem to make as much difference in aggressive outcomes as whether spanking happened at all. Strassberg et al. (1994) pointed out that this could be interpreted to mean that children have a very low threshold for turning the experience of aggressive punishment into their own aggressive behavior. *Threshold* is a concept that you will encounter in many domains of psychology and it is one that you should understand. This concept is derived from an analogy with the threshold at the bottom of a door, leading into a room. With doors, a threshold is a boundary between two different areas: in or out of a room. In psychology, it is a boundary between different states of behavior, such as nonaggression or aggression. When the threshold is low, aggression happens readily; it is easy to cross into that state. In order to fully understand this concept, you should reflect on some examples from your own life. When we read something that is boring, many of us find we have a low threshold for daydreaming, which happens easily and readily. On the other hand, many of us have a high threshold for using physical violence; we would have to be severely provoked before we would physically attack someone. The findings reported here suggest that even a few spankings are enough to predispose aggressive behavior in children. The threshold is low. It is not only the frequently punished child who is aggressive on the playground.

Although the data presented are broken down into different types of aggression, the overall pattern is the same for boys and girls and mothers and fathers. A scan of Figures 9.3 and 9.4 would suggest the conclusion that increasing the violence of punishment type is associated with increases in aggressive behavior. This conclusion is the type of interpretation that we have called a story because the differences are not statistically significant for every comparison. Nevertheless, some of the differences are significant and the others point in the same direction. Although we might be less confident in the discussion of any particular association between punishment type and aggression type, we are fairly confident that there was an important relationship demonstrated by the data in this study.

The correlations with SES and punishment suggested that lower SES families were more likely to use spanking or violence. SES usually measures parental income and educational levels. There are a variety of stories one might tell about this finding, but further investigation would be required to confirm any of them. It is imaginable, for example, that parents with less income might have to spend more hours at less rewarding work in order to survive financially. They might not be willing to take the time required for negative punishment—such as time out—and discussion with the child. There are statistical tactics that allow researchers to numerically remove the effects of, or control for, a particular variable in doing a data analysis. This means that the impact of this variable is mathematically eliminated in order to see if other variables continue to make a difference in its absence. When Strassberg et al. (1994) controlled for SES, the use of physical punishment continued to be associated with aggressive behavior. This continued association points to the robustness of the main findings. Aggression leads to aggression, regardless of SES differences among parents.

Physical punishment is not the only factor leading to aggression. Other factors in the life of a child such as observed aggression (Bandura, 1991) and martial conflict (Hughes, 1988; Jaffe, Wolfe, Wilson, & Zak, 1986) have also been shown to make a difference. Because boys have been repeatedly shown to be more aggressive than girls, we are willing to believe that biological factors almost certainly play a role as well. In spite of the multidetermined nature of child aggressive behavior, we believe that the study by Strassberg, et al. (1994) pointed with confidence to one interesting component of childhood aggression.

CRITICAL THINKING TOOLKIT ITEMS

Assess research studies for both internal and external validity. Internal validity involves such things as avoiding confounds while providing adequate operational definitions, measures, and controls in the design of the research. External validity is the extent to which results may be applied to situations beyond the study itself. No study will have perfect internal or external validity but the assessment of these characteristics should be part of your evaluation of research.

Some data are more robust than others. Robustness refers to the rigor of the methods and quality of the data analysis. When data are not robust, you should be less confident about conclusions based on them.

It can be useful to interpret study findings, even weak ones, by telling stories about the data. Organizing data into stories makes them easier to remember. While engaged in this task it is crucial to speak cautiously when data are not robust.

REFERENCES

Bandura, A. (1991). Social cognitive theory of moral thought and action. In W. Kurtines & J. Gewirtz (Eds.), *Handbook of moral behavior and development: Vol. 1* (pp. 45–104). Hillsdale, NJ: Erlbaum.

Eisenberg, N., Fabes, R. A., Nyman, M., Bernzweig, J., & Pinuelas, A. (1994). The relations of emotionality and regulation of children's anger-related reactions. *Child Development, 65,* 109–128.

Eron, L. D. (1987). The development of aggressive behavior from the perspective of a developing behaviorism. *American Psychologist, 42,* 435–442.

Gerbner, G., Gross, L., Morgan, M., & Signorielli, N. (1994). Growing up with television: The cultivation perspective. In J. Bryant & D. Zillman (Eds.), *Media effects: Advances in theory and research* (pp. 17–42). Hillsdale, NJ: Erlbaum.

Gottfried, A. (1985). Measures of socioeconomic status in child development research: Data and recommendations. *Merrill-Palmer Quarterly, 31,* 85–92.

Hughes, H. (1988). Psychological and behavioral correlates of family violence in child witnesses and victims. *American Journal of Orthopsychiatry, 58,* 77–90.

Huesmann, L. R., Eron, L. D., Lefkowitz, M. M., & Walder, L. O. (1984). Stability of aggression over time and generations. *Developmental Psychology, 20,* 1120–1134.

Jaffe, P., Wolfe, D., Wilson, S., & Zak, L. (1986). Similarities in behavioral and social maladjustment among child victims and witnesses to family violence. *American Journal of Orthopsychiatry, 56,* 142–146.

Kagan, J., Arcus, D., Snidman, N., Feng, W., Hendler, J., & Greene, S. (1994). Reactivity in infants: A cross-national comparison. *Developmental Psychology, 30,* 342–345.

Loeber, R., & Hay, D. F. (1993). Developmental approaches to aggression and conduct problems. In M. Rutter & D. F. Hay (Eds.), *Development through life: A handbook for clinicians* (pp. 488–516). Oxford: Blackwell Scientific.

Olweus, D., Mattson, A., Schalling, D., & Low, H. (1988). Circulating testosterone levels and aggression in adolescent males: A causal analysis. *Psychosomatic Medicine, 50,* 261–272.

Patterson, G. R. (1995). Coercion—A basis for early age of onset for arrest. In J. McCord (Ed.), *Coercion and punishment in long-term perspective* (pp. 81–105). New York: Cambridge University Press.

Smith, S. L., & Donnerstein, E. (1998). Harmful effects of exposure to media violence: Learning of aggression, emotional desensitization, and fear. In R. G. Geen & E. Donnerstein (Eds.), *Human aggression: Theories, research, and implications for social policy* (pp. 167–202). San Diego, CA: Academic.

Strassburg, Z., Dodge, K. A., Pettit, G. S., & Bates, J. E. (1994). Spanking in the home and children's subsequent aggression toward kindergarten peers. *Development and Psychopathology, 6,* 445–461.

Straus, M. A. (1979). Measuring infrafamily conflict and violence: The Conflict Tactics Scale. *Journal of Marriage and the Family, 41,* 75–88.

Straus, M. A. (1987). *Measuring physical and emotional abuse of children with the Conflict Tactics Scale.* Unpublished report, Family Violence Research Program of the Family Research Laboratory, University of New Hampshire, Durham.

CHAPTER 10

REACH FOR THE SKY!

A predominant view of cognitive immaturity in young children incorporates the belief that they are inescapably disadvantaged in the world because their cognitive systems are not fully functioning. According to this view, children must undergo considerable development before these deficits can be overcome. Gould (1977) described human babies as "helpless and undeveloped at birth." It is not a profound observation that newborns appear helpless when compared to older humans. Recently, however, interest has been kindled among psychologists and biologists to attempt to find out why human newborns are so seemingly helpless, particularly when compared to the newborns of other species. The traditional answer has been that humans are immature at birth because of the biological necessity to be born before the large human brain has developed to the point where the head is too big to fit through the birth canal. While this may be a component of the immaturity of newborn humans, new thinking has sought other, associated, benefits of immaturity in infancy. The contemporary psychological view of infants combines an improved understanding of evolution with new demonstrations of competence in small children. As we mentioned in Chapter 6, current psychological thinking contends that children's cognitive and motor immaturity may serve as evolutionarily adaptive mechanisms that play necessary and important functions in a child's development (Bjorklund & Green, 1992).

Some proponents of this adaptationist view (Lenneberg, 1967; Oppenheim, 1981) have proposed that certain cognitive-social abilities, for example, language and attachment, may be more readily acquired by an immature cognitive system. Cognitive limitations make it difficult to store large chunks of language as single units, so language tends to be stored in smaller pieces. Later in life, the small fragments stored by an immature cognitive system can be used in flexible ways to create a wide variety of new phrases. In contrast, when an adult learns a new language, large phrases may be stored together, resulting in a diminished ability to use the small parts in novel ways. Additionally, immature sensory capacities, such as limited visual acuity, may help infants interpret a very complex world by focusing attention on nearby objects and events (Turkewitz & Kenny, 1982).

Additional support for the view that cognitive immaturity may have benefits comes from research studying *metacognition,* or a person's awareness and monitoring of their own thought processes. Thinking about one's own memory, decision making, attention, and problem solving are examples of metacognitive tasks. In a study of metamemory, Flavell,

Incorporating the research of J. Plumert, "Relations between Children's Overestimation of Their Physical Abilities and Accident Proneness," 1995, *Developmental Psychology, 31,* pp. 866–876.

Friedrichs, and Hoyt (1970) demonstrated that 5- and 6-year-old children tended to over-estimate how much they could remember. One of the hallmarks of immature thinking is overestimation. Similarly, other metacognitive research has suggested that young children often remain confident about their memory abilities, even after they experience failure on memory-related tasks (Yussen & Levy, 1975).

In the domain of motor performance, Bjorklund, Gualtney, and Green (1992) found that children often overestimated the extent to which they could imitate a given behavior, such as juggling, and consistently made inaccurate assessments of their performance even after they had attempted to perform the task. Therefore, the tendency for young children to overestimate their abilities may apply not only to metacognitive tasks, but to physical tasks as well.

Bjorklund et al. (1992) argued that poor metacognitive abilities might serve an adaptive function. Children's overestimation and overconfidence in their abilities may protect them from the effects of failure and generate the necessary motivation to allow them to persist at tasks when they might otherwise have given up. Giving up is sometimes called *learned helplessness* and it is discussed more fully in Chapter 14.

Some aspects of cognitive and physical performance in small children have now been shown to be more competent than was previously realized. Earlier chapters, such as Chapters 1, 5, and 8, illustrate some of this research in cognitive development. These were primarily demonstrations of cognitive development, but they also required some physical competence. Several recent studies have investigated performances requiring significant physical components, in addition to cognitive processing. J. J. Gibson (1979) pointed out that a great deal of adaptive functioning requires the perception of *affordances:* the fit between a person's behavior and the properties of the environment in which the behavior takes place. Even very young children may be able to accurately perceive the relationship between the situational demands of a task and their physical abilities. For example, walking infants change to crawling when they move from a rigid surface to a nonrigid surface, such as a waterbed (Gibson et al., 1987). Adolph, Epler, and Gibson (1993) found that infants changed their behavior from walking to crawling or sliding as the slope of a surface changed. Consistent with previous findings involving ability estimation, they found that even though considerable competence was displayed in judging affordances, infants tended to overestimate their ability to walk on slopes.

Plumert (1995) designed a quasi-experiment to test the estimation of affordances on several engineered tasks in two age groups of children and in adults. To connect this research to the real world, she also examined the extent to which this cognitive skill might be related to children's previous accident history.

STUDY 1

Participants

Three different age groups were examined in this study: 6-year-olds (6 years to 6 years, 10 months), 8-year-olds (8 years, 2 months to 8 years, 11 months), and adults. Each age group consisted of 20 participants, with equal numbers of males and females in each age category. The researcher used college students as the adult participants in the study and awarded them course credit in exchange for their participation. (The issue of college students as participants is discussed in Chapter 21.) The children's parents were contacted from a list of potential volunteers. Informed consent procedures were administered. Most of the children who participated in the study were white and came from middle- to upper-middle-class backgrounds.

Design and Procedure

Children were presented with four different physical tasks. The researcher used each task to distinguish between the children's perceived physical abilities (whether they thought they could perform a physical task) and their actual physical abilities (whether they could perform the physical task). _

Figure 10.1, from Plumert (1995), shows the equipment used to perform each of the physical tasks. The four physical task activities can be described as follows:

1. *Vertical Reach Task:* Participants reach above their heads, while on tiptoes, and try to grab a small toy from a shelf.
2. *Horizontal Reach Task:* Participants squat on top of a flat wooden board with toes positioned against a raised edge on one side of the board. While in this squatting position, participants reach out in front of themselves and try to grab a toy duck off the top of a wooden block. This task was judged successful if participant's hands or knees did not come into contact with the ground while reaching for the duck.
3. *Stepping Task:* Participants line up their toes against the edge of one of two parallel wooden sticks. Participants then attempt to step over the gap between the wooden sticks.

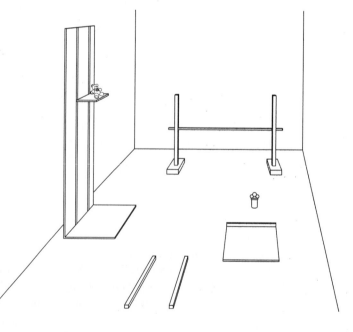

**FIGURE 10.1   Apparatus
Used for Testing Affordances.**

From J. Plumert. (1995) Relations between children's overestimation of their physical abilities and accident proneness. *Developmental Psychology, 31,* 866–876. Copyright © American Psychological Association. Reprinted with permission.

4. *Clearance Task:* Participants squat parallel to a wooden bar held in place by two adjoining supports. This task was judged successful if participants could crawl underneath the wooden bar without jarring it loose from the supports or touching a hand or knee to the floor.

For the study, these tasks were presented in each of four different levels of difficulty. The author refers to these four levels of difficulty as *task versions.* The four task versions were as follows:

1. *Well Within:* The task could easily be performed by the participant.
2. *Just Within:* The task could be performed but required the participant's full physical ability.
3. *Just Beyond:* The task could not be performed. The task apparatus was set 8 percent above the full physical abilities of the participant.
4. *Well Beyond:* The task could not be performed. The task apparatus was set 13 percent above the full physical ability of the participant.

Prior to any test trials, baseline measures were obtained outside the laboratory room in order to gauge each participant's maximum level of physical ability. At baseline, participants were asked to perform the task-related movements, but none of the laboratory equipment was used. During the testing procedures, both task activity (vertical reach, horizontal reach, etc.), and task version (well within, just within, etc.) were presented in random order.

Participants were individually brought into the laboratory and a researcher explained to them that they would be playing a game that involved making decisions about their ability to perform physical activities using four different pieces of lab equipment. The researcher told the participants that the game would be scored in the following manner:

A point would be added to their score if they believed they were capable of performing a specified task activity and could subsequently meet the demands of the task by executing the proper physical action.

A point would be deducted from their score if they believed they could perform a given task activity, but then could not successfully complete the proper physical action required by the task.

If participants believed they were capable of performing an activity, they were asked to perform it. However, if they believed they were incapable of performing an activity, they were not asked to try it. Points were tabulated on a chalkboard in the laboratory. At the end of all testing trials, participants were asked to try to perform those activities they had previously indicated were beyond their physical abilities. This was done so that comparisons could be made between participant's beliefs about their physical abilities and the true nature of their physical abilities.

Before participants were required to make a judgment about a particular activity, the researcher told them how a successful activity could be performed on each piece of equipment. Participants were then requested to assume a specified starting position for each activity. Once a participant had assumed the proper starting position, the researcher then asked them if they believed they were capable of performing the given task activity. The time that elapsed following the researcher's question and the participant's Yes or No response was recorded. This elapsed time interval is known as a *latency* period. Latencies are common outcome measures in many types of research, and we feel it is important that you familiarize yourself with this term. A latency period always represents some interval of time that elapses between two events. The time it takes a runner to finish a marathon is an example of a latency period: It is the recorded time interval between the start of the race and the point where the runner crosses the finish line.

Each participant was removed from the laboratory room after he or she had completed four test trials so that the laboratory equipment could be adjusted to a different level of difficulty by a second researcher. This procedure ensured that participants were unaware of whether task difficulty had changed. Throughout the trials, participants were videotaped through a one-way mirror. Parents were asked to fill out the Accidental Injury Questionnaire for their children while they waited for their children to finish the testing. The questionnaire requested various information about serious injuries requiring medical attention their children had encountered in the past.

The accuracy of the participants' judgments about their physical abilities was recorded. A judgment was considered correct if the participant had responded Yes to the researcher's question regarding their ability to perform a well within or just within task. Furthermore, a judgment was deemed correct if the participant had responded No to the researcher's question about the just beyond and well beyond tasks. All other responses were considered incorrect. Overall accuracy scores were then calculated.

Results

A primary question the author wanted to answer was if there is a significant difference between the age groups in terms of their ability to accurately estimate their physical abilities for the task. Figure 10.2 presents these findings. The children were significantly more accurate in judging their ability to perform the well within and just within task versions than they were at judging their ability to perform the just beyond and well beyond task versions. This pattern of response suggests that young children tend to overestimate their physical

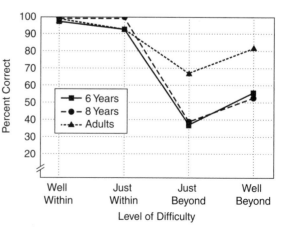

FIGURE 10.2   Mean Percentage of Correct Judgments as a Function of Age and Difficulty Level.

Source: From Plumert, J. (1995). Relations between children's overestimation of their physical abilities and accident proneness. *Developmental Psychology, 31,* 866–876.

abilities, but are less likely to underestimate them. When all judgments were considered together, there was an overall effect of age; adults performed better. However, the group of adults performed less well on the just beyond task than the others.

The participants' mean response latencies were also investigated based on which task version had been presented to them. For this analysis, the data for all three age groups were averaged together. These findings are shown in Figure 10.3. Participants took significantly less time to decide whether they could perform the well within task version compared to the other three task versions. Also, it took participants significantly more time to respond to the researcher's question about the just beyond task version than it did for the just within task version.

Before the mean response latencies in Figure 10.3 were statistically computed, the extreme scores in each age category were removed from the data analysis. These scores were at least three standard deviations above the mean, and the number of 6-year-old, 8-year-old, and adult participants whose data were excluded from this analysis was six, nine, and five, respectively. A simplified description of the calculation of the standard deviation *(SD)* is that it involves subtracting each score from the mean, literally finding out how much it deviates or differs from the mean, and then averaging these differences. The formula is a little more complex than this, but conceptually the *SD* is an average of the amount that scores in a group differ from the mean. An individual's raw score can also be expressed as the number of standard deviations it is away from the mean.

We will not attempt to teach you at length about the standard deviation because that would be beyond the scope of this book. We will provide a brief introduction to the SD that should suffice for our purposes. You will encounter the standard deviation in other chapters in this book and in many original journal articles.

The standard deviation is a measure of variation within a distribution of scores. It is an improvement on the range as a measure of variation because the range is very sensitive to extreme scores. The range is exactly what it sounds like: the lowest score and the highest score. If all the scores in a group were clustered tightly around a mean but there was one extreme score, the range would be dramatically affected by this extreme score. Because the *SD* averages the differences between each score and the mean, one extreme score would not change the *SD* much, particularly in a large group of scores. For a whole

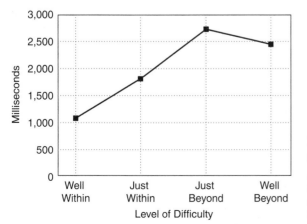

FIGURE 10.3   Mean Response Latencies as a Function of Difficulty Level.

Source: From Plumert, J. (1995). Relations between children's overestimation of their physical abilities and accident proneness. *Developmental Psychology, 31,* 866–876.

distribution of scores, when the *SD* is large, there is a lot of variability in the population; when it is small, there is little variation. By definition, 68 percent of the scores in a distribution fall between one standard deviation below the mean and one standard deviation above the mean. Ninety-five percent of the scores in a normal bell-shaped distribution fall between plus and minus two standard deviations (± 2 *SD*) and 99 percent of the scores occur between −3 and +3 *SD*. In the cases where data were dropped in this study, the dropped scores were three standard deviations above the mean; they were much higher than the other scores, suggesting that these people took an extraordinary amount of time to make decisions.

As part of your critical thinking when reading scientific research, it is important to recognize manipulations in data similar to those described here. In this case, based on your assessment of the importance of the participants who were dropped from the analysis, you may adjust your confidence in a particular finding. For example, in this study it is important to remember that the number of participants in each age group was 20. Thus, for the 8-year-olds' data, nine outliers were excluded from this analysis, just less than half of all the participants in this age category. The data set in this study must have been unusual to have so many participants with very extreme scores. Faced with this, a naive thinker might jump to the conclusion that the data are worthless, but such an extreme reaction would indicate a lack of scientific understanding. This situation might, however, justifiably modify your confidence in the findings because they resulted from highly selected data. In this case, we have some doubts about the value of the latency data because it seems as if some of the participants took a very long time to respond compared to others. This is our judgment, not some absolute right or wrong. One of the things we want you to be able to do is to make a judgment about how much confidence you can have in any particular data set and be able to support that judgment with some good reasons.

We have concerns when a high percentage of participants are dropped before a particular data set is analyzed. Sometimes there may be good reasons for dropping a participant, as when a piece of equipment fails or when it is obvious that a participant is not paying attention to the task. In the case of the response latencies in this study, participants seem to have been dropped from the analysis because they were extreme outliers: people with scores dramatically different from the mean. This undermines our confidence in these data and we would, at least, like to have some more information about why so many people were so different from the average time for the group. The lack of confidence that we might have in the response latency data do not necessarily generalize to the other findings in the study, however. When research studies have a number of different outcome measures, it is usually possible to critically evaluate each on its own merits. Sometimes outcomes that, considered alone, are weak can nevertheless help to support a number of stronger findings that point in the same direction.

Another question addressed by the researcher was if there is a relationship between the children's ability to make accurate judgments regarding their physical abilities and how vulnerable they have been to accidents in the past. To examine this relationship, a correlation was computed between children's judgment accuracy for tasks that were beyond their physical abilities and the number of previous accidents requiring medical attention, as reported by mothers on the Accidental Injury Questionnaire. A significant correlation was obtained for the 6-year-olds' data ($r = -.44$, $p = .05$). For 8-year-olds, no significant relationship was obtained on this measure ($r = .10$, *ns*).

STUDY 2

An additional experimental manipulation was implemented in a related study in order to evaluate the influence of practice on children's estimation of their physical abilities; the researchers wanted to know if prior successes and failures would influence how accurately children would estimate their ability to perform the different task versions. The same set of procedures was followed as in Study 1, except twenty-four 6-year-olds and twenty-four 8-year-olds were recruited and given four practice trials with the test apparatus prior to the actual testing session. When children were presented with the practice trials, they were not asked to make any assessment of their physical abilities. Children were randomly assigned to one of the two following practice conditions:

> *Success Condition:* Each of the four practice trials prior to the testing session could be accomplished and each task was set to be 10 percent more achievable than the participants' maximum abilities.

> *Failure Condition:* Each of the four practice trials prior to the testing session could not be accomplished and each task was set to be 10 percent less achievable than the participants' maximum abilities.

Results

The independent variable success or failure did not result in any important outcomes; however, this study produced other interesting findings. In order to evaluate the influence of age and practice on children's judgment of their physical abilities, children's responses to whether they could perform a particular task were compared across the four task versions. The results are presented in Figure 10.4.

Once again, 6-year-old children were significantly better at estimating the nature of their physical abilities for the well within and just within task versions than the just beyond and well beyond task versions. The success or failure comparison did not lead to significant differences between the conditions. However, a difference appeared between the two age

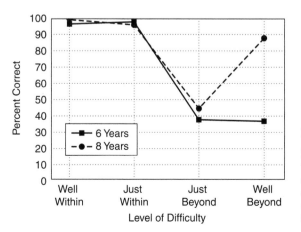

FIGURE 10.4   Mean Percentage of Correct Judgments as a Function of Age and Difficulty Level.

Source: From Plumert, J. (1995). Relations between children's overestimation of their physical abilities and accident proneness. *Developmental Psychology, 31,* 866–876.

categories that had not been found in Study 1. Eight-year-old children were significantly more accurate in estimating their physical abilities for the well beyond task version than the just beyond task version. In Study 1 these were not significantly different. The author believed that these findings implied that 8-year-old children were able to incorporate information from their prior experiences, successful or failed, during the practice trials and use it to their advantage in the test trials, whereas younger children were not able to incorporate this information.

As in study 1, the researcher collected latency response times from each participant and excluded data from those participants who exceeded the mean by at least 3 standard deviations. Ten 6-year-olds and five 8-year-olds had their data removed from analysis. The data for the remaining sample is presented in Figure 10.5.

Six-year-olds had mean response latencies that were significantly less when asked about tasks that were just within and well within their range of abilities than they were for tasks that were just beyond and well beyond their physical limits. Moreover, mean response latencies for 8-year-olds were significantly lower for tasks well within their physical boundaries than for the other three task versions. Plumert concluded: "Compared with 6-year-olds, however, 8-year-olds exercised more caution in their decisions about tasks that were just within their ability" (p. 873).

As in the first study, the relationship between children's estimation of their physical abilities and the number of accidents they had experienced in the past was explored. The researchers found a significant negative correlation for 6-year-olds on this measure ($r = -.48$, $p < .05$) but, once again, there was no significant relationship obtained for the 8-year-olds ($r = -.02$, ns).

DISCUSSION

Both studies reported in this chapter tested participants' estimations of affordances. The data presented here suggested that there are developmental differences in accuracy of judging the match between physical abilities and the demands of a task. Specifically, both 6- and 8-year olds in the first study tended to overestimate their physical abilities for the just beyond and well beyond tasks versions. However, in the second study, 8-year-olds appeared

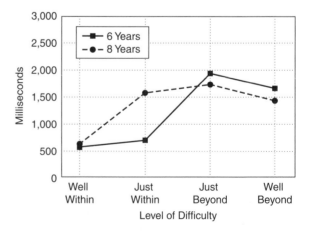

FIGURE 10.5   Mean Response Latencies as a Function of Age and Difficulty Level.

Source: From Plumert, J. (1995). Relations between children's overestimation of their physical abilities and accident proneness. *Developmental Psychology, 31,* 866–876.

to benefit more from practice and were significantly more accurate in estimating their performance on the well beyond task. The findings imply that within these age ranges, as children age they are more capable of incorporating information from previous experiences into future judgments of their abilities. The amount of additional experience provided in Study 2 was minimal: children were given four additional practice trials. Plumert (1995) was appropriately cautious in saying that these findings "suggest that 8-year-olds, not 6-year-olds benefited from prior experience with performing the task" (p. 873). This conclusion should be treated carefully because it is derived from a comparison between groups of 8-year-olds from two different studies. The internal validity might have been higher if all the children had been in one study and randomly assigned to extra experience or no extra experience as a manipulation.

A significant relationship was found between the number of accidents 6-year-olds had been involved in and the accuracy of their estimation of affordances. This finding could be of practical importance if it were able to be replicated and better understood. Of course, many accidents do not require the professional medical attention included in the operational definition of accidents in this study. It would be interesting to know more about affordance-judging ability and routine home bumps and falls. Other future directions for research might include training programs to help children appreciate affordances in specific situations, such as road traffic, where serious harm can result from the type of ability overestimation demonstrated in this study. For 8-year-olds, this study suggested that relatively little experience may enhance judgment quality, but this finding should be replicated in situations with a wider variety of experience manipulations. At the least, the findings of this research suggest that the overestimation of 6-year-olds, and presumably younger children, may place them at greater risk for affordance-based accidents than children 8 years and older.

CRITICAL THINKING TOOLKIT ITEMS

Evaluate the reasons why participants have been dropped from a study. Your confidence in the findings of part or all of the study may be modified based on the reasons given. This critical evaluation is particularly important when a large proportion of participants have been dropped.

REFERENCES

Adolph, K. E., Epler, M. A., & Gibson, E. J. (1993). Crawling versus walking infants' perception of affordances for locomotion over sloping surfaces. *Child Development, 64,* 1158–1174.

Bjorklund, D. F., Gualtney, J. F., & Green, B. L. (1992). "I watch therefore I can do": The development of meta-imitation over the pre-school years and the advantage of optimism in one's imitative skills. In M. L. Howe & R. Pasnak (Eds.), *Emerging themes in cognitive development* (Vol. 2). New York: Springer-Verlag.

Bjorklund, D., & Green, B. L. (1992). The adaptive nature of cognitive immaturity. *American Psychologist, 47,* 46–54.

Flavell, J. H., Friedrichs, A. G., & Hoyt, J. D. (1970). Developmental changes in memorization processes. *Cognitive Psychology, 1,* 324–340.

Gould, S. J. (1977). *Ever since Darwin.* New York: Norton.

Gibson, J. J. (1979). *The ecological approach to visual perception.* Hillsdale, NJ: Erlbaum.

Gibson, E. J., Riccio, G., Schmuckler, M. A., Stoffregen, T. A., Rosenberg, D., & Taormina, J. (1987). Detection of the traversability of surfaces by crawling and walking infants. *Journal of Experimental Psychology: Human Perception and Performance, 13,* 533–544.

Lenneberg, E. H. (1967). *Biological foundations of language.* New York: Wiley.

Oppenheim, R. W. (1981). Ontogenetic adaptations and retrogressive processes in the development of the nervous system and behavior. In K. J. Connolly & H. F. R. Prechtl (Eds.), *Maturation and development: Biological and psychological perspectives* (pp. 73–108). Philadelphia: International Medical Publications.

Plumert, J. (1995). Relations between children's overestimation of their physical abilities and accident proneness. *Development Psychology, 31,* 866–876.

Turkewitz, G., & Kenny, P. (1982). Limitations on input as a basis for neural organization and perceptual development: A preliminary theoretical statement. *Developmental Psychology, 15,* 357–368.

Yussen, S., & Levy, V. (1975). Developmental changes in predicting one's own span of short-term memory. *Journal of Experimental Child Psychology, 19,* 502–508.

CHAPTER 11

SOME RESTRICTIONS MAY APPLY

A number of chapters in this book are concerned with behavioral or psychological outcomes associated with some form of deprivation. Most of our knowledge about patterns of development has resulted from studies of normal people from normal backgrounds; yet, some of what we know comes from the study of children whose developmental circumstances were suboptimal. The fetal alcohol syndrome (FAS) children in Chapter 3 might fit into this category because they were deprived of the opportunity for normal physical development by the presence of alcohol in their mother's bloodstream. Later, in Chapter 17, we discuss what can happen if an individual is deprived of the opportunity to hear language early in life.

Past studies of deprivation in humans almost always drew on conditions of deprivation that were preexisting and beyond the control of the researcher. A few of the well-known cases of children who were horribly deprived of stimulation in early childhood are presented in Chapter 17. Today, there are strictly enforced ethical guidelines for psychological research. Scientists must have permission from committees established at their institutions to undertake any psychological research and those committees are vigilant in their mission to protect human participants. Even the most seemingly innocuous questionnaire study has to be scrutinized and approved. Approval would not be given for a study that might harm participants in any way. Another layer of permission is also required: the permission of the participant. Participants must be informed of the nature of the study. They must be told that they have a right to refuse to participate in the study and can leave the study at any point. Participants must give informed consent for their participation; they are told what will happen to them before the study begins and then are debriefed following the study. As you can imagine, these ethical guidelines make some kinds of research impossible.

In the previous paragraph, you may have noticed that we said that human deprivation research "almost always" drew on preexisting deprivation. There is at least one clear example where it did not. We searched a number of textbooks to see if any of them referred to this example, but could not find a single direct reference. There may be several reasons why this study has been omitted from standard textbooks such as the age of the study, quality

Incorporating the research of J. W. Fantuzzo, A. D. Weiss, M. Atkins, R. Meyers, and M. Noone, "A Contextually Relevant Assessment of the Impact of Child Maltreatment on the Social Competencies of Low-Income Urban Children," 1998, *Journal of the American Academy of Child and Adolescent Psychiatry, 37*, pp. 1201–1208.

of methodology, and current theoretical relevance. However, we are inclined to believe the primary reason for the exclusion of this study is that there is an attempt to cover up blatantly unethical research published in a mainstream scientific journal, before ethical guidelines existed. The work to which we refer was a series of studies by psychologist Wayne Dennis (1941).

Dennis published several reports (e.g., Dennis, 1936; Dennis 1938) on a pair of female fraternal twins. In 1941, Dennis wrote of being able to "secure" the twins who were "proffered" by their mother. Dennis (1941) stated that he was able to "obtain the twins as subjects [participants] because the mother was unable to look after them.… The mother understood that we offered temporary care of the twins in return for the privilege of studying them. She understood the nature of our research and was cooperative at all times" (p. 149). The fact that these children were fraternal twins had no impact on the data other than presenting the opportunity for Dennis to observe two children at once. Both girls experienced conditions that were similar during the research.

The goal of the research was to see what would happen if social stimulation and motor stimulation were kept at a bare minimum during the first year of life. The girls were observed from the start of their second month of life until they were 14 months old. Dennis described the research procedure as follows:

> The two experimenters (Mrs. Dennis and the writer) exercised the sole care of the subjects. The subjects saw no other children and saw very few adults aside from the experimenters. We refrained from performing any infant responses in the subjects' presence. We did not reward or punish the subjects for any response nor instruct them in any way. Furthermore, the environment of the children was such that in respect to many responses there was little or no opportunity to engage in practice. The aim of the study was to determine what behavioral development would occur when the care of the infants was reduced to the minimum attention which would insure their comfort and well-being. (p. 147)

Until 26 weeks, Dennis and his wife never spoke to the infants, nor did they cuddle or show any affection during that time. No toys were provided until the 49th week. The twins were kept isolated in cribs in a room with no view. They were fed and changed, but otherwise their needs and wants were ignored. They were observed carefully because the hypothesis, if there was one, was that social and motor development would be controlled by biological factors and therefore stimulation from the environment would make no difference. In developmental psychology, development that is supposed to be the result of biological factors is called *maturation*. While this word is used to mean many things in the vernacular, in psychology it refers to development that is influenced by genetic instructions. We find this to be an archaic concept, because it is now understood that all development has many components. Nevertheless, older research was often based on the mistaken idea that some behavior was simply genetic in origin.

Surprisingly, some of the development of these infants appeared to be similar to the development of children in normal environments. For example, without encouragement or responses from the researchers, the infants began to smile around 6 weeks of age. The initial appearance of several other behaviors was also carefully noted by the researchers. At the end of the observations, when the girls were 14 months old, Dennis believed that the girls were quite normal in their development and felt that he had gathered support for the idea that during the first year of life behavior develops normally even with very restricted stimulation. The girls were returned to their mother and disappeared from the annals of psychology. By 1960, Dennis had made further observations of maturation, this time of severely deprived children in Iranian orphanages. At that time, he recanted his earlier views concluding that the results of his orphanage study "challenge the widely held view that motor development consists in the emergence of a behavioral sequence based primarily upon maturation. These facts seem to indicate clearly that experience affects not only the ages at which motor items appear, but also their very form…Maturation alone is insufficient to bring about most post-natal developments in behavior" (p. 57).

In his earlier work with the twin girls, Dennis seemed to be primarily concerned with motor development. Even the social responses he observed, such as reaching out to people, were interpreted in motor terms. In the time since Dennis observed the twins, an interest in cognitive development has appeared within the field of developmental psychology. Much of this interest in cognition was probably initiated by the writings of Piaget. We are horrified by the cavalier treatment of the twins in Dennis's research but, at that time, almost nothing was understood about cognitive development and the extent to which it depended on experience. The Bayley Scales, the first valid instrument specifically designed to assess cognitive development in infants was developed only shortly before Dennis's early research (Bayley, 1933). If Dennis had used the Bayley Scales to assess the twins, it is likely that he would have found some striking differences between the twins and children raised in nonrestrictive environments. We might suspect, for example, that the twins would have demonstrated deficits in language development. As will be discussed in Chapter 17, today we know that very early experience is essential for the development of language.

Although research ethics now absolutely forbid the type of study undertaken by Dennis, conditions of deprivation and restricted stimulation unfortunately remain part of everyday life for many children. Psychologists study this deprivation in quasi-experimental ways, either with a control group selected for study or by using norms from large populations of nondeprived individuals as the controls. You will remember that this latter strategy was described in Chapter 3, when the IQ of children with FAS was compared to population IQ statistics.

Child neglect and abuse is quite common. According to the U.S. Department of Health and Human Services (DHHS; 2000) in 1997 as many as 3 million children were reported as having been maltreated in some way—about one child in every 24. We can surmise that the actual number of abusive incidents was almost certainly higher because not all maltreatment would have been reported.

Research has identified a number of factors associated with high risk for maltreatment. These factors are not independent; that is, they are entangled with one another in a web of causation. Age of child, ethnic status, poverty, and living in an urban environment are all part of this web (Garbarino & Kostelny, 1992). Among maltreated children in 1997, more than half were under 7 years old. Nine hundred sixty-seven American children were known to have died as a result of abuse or neglect. Seventy-seven percent of these children were 3 years old or younger. Because these factors are not independent, some of them, for example poverty, may be components of others. Despite the changes that have occurred in

America since the civil rights movement, the national scandal of linkage between ethnic minority status and poverty continues. We believe that it is racist to assume that these two are causally linked and, indeed, the available evidence does not support the bigoted assertion that ethnic status is the cause of poverty or, for that matter, maltreatment. To think critically about this assertion, it is important to understand that the data are correlational and conclusions about cause are unwarranted. This general issue will be discussed again in Chapter 15. One of the reasons educated people should understand science is that this knowledge can help prevent drawing inappropriate conclusions, racist or otherwise, from scientific data.

We doubt that anyone believes that child abuse or maltreatment should be permitted to exist. In order to design effective interventions to prevent abuse or overcome its effects, we need good-quality research that helps us understand the nature of the problem. Although there has been considerable research on this topic, much of it has been flawed in various ways, possibly owing to limitations of funding or practicality (Ammerman, 1998). Past studies have suffered from problems of internal validity as well as external validity. You will remember from Chapter 9 that internal validity includes quality aspects of research design, such as the avoidance of confounds within the study. External validity refers to applicability or generalizability of outcomes to other populations, other environments, and other times. A related, but slightly different concept is ecological validity. A study has ecological validity if the setting in which the research is conducted is similar to real-world settings. One way to achieve this is to conduct the research in real-world settings, rather than laboratories. It is likely that a study that has ecological validity will also have external validity.

Fantuzzo, Weiss, Atkins, Myers, and Noone (1998) described the general problems associated with internal and external validity in past studies about maltreatment. Internal validity has been threatened by the difficulty of finding comparable groups. Groups to be compared should be different in maltreatment but similar in factors such as sex, ethnicity, socioeconomic status (SES), and family constellation, otherwise it is impossible to separate effects of maltreatment from these other factors. Practically, it is often easier to compare maltreated children with groups of nonmaltreated children who are also different in many other ways, for example, from a much higher SES background. Such expedient comparisons threaten internal validity because SES is a potential confound when making statements about maltreatment. A second threat to internal validity mentioned by Fantuzzo, Weiss, Atkins, et al. (1998) is the lack of clear operational definitions of maltreatment. One operational definition that has been used is parent self-report. Parents are sometimes willing to self-report child abuse, as we saw in Chapter 9, but common sense suggests that fear of action by authorities might undermine the validity of these reports. The internal validity of a study would be increased if these self-reports were verified by some other means.

In studies of maltreatment, ecological validity has been compromised by the use of artificial measures presented in artificial settings such as rating scales based on lab observations. This can be improved by using information from the settings in which the child actually lives, supplied by a number of people who normally interact with the child in those settings (Fantuzzo, Weiss, & Coolahan, 1998). It is important that outcome measures be appropriate to the characteristics of the children being studied, such as age, language background, or SES. For preschool children, measures used in past research have sometimes been inappropriate (Martin, 1986), particularly for culturally diverse children or children from low SES homes (Coll et al., 1996).

Using a design that attempted to overcome these problems, Fantuzzo, Weiss, Atkins, et al. (1998) conducted a study of the extent to which child maltreatment is related to competent social behavior in children. The acquisition of social competence is one of the primary tasks of the preschool years (Levy-Schiff & Hoffman, 1989). It is pervasive in the life of the child because problems with social adjustment impact most of the settings in which preschoolers operate. Academic difficulties, for example, may be magnified by poor social competence. A number of studies have suggested that children who were maltreated were also likely to have problems with social competence (Aber & Allen, 1987; Alessandri, 1991).

PARTICIPANTS

The participants were 108 preschoolers from a large urban Head Start program in the Northeast. Head Start is a federally funded program designed to help disadvantaged children acquire the skills required for formal learning. The particular Head Start centers in the study were selected because they were located in regions that had high levels of reported child abuse, according to data provided by the local department of human services. Most of the children were African American (95 percent) and the remainder were of Caucasian, Hispanic, or Asian descent. The mean age of the children in the study was 3.9 (range = 2.9 to 4.8). The maltreatment group was composed of 22 boys and 32 girls. Once the maltreatment group had been identified, the comparison group was selected from 500 potential participants to match the maltreatment group on demographic variables such as age, gender, birth order, family constellation, and family income. The comparison group, who had no obvious maltreatment, consisted of 24 boys and 30 girls. Both groups of children were drawn from the same classrooms. Overall, 62 percent of the children came from single-parent families and 22 percent of the families were headed by two adults. The rest of the children were being raised by others, such as grandparents or friends. A statistical analysis showed no significant differences between the groups on the matched characteristics, suggesting that the matching process had been successful.

In order to avoid the kinds of influences usually called experimenter expectancy effects, none of the staff at Head Start or any of the research assistants on the project knew of the group membership for any individual child. In addition to avoiding threats to the internal validity of the study, this procedure provided ethical protection for the children by helping to keep this information confidential.

For the purposes of the study, *physical abuse* and *physical neglect* were defined in accordance with the legal definitions in the state of Pennsylvania (Knapp & VandeCreek, 1992):

> *Physical Abuse:* "physical injury caused by the acts or omissions of a perpetrator that does one or more of the following:
> (a) causes the child severe pain,
> (b) significantly impairs the child's physical functioning, either temporarily or permanently, or
> (c) is accompanied by physical evidence of a continuous pattern of separate, unexplained injuries to the child."

Physical Neglect: "a physical condition caused by the acts or omission of a perpetrator which endangers the child's life or development or impairs his functioning and is the result of one of the following:
  (a) prolonged or repeated lack of supervision
  (b) failure to provide the essentials of life, including adequate medical care." (pp. 71–72)

Among the children in the maltreatment group, nonphysical neglect was most common, having been experienced by 57.4 percent of the participants. Nonphysical neglect was any neglect that did not result in obvious bodily harm, such as tissue damage. Emotional problems might be an example of an outcome of nonphysical neglect. Physical neglect had been experienced by 16.7 percent of this group. As a result of abuse, 9.3 percent had experienced bodily injury and 5.6 percent had been sexually abused. The average number of reported incidents per child was one. In 66 percent of the cases, the abuse was perpetrated by the primary caregiver, mother or otherwise. The authors note that because the primary caregivers in this study were either relatives or friends, the levels of abuse seen here might be lower than in other situations, such as in a poorly run foster home.

PIPPS MEASURE

A specialized system for coding the amount and quality of interactions between children, the Penn Interactive Peer Play Scale (PIPPS), was used as a means to quantify behavioral observations made by teachers. This scale has 32 items that describe common behaviors used by preschool children in play situations. These behaviors either promote social interaction or decrease it. The other measures in the study helped to establish the validity of the PIPPS by collecting related ratings. This type of validity is called *concurrent validity,* denoting that validity is being checked at the same time by using other measures.

Good rating scales, questionnaires, or surveys should be accompanied by some evidence that the questions being asked are valid. Concurrent validity is one approach to this. Another common approach is to cite a statistic called an *alpha* (α). Scaled from 0 to 1.00, alpha is a measure of internal consistency. Imagine that a survey had four questions about an individual's self-esteem. The alpha statistic would tell us whether an individual answered all four questions in the same manner, that is, asserting the same level of self-esteem in each answer to each question. If this were characteristic of the self-esteem survey, the alpha level would be high.

The alpha statistic measures the reliability, or consistency, that is used to make a case for the validity of the survey. We do not see anything particularly subversive in this usage, but in order to think clearly about these concepts you should know that while an alpha is a way to infer validity, it is not a direct assurance of validity. Like so many other statistics, alpha is sensitive to the number of questions being considered. With more questions, it is easier to achieve high alphas. When there are fewer items, one might expect somewhat lower alpha ratings. There is no generally accepted level of alpha that is considered to be the threshold of adequacy, but in our experience studies commonly report alphas above .70. Consequently, below this level, one should begin to wonder about the findings, while, at the same time, taking account of the number of questions under analysis.

The overall alpha of the PIPPS was .93. Three particular aspects of behavior were measured by parts of the PIPPS and were used as outcomes in this study. Their alphas were play interaction, .92; play disruption, .91; and play disconnection, .89.

SOCIAL SKILLS RATING SYSTEM MEASURE

The Social Skills Rating System (SSRS; Gresham & Elliott, 1990) is available in a version for teachers and a version for parents; both were used in this study. The SSRS was designed to measure not only social skills in classroom settings, but also problem behaviors. For the teacher version, the measures used as outcomes, with their alphas, were self-control (.90), verbal assertion (.84), and interpersonal skill (.88). Two other behavioral outcomes that were measured by this scale were the extent to which behavior was externalizing or internalizing. *Externalizing behaviors* are easy to see, and include such actions as wiggling around in a chair, shouting out comments in class, and interrupting others. *Internalizing behaviors* are the opposite, including such responses as being withdrawn, sad, depressed, or quiet. The alphas for internalizing and externalizing for the teacher version were .88 and .77, respectively; for the parent version of the SSRS, alphas were .68 and .75. The only measures from the parent version of the SSRS that were included in the study were those for internalizing and externalizing behavior.

SOCIOMETRIC RATING MEASURE

A tactic used in the study, modified from Howes (1987), asked children to state their preferences for interacting with other children. These ratings were collected from entire classrooms of children, probably to ensure that children who were participants in the study would not be seen to receive different treatment than the rest of their classmates. Because these ratings were only available for 60 percent of the classrooms, there were 34 nonmaltreated children and 32 maltreated children contributing to the data for this analysis. As part of an interview, the children were given photographs of their classmates and asked to place them in one of a series of bowls denoting the extent to which the child in the photo fit the categories "Like to play with" or "Do not like to play with."

The scores on this measure were the percent of peers who rated the target child the most positively and the percent of peers who rated the child the most negatively. Fantuzzo, Weiss, Atkins, et al. (1998) refer the reader to a review paper by Howes (1987) where they say this measurement was found to have "acceptable levels of reliability and validity" (p. 1204). Because Howes (1987) is a review article, the actual evidence cited is scattered over a number of individual sources and is difficult to find. This is too bad because one should always be interested in evidence of validity. Good evidence for the validity of measures is usually missing. If you persistently ask for evidence of validity when presented with findings from psychological scales, you will probably be considered a pain in the neck, or some other body part. That is what sometimes happens to critical thinkers and we think you should get used to it—we have.

RESULTS

The means for the outcome measures are presented in Table 11.1. Presented here as T scores, the scores have been mathematically transformed so that the mean is 50 and the standard deviation (*SD*) is 10. This is done to make scores from different scales, with different pretransformation means, easy to compare visually. You will remember from the discussion in Chapter 10 that if the *SD* equals 10 and the mean equals 50, 68 percent of the scores will fall between 40 and 60. Scores in Table 11.1 that approach 40 or 60 are fairly low, or high, respectively—compared to the rest of the scores in the distribution.

Observational coding of behavior with the PIPPS showed that maltreated children were significantly less interactive with other children in play behavior. Teacher's ratings with the SSRS showed that the maltreated children had significantly less self-control and significantly lower interpersonal skill levels than nonmaltreated children. The teachers rated the maltreated children as more prone to internalizing behaviors. It is noteworthy that teachers' ratings for externalizing behaviors were not significantly different when one group was compared to the other. The same trend was found in parents' ratings using the SSRS. There was significantly more internalizing on the part of maltreated children but no significant difference for externalizing.

TABLE 11.1   Means for Outcome Measures

	MALTREATMENT GROUP	NONMALTREATMENT GROUP	PROBABILITY LEVEL
Interactive Peer Play (PIPPS)			
Play interaction	47.14	53.24	$p = .005$
Play disruption	53.20	51.72	NS
Play disconnection	54.50	51.24	NS
Social Skills—Teacher (SSRS)			
Self-control	47.31	53.31	$p < .05$
Interpersonal skill	48.11	58.15	$p < .01$
Verbal assertiveness	49.38	53.61	NS
Internalizing problems	58.43	53.89	$p = .001$
Externalizing problems	54.48	52.63	NS
Social-Skills—Parent (SSRS)			
Internalizing problems	60.37	52.61	$p = .001$
Externalizing problems	58.61	51.94	NS
Peer Sociometric Ratings			
Lowest peer rating	53.72	47.23	$p = .001$
Highest peer rating	46.12	52.79	$p < .01$

Note: NS—not significantly different.

Source: From Fantuzzo, J. W., Weiss, A. D., Atkins, M., Meyers, R., & Noone, M. (1998). A contextually relevant assessment of the impact of child maltreatment on the social competencies of low-income urban children. *Journal of the American Academy of Child and Adolescent Psychiatry, 37,* 1205.

Peer sociometric ratings indicated that the maltreated children were significantly more likely to be placed in the lowest category, the one labeled "Do not like to play with." The reverse was also true: The maltreated children were significantly less likely to be placed in the top category "Like to play with" when compared to nonmaltreated children.

DISCUSSION

We chose this study as a representative investigation of child abuse because it seemed to us superior to many of the studies in the field. While child abuse is a high-interest topic, to which whole journals are dedicated, much of the research is weak. One could say that inherent difficulties almost preclude good studies of the long-term effects of abuse or neglect. To make an analogy, if we wanted to know the temperature of the surface of the moon, we could go out on a moonlit night and hold our hands up so that our palms face the moon, trying to feel the temperature. While this might result in some subjective impressions, it has no validity. The temperature of the moon cannot be studied using the hands as instruments. It may be that many of the important long-term questions about abuse and neglect are similar in that they cannot be studied in any valid way with the instruments available.

The long-term effects of child abuse have often been studied by asking adults to recollect childhood events. Studies of this sort are examples of retrospective research methodology, in which associations are sought between childhood events and the circumstances of the adults (e.g., see Wyatt, Loeb, Solis, & Carmona, 1999; Westbury & Tutty, 1999). If we know anything at all about memory, we know that it is reconstructive: new experiences are added and actual occurrences are deleted. Even when there is considerable emotion involved, memory is not improved. Confidence in memory does not ensure accuracy (Neisser & Harsch, 1992). Studying childhood abuse through adult recollections may be like studying the temperature of the moon with your hands.

This study used social services records to identify maltreated children and used a number of different measures to find an association between maltreatment and the children's social interaction skills. While this is a much more modest goal than the tracking of adult psychological problems to their purported childhood roots, it is more realistic. Indeed, in a review of the literature that examined 80 studies, Paris (1998) concluded that childhood trauma does not necessarily lead to adult personality disorders. Many children are resilient and will form attachments and persist in their goals in spite of trauma. Others may even demonstrate "steeling," in which negative circumstances lead them to become even more adaptable in the face of problems. The scientific research gives some reason to doubt the certainty of long-term negative personality outcomes of abuse that are often featured on television talk shows and in the popular press.

CRITICAL THINKING TOOLKIT ITEMS

Not everything can be studied using scientific methodology. For example, it is sometimes asserted that psychic powers fade away when they are exposed to the controlled conditions typical of scientific scrutiny. If that is so, then the existence of psychic powers cannot be confirmed or denied by scientific studies. In addition, it may be so difficult to adequately operationalize some human events and responses, that trying to study them becomes similar to trying to detect the temperature of the moon with one's hands.

REFERENCES

Aber, J., & Allen, J. (1987). Effects of maltreatment on young children's socioemotional development: An attachment theory perspective. *Developmental Psychology, 23,* 406–414.

Alessandri, S. (1991). Play and social behaviors in maltreated preschoolers. *Developmental Psychopathology, 3,* 191–205.

Ammerman, R. (1998). Methodological issues in child maltreatment research. In J. Lutzker (Ed.), *Handbook of child abuse research and treatment* (pp. 117–132). New York: Plenum.

Bayley, N. (1933). *The California first-year mental scales.* Berkeley: University of California Press.

Coll, C. G., Crnic, K., Lamberty, G., Wasik, B. H., Jenkins, R., Garcia, H. V., & McAdoo, H. P. (1996). An integrative model for the study of developmental competencies in minority children. *Child Development, 67,* 1891–1914.

Dennis, W. (1936). Infant development under minimal social stimulation. *Psychological Bulletin, 33,* 750.

Dennis, W. (1938). Infant development under conditions of restricted practice and of minimum social stimulation: A preliminary report. *Journal of Genetic Psychology, 53,* 149–158.

Dennis, W. (1941). Infant development under conditions of restricted practice and of minimum social stimulation. *Genetic Psychology Monographs, 23,* 143–189.

Dennis, W. (1960). Causes of retardation among institutionalized children: Iran. *Journal of Genetic Psychology, 96,* 47–59.

Fantuzzo, J. W., Weiss, A. D., Atkins, M., Meyers, R., & Noone, M. (1998). A contextually relevant assessment of the impact of child maltreatment on the social competencies of low-income urban children. *Journal of the American Academy of Child and Adolescent Psychology, 37,* 1201–1208.

Fantuzzo, J., Weiss, A., & Coolahan, K. (1998). Community-based partnership-directed research: Actualizing community strengths to treat child victims of physical abuse and neglect. In J. Lutzker, (Ed.),

Handbook of child abuse research and treatment (pp. 213–237). New York: Plenum.

Garbarino, J., & Kostelny, K. (1992). Child maltreatment as a community problem. *Child Abuse and Neglect, 16,* 455–464.

Gresham, F., & Elliott, S. (1990). *The Social Skills Rating System.* Circle Pines, MN: American Guidance Service.

Howes, C. (1987). Social competence with peers in young children: Developmental sequences. *Developmental Review, 7,* 252–272.

Knapp, S., & VandeCreek, P. (1992). *Pennsylvania law and psychology.* Harrisburg: Pennsylvania Psychological Association.

Levy-Schiff, R., & Hoffman, M. (1989). Social behavior as a predictor of adjustment among three-year-olds. *Journal of Clinical Child Psychology, 18,* 65–71.

Martin, R. (1986). Assessment of the social and emotional functioning of pre-school children. *School Psychology Review, 15,* 216–232.

Neisser, U., & Harsch, N. (1992). Phantom flashbulbs: False recollections of hearing the news about *Challenger.* In E. Winograd & U. Neisser (Eds.), *Affect and accuracy in recall: Studies of "flashbulb" memories* (pp. 9–31). New York: Cambridge University Press.

Paris, J. (1998). Does childhood trauma cause personality disorders in adults? *Canadian Journal of Psychiatry, 43,* 148–153.

U.S. Department of Health and Human Services (DHHS). (2000). *Child maltreatment 1995: Reports from the states to the national center in child abuse and neglect.* Washington, DC: U.S. Government Printing Office.

Westbury, E., & Tutty, L. M. (1999). The efficacy of group treatment for survivors of childhood abuse. *Child Abuse and Neglect, 2,* 31–44.

Wyatt, G. E., Loeb, T. B., Solis, B., & Carmona, J. V. (1999). The prevalence and circumstances of child sexual abuse: Changes across a decade. *Child Abuse and Neglect, 23,* 45–60.

CHAPTER 12

CHIP OFF THE OLD BLOCK

In earlier chapters we have repeatedly stressed the notion that behavior is multidetermined; that behaviors cannot be reduced to a single cause. This chapter will deal with genetic influences on behavior. In discussions at family gatherings, all of us have heard people say things like: "She gets her stubbornness from her Aunt Maud. That whole branch of the family was stubborn as a bunch of mules—it's genetic." You already know how we would respond to that attribution: All behavior has genetic components, but many other factors influence it as well.

For a long time psychologists and biologists tried to force behaviors into one of two categories, behaviors caused by genes or those caused by learning. The behaviors that were supposed to be genetic in origin were sometimes called *instincts,* and for years debates raged about the extent to which humans had instinctive behaviors. Instinctive behaviors were thought to automatically occur in response to certain stimuli. For example, proponents argued that all humans posses an instinct to behave aggressively and fight over territory, which would account for why humans have wars. Opponents argued that aggressive behavior is not innate, but rather learned from others in the environment. Though this kind of nonsensical nature-nurture dichotomy is gone from contemporary psychology, it still has a vigorous life in daily conversations, such as the one about Aunt Maud.

You will probably remember from biology classes that genes are arrangements of chemicals that occur along very large molecules called deoxyribonucleic acid, or DNA. Our genetic material is found in structures called chromosomes. Each chromosome consists of a DNA molecule and proteins. The chromosomes are found in pairs. Humans have 23 pairs of chromosomes. Copies of these 46 chromosomes are found in almost every cell in the body, the exceptions being eggs or sperm. These sex cells, or gametes, are haploid, meaning that they have half the usual number of chromosomes. When sex cells combine to create new human beings, the 23 individual chromosomes in the egg become paired with those in the sperm, restoring the total to 23 pairs.

As this description indicates, half of a person's chromosomes come from one parent and half from the other. This is why the proportion of genes we share with a parent is 50 percent. Among full biological siblings, the situation is different. Single parental chromosomes

Incorporating the research of R. Plomin, D. W. Fulker, R. Corley, and J. C. DeFries, "Nature, Nurture, and Cognitive Development From 1 to 16 Years: A Parent-Offspring Adoption Study," 1997, *Psychological Science, 8,* pp. 442–227.

are, in effect, randomly assigned to eggs or sperm. Because each sibling will get a copy of either one or the other chromosome from each parental pair, the chance that two siblings will get a copy of the same chromosome from a specific parental pair is 50 percent. As a result, the average genetic relatedness between full siblings is 50 percent. It is important to stress that this is the average and that any two particular siblings may not share exactly half of their genes.

Imagine the extreme case in which one sibling received a chromosome from each parental pair but by chance the other sibling received the other chromosome from each parental pair. In this case, because the siblings share no genes, they are technically considered unrelated genetically—even though they have the same biological parents. The reverse is also theoretically possible—two siblings might share all their genes, each happening by chance to have drawn each of the same 23 chromosomes from mother and from father. While theoretically possible, neither of these extremes is at all likely. Remember, siblings only share 50 percent of their genes on the average while individual cases may diverge widely from this figure.

Recently, considerable attention has been paid to attempts to assess the extent of the genetic contribution to behaviors. One of the best-known studies in this area is the Minnesota Twin Study (e.g., see Bouchard & McGue, 1990). The Minnesota Twin Study investigated pairs of monozygotic and dizygotic twins who had been reared apart. Monozygotic twins share all their genes because they are the result of a single fertilized egg splitting into two individuals. In contrast, dizygotic twins are genetically like full siblings: Two different sperm have fertilized two different eggs, resulting in an average genetic commonality of 50 percent. The Minnesota Twin Study is a very large and very carefully constructed study that has overcome many of the methodological flaws that marred earlier studies of separated twins. Obviously, separated monozygotic twins can make important contributions to our understanding of genetics and behavior. In the Minnesota study, a measure of the interaction climate of the rearing homes for separated twins showed effectively zero correlation, suggesting that similarity between twins was not merely a matter of both having been sent to homes that happened to be quite similar. However, on various measures of personality the correlations found between members of a monozygotic twin pair were between $r = .44$ and $r = .68$. For the separated dizygotic twins, the correlations were lower, ranging from $r = -.28$ to $r = .39$. This implies a large genetic component for personality. While the Minnesota study is important, it cannot give us a picture of behavior development because the twins were only contacted as adults.

Fortunately, another well-known study, the Colorado Adoption Project (CAP; Plomin, Fulker, Corley, & DeFries, 1997) does provide us with high-quality evidence about the role of genetics in the development of psychological characteristics. The CAP is not the only psychological study of adopted children. Plomin and DeFries (1985) reviewed 19 other adoption studies spanning the years from 1924 to 1982. Unfortunately, many of these had substantial deficiencies in research design.

Adoption studies are extraordinarily difficult to conduct because of ethical and sampling limitations, but they can produce evidence about the role of genetics in behavior that may not be able to be researched in any other way. You will remember from Chapter 1 that random assignment is used in research design as a way of canceling out potentially confounding differences among participants. Adopted children's genes remain similar to their biological parents, but their environments often do not. Environmental effects are randomized by placing adoptees with a diverse group of adoptive parents, who are likely to be different from the biological parents in many ways. In another comparison that can be made within the adoption situation, heredity is randomized as individuals of different genetic background—adoptive parents and their adopted children—are placed in the same environment. Correlations can be sought between the behavior of adoptees and both biological and adoptive parents. Correlations between the behaviors of adoptees and their biological parents will be higher if genetic factors play a large role. On the other hand, if correlational measures of behavior between adoptive parents and adoptees are strong, then the behavior might be thought to have a large experiential component.

METHOD

The CAP is an enormous undertaking. It is not possible for us to begin to do justice to the entire study in this brief discussion. We have chosen one current study from the CAP data as the focus of this chapter and we will limit our description of the CAP to the material you need to know in order to interpret the results of this single study. If you have additional interest in this topic, we refer you to DeFries, Plomin, and Fulker (1994) and Plomin and DeFries (1985), both of which are book-length monographs about the CAP that contain excellent introductory text describing the basic genetic rationale for adoption studies.

Methodologically, Plomin and DeFries (1985) described the CAP as a "fishing expedition, rather than a test of specific developmental theories" (p. 48). An overview of the method was that biological and adoptive parents were tested for a variety of attributes such as intelligence and personality. The adopted children were repeatedly tested for the same or similar attributes over the course of their childhood. Among other outcomes, the CAP sought to assess correlations between the adopted children's scores and those of their adoptive and their biological parents.

The sample of children for the CAP came from Denver, Colorado, between 1975 and 1982. Two adoption agencies, both church-affiliated, were willing and eager to participate because the directors and others in charge of making decisions recognized that valuable information could come from a thorough study of adoption. It is not a small point that the CAP may be the last big study of its kind because there is a national trend toward fewer children being available for adoption. This trend is thought to be a result of better sex education among teenagers and more social support for single parents (Plomin & DeFries, 1985).

Pregnant women who were in touch with the adoption agencies, and therefore probably planning to give their children up for adoption, were approached and asked if they would be willing to take part in the study. If they were willing to participate, an extensive battery of psychological tests was administered to them prior to the birth of the child. When possible, the biological fathers were also tested. This effort resulted in data for about 20 percent of the biological fathers. The operational definition of biological paternity was verbal agreement on this point between the mother and the father. No biological testing was undertaken to ensure paternity because of the presumed negative effects that would be associated with such a request from researchers. Plomin and DeFries (1985) argued that it is likely that the putative fathers were the real biological fathers because verification of paternity makes the father liable for support payments. A paternity claim is not, therefore, something that would be done without serious consideration on the part of the fathers.

There was an issue of ethics involved in seeking participation from the adoptive parents. It was felt that if the parents were asked to participate before adoption took place, they would feel coerced, thinking in some way that willingness to participate might increase the probability that a child would be found for them. Ethical standards in psychology rightly forbid the coercion of research participants even in subtle forms. Because of this, adoptive parents were not contacted until the courts had made final decisions about custody of a child, usually when the child was between 7 and 9 months old. Most infants were not tested until they were around a year old. About 75 percent of the adoptive parents agreed to participate, which meant that they would permit their adopted child to be tested at intervals and that they, themselves, would also be tested with the battery of adult tests. A control group of biological parents rearing their nonadopted biological children were selected by matching each family to an adoptive family on such characteristics as sex of child, number of children in family, age of father, occupation of father, and father's total years of education. In an attempt to avoid confusion, we will refer to this group as nonadoptive, or control, parents. We reserve the term *biological parents* for the parents in the study whose children were given up for adoption.

PARTICIPANTS

The participants consisted of 245 biological mothers who gave their children up for adoption at birth, as well as the parents who adopted these children. The children were also participants as were the 245 nonadoptive matched control families. Ninety percent of the biological parents and 95 percent of the adoptive parents were European American based on self-report. Socioeconomic status (SES) was measured in a number of highly intercorrelated ways, such as the Hollingshead scheme, described earlier in Chapter 9. Both groups were a bit above the national average SES for the American population; however, the variability in SES was about the same as the American population. The individuals in the study were effectively middle class. The SES of the biological parents was somewhat lower than that of the adoptive parents and the biological parents were younger (biological mothers, $M = 19.4, SD = 3.0$, adoptive mothers, $M = 32.5, SD = 3.5$). The SES differences were not unexpected because many of the biological mothers were teenagers. When reports about grandfathers, the fathers of both biological and adoptive mothers, were compared on education and occupational status, the results were very similar, debunking the stereotype that the biological parents who put children up for adoption are of low SES, at least in this study (Plomin & DeFries, 1985).

SELECTIVE PLACEMENT
AS A POTENTIAL CONFOUND

Unless care is taken, selective placement can be a confound in adoption studies. The biological parent-child comparison holds heredity constant while adoption randomizes environment. If children had been selectively placed, by giving them to adoptive parents who were similar in many ways to their biological parents, then both heredity and environment would be similar between children and biological parents, even though the biological parents were not present in the rearing environment. This would confound the interpretation of any similarities found between biological parents and children: The similarities could be a result of heredity, environment, or both. The adoption agencies used in the CAP did not practice selective placement, except in some attempts to avoid dramatic mismatches in height. The only other systematic selection in placement involved purposely moving children away from the locality of the biological parents' residences. There was no attempt to selectively place children based on mental ability, SES, or parental education. When correlations were done seeking evidence of selective placement using data for SES and educational levels of parents and grandparents, the median correlation was $r = .02$, suggesting that selective placement had been avoided; environment had been successfully randomized.

MEASURES

A very comprehensive battery of tests was given to participants in the CAP. The adults took a 3-hour long battery of surveys and tests measuring intelligence, personality, interests, likes and dislikes, talents, drug use, and things such as whether they were left- or right-handed. Several standardized measures of the environment such as the Home Observation for the Measurement of the Environment (HOME; Caldwell & Bradley, 1978) and the Family Environment Scale (FES; Moos, 1974) were conducted on the adoptive and nonadoptive control families to permit comparisons between these groups. The HOME measures things such as sources of stimulation in the home, from interpersonal interaction to the variety and types of toys. The FES measures personal family interaction styles, such as extent of conflict and organizational structures of the family (Moos & Moos, 1981). Videotapes were made of ordinary situations in the home for later coding.

The children were tested for cognitive ability at 1, 2, 3, and 4 years of age in their homes. They were subsequently tested in the laboratory between the ages of 7 and 16 years old. At ages 1 and 2, they were tested with the Bayley Scales (Bayley, 1969), a test of cognitive and motor development mentioned in Chapter 11. At ages 3 and 4, children were given a standard IQ test for small children, the Stanford Binet Form L-M (Terman & Merrill, 1973). By 7 and 12, an intelligence test appropriate for older children, the Wechsler Intelligence Scale for Children-Revised (WISC-R, often pronounced "wisk-are"; Wechsler, 1974) was used, and at age 16, the adoptees were given an adult intelligence test, the Wechsler Adult Intelligence Scale (WAIS, often pronounced like "waist" without the t; Wechsler, 1972).

To protect the parents who were giving their children up for adoption, biological parents, if they consented to be in the study, were tested only once, a condition imposed on the researchers by the adoption agencies. The researchers were not permitted to contact the biological parents again. The battery of tests given to biological parents in the single testing session was thorough. Adoptive and nonadoptive parents were given this same test battery but, in addition, these two groups were tested specifically for IQ. While the biological parents were tested for general cognitive ability, they were not tested for IQ per se. The test that was used for adult IQ testing was the WAIS. It was only administered to the adoptive parents and the nonadoptive control group. For all adoptive parents together the WAIS IQ mean was 112.5 for fathers, and 107.6 for mothers. For nonadoptive control parents the WAIS means were 114.9 for fathers and 110.4 for mothers. When children were tested with the WAIS at age 16, the group means were 104.8 for adopted children and 108.5 for nonadoptive control children. These were probably not important differences in IQ.

RESULTS AND DISCUSSION

Sometimes the outcomes of psychological research are intuitively obvious, meaning that you could have guessed the findings even before the research was conducted; the findings from the CAP do not strike us as such. Because adoptive and nonadoptive control parents were tested for IQ, it is possible to correlate the WAIS IQs of these parents with the longitudinally measured IQ of their children generated by the Bayley Scales, the WISC-R, and, at age 16, the WAIS itself. These correlations are presented in Figure 12.1.

As you can see, the correlation for IQ between adopted children and their adoptive parents starts out somewhat lower than the correlation for control children who are living with their biological parents. This, and the subsequent steep initial increase in correlation to age 3, may not be a complete surprise because in the first three years a great deal can be learned from the parents. The IQ assessments at that age were likely detecting the differences between higher IQ adoptive parents who may spend more time teaching their children and lower IQ parents who may not. During the first few years, it appears that the environment provided by adoptive parents can result in their children becoming similar to them, at least in terms of IQ. The most interesting trend happens after about age 4. While the children living with biological parents continue to increase in IQ resemblance to their parents, the adopted children do not. Not only do the correlations fail to increase, they fall

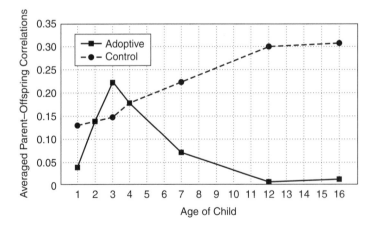

FIGURE 12.1   Parent-Offspring IQ Correlations. Correlations between the IQs of adoptive parents and their adopted offspring, compared to parent-child IQ correlations in nonadoptive control families, where parents are living with their biological offspring.

Source: From "Nature, Nurture, and Cognitive Development from 1 to 16 Years: A Parent-Offspring Adoption Study," by R. Plomin, D. W. Fulker, R. Corley, and J. C. DeFries, 1997, *Psychological Science, 8,* p. 444. Copyright © American Psychological Society. Reprinted with permission.

away, coming to a rest at about zero. Both groups of children share a home environment with parents, but only the nonadopted children show increasingly stronger correlations with parental IQ. At the least, this seems to argue that parental practices are not responsible for increased IQ similarity between parents and children, otherwise correlations would increase for both groups over time.

Further explanation of these data comes from considering the trends that emerge when adopted children are compared with their biological parents. This comparison was not possible for WAIS IQ because, as noted earlier, the biological parents whose children were placed for adoption were not tested with the WAIS. They were, how ver, given an extensive battery of cognitive tests that measured a variety of aspects of men l functioning. Although you may have heard the terms *IQ* and *intelligence* used intercha eably, within psychology IQ specifically refers to the outcome of one of several particul standardized IQ tests. *Intelligence* is a more general term and IQ is often considered to be he operational definition of intelligence. Cognitive ability is not the same as IQ but it is a related set of skills. The difference is that IQ is generally considered to be a particular test score whereas cognitive ability refers to almost any aspect of thinking including those not usually measured by IQ tests. For example, ability to reproduce a musical note on key is a cognitive ability, but it is not part of ordinary IQ testing. For the purposes of interpreting the results in Figure 12.1, however, we will stress that cognitive performances certainly underlie IQ; the two are related measures that both assess intellectual performance.

Figure 12.2 shows the CAP data for cognitive ability correlations between adopted children and their biological parents, as well as with their adoptive parents. In addition, correlations are shown for the nonadoptive control children and their parents.

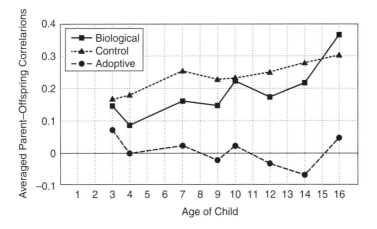

FIGURE 12.2   Summary Cognitive Ability Scores. Parent-offspring correlations for general cognitive ability comparing adoptive parents and their adopted offspring, biological parents and offspring they gave up for adoption, and nonadoptive control families.

Source: From "Nature, Nurture, and Cognitive Development from 1 to 16 Years: A Parent-Offspring Adoption Study," by R. Plomin, D. W. Fulker, R. Corley, and J. C. DeFries, 1997, *Psychological Science, 8,* p. 443. Copyright © American Psychological Society. Reprinted with permission.

Presumably, the reason why there are no data for the children until age 3 is that it makes no sense to measure broad-ranging cognitive ability until after infancy, when it ceases to be seriously confounded with motor skills. The picture of adoptive and nonadoptive control parent-child correlations in Figure 12.2 shows considerable resemblance to the post-3-year-old data for these groups as depicted in Figure 12.1. The control group correlations increase to about $r = .30$, whereas the adoptive correlations quickly approach 0. Perhaps the most interesting aspect of Figure 12.2 is the data for the biological parents. Even though they gave their children up at birth, their children come to increasingly resemble them in general cognitive ability as the years go by. This similarity is almost certain to be an effect of heredity because parent and child do not know each other or live together. Environment has been randomized, so it is difficult to see this finding as some systematic effect of chance similarities in environments.

These outcomes imply that the increasing correlations for nonadoptive control families seen in both Figure 12.1 and Figure 12.2 are likely to be the result of heredity, rather than parenting or other environmental characteristics. In other words, children growing up in homes with their biological parents become more similar to their parents in cognitive ability over time because of their shared heredity, not because of prolonged exposure to aspects of the environment created by their parents. Looking at Figure 12.2 it almost does not seem to matter who children are raised by—they end up with cognitive ability that resembles their biological parents regardless. This finding echoes the finding of the Minnesota Twin Study that monozygotic twins reared separately were very similar in personality, but this similarity was not greater in another group of monozygotic twins who were raised together (Bouchard & McGue, 1990).

Cognitive ability can be broken down into subcomponents such as speed of information processing, ability to imagine spatial relationships, memory enabling recognition of past stimuli, and verbal skill. The battery of tests given to all parents, including the biological parents, measured these cognitive skills as well as others. Plomin, et al. (1997) focused on processing speed, recognition memory, spatial ability, and verbal ability because an analysis of the test battery suggested that these skills were measured by a number of different items in the battery. The correlational outcomes for these measures are shown in Figure 12.3.

In one way or another, each of the graphs in Figure 12.3 shows overall similarities to the data presented in Figure 12.1 and Figure 12.2. Biological and control parents are more similar to their children than are adoptive parents. Furthermore, this gap widens during middle childhood. In two cases, recognition memory and speed of processing, the gap between biological and adoptive parents appears to be closing when children are measured at age 16. However the differences in correlations for spatial ability and, even more surprisingly, verbal ability seem to continue to widen at the 16-year-old measure. The gap in verbal ability is striking because common sense might dictate that verbal ability is largely a matter of operant reinforcement and social learning through imitation. In contrast, the striking similarity of correlations for nonadoptive families compared to those for biological parents and the children they gave up for adoption attests to a major genetic component for verbal behavior.

Another somewhat surprising finding from the data shown in the figures is that, excepting speed of processing, heredity appears to exert a greater influence as children get older. It is often mistakenly believed that the effects of genes are stable and binary—either

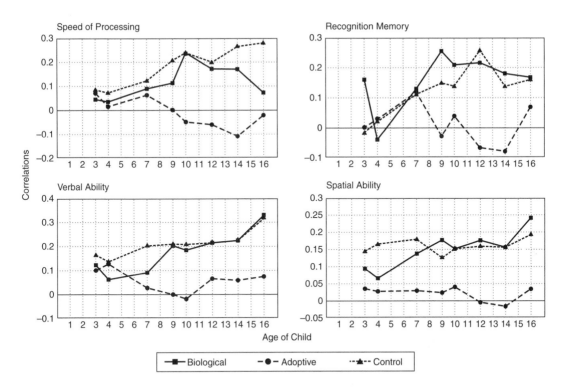

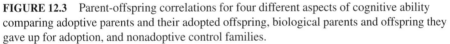

FIGURE 12.3   Parent-offspring correlations for four different aspects of cognitive ability comparing adoptive parents and their adopted offspring, biological parents and offspring they gave up for adoption, and nonadoptive control families.

Source: From "Nature, Nurture, and Cognitive Development from 1 to 16 Years: A Parent-Offspring Adoption Study," by R. Plomin, D. W. Fulker, R. Corley, and J. C. DeFries, 1997, *Psychological Science, 8,* p. 445. Copyright © American Psychological Society. Reprinted with permission.

they are there or they are not. Instead, what we see is the genetic component of behavior increasing over time. We assume that the children in the CAP will continue to be studied for quite some time into the future and it will be interesting to see if the initial trend of increasing genetic influence over time continues in later life.

CONCLUSIONS

As you read this, you may be thinking that we have given up our stance that behavior is multidetermined and that we now view heredity and environment as single causes of behavior with varying strengths. We do not. First, the data presented here are correlations. As you will remember from Chapter 2, a quick way to assess the magnitude of a correlation is to square it. The outcome tells you what percent of the variance in one factor is accounted for by variability in the other factor. The largest correlation we have presented is $r = .38$—the correlation for verbal ability between biological parents and the children they gave up for adoption (when those children were tested at 16 years of age). The variation in biological parent verbal behavior accounts for about 14.4 percent of the variance in adopted child behavior. That was the extent of genetic influence in this study. This does not seem to be a great deal, but maybe it is. There are no other obvious factors that account for more of the variance. Whatever else is going on, parenting and home environment do not seem to account for much, judging by the near-zero correlation between adoptive parents and adopted children. Frustratingly, the bulk of the variance in verbal behavior is accounted for by unknown factors, probably many of them unique to individuals' personal interactions with their environment. In spite of the small percent of the variance that is accounted for, heredity is a big factor, but it is only big because it is likely that any other single factor is much less influential than heredity.

Another caution is that correlations between variables such as heredity and verbal behavior should not, as you know, be interpreted as certain evidence that the relationship is causal. In this case, because of the elegance of the adoption-study design, it seems likely that the relation is causal, that heredity does substantially contribute to cognitive ability. Nevertheless, this is an interpretation of the data, and is not conclusively demonstrated by the discovery of correlations.

In the past, explanations of behavior involving genes have evoked pictures of rigid instinctive behavior and have been associated with Nazi-like notions of superiority and inferiority. The principal CAP researchers Plomin and DeFries (1985) pointed out that the study of genetic influences has also been a very good way to find out about behavior flexibility. Apparently, genes should not be associated with static levels of behaviors, as has been demonstrated by the CAP. Further, although genes explain a small amount of variance, most of the variance in behavior has yet to be explained. This is an important task for psychology in the new century.

CRITICAL THINKING TOOLKIT ITEMS

In contrast to what may be commonly believed, behavior does not have single causes or even many particularly large components.

An object or event that accounts for, let us say, 20 percent of the variance in a behavior could be a very large component indeed, if the next largest component only accounted for a fraction of 1 percent. Although we have made up the numbers, the orders of magnitude in this example may be quite typical of real behavior.

REFERENCES

Bayley, N. (1969). *Manual for the Bayley Scales of Infant Development*. New York: Psychological Corp.

Bouchard, T., & McGue, M. (1990). Genetic and rearing environmental influences on adult personality: An analysis of adopted twins reared apart. *Journal of Personality, 58,* 263–292.

Caldwell, B. M., & Bradley, R. H. (1978). *Home observation for the measurement of the environment*. Little Rock: University of Arkansas Press.

DeFries, J. C., Plomin, R., & Fulker, D. W. (1994). *Nature and nurture during middle childhood*. Cambridge, MA: Blackwell.

Moos, R. H. (1974). *Preliminary manual for Family Environment Scale, work environment scale, and group environment scale*. Palo Alto, CA: Consulting Psychologists Press.

Moos, R. H., & Moos, B. S. (1981). *Family Environment Scale manual.* Palo Alto, CA: Consulting Psychologists Press.

Plomin, R., Fulker, D. W., Corley, R., & DeFries, J. C. (1997). Nature, nurture, and cognitive development from 1 to 16 years: A parent-offspring adoption study. *Psychological Science, 8,* 442–447.

Plomin, R., & DeFries, J. C. (1985). *Origins of individual differences in infancy: The Colorado Adoption Project.* New York: Academic.

Terman, L. M., & Merrill, M. A. (1973). *Stanford-Binet Intelligence Scale: 1972 norms edition.* Boston: Houghton Mifflin.

Wechsler, D. L. (1972). *Examiner's manual: Wechsler Intelligence Scale for Adults.* New York: Psychological Corp.

Wechsler, D. L. (1974). *Examiner's manual: Wechsler Intelligence Scale for Children-Revised.* New York: Psychological Corp.

CHAPTER 13

WATCHING AND WEIGHTING

Obesity can be a problem for people at any stage in life. In recent years, it has become a health concern for many Western societies. Particularly in the United States, there has been a dramatic increase in the frequency of overweight people. Despite the extent to which obesity contributes to other health problems, many healthcare providers do not consider it to be a significant problem. While it may sound like state interference in personal choice, the government has been successful with other health issues and might provide help combating obesity. The success of government attempts to increase awareness about health issues is illustrated by the reductions in both smoking and HIV infection in America (Hill, 1998).

A standard measure of the amount of body fat, called *adiposity,* is body mass index (BMI). Although not without its detractors, BMI is probably the most widely accepted index of obesity. BMI has been examined and found to be a good measure of fatness in children or adults considered as a group. One should be cautious, however, because it may be a less good predictor of actual fatness for any individual. (Pietrobelli, 1998). BMI is the weight in kilograms divided by the square of the height in meters. BMI is not a perfect measure of body fat. However, BMI is sensitive to lean body size whereas other measures, such as trunk skinfold, are less so. (Stafford, Wells, & Fewtrell, 1998).

In an article about the obesity epidemic in the United States, Hill (1998) reported that 54 percent of the adult population is overweight (BMI greater than or equal to 25) and 22 percent is obese (BMI greater than or equal to 30). Much of this problem is associated with the "essentially unlimited supply of energy-dense foods, coupled with a lifestyle requiring only low levels of physical activity…" (Hill, 1998, p. 1371). As environmental factors, Hill included food availability and portion size as well as high-fat diets. Technology and transportation, aided and abetted by televisions and computers, have permitted a sedentary lifestyle. Obesity also clearly has genetic components (Stunkard, 1988). In this sense it shows the same kind of multidetermination that we have seen in earlier chapters. The genetic component is not likely to be responsible for the rapid increase in obesity in the United States because the gene pool does not change rapidly.

Indeed, one reason why obesity can be so difficult to treat is that there is no single cause. In order for a treatment to be effective, it may have to cover a wide variety of do-

Incorporating the research of T. H. Robinson, "Reducing Children's Television Viewing to Prevent Obesity: A Randomized Controlled Trial," 1999, *Journal of the American Medical Association, 282,* pp. 1561–1567.

mains. Simple single solutions such as skipping meals, or increasing exercise, or taking certain drugs are not, by themselves, likely to lead to permanent changes. Obese adults can lose considerable amounts of weight as a result of weight loss programs, but it is by far the most usual case that this loss is not maintained over a long period of time.

Obesity is not merely a problem for adults. The U.S. Surgeon General has determined that one in five children in the United States is significantly overweight. This represents a two-fold increase during the past 20 years. For children, obesity can have psychological consequences as well as physical ones. Obese children may be teased or rejected by peers. They have fewer friends than their peers. They may have lower levels of measured self-esteem and even show signs of depression (Strauss, Smith, Frame, & Forehand, 1985). Demonstrating the prejudice that may be directed toward obese young people, one study found that young women seeking admission to highly selective New England colleges were less likely to be accepted by those institutions if they were overweight (Canning & Mayer, 1966).

As a health issue, childhood obesity has been found to have comorbidity with a number of other disorders. This means that incidences of some medical problems are positively correlated with the incidence of obesity. Asthma is affected by overweight conditions because it is harder for the obese child to breathe and it takes longer for a child in this situation to get over asthma attacks. There has also been an increase in Type II diabetes, a disorder that is normally associated with adults. In the childhood form of the disease, excess adiposity means that the body cannot make enough insulin. Overweight in children is also associated with sleep apnea. In this disorder, the difficulty in breathing that accompanies obesity leads to a lack of adequate oxygen supply that can wake a child numerous times during the night. It may even be that some cases of children who have been diagnosed as attention deficit hyperactivity disorder (ADHD) are lethargic and distractible because they are sleep-deprived by apnea, rather than because of neurological chemical imbalances (Monaco, 1999).

Treatment of obesity in children must be managed carefully so as to avoid interrupting normal linear growth. Drastic calorie intake reduction as an attempt at treatment has been linked to the appearance of eating disorders in some individuals (Epstein, Myers, Raynor, & Saelens, 1998).

In a review of the treatment literature, Epstein et al. (1998) suggested reasons why treating children may be more likely to be successful than treating adults:

Family Support: Ideally, it may be easier to find support for children from families.

Short History of Obesity: Unlike adults, children do not have 20 or more years of unhealthy eating habits behind them.

Rapid Growth: Children are growing quite rapidly. Energy demands may be high, helping children to "grow out of" obesity in a way that is not available to older persons.

Less Adipose Cell Development: Treatment early in life may be able to prevent the development of excess fat cells in the body and this is likely to make it easier for a child to maintain body size following weight loss.

The standard approach to treatment has been that both physical activity and dietary intervention are important. There has been considerable focus in our society on low-fat foods and healthy eating. This might seem to be part of one approach to weight loss because in studies of nutrition, participants have tended to eat the same weight of food whether on high-fat diets or low-fat diets (Hill, 1998). Usually, the most calorie-dense foods also contain quite a bit of fat. Some of the newest low-fat foods are, however, quite high in calories. Although they are low in fat, they contain a lot of sugar. As far as weight goes, a calorie is a calorie, no matter what kind of food it comes from.

It has been shown that extra exercise may not affect weight in the absence of modifications to the diet. However, there is growing evidence for the value of so-called lifestyle exercise. In one study lasting 17 months, lifestyle exercise was shown to be associated with superior weight loss when compared to programmed aerobic exercise. There may be value in teaching children more general principles for increasing physical activity in their day-to-day lives. This might include walking as a means of transportation and using the stairs when going up only a few floors.

In the past, obesity was sometimes viewed as an indication of inadequate self-control. Studies have attempted to manipulate this by intensive training in self-control. This training had no significant effects on subsequent ability to lose weight, suggesting that this was the wrong way to think about excess body weight (Epstein et al., 1998).

There are life span trends in body weight but until middle childhood it is difficult to use weight measured early in life to make accurate predictions about later weight. Being an overweight baby does not necessarily mean that one will be overweight later in life. The correlations that have been found, at least across early childhood, have been small (Shapiro et al., 1984). In another study, a large group of 5,016 ethnically diverse middle-aged children was measured for body weight at age 9 and again at age 11. The strongest predictor of weight status at 11 years was overweight at 9 years, suggesting that weight patterns are beginning to stabilize by these ages (Dwyer et al., 1998).

TELEVISION AND CHILDHOOD OBESITY

Recent research suggested that television viewing may play a role in childhood obesity in America. A study by Gortmaker, Must, et al. (1996) found that children who watched more than 5 hours of television per day were five times more likely to be overweight than children who watched 0 to 2 hours of television. The average amount of television watched by children was 4.8 hours per day; 33 percent watched more than 5 hours each day and 11 percent watched for 2 hours or less per day. The American Academy of Pediatrics recommends that children watch no more than 2 hours of television per day.

Gortmaker, Peterson, et al., (1999) evaluated a program called Planet Health. Five schools took part in the program and five schools were designated control schools. A total of 1,295 children participated. The program gave instruction about health and fitness, including dietary recommendations and a suggested decrease in television viewing. Participants in the program improved their diets and watched less television. The reduction in television viewing made the most difference in decreasing obesity. This is not an isolated finding.

Sex has also been found to be a variable in some studies. Time spent watching television was significantly related to BMI in girls and to percentage of body fat in both boys and girls (Moreno, et al., 1998). The National Health and Nutrition Examination Survey III examined a national sample of 4,063 children between 8 and 16 years old. Twenty-six percent of the children reported watching 4 or more hours of television per day. These children also engaged in some physical activity, with almost 80 percent of them responding that they had three or more instances of vigorous physical activity per week. Perhaps surprisingly, BMI and skinfold measurements were not associated with physical activity in girls. Perhaps even more surprisingly, for the boys, the trend was that more activity was associated with greater BMI. While this seems counterintuitive—one might guess that more activity would be associated with lower BMI—it is a precursor to the findings that will be presented in this chapter. It was noteworthy that both boys and girls with the greatest BMI and skinfold levels were more likely to claim that they had watched television on the day before the survey (Andersen, Crespo, Bartlett, et al., 1998).

There may be several reasons why television watching is associated with obesity. Socioeconomic status (SES) may be a factor. A study in Spain showed that the lowest SES children were the most sedentary and spent more time watching television than higher SES children. Unfortunately, in large samples, ethnicity continues to show some association with SES. However, in a large national sample of children in America, it was found that SES did not fully account for differences in physical activity seen among different ethnic groups. Cultural beliefs about the value of activity and neighborhood safety were also factors (Andersen, Crespo, Bartlett, & Pratt, 1998). It will come as no surprise that advertisements for high-calorie foods on television were likely to result in children wanting and eating these kinds of foods (Gorn & Goldberg, 1982).

If the data are correlational, body weight and television watching might be measured at the same time, for example on a questionnaire. But as you know, you cannot determine if television causes children to be overweight from correlational data. It may also be that overweight children spend more time watching television because it is more rewarding than more vigorous activities. Further, it is not possible to eliminate some third variable, such as the food that is eaten while watching television. Prospective studies might be able to help illuminate this question by measuring television watching earlier in life and then, somewhat later, measuring body size. The two prospective studies that have examined whether television watching preceded overweight had inconclusive results (Robinson, 1998).

Robinson (1999) did an experiment designed to investigate the relationship between television watching and weight gain in children. It can be difficult to conduct an experiment in a real-world setting, but, as you know, it is the only way to make a determination about cause and effect. For the issue of television and obesity, causal conclusions are particularly important, given the recent population increases in child obesity.

PARTICIPANTS

The participants in this study were third- and fourth-graders from two different schools in San Jose, California. Schools were selected to be as similar as possible in characteristics such as the SES and ethnic backgrounds of the students. School officials and teachers had to agree that their students could take part in the study. Additionally, a parent of each child had to give consent in order for the child to be included as a participant. The participants and the school employees were given general information about the programs that children would experience, but they were not told the specifics of the hypothesis.

Ideally, it would have been desirable to randomly assign single individuals to conditions, but practical limitations probably made this unfeasible. Children were going to experience different programs as part of an intervention and, as you can imagine, there would be tactical problems associated with presenting different programs to children who were in the same classroom. Even if these problems could be overcome by complex scheduling, there would also be the potential that the children in the experimental condition might discuss their experiences with children from the control condition. Instead of random assignment of individual children, a random assignment was made in which one school was put in the experimental condition and the other was put in the control group. In this kind of random assignment the groups should be similar at the start of the study. As an illustration of the group similarities in this study, some of the characteristics of the participants are presented in Table 13.1.

EXPERIMENTAL INTERVENTION

The goal of the study was to "assess the effects of reducing television, videotape, and video game use on changes in adiposity, physical activity and dietary intake" (Robinson, 1999, p. 1561). The experimental group received some special learning units that were inserted into the regular school day. In all, these intervention classes consisted of 18 sessions lasting between 30 and 50 minutes. This intervention program was taught by the children's regular teachers. In the first part of the intervention, the children were trained how to record the amount of time that they spent watching television (prerecorded and otherwise) and playing video games. Part of the reason for having the children do this themselves was to use the reported levels of watching and playing to help convince the children that too much time was being spent in these activities.

After children had learned to record their screen time, the children in this group were told to try to see if they could turn the television off for 10 straight days. After this "TV turn-

TABLE 13.1   Characteristics of Control and Intervention Group Participants

	INTERVENTION	CONTROL
Age	M = 8.95	M = 8.92
Percent females	44.6%	48.5%
Number of TVs in home	M = 2.7	M = 2.7
TV in child's room	43.5%	42.7%
Complete phone interviews	71.6%	72.8%
Parent attended college	45.0%	21.0%*
Parent married	77.0%	67.0%

*This difference was significant ($p = .01$) but the others in this table were not.

Source: From Robinson, T. H. (1999). Reducing children's television viewing to prevent obesity: A randomized controlled trial. *Journal of the American Medical Association, 282,* 1561–1567.

off," the children were instructed to restrict their television viewing and game playing to no more than 7 hours each week. Subsequently, the children were taught to make careful judgments about television viewing and game activity so that their 7-hour budget consisted of careful selections from the choices available. In the concluding intervention sessions, attempts were made to teach the participants to promote the wise use of television to other children.

The intervention group parents were provided with information about ways in which television watching could be budgeted. In addition, an electronic device that helped to control television watching was given to the families of the intervention group. These control units were available for every television set in an intervention home. Called a TV Allowance (from Mindmaster Inc., Miami, FL), the device controlled access to the television by permitting predetermined amounts of television to be watched. Household members were given a personal identification number (PIN) for the TV Allowance and when the time allotted to that PIN ran out, the TV Allowance would disconnect the power to the television set. Data collected suggested good, though not perfect, compliance with the various phases of the intervention. For example, 91 percent of the intervention group children participated in some of the TV turnoff and 67 percent of them turned the television off for the full 10-day period.

DEPENDENT MEASURES

Near the beginning of the school year, a researcher came to each school to collect baseline information on the children in both groups. Near the end of the school year, research staff collected the outcome information. The parents, teachers, and students were unaware that the main purpose of the study was to investigate body fat levels. The researchers who interacted with children in schools were purposely unaware of group assignment. In order to preserve this control for bias in the data, the children's teachers did not take part in data collection. The outcome data consisted of a questionnaire that was read to the students. Before any of the real questions were asked, the children were given a practice session in which they were asked questions that were similar to the real questions to sharpen their skills at estimation of past events.

Students were asked about how much time they spent "watching television," and "watching movies or videos on a VCR." They were also asked to report about playing video games. They were asked to recall these events "separately for before school and after school,… 'yesterday,' and 'last Saturday'" for baseline and only "yesterday" in the follow-up data collection in April (quoted from Robinson, 1999 p. 1562). As part of the data collection, a structured telephone interview was conducted with the parents. The parents were asked to report the amount of time that the target child spent in activities that involved watching television.

Both parents and students were asked to report the amount of time that the children spent in activities, other than television, that did not involve much physical effort. This included pastimes such as doing schoolwork, listening to music, talking with others, and engaging in hobbies and quiet games. Both parents and students estimated the physical activity undertaken by the student on the day before the data collection. The children filled out a standard questionnaire that listed activities and the parents reported amounts of time the children spent in physical activity. Participant children were given a list of 60 foods likely to be eaten by young people and they were asked to identify those that they had eaten on a previous day. One of the impressive things about this research is the extent to which Robinson sought out and employed instruments that had been subject to some prior validation. For example, the questionnaire used to assess food types was developed from scales that had been validated in previous studies (Baranowski, et al., 1986; Simons-Morton, Baranowski, Parcel, O'Hara, and Matteson, 1990). Unfortunately, it is common in psychology that researchers merely construct measurement scales as they are needed with no evidence for validity whatsoever. Some validation of scales should increase your confidence in a study's findings. Robinson (1999) used a version of previously evaluated scales for most of the measurements in the study, a hallmark of high-quality research.

The same researchers went to both schools to take physical measures while the children were in their regular gym classes. Height and weight were carefully measured using standard instruments. Another measure of body fat was the tricept skinfold thickness on the right arm. This was measured with a standard caliper designed for the purpose. To check for accuracy these measures were repeated on the same individual. The test-retest reliability was $r = .99$ for all three. The children's waist and hips were measured with a tape measure at the level of the navel and, in addition, at the position on the body where the buttocks were maximal. These measurements all correlated strongly and positively with the BMI at levels between $r = .72$ and $r = .90$. Heart and lung fitness was tested with a shuttle run test, in which the individual runs back and forth between specified points for a standard amount of time. This has been found to be a reliable and valid measure. Perhaps more importantly for this study, this test has been shown to be useful in measuring changes in the cardiorespiratory functioning of children (Ahmaidi, Varray, Savy-Pacaux, & Prefaut, 1993).

Children and parents both reported the frequency with which the children ate a morning and/or evening meal in a room with a television turned off. They also estimated the proportion of time spent eating or drinking between-meal snacks while in front of the television.

BASELINE COMPARISONS

The intervention and control groups were very similar at the time of baseline measurements before intervention. Some of these similarities can be seen in Table 13.1. The groups were also not significantly different in any of the physical measurements. Of all the measures taken of hours of television watching, frequency of eating, and measures of physical activity, the only significant group difference prior to intervention reported by the children was that the intervention group ate more meals in front of the television ($p < .05$). In the reports from the parents about the children, only overall household television use and children's other sedentary behaviors were significantly different when reports of intervention parents were compared to control parents. In these data, overall household television use was higher in the control group ($p < .05$) and hours per week in other sedentary behaviors were higher in the intervention group.

RESULTS

The outcomes in this study consist of the differences between baseline measures—taken before intervention—and postintervention measures of the same characteristics. For example, each child's BMI was measured before and after intervention. It was important to remove the effects of normal growth. This study spanned most of a school year, during which time we would expect BMI to increase for all children in this age group because they were growing quite rapidly. To account for this expected growth, the mean change in each measure over the duration of the study was calculated. Then the amount of this change was compared by subtracting the control group value from the intervention group value. In other words, the growth of the control group was subtracted from the weight gain of the intervention group. Whatever was left over can be attributed to the intervention, because that was the only difference between the groups. A relative decrease was said to have occurred if the intervention group showed less change than the control group, and was indicated with a negative sign. Table 13.2 shows the relative change data for BMI.

As you can see from this table, both groups increased in BMI owing to normal growth but there was a relative decrease in BMI for the intervention group. BMI, tricept skinfold thickness, waist circumference, and waist-to-hip ratio all showed significant relative decreases indicating a loss in adiposity for the intervention group. The other body measurement, hip circumference, decreased, but not significantly.

Postintervention data were collected to permit comparisons with all the other baseline data from parents and children. You will remember that this was largely questionnaire information but the data also included the performance of children in the shuttle test. The questionnaires asked about relevant behaviors such as snacking, physical activity, sedentary activities, servings of highly advertised, high-fat foods, and hours spent watching different kinds of television. The only finding that changed significantly following intervention was that both parents and children in the intervention group reported that children watched significantly fewer hours of television each week. The parents reported a change from 15.35 hours per week before intervention to 8.80 hours per week following intervention. Children reported a decrease in their own watching from 12.43 hours to 8.86 hours. The control group levels did not change significantly over this period of time. It is noteworthy that no significant decrease was found for watching videos or playing video games; however, less than 5 hours a week was spent on each of these activities at baseline.

DISCUSSION

Because this research was an experiment, it is possible to conclude that there is some sort of causal link between watching television and weight gain in children. Initially, it may seem

TABLE 13.2   Relative Change in BMI for Both Groups across the Study

	Baseline		*Postintervention*		
	INTERVENTION	**CONTROL**	**INTERVENTION**	**CONTROL**	**RELATIVE CHANGE**
BMI	18.38	18.10	18.67	18.81	−0.45

Source: From Robinson, T. H. (1999). Reducing children's television viewing to prevent obesity: A randomized controlled trial. *Journal of the American Medical Association, 282,* 1561–1567.

puzzling that there were not also associated differences in factors such as eating snacks, amount of other exercise, amount of sedentary activity, and consumption of high-fat foods. At least tentatively, this study has shown that hours of television watching causes weight gain. Phrased another way, the intervention program designed to decrease television watching resulted in less weight being gained. It would be possible to leave it at that and to simply consider turning off the television to be an effective treatment for obesity. Presented with this information, we believe most people would want to know why less television leads to weight loss. The other measures in this study allow us to rule out some explanations, but they do not provide explanations. Snacking and food advertisements were not found to be factors.

In another study, Epstein, Valoski, et al. (1995) randomly assigned children to one of two groups: a group reinforced to be more active and a group reinforced to be less sedentary. One year later, the percentage of overweight children was less in the sedentary reward group. There was also a greater decrease in the percentage of body fat measured in this group. Another study had more modest findings. Epstein, Paluch, Gordy, and Dorn (2000) found that encouraging children to undertake physical activity achieved about the same levels of weight loss as working with children to limit sedentary activities. In any event, it appears as if decreasing sedentary activities may be an important component of weight loss programs for children.

The findings from these two studies mirror the findings reported by Robinson (1999). Television watching is one kind of sedentary activity and these studies found decreased weight associated with decreases in sedentary activity. Robinson (1999) noted that his measures only recorded vigorous and moderate levels of physical activity so it is possible that the time that was previously spent watching television was, instead, used in levels of physical activity too low to be detected in the study. As further evidence for the value of decreasing sedentary activity, past research would certainly support the generalization that programs designed only to increase physical activity and decrease fat intake have not been very effective in weight reduction (Resnikow, 1993).

It is difficult to know what other conclusions to draw at this point. In our view, this study was particularly carefully conducted and its findings are robust. We have little doubt that from these solid beginnings, this area will be a topic of additional research efforts.

CRITICAL THINKING TOOLKIT ITEMS

There are circumstances in which it is not practical to randomly assign participants as individuals to experimental conditions. Instead, groups are randomly assigned to conditions. It is particularly important in these cases to seek confirmation that groups are similar in characteristics that otherwise might confound the study.

REFERENCES

Ahmaidi, S. B., Varray, A. L., Savy-Pacaux, A. M., & Prefaut, C. G. (1993). Cardiorespiratory fitness evaluation by shuttle test in asthmatic subjects during aerobic training. *Chest, 103,* 1135–1141.

Andersen, R. E., Crespo, C. J., Bartlett, S. J., Cheskin, L. J., & Pratt, M. (1998). Relationship of physical activity and television watching with body weight and level of fatness among children: Results from the Third National Health and Nutrition Examination Survey. *Journal of the American Medical Association, 279,* 938–942.

Andersen, R. E., Crespo, C., Bartlett, S. J., & Pratt, M. (1998). Television watching and fatness in children: A reply to Moreno et al. *Journal of the American Medical Association, 280,* 1230.

Baranowski, T., Dworkin, R., Henske, J. C., Clearman, D. R., Dunn, J. K., Nader, P. R., & Hooks, P. C. (1986). The accuracy of children's self reports of diet: Family health project. *Journal of the American Dietetic Association, 86,* 1381–1385.

Canning, H., & Mayer, J. (1966). Obesity—Its possible effects on college acceptance. *New England Journal of Medicine, 275,* 1172–1174.

Dietz, W. H., & Bellizzi, M. C. (1999). Introduction: The use of body mass index to assess obesity in children. *American Journal of Clinical Nutrition, 70,* 123–125.

Dwyer, J. T., Stone, E. J., Yang, M., Feldman, H., Webber, L. S., Must, A., Perry, C. L., Nader, P. R., & Parcel, G. S. (1998). Predictors of overweight and overfatness in a multiethnic pediatric population. *American Journal of Clinical Nutrition, 67,* 602–609.

Epstein, L. H., Myers, M. D., Raynor, H. A., & Saelens, B. E. (1998). Treatment of pediatric obesity: The causes and health consequences of obesity in children and adolescents. *Pediatrics, 101,* 554–570.

Epstein, L. H., Paluch, R. A., Gordy, C. C., and Dorn, J. (2000). Decreasing sedentary behaviors in treating pediatric obesity. *Archives of Pediatrics & Adolescent Medicine, 154,* 220–226.

Epstein, L. H., Valoski, A. M., Vara, L. S., McCurley, J., Wisiewski, L., Kalarchian, M. A., & Shrager, L. R. (1995). Effects of decreasing sedentary behavior and increasing activity on weight change in obese children. *Health Psychology, 14,* 109–115.

Gorn, G. J., & Goldberg, M. E. (1982). Behavioral evidence for the effects of televised food messages on children. *Journal of Consumer Research, 9,* 78–93.

Gortmaker, S. L., Must, A., Sobol, A. M., Peterson, K., Colditz, G. A., & Dietz, W. H. (1996). Television viewing as a cause of increasing obesity among children in the United States. *Archives of Pediatrics & Adolescent Medicine, 150,* 356–362.

Gortmaker, S. L., Peterson, K., Wiecha, J., Sobol, A. M., Dixit, S., Fox, M. K., & Laird, N. (1999). Reducing obesity via a school-based interdisciplinary intervention among youth. *Archives of Pediatrics & Adolescent Medicine, 153,* 409–418.

Hill, J. O. (1998). Environmental contributions to the obesity epidemic. *Science, 280,* 1371–1374.

Monaco, J. E. (1999). Childhood obesity: A national epidemic. *Pediatrics for Parents, 18,* 6.

Moreno, L. A., Fleta, J., Mur, L., Stafford, M., Wells, J. C. K., Fewtrell, M., Anderson, R. E., Crespo, C., Bartlett, S. J., & Pratt, M. (1998). Television watching and fatness in children. *Journal of the American Medical Association, 280,* 1230–1231.

Pietrobelli, A. (1998). Body mass index as a measure of adiposity among children and adolescents: A validation study. *Journal of Pediatrics, 132,* 204–210.

Resnikow, K. (1993). School-based obesity prevention: Population vs. high risk interventions. *Annals of the New York Academy of Science, 699,* 154–166.

Robinson, T. N. (1998). Does television cause childhood obesity? *Journal of the American Medical Association, 279,* 959–960.

Robinson, T. N. (1999). Reducing children's television viewing to prevent obesity: A randomized control trail. *Journal of the American Medical Association, 282,* 1561–1567.

Shapiro, L. R., Crawford, P. B., Clark, M. J., Pearson, D. L., Raz, J., & Huenemann, R. (1984). Obesity prognosis: A longitudinal study of children from the age of 6 months to 9 years. *American Journal of Public Health, 74,* 968–972.

Simons-Morton, B. G., Baranowski, T., Parcel, G. S., O'Hara, N. M., and Matteson, R. C. (1990). Children's frequency of consumption of foods high in fat and sodium. *American Journal of Preventative Medicine, 6,* 218–227.

Stafford, M., Wells, J. C. K., & Fewtrell, M. (1998). Television watching and fatness in children: A reply to Moreno, et al. *Journal of the American Medical Association, 280,* 1231–1232.

Strauss, C. C., Smith, K., Frame, C., & Forehand, R. (1985). Personal and interpersonal characteristics associated with childhood obesity. *Journal of Pediatric Psychology, 10,* 337–343.

Stunkard, A. J. (1988). Some perspectives on human obesity: Its causes. *Bulletin of the New York Academy of Medicine, 64,* 902–923.

CHAPTER 14

BOLDFACE LETTERS

Over the years, many research studies in human development have added to our understanding of the phenomenon known as *learned helplessness.* Learned helplessness describes the situation in which an acquired expectation of failure prevents activity that might overcome the failure. The classic description of learned helplessness came from a laboratory study examining learning in dogs by Seligman and Maier (1967). Since that time, the work of Seligman and others on learned helplessness has included human participants and evolved to incorporate an interest in the opposite of learned helplessness: *learned optimism.* With a number of colleagues, Seligman also has designed a program supported by good psychological research that can be used to diagnose and treat the pessimistic attitudes that may be expressions of helplessness in children (Seligman, 1991). We do not know whether to be amused or alarmed that Seligman's wonderful book on this topic often finds itself in mall bookstores tucked between pop psychology titles such as *Thirteen Steps to Total Self-Esteem, How to Raise Flawless Children Who Will Make Your Neighbors Green with Envy,* and *Becoming a Perfect Person through the Cabbage Diet.*

Since the early 1970s, Carol Dweck has been a leading researcher in the area of learned helplessness in children. Her work has linked this concept with several other bodies of thought, perhaps most notably *attribution theory.* Attributions are ways in which an individual interprets the causes of events. Hence, attribution theory states that the way individuals think about these causes can lead them to behave in certain ways. Notice that the focus is on individual differences. Different individuals make different types of assertions about the factors that cause behavior. For an illustration, listen to other students talking about an exam they have taken. Those who did poorly on the exam may make statements of cause, or attributions, ranging from "I did not study enough" to "the test was completely unfair." Note that in the first statement the student is assuming responsibility for a bad grade, whereas in the second, the test itself is the culprit. Our understanding of attributions might lead us to expect that different behaviors might follow from these different views. The student who believes that lack of effort caused failure might work harder next time. The student who blamed the exam might be a candidate for helplessness. There is nothing much that can be

Incorporating the research of C. Erdley, K. M. Cain, C. C. Loomis, F. Dumas-Hines, and C. S. Dweck, "Relations among Children's Social Goals, Implicit Personality Theories, and Responses to Social Failure," 1997, *Developmental Psychology, 33,* pp. 263–272.

done about an unfair exam, so instrumental activity comes to a halt. In contrast to taking initiative and responsibility for one's actions, helplessness offers no productive solutions.

Past research has found that there are other related attributions often associated with helplessness. One of these addresses the extent to which traits such as intelligence or personality are believed to be malleable, meaning changeable. A person who believes intelligence is a fixed quantity that cannot be changed is called an *entity thinker* or *entity theorist.* That person treats intelligence as a permanent trait in the same way that eye color is permanent. An entity theorist believes each person has a certain amount of intelligence and, although a person may not work up to full potential, the actual amount of intelligence possessed will not change. In contrast, an *incremental thinker* or *incremental theorist* thinks that intelligence is like learning to play basketball—the harder you work at it, the better you will get. Of course, incremental theorists do not hold the absurd view that intelligence is limitless, but they do believe that intelligence can usually be increased through hard work.

Not surprisingly, entity thinkers easily become helpless. Children who are entity thinkers are among those who give up prematurely: If they experience failure, they believe that they simply cannot do the task at hand and stop trying. Their entity thinking predisposes them to assume that their ability has reached its permanent limits. Often, they are discouraged after these failures and are unlikely to try again in the future. In contrast, incremental thinkers are more likely to consider a failure to be an opportunity to learn. Instead of becoming helpless, these children are likely to try again, build new skills, and eventually succeed (Cain & Dweck, 1995).

The opposite of helplessness is often described as a *mastery orientation,* because the person feels that he or she can master the problems at hand. Mastery-oriented children are "undaunted by failure" (Diener & Dweck, 1980, p. 950). This is in marked contrast to the helpless child who takes a very different view, not only of failure but also of success. The helpless child does not seem to remember past successes and, in this way, has a difficult time benefiting from previous achievements. In addition, the helpless child does not believe that current success is likely to indicate future successes (Diener & Dweck, 1978, 1980). Because the helpless child believes that factors such as luck, rather than effort, are responsible for outcomes, a few successes are not likely to motivate the helpless child.

The goals that are typically held by entity or incremental thinkers are referred to, respectively, as *performance* and *learning* goals. A person with a performance goal is focused on the quality of the particular performance and does not see the learning opportunity offered by mistakes. Instead, mistakes are seen as evidence of a permanent inability to do some particular behavior. A person with a learning goal recognizes that while mistakes may have some negative consequences, they are also opportunities to learn.

Table 14.1 presents a diagram to help you to sort these terms. Note that learning and performance goals are not the same as incremental and entity thinking, respectively, but they do have some shared elements and are often found in the same people. The entity thinker who has performance goals is likely to treat mistakes and failures as evidence of limited innate ability. The incremental thinker with learning goals sees mistakes as a chance to change and improve, using the mistake to understand what can go wrong.

Where do these styles come from? The evidence is still coming in, but in one study Heyman, Dweck, and Cain (1992) observed children experiencing criticism through role-play with dolls. Some children reacted negatively to criticism, refusing to persist after mistakes

TABLE 14.1   **Clusters of Terms Used in Attributions about Success and Failure Experiences**

Mastery-Oriented	Helpless
Persists at tasks	Gives up easily
Tries new approaches to old failures	Fails to explore for new solutions
Incremental Thinking	**Entity Thinking**
Ability is changeable with effort	Ability is a fixed and unchangeable quantity
Learning Goal	**Performance Goal**
Mistakes or failures are opportunities to learn to do better next time	Mistakes or failures (poor performance) indicate inadequate ability

had been pointed out. These same children also anticipated negative parental response to mistakes, such as telling the children that they had done a "bad job" or "bad work." They even anticipated punishment from parents for what amounted to very trivial errors in assigned tasks. The implication was that parent responses to the child's behavior played a role in the child's implicit theories about behavior. The lack of persistence or willingness to try again observed in these children was a form of learned helplessness. A number of research projects have highlighted the difference between children with this behavioral style—who tend to attribute their failures to lack of ability—compared to children who adopt a mastery approach in which competence is thought to be improved by effort. Furthermore, as mentioned above, when the helpless children do succeed, they are likely to attribute their success to fate or luck (Elliott & Dweck, 1988). It is easy to imagine that helpless children can end up in a downward spiral in which failure is seen as meaning that they cannot perform adequately, which leads to unwillingness to try harder, leading to more failure, and so on (Heyman & Dweck, 1992).

In a 1997 investigation, Erdley, Cain, Loomis, Dumas-Hines, and Dweck examined the response of children to social failure. Their original work was reported as two separate studies but we will only consider the first study they reported. As with other research cited in this book, we encourage you to consult the original journal article for a complete report of the research.

PARTICIPANTS

The participants lived in a small city in the Midwest. They were recruited from two elementary schools, and were in fourth or fifth grade. Sixty-three children participated, 33 girls and 30 boys; about 70 percent of them were Caucasian. Parental permission for participation was required.

GROUP ASSIGNMENT

Two questionnaire measures were taken to provide the information used to assign participants to research groups. The goal of these measures was to control potentially confounding preexisting variables by measuring them and then creating experimental groups that consisted of children with a mix of these relevant characteristics. In an ideal world, random assignment might have taken care of this, but with a total study sample as small as 63 and potentially strong and important preexisting differences, random assignment might not have been sufficient to distribute important subject variables. Despite the lack of complete random assignment to conditions, we believe that parts of this study qualify it to be classified as an experiment.

The first of the two measures used for group assignment was developed specifically for this study and was called the Implicit Personality Theory Questionnaire. This questionnaire measured the extent to which an individual child was an entity or incremental thinker. On this instrument, the children rated three statements on a scale running from 1 (*really agree*) to 6 (*really disagree*). The statements were:

You have a certain personality and it is something that you can't do much about.

Your personality is something about you that you can't change very much.

Either you have a good personality or you don't and there really is very little you can do about it. (Erdley et al., 1997, p. 265).

You will note that each of these statements reflects an entity orientation—the view that personality cannot be changed. The reason why the questionnaire was constructed this way was because previous research has found that when people are offered a mix of entity and incremental statements on a scale such as this, they will tend to agree with the incremental statements. There is something attractive and compelling about the incremental orientation that tends to make people agree with statements phrased in that direction. Erdley et al. (1997) argued that by presenting only entity statements, some of this bias could be overcome. The more incrementally oriented people were still free to disagree with the statements, but children who were inclined to entity thinking would not be as easily swayed by inherently more attractive incremental assertions. Putting only entity phrasing in front of the children was done to balance out or overcome the seeming tendency to choose incremental statements. The authors defended this procedure by citing unpublished data that showed that in the domain of intelligence, people who saw intelligence in an incremental way would reject entity statements.

Children also completed a second questionnaire that measured social confidence (Erdley & Pietrucha, 1995). This instrument had four items each consisting of a pair of statements reflecting rival views of social confidence. For example, one item might state, "It is good to be liked by other people," while the other might state, "I do not expect to be liked by others." The children rated each statement as being "a little true" "true," or "very true," based on their own social interactions. The overall social confidence of the children was measured by the researchers, who assigned a numerical score ranging from 1 for children who indicated low confidence statements were "very true," to a score of 6 for children who indicated high confidence statements were "very true." In addition, during the data collection session, children were asked to identify topics from a list that represented their favorite activities. They were told these topics would be used to help choose pen pals for them.

Once this information was collected, children were assigned to research groups. The researchers wanted to control for the implicit personality theories held by the children, so they assigned them to groups in such a way that each experimental group contained children with a mix of attitudes about personality malleability. The mean score on the Implicit Personality Theory Questionnaire was 3.33. Approximately equal numbers of children scoring above the mean and below the mean were randomly assigned to each experimental group. There were 10 children who scored very near the mean and they were randomly assigned to one or the other experimental condition. The mean score for the social confidence questionnaire was 3.86. The experimental groups were also constructed so that they represented a mix of social confidence levels. About half of the children in each group scored above the mean in social confidence and about half of them scored below the mean.

PEN PAL PROCEDURE

Two researchers took part in the experiment. They were referred to as the "research lady" and the "pen pal lady." When the children appeared for the experiment the research lady told them that a pen pal club in another state was seeking pen pals for its members. They were told that the club was too far away for members to visit, but that a representative of the club would listen to a letter that the child could send orally over a radio transmitter operated by the pen pal lady. The research lady pointed out that the club representative would then select the child to become a pen pal based on this radio-transmitted letter. The research lady had access to the social confidence questionnaire outcomes and specifically reminded the child of his or her own self-rated social confidence. She said either: "Looking at your answers I can see you're pretty sure about your ability to make friends"(p. 265) or "Looking at your answers, I can see that you are not sure about your ability to make friends"(p. 265). Both were then told "by communicating with the person in the pen pal club you'll actually have a chance to make a new friend"(p. 266).

Each of the research groups received one of two manipulations: the performance goal or the learning goal. The performance goal was consistent with entity thinking and was given to the child by the research lady who said: "The important thing is, we'd like to see how good you are at making friends. Think of it as a chance to see how good you are at making friends too"(p. 266). Notice that the emphasis here is on the presence or absence of a fixed ability—the ability to make friends. There is no suggestion to the child that this ability will be able to be improved with practice. In contrast, the learning goal, consistent with incremental thinking, was communicated to the children in the other experimental group by the research lady who said: "The important thing is, this will give you a chance to practice and improve your ways of making friends. So think of it as a chance to work on your skills and maybe learn some new ones"(p. 266).

To be sure that the goal was understood, it was repeated for the child and the child was asked to repeat it back. It was also written on an index card, which the child was asked to keep on his or her lap as a memory aid for the goal. Following this presentation of the independent variable, the child was brought to the pen pal lady. The pen pal lady chatted with the child about which topics might be interesting to a pen pal. The child was told to make notes for a radio "letter" to the representative of the pen pal club. The pen pal lady was not aware of which experimental group the child was in or of the child's social confidence level. The pen pal lady wore headphones, ostensibly to receive the sound, and twiddled with the dials on a realistic-looking radio transmitter, seeming to talk to the representative of the pen pal club.

Each child relayed his or her radio letter to the transmitter. After the end of the letter, the pen pal lady seemed to listen to the headphones for a short while and then told the child that the club representative was not sure yet whether the child would be given a pen pal. This was a mild rejection, and following it the pen pal lady suggested that the child transmit another letter. Following the second letter the child was always accepted for a pen pal. Even though the pen pal club was a sham, the children were given real pen pals at the end of the study as a payoff for their participation.

Once the children had been accepted for a pen pal, the pen pal lady said that she wanted to know what the child thought when he or she heard that there was some doubt about whether a pen pal would be assigned. She told the children that she had collected the thoughts of other children and put four of them on a wheel that had four movable sections, like an adjustable pie chart. These thoughts were

Am I a likeable person?
Am I not so good at making new friends?
Are we too different?
Did I not try hard enough?

Note that the first two of these concern social ability, the third suggests a reason beyond personal control, and the fourth involves effort expended. The participants were asked to move the sections of the pie chart around until their sizes represented the extent to which each of the four ideas had been in their thoughts. The pie chart wheel had 32 evenly spaced graduations around the edge, making it possible to convert the responses of the children into numbers between 1 and 32. Although the radio transmitter and the pie chart wheel might seem rather contrived as they are described, the children showed no sign that they did not believe the cover stories.

Following data collection, the children returned to the research lady who gave them some encouragement about their performance during the radio transmission and discussed methods for making new friends.

CODING THE DATA

The radio letters written by the participants were taped and transcribed word for word. Individual units of information were counted. An information unit was a statement such as "I like to play basketball." The content of the information units was also coded into strategy categories; for example, the statement about basketball was counted in the category labeled *activities*. The rater who coded the letters was unaware of the individual child's assignment to a research group or to the child's measured social confidence level. A second coder rated a randomly selected 50 percent of the letters. Interrater reliability was 86 percent.

RESULTS AND DISCUSSION

Content of Letters

There were no systematic differences found in the letter content that related to the gender of the participant children, even though each group contained a gender mix. There were, however, some interesting findings with respect to the number of different strategy categories that were used by children. These strategies were the outcomes of the coders' work on the letters and included categories such as greetings and closings, questions, comparison between self and other children, activities, possessions, self-evaluations, and feelings. In their first letters, before the mild rejection, the performance goal group and the learning goal group used almost the same number of strategies ($M = 3.28$; $M = 3.47$). Here and elsewhere in reporting the results of this study, the first mean mentioned in the text will be the mean that appears first in the parentheses. Following the mild rejection, the children in the performance goal group used what Erdley et al. (1997) reported as "fewer strategies" than did the children in the learning goal group ($M = 2.36$; $M = 3.14$; $p < .06$). Following the work of Goetz and Dweck (1980) this was interpreted as a sign of learned helplessness.

In a further comparison of the first and second letter, the performance goal group also put less information in letter two ($M = .28$; $M = .49$; $p < .025$). This could be another sign of giving up because the amount of information did not differ significantly when the first letters were compared. In response to the mild rejection, the performance goal children might have produced less information as a means of protecting themselves from further negative evaluation.

Compared to their first letters, in their second letters, the learning goal children increased their expression of positive feelings by making statements such as "I like to meet new people" and "I like this school" ($M = .07$; $M = .18$; $p < .01$). This greater expression of positive feelings might be seen as a useful strategy in trying to make the second letter more attractive to the pen pal representative than the first had been. It demonstrated that the learning goal children were willing to keep on trying to overcome the mild rejection, to a greater extent than was seen for the performance goal children. The learning goal children also asked fewer questions in their letters compared to the performance goal group. This could be seen in the first letters ($M = .18$; $M = .34$; $p < .05$) as well as in the second letters ($M = .07$; $M = .26$; $p < .01$). Asking questions might not seem to be a very good strategy to use in this situation. The purported pen pal representative had the decision-making power and was seeking information about the applicant child. The only information that would be conveyed by question asking would be that the applicant was inquisitive. The higher levels of question asking were interpreted by Erdley et al. (1997) as a means for the performance goal children to avoid talking about themselves, thereby enabling them to avoid negative evaluation by the supposed pen pal representative at the other end of the radio link. Diener and Dweck (1978, 1980) looked at helpless and mastery-oriented children in a situation that involved solving visual puzzles and found that helpless children used statements that had the function of diverting the attention of a person evaluating their poor performance.

Classically, learned helplessness is manifested by refusal to act and it is noteworthy that a higher absolute number of performance goal children flatly refused to send a second message (19 percent, $n = 6$; 6 percent, $n = 2$). This difference was not statistically significant but it was in the direction that would be predicted if the performance goal children were showing learned helplessness.

Incremental and Entity Theorists—
Quasi-Experimental Outcomes

You will remember that the children were originally tested using the Implicit Personality Theory Questionnaire to determine the extent to which they held previously established entity or incremental beliefs. Even though both kinds of theorists were purposely spread over both goal conditions it was possible, following data collection, to regroup the data from the children based on their preexisting entity or incremental thinking. This was a quasi-experimental procedure embedded in what was otherwise an experiment. It was found that the preexisting theories the children held about personality before the research manipulation had a relationship to their response in the face of mild social failure no matter which goal condition they received as the independent variable in the experimental manipulation.

Children originally identified as incremental theorists were more likely to express positive feelings in their letters than were those who were entity theorists ($M = .17$; $M = .07$; $p < .05$). Perhaps not surprisingly, the subgroup of incremental theorists who also happened to get the learning goal as the independent variable did best of all in the communication of positive feelings ($p < .05$). The goal given to these children—opportunity to learn–was consistent with attributions that they held before any participation in the research.

It may be surprising that the preexisting implicit personality theories made any difference at all, given that individuals near the mean on the measurement scale were randomly assigned to the incremental or entity group, which likely increased the variability of the groups with respect to their actual beliefs. Probably, these findings would have been even more pronounced if only the extremes had been compared, discarding the participants scoring near the mean.

Attributions on the Adjustable Pie Chart

As Erdley et al. (1997) expected, compared to the performance goal children, children who received the learning goal adjusted the pie chart so that more of the area was taken up by the concern that they had not tried hard enough ($M = 7.03$; $M = 13.09$; $p < .01$).

Compared to the children who were given a learning goal, children who received a performance goal were more likely to use the adjustable chart to indicate that they believed their initial rejection by the pen pal representative was a result of a factor they could not control: being too different from the representative ($M = 4.09$; $M = 8.20$; $p < .01$).

The results of the quasi-experimental regroupings showed that the preexisting theories held by the children at the beginning of the study also had a relationship to their attributions for the mild rejections. Children who were entity theorists at the start were more likely to believe that their initial rejection was a result of their inability to make friends than were the incremental theorists ($M = 8.42$; $M = 4.97$; $p < .01$). If these entity theorists were to use this as a reason for not bothering to exert effort, their failure to make friends could become a self-fulfilling prophecy: If they believe they cannot make friends, they may not try to do so.

The findings of this study support the majority of similar research in this area. Children who experienced the performance goal seem to have taken it to heart. They were told that their mistakes were an indication of their ability and they acted accordingly, making less effort and even refusing to try again. One of the most striking things about this study was the extent to which a mere statement of goals, repeated several times, was enough to change behavior. This happened even in incremental theorist children who were predisposed to think that their ability could be improved through effort. There is no way to tell from the data in this study how long lasting these attitude shifts were, nor the extent to which they would transfer to other tasks. This information should serve as a cautionary tale to all of us who deal with children or who plan to do so. We need to be careful about what we say. Even brief statements of goals can affect child behavior.

Further, the findings suggest that in dealing with children it is important to stress the value of effort in finding solutions to problems. Parents and teachers should exercise caution when talking to children about failure performances. Failure cannot be avoided. This research suggests that children should not be protected from situations where they may experience failure. What is more important is to teach children how to deal with criticism and failure. The child who becomes mastery-oriented, who believes that effort matters, has a life skill that is likely to lead to success.

CRITICAL THINKING TOOLKIT ITEMS

Random assignment is usually the best way to create groups for an experiment. However, when groups are quite small and when there are potentially powerful and confounding pre-existing differences among participants, it may be better to take steps to ensure that these differences are spread evenly over groups. This may improve internal validity, even though assignment to groups may no longer be totally random.

REFERENCES

Cain, K. M., & Dweck, C. S. (1995). The relation between motivational patterns and achievement cognitions through the elementary school years. *Merrill-Palmer Quarterly, 41,* 25–52.

Diener, C. I., & Dweck, C. S. (1978). An analysis of learned helplessness: Continuous change in performance, strategy, and achievement cognitions following failure. *Journal of Personality and Social Psychology, 36,* 451–462.

Diener, C. I., & Dweck, C. S. (1980). An analysis of learned helplessness: 2. The processing of success. *Journal of Personality and Social Psychology, 39,* 940–952.

Elliott, E. S., & Dweck, C. S. (1988). Goals: An approach to motivation and achievement. *Journal of Personality and Social Psychology 54,* 5–12.

Erdley, C., Cain, K. M., Loomis, C. C., Dumas-Hines, F., & Dweck, C. S. (1997). Relations among children's social goals, implicit personality theories,

and responses to social failure. *Developmental Psychology, 33,* 263–272.

Erdley, C. A., & Pietrucha, C. A. (1995, April). *The relation of children's attributions and social goals to their responses to social failure.* Paper presented at the annual meeting of the American Educational Research Association, San Francisco.

Goetz, T. S., & Dweck, C. S. (1980). Learned helplessness in social situations. *Journal of Personality and Social Psychology, 39,* 246–255.

Heyman, G. D., Dweck, C. S. & Cain, K. (1992). Young children's vulnerability to self blame and helplessness: Relationship to beliefs about goodness. *Child Development, 63* 401–415.

Seligman, M. E. P. (1991). *Learned optimism.* New York: Knopf.

Seligman, M. E. P., & Maier, S. F. (1967). Failure to escape traumatic shock. *Journal of Experimental Psychology, 74,* 1–9.

CHAPTER 15

IT ALL ADDS UP

During the past decade, researchers have spent considerable energy investigating the academic performance of children who represent different ethnic groups within American schools. One of the most consistent findings to emerge from this effort has been that Asian American students, as a group, tend to outperform other ethnic groups, particularly in mathematics. In the National Educational Longitudinal Study (NELS), Hafner, Ingels, Schneider, and Stevenson (1990) found that Asian American students excelled in a number of mathematical performance measures when compared to all other ethnic groups in the country. This finding was supported by another study which found that in the 7th and 11th grades Asian American students outperformed other ethnic groups on standardized math proficiency exams (Dossey, Mullis, Lindquist, & Chambers, 1988). In this investigation, superior mathematics grades were typically achieved in school classes by Asian Americans. They also chose to take optional upper-level math courses in school more frequently than other ethnic groups.

In thinking about these cultural differences, it is important to realize that a potential problem exists in studies of Asian Americans, namely, that the label *Asian American* does not necessarily specify a common cultural group. Chinese, Filipinos, Japanese, Koreans, and Vietnamese might all be included as *Asian Americans,* yet these cultural groups might be quite different. Also, populations of so-called Asian Americans drawn from specific areas may not be diverse with respect to their background nationality.

The reasons for the observed differences in academic performance that exist between Asian Americans and other ethnic groups are probably complex, but are likely to include factors such as cultural values, neurological functioning, parental training, peer group influences, and genetics (d'Ailly, 1992; Sue & Okazaki, 1990; Whang & Hancock, 1994). Contextual influences that are beyond the classroom have also been strongly implicated in explaining these academic differences. For example, Stevenson and Lee (1990) found a relationship between the achievement of Asian students living in Taiwan and Japan and the learning environment that was established at home. The values of parents, which stressed achievement, were found to be part of this relationship, as were the expectations about school performance that the students shared with parents, teachers, and peers.

Incorporating the research of S. L. Huang and H. C. Waxman, "Motivation and Learning-Environment Differences between Asian-American and White Middle School Students in Mathematics," 1995, *Journal of Research and Development in Education, 28,* pp. 208–219.

Evidence that these cultural values exist among Asian Americans can be seen in the finding that Asian Americans tend to do more homework than other ethnic groups (Hafner, et al., 1990); twice as much in one analysis of the data (Kennedy & Park, 1994). They are also more likely to think that school is a good learning environment, with fair discipline, and good teachers who listen to the needs and questions of students.

In a study of different ethnic groups within the United States, Steinberg, Dornbusch, and Brown (1992) found that Asian American students were more likely to have peers who supported their academic aspirations when compared to other ethnic groups. In this study, all ethnic groups responded positively when asked if they thought that a good education would lead to a good job. Thus, all of the ethnic groups studied seemed to value education equally. However, the Asian American students were more likely than others to agree with the statement that failing to get a good education would lead to difficulty in getting a good job. The other ethnic groups tended to be more optimistic; believing that even if education was not first-rate, there still might be an opportunity for occupational success. The pessimism found among Asian Americans considering the consequences of a poor education may provide them with an additional motive to perform.

The academic success of Asian American young people is disproportionate to their numbers. They represent only 2.1 percent of the U.S. population, but they are strongly represented in the freshman classes at the colleges and universities recognized for excellence: 12 percent at Harvard, 19 percent at Massachusetts Institute of Technology, and 20 percent at Berkeley.

Huang and Waxman (1995) conducted a large study using Asian American and Caucasian middle school–aged children. They were interested in examining behavioral as well as cognitive differences between the two ethnic groups. In the cognitive domain, the researchers investigated the psychological factors influencing motivation. They also examined how the students perceived the learning environment. Past research has demonstrated that the attitudes students have about the classroom as a learning environment are likely to influence their performance. For example, a classroom that appears on the surface to be "the same environment" for students from different ethnic groups may actually be experienced in quite different ways depending upon the attitudes of the student (Waxman, 1991). Knight and Waxman (1990) found that the perception of the classroom learning environment was so closely related to motivation that these two measures had to be investigated together.

Huang and Waxman (1995) restricted their investigation to a single public school district. One reason for this was to avoid a potential confound that had been found in previous studies: Asian American students are more likely to attend private schools. For example, in the 1988 NELS, Asian American students were more likely to be enrolled in parochial or independent private schools than other ethnic groups and, therefore, less likely to be in public educational systems. Because the sample of participants in Huang and Waxman (1995) was so large, it was also possible for them to investigate the effects of gender and grade level among the middle school children they studied.

PARTICIPANTS

Sixth-, seventh-, and eighth-grade middle school children from a large city in the south-central United States were the population from which the participants were drawn. This particular area was chosen because a large percentage of the students in the schools were Asian American. Ethnic groups within this school district existed in about the following proportions: 20 percent Asian American, 31 percent white, 26 percent African American, and 23 percent Hispanic. In order to select participants from the district, a student survey was given to all the middle school students in the school district ($N = 7,000$).

The participants in this study were a *stratified sample,* meaning that the entire population was treated as several subpopulations from which participants were then randomly selected. For example, if you knew that a school district had a population of 56 percent girls and 44 percent boys, you might want your research sample to reflect these proportions. Selecting a random sample from the entire population might not preserve this ratio because you might produce more boys than girls just by the luck of the draw. To correct for this, you could first subdivide your population into two gender groups—male and female, and then select the correct number of people from each to achieve a 56 to 44 ratio of females to males. This would be a stratified sample. Huang and Waxman (1995) used a stratified sample that consisted of 1,200 whites and 1,200 Asian Americans, with an equal representation of students from each of the three grade levels and an equal number of male and female participants.

The students in the study came from lower to middle-income homes. The level of school achievement across the school district was slightly higher than national samples. The Asian American students from this particular middle school scored higher than all other ethnic groups in the district on both district- and state-conducted tests of mathematical performance.

MEASUREMENTS

The psychological scales used in this study were modifications of three standardized instruments.These newly modified pencil-and-paper scales were used to measure motivation in this study. They were the Multidimensional Motivational Instrument (MMI; Uguroglu, Schiller, & Walberg, 1981), the Classroom Environment Scale (CES; Fraser, 1982, 1986), and the Instructional Learning Environment Questionnaire (IEQ; Knight & Waxman's report, as cited in Huang & Waxman, 1995).

The MMI was designed to measure internal psychological states relating to motivation. In its intact form, Huang and Waxman (1995) noted that it had test-retest reliability as well as construct validity and predictive validity. *Test-retest reliability* is what it sounds like: If the test is given again to the same people, they will get about the same scores. *Construct validity* means that the test measures the particular psychological state it is designed to measure. In psychology, constructs are usually internal cognitive factors such as attitudes, thoughts, or feelings that are supposed to influence behavior. *Predictive validity* means that the instrument can predict some future performance that is consistent with the construct: An individual who scores high on a test of achievement motivation should achieve his or her goals in the future. For this study, the MMI scales that were used were the ones from the original instrument that measured achievement motivation, the intrinsic desire to succeed, and academic self-concept, the exhibition of pride and the expectation of good performance in class work.

The CES normally contains six scales and has been shown to have content validity as well as concurrent validity. *Content validity,* also called face validity, presumes that a measure is valid simply because the measure makes sense. A measure of class participation would not have content validity if it recorded the frequency of nail biting among students in a class. Frequency of hand raising would appear to have more content validity. However, you will notice that we have said that content validity "presumes" a measure is valid because it makes sense. We have used this phrasing because content validity, by itself, does not necessarily indicate that a measure is truly valid. The introversion-extroversion survey in the latest issue of *Young Drooling Teen Magazine* may appear to measure these traits, but it may not be a valid measure. *Concurrent validity* means that some other measure, taken at the same time, indicates that the test is valid. For example, if the test is supposed to measure classroom involvement, students who score high on it will also be frequent participants in class discussions. The CES has also been shown to be *internally consistent*. As you will remember from Chapter 11, this means that responses to items that are supposed to measure a particular characteristic are strongly correlated. For example, a student who gives high ratings to one item suggesting high involvement in the classroom will also rate highly other items suggesting involvement (Fraser, 1982; Moos, 1979). Two scales of the CES were used in the study under discussion: involvement, active participation and attentiveness in class, and affiliation, knowing, helping, and being friendly toward other students.

The ILEQ measures the perceptions of students about the places in which they learn. Intact, it has been shown to have adequate test-retest reliability and internal consistency (Knight and Waxman, 1990; Waxman, Huang, Knight, & Owens, 1992). In the present study, two scales from the ILEQ were used: satisfaction, enjoyment of class and schoolwork, and parent involvement, students' reports of their parents' interest and involvement in schoolwork.

Each of these three modified scales contained four items. Each of the items was designed to be rated on a 4-point Likert scale, where 1 = not at all true, 2 = not very true, 3 = sort of true, and 4 = very true. Responses to the four items within each scale were averaged to give a score for that particular scale. The result was that the highest possible score for an instrument was 4, indicating that all items had been rated as very true, and the lowest was 1, meaning that all items had been rated not at all true. The scales described above were combined into a single instrument together with some additional items from the NELS (Hafner et al., 1990). These items asked about things such as amount of time spent on homework and other activities.

As part of your critical thinking about psychology, it is important to understand that when scales are modified, such as when a few items are selected from a scale and reused for the measurement of a specific characteristic, quality statements about the original, intact scale may no longer apply. Information about reliability and validity, which were discussed in Chapter 4, or other psychometric qualities that may have originally applied to the entire scale, may not apply to selected parts of the scale, particularly when they are recombined with items from other instruments. This is not to say that the new scale is, of necessity, unreliable or invalid. Rather, it means that any previous standardization demonstrating the reliability or validity of this measure may no longer apply.

An easy way to understand this concept is to imagine a 50-question exam covering some assigned reading. You have done the reading carefully and learned the material. Assume that the exam is a reliable and valid measure of what you know about the material. If only three questions are selected to represent this reading material, those questions may no longer measure your knowledge: they could be the only three things you did not know from all the reading material. On the other hand, three questions might measure your knowledge perfectly well—you have learned the reading thoroughly and are able to correctly answer those three questions, demonstrating your learning. The point is that even if the 50-question test was valid, you cannot assume that items pulled from it and used separately will also be valid.

While it might have been better for the researchers to use the complete original scales rather than parts selected from them, there was a practical constraint: The school district only permitted the researchers to have 45 minutes to collect all the survey data. A further practical constraint was the length of time middle school students could be expected to pay attention to a survey.

RESULTS

The data in this study were separated by ethnicity, sex, and grade in school. The ethnicity outcomes on items from the three scales are shown in Figure 15.1. All of the differences shown in Figure 15.1 were statistically significant at levels exceeding $p < .004$. The mean scores in Figure 15.1 are the averaged scores of all individuals from each ethnic group on each of the subscales. Given that the scales used 4-point Likert scales, these averages could have ranged between 1 and 4. Asian American students reported higher active participation or involvement in the classroom. In contrast, they reported less affiliation: a measure of knowing, liking, and working with other students. The Asian American students scored higher on all of the other measured outcomes: satisfaction, parental involvement, self-concept, and achievement motivation.

Other self-reported outcomes also highlight differences between the Asian American students and the white students. Four of these are shown in Figure 15.2. An interpretation of Figure 15.2 might suggest that the Asian Americans are different from the whites in a number of reasonably concrete ways. They have higher educational aspirations ($p < .001$), they spend more time on homework ($p < .001$), they are absent from school less often ($p < .001$), and

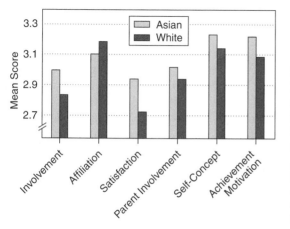

FIGURE 15.1   Ethnicity and Outcome Measures. Ethnicity differences for the outcome measures in mathematics classrooms of involvement, affiliation, satisfaction, parental involvement, academic self-concept, and achievement motivation.

Source: From Huang, S. L., & Waxman, H. C. (1995). Motivation and learning-environment differences between Asian-American and White middle school students in mathematics. *Journal of Research and Development in Education, 28,* 216.

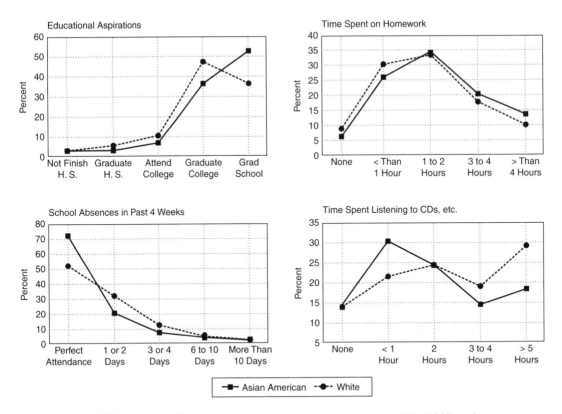

FIGURE 15.2   Differences found between a group of Asian American students ($N = 1,200$) and a group of white students ($N = 1,200$) on variables that are part of academic performance.

Source: From Huang, S. L., & Waxman, H. C. (1995). Motivation and learning-environment differences between Asian-American and White middle school students in mathematics. *Journal of Research and Development in Education, 28,* 214.

they spend less time listening to CDs, tapes, and the radio ($p < .001$). Although not shown in this figure, the Asian Americans also spend less time watching television ($p < .01$).

In a study such as this, where researchers have a great deal of data, the participants may be regrouped to show the effects of other quasi-experimental variables. These researchers used this tactic to provide information about gender differences and grade differences. The issue of regrouping was discussed earlier in Chapter 6. You will remember from that chapter that there should be some logic to the new groups. The new groups under discussion here have the clear logic of representing sex or grade. Sex differences were investigated by dividing the entire sample into males and females, regardless of ethnicity and grade level. In considering these data it may be important to remember that these children were part of a sample originally stratified to produce two ethnic groups. The recombined sample, although large, does not represent the diversity found in the schools in a large city because only Asian Americans and whites are included. These data are presented in Table 15.1. In each case where there were significant differences between girls and boys,

TABLE 15.1   Mean Scores for Outcome Measures Grouped by Sex

OUTCOME MEASURE	BOYS MEAN SCORE	GIRLS MEAN SCORE	p VALUE
Involvement	2.88	2.97	.0001
Affiliation	3.07	3.21	.0001
Satisfaction	2.78	2.91	.0001
Parent involvement	2.98	3.01	.2880
Academic self-concept	3.18	3.17	.7410
Achievement motivation	3.08	3.20	.0001

Source: From Huang, S. L., & Waxman, H. C. (1995). Motivation and learning-environment differences between Asian-American and White middle school students in mathematics. *Journal of Research and Development in Education, 28,* 216.

the direction favored the girls. Girls were significantly higher than boys on all measures except parental involvement and academic self-concept. These last two measures did not produce significant differences.

In another analysis, the entire sample was divided into three groups, sixth grade, seventh grade, and eighth grade. This cross-sectional analysis suggested some developmental changes in variables measured across the three grades. These data are found in Table 15.2. Although the trends are not always significant, each of the measured variables except academic self-concept showed a decrease in absolute value from sixth grade to eighth grade. Given the nature of the variables measured, this is an unfortunate trend. If these data can be generalized to other populations, it should be a matter of national concern that factors such as involvement, academic self-concept, and achievement motivation decrease during the middle school years.

TABLE 15.2   Mean Scores for Outcome Measures Grouped by Grade Level

OUTCOME MEASURE	SIXTH GRADE MEAN	SEVENTH GRADE MEAN	EIGHTH GRADE MEAN	p VALUE
Involvement	3.06a	2.96b	2.76c	.0001
Affiliation	3.20a	3.11b	3.11b	.0034
Satisfaction	2.96a	2.88b	2.70b	.0001
Parent involvement	3.11a	3.00b	2.86b	.0001
Academic self-concept	3.18	3.18	3.16	.7220
Achievement motivation	3.22a	3.12b	3.08b	.0001

Note: Mean values with the same letter are not significantly different from each other.

Source: From Huang, S. L., & Waxman, H. C. (1995). Motivation and learning-environment differences between Asian-American and White middle school students in mathematics. *Journal of Research and Development in Education, 28,* 216.

DISCUSSION

The results of this study present an interesting picture of the personal motivations and other variables that affect performance in middle school. Both self-reports of behavior and reports of personal motivations indicate differences between ethnic groups. With reference to the Asian American ethnic group, past research (Oxnam, 1986) has indicated four clear differences found in Asian cultures that may have influenced the Asian-American children in this study:

1. Parents are likely to expect high levels of academic performance from their children and they are not easily satisfied unless these expectations are met.
2. Asian parents have high standards for school curricula and exert considerable pressure for improvements in schools.
3. Asian cultures place a very high value on effort. Euro-American culture, in contrast, is more likely to stress natural ability. If academic outcomes are believed to be a result of ability, students and parents may accept poor performance, thinking that increased effort is a waste of time.
4. Time-on-task is likely to be different. Students from Asian cultures are more likely to spend more time on homework, have an appropriate quiet place to work such as their own desk at home, and do few chores around the house so as to be able to focus on school work.

The consistently higher grades for students in this earlier study were received regardless of the SES of the family or the educational level of the parents (Oxnam, 1986). The findings of this study suggest that values from the parents and home, as well as behavior consistent with these values, are crucial components of school performance.

GENETICS AND ETHNICITY

Huang and Waxman (1995) presented evidence for performance differences when Asian Americans are compared to whites. A number of fairly concrete reasons for this have been identified. This study is similar to many other studies of academic performance in ethnic groups in that there is no evidence presented for genetics as a factor. A naive reader might assume that a considerable amount of the variability observed among ethnic groups was the result of genetic differences. Indeed, there has been a major controversy over the origin of these differences in the past few years.

Although the issue has ancient roots, it was brought to life again by the publication of *The Bell Curve* (Herrnstein & Murray, 1994), a book which asserted that differences in IQ between Asian Americans and others were largely caused by genes. This stance was taken up by others including J. Philippe Rushton of the University of Western Ontario and Richard Lynn of the University of Ulster. Details of their positions can be found in several books about the subject (e.g., Jacoby & Glauberman, 1995) or by searching the Internet. The arguments on both sides are heated, voluminous, and complex. Nevertheless, it is our opinion that, given the existing data, it is inappropriate to conclude that differences observed in behaviors as complex as school performance are the result of genetic factors.

Probably the best evidence we have about the genetics of intelligence comes from careful studies of twins who have been reared in separate homes and children who have been adopted, as discussed in Chapter 12. However, there is no evidence parallel to these twin studies that addresses the genetic contributions of intelligence to differences between ethnic groups. This is because the role of genes dictates that genetic influences can only be studied within a group. The clearest findings come from groups that contain very closely related individuals. Good studies of twins have shown that about 50 percent of the variance in IQ is a result of genetic factors. This means that 50 percent of the IQ variability that can be observed in this population (separated twins) is explained by, or attributable to, variation in genes (Bouchard & McGue, 1981).

It is important to think critically about these data. People who do not understand the issues may quickly jump to the conclusion that IQ is genetic and, therefore, school performance differences among ethnic groups is also genetic. There are a number of problems with asserting genetic control; we will present two of them. First, IQ is correlated with school performance, but it is not the same thing. Common sense, as well as careful research, both indicate that IQ—the outcome of taking a test—may explain some of the variance in school performance, but much of the rest of it is accounted for by contextual or environmental factors (Scarr, 1992). Second, the variability in IQ within a group says nothing about the level of IQ within a group. The studies of ethnic groups discussed here are concerned with one group outperforming another, that is, with average level of performance, not with variability of performance within a single group. There is no evidence in studies of separated monozygotic twins to demonstrate that the differences routinely observed between ethnic groups are the result of genes. The twin studies present us with estimates of genetic effects within a group of twins. It is not appropriate to take estimates derived in this way and assume that they also account for the differences between groups of people.

Despite all the social and cultural importance that they carry, labels such as Asian American, Hispanic, white, and African American have no genetic meaning. These populations are genetically very diverse. The ancestry of any of these groups is anything but homogenous. Scarr (1981) reported one of the few instances in which genetic analysis went beyond merely asking people about their ancestors. In this study, biological analyses of blood groups and serum proteins were conducted in an attempt to identify groups that were meaningfully genetically diverse. It was found that mental test scores between groups were not different.

Huang & Waxman (1995) have identified a number of interesting ways in which Asian American students are different from white students. There is no evidence in this study that genetic differences account for performance differences between Asian Americans and it was not the intent of these authors to support genetic assertions. What they have given us is a list of other factors that are likely to make a difference, ranging from family values to various measures of time-on-task.

CRITICAL THINKING TOOLKIT ITEMS

Be cautious about the assumption that reliability and validity estimates derived for complete scales also apply to parts of those scales.

When assessing psychological tests or scales, look for evidence about the different kinds of reliability and validity.

Differences observed when comparing ethnic groups do not necessarily reflect genetic differences.

REFERENCES

Bouchard, T. J., & McGue, M. (1981). Familial studies of intelligence: A review. *Science, 212,* 1055–1059.

d'Ailly, H. H. (1992). Asian mathematics superiority: A search for explanations. *Educational Psychologist, 27,* 243–261.

Dossey, J. A., Mullis, I. V. S., Lindquist, M. M., & Chambers, D. L. (1988). *The mathematics report card: Are we measuring up?* (Rep. No. 17-M-01). Princeton, NJ: Educational Testing Service.

Fraser, B. J. (1982). Development of short forms of several classroom environment scales. *Journal of Educational measurement, 19,* 221–227.

Fraser, B. J. (1986). *Classroom environment.* London: Croon Helm.

Hafner, A., Ingels, S., Schneider, B., & Stevenson, D. (1990). *A profile of the American eighth grader: NELS:88 Student descriptive summary.* Washington DC: U.S. Department of Education, National Center for Educational Statistics.

Herrnstein, R. J., & Murray, C. (1994). *The bell curve.* New York: Free Press.

Huang, S. L., & Waxman, H. C. (1995). Motivation and learning-environment differences between Asian American and White middle school students in Mathematics. *Journal of Research and Development in Education, 28,* 208–219.

Jacoby, R., & Glauberman, N. (1995). *The bell curve debate.* New York: Times Books.

Kennedy, E., & Park, H. -S. (1994). Home language as a predictor of academic achievement: A comparative study of Mexican- and Asian-American youth. *Journal of Research and Development in Education, 27,* 188–194.

Knight, S. L., & Waxman, H. C. (1990). Investigating the effects of the classroom learning environment on students' motivation in social studies. *Journal of Social Studies Research, 14,* 1–12.

Moos, R. H. (1979). *Evaluating educational environments, procedures, measures, findings, and policy implications.* San Francisco; Jossey-Bass.

Oxnam, R. B. (1986, November 30). Why Asians succeed here. *New York Times Magazine* 71–74.

Scarr, S. (1981). Toward a more biological psychology. In M. S. Collins, I. W. D. Wainer, & T. A. Brenner (Eds.), *Science and the question of human equality.* Boulder, CO: Westview.

Scarr, S. (1992). Developmental theories for the 1990s: Development and individual differences. *Child Development, 63,* 1–19.

Steinberg, L., Dornbusch, S., & Brown, B. (1992). Ethnic differences in adolescent achievement: An ecological perspective. *American Psychologist, 47,* 723–729.

Stevenson, H. W., & Lee, S. -Y. (1990). Contexts of achievement: A study of American, Chinese, and Japanese children. *Monographs of the Society for Research in Child Development, 55* (1–2, Serial No. 221).

Sue, S., & Okazaki, S. (1990). Asian American educational achievements: A phenomenon in search of an explanation. *American Psychologist, 45,* 913–920.

Uguroglu, E. M., Schiller, D. P., & Walberg, H. J. (1981). A multidimensional motivational instrument. *Psychology in the Schools, 18,* 279–285.

Waxman, H. C. (1991). Investigating classroom and school learning environments: A review of recent research and developments in the field. *Journal of Classroom Interaction, 26,* 1–4.

Waxman, H. C., Huang, S. L., Knight, S. L., & Owens, E. W. (1992). Investigating the effects of the classroom learning environment on the academic achievement of at-risk students. In H. C. Waxman & C. D. Ellett (Eds.), *The study of learning environment* (Vol. 5, pp. 92–100). Houston: University of Houston.

Whang, P. A., & Hancock, G. R. (1994). Motivation and mathematics achievement: Comparisons between Asian American and non-Asian students. *Contemporary Educational Psychology, 19,* 302–322.

CHAPTER 16

WATCH YOURSELF

Because of the high frequency of attention deficit hyperactivity disorder (ADHD), you probably know, or know of, someone who has experienced it. Although our understanding of ADHD is very recent, one of its most successful treatments has roots deep into the last century. Around the turn of the twentieth century, the prevailing psychological school known as functionalism accepted both mental processes and behavior as legitimate subject matter for psychology. As noted in Chapter 2, in the 1920s a movement called behaviorism appeared within psychology and radically shifted the focus of psychology toward a science of behavior. Its founder, John B. Watson (1878–1958), took the very radical stance that behavior was almost exclusively the result of learning. Watson did not deny that some reflexes and certain species-typical behaviors, such as walking, might have a genetic foundation; however, he believed that the important differences found among individuals were the direct result of experience.

Watson and his followers wanted to discard any consideration of mental processes in the study of psychology; they believed mentalistic or cognitive concepts such as "thinking" or "willing" were nonsensical and should be rejected. These behaviorists maintained that observable behavior was controlled by observable environmental events and that mental processes were not required for an understanding of behavior. This paradigm shift in psychology attracted many adherents, probably the best known of whom was B. F. Skinner (1904–1990). Skinner rode the tidal wave formed by these early behaviorists. Although the strident tone of behaviorism (Skinner, 1953) has been softened by new research, particularly in the cognitive domain, it has left a permanent legacy in the form of a powerful behavior technology.

Behavior modification is the name given to attempts to change behavior using principles of learning. This term is used to describe learning-based treatment programs designed to eliminate problem behaviors that occur in real-world settings. Behavior modification is most likely to depend on operant conditioning, in which the frequency of behavior is affected by the consequences of behavior. Chapter 9 described two kinds of consequences that decrease the frequency of behavior: positive and negative punishment. Operant conditioning also employs two types of consequences that can increase the frequency of behavior: positive and negative reinforcement. By definition, a *reinforcement* is a consequence

Incorporating the research of K. E. Hoff & G. J. DuPaul, "Reducing Disruptive Behavior in General Education Classrooms: The Use of Self-Management Strategies," 1998, *School Psychology Review, 27,* pp. 290–303.

that increases behavior frequency. Positive and negative are used in the same way they were used in our earlier descriptions of punishment. Positive means a stimulus has been added, negative means a stimulus has been removed. Positive reinforcement is usually a reward of some sort. In negative reinforcement, usually some aversive stimulus is removed. If your alarm clock makes an annoying noise, you have probably been conditioned to turn it off quickly. The removal of the irritating noise reinforces and maintains the rapid-alarm-shut-off behavior at a high frequency. Those who are less savvy about psychology may use the term *negative reinforcement* when they are, in fact, talking about decreasing the frequency of behavior with some kind of punishment.

Unlike the radical behaviorists, most psychologists today are likely to give some consideration to cognitive factors, even in programs aimed at behavior change. Nevertheless, the main power of behavior modification is that it does not depend on an in-depth understanding of the mind. In behavior modification, environmental consequences are carefully manipulated and behavior frequencies change. Skinner (1956) noted that large groups of animals were not required to demonstrate the effects of operant conditioning. Even the species of organism did not always make a difference. He presented learning curve data generated by three different species of animals, a pigeon, a rat, and a monkey, who received the same schedule of reinforcements for a simple key-pressing behavior. The graphs of response frequencies were virtually identical.

Behavior modification has been used to address a wide variety of behavior problems. Recently, it has been an approach of choice for small children and people with serious intellectual or communication deficits because it does not depend greatly upon the participant's understanding of detailed instructions or other cognitive skills. Pelham, Wheeler, and Chronis (1998) reviewed about 50 different studies from the treatment literature on attention deficit hyperactivity disorder (ADHD) and concluded that behavioral treatments are common and have often been shown to be efficacious. DuPaul, Eckert, and McGoey (1997) urged caution in thinking that all children with ADHD should receive the same treatment regime. While this chapter will deal with a behavioral approach to treatment, you are probably aware that stimulant medication is another very common method for addressing this disorder.

The *Diagnostic and Statistical Manual 4th Edition* (*DSM-IV*; American Psychiatric Association, 1994) defines the different types of ADHD. It is a disturbance of at least 6 months duration during which specific symptoms are present. *DSM-IV* recognizes two distinct subtypes of ADHD: the hyperactive-impulsive type and the inattentive type. In addition, some people have a combination of the two types.

In the hyperactive-impulsive type the following kinds of behaviors are exhibited:

- fidgets or squirms in seat
- has difficulty remaining seated
- is easily distracted
- has difficulty in awaiting turn in group situations
- blurts out answers to unfinished questions
- has difficulty playing quietly, talks excessively
- interrupts others, does not listen to others

For comparison, the following are examples of behavior from the inattentive type of ADHD:

- has difficulty following instructions
- has difficulty sustaining attention
- shifts from one uncompleted activity to another
- loses things necessary for task performance

These behaviors listed above are called *externalizing behaviors,* meaning that they are behaviors that impinge on other people and contexts external to the individual. These can be contrasted to *internalizing behaviors* such as depression. You will remember that there was an earlier discussion of internalizing and externalizing behaviors in the chapter *Some Restrictions May Apply,* where the participants were children who had been maltreated.

According to *DSM-IV*, onset of ADHD occurs before age 7. ADHD is common and occurs in about 3 percent of children. It is six to nine times more common in boys than in girls. Other literature gives prevalence figures as high as 5 percent (Pelham et al., 1998). School failure is one of the most common accompaniments of the disorder. It is often associated with another problem, oppositional defiant disorder (ODD) which is characterized by being angry, argumentative, defiant, and vindictive. About one third of the children with ADHD show some evidence of problems with the disorder later in life, even in adulthood. No single cause for ADHD has been found but *DSM-IV* lists neurological factors as well as disorganized or abusive/neglectful environments.

Hoff and DuPaul (1998) conducted a study of the use of self-management techniques to deal with behavior associated with ADHD in classroom settings. This was a field study conducted in several real life settings within the participants' school. The basic idea was to use the reward tactics of behaviorism to train the children to pay attention to their own behavior. They were also trained to increase the frequency of behaviors that were consistent with academic performance while decreasing behavior that interfered with education. In a busy school setting it is impractical to expect a teacher to be able to pay continuous careful attention to one or a few problem children in order to manipulate their behavior with rewards. The self-management component of this study meant that although more intensive teacher attention was required at first, eventually the child would be able to monitor his or her own behavior. As the child gradually took responsibility for this, the teacher was able to concentrate on other classroom issues.

PARTICIPANTS

The participants were three children, each 9 years of age. It is quite usual that behavior modification studies have few participants. Sometimes these are referred to as *single subject designs* because among a few participants, each one is compared to himself or herself. Following the precepts of B. F. Skinner, if the outcomes of the modification are similar for a few participants, they are thought to be likely to be applicable to other individuals who are sufficiently similar to the study sample. Usually a single subject design is a treatment as well as a research project and this is another reason why it may be reasonable to relax the usual strictures about sample size. The three participants were selected from a total of nine children who had been identified as disruptive and aggressive in classroom situations. The original nine children were tested with the Systematic Screening for Behavior Disorders (SSBD; Walker & Severson, 1990), a psychological instrument used to identify students who have externalizing behavior problems. This instrument included teacher ratings as well as direct observations of the child.

Students identified as externalizing were then rated by teachers using the Child Behavior Checklist-Teacher Form (TRF; Achenbach, 1991), which identified the clinical significance of the externalizing behavior for each child. Because a goal of the study was to treat aggression as well as other aspects of ADHD, children were chosen who scored above the 93rd percentile for aggression on the TRF.

The last component of the participation selection procedure involved an interview with parents about the extent to which the behavior of the child was similar to the *DSM-IV* descriptions of ADHD and ODD. Based on the account of the parents, only children who conformed to the *DSM-IV* descriptions were included in the final group of three participants. No distinction was made between subtypes of ADHD in this study.

PROCEDURE

The general procedure in this study consisted of elements that are common in behavior modification studies. First, baseline observations were made to determine the frequencies of the behaviors that were targeted for change. Once the target behavior frequency was known, some interventions were undertaken that attempted to change the behavior frequencies. When possible in this type of study, a period of observations with no intervention typically follows to determine if changes have been maintained.

The purpose of the study by Hoff and DuPaul (1998) was to demonstrate the efficacy of a behavior modification strategy called *self-management* or *self-evaluation*. These terms refer to a situation in which the children learn to pay attention to their own behavior and to self-record frequencies of disruptive behavior. The goal was to train the children to make accurate self-recordings. These recordings became the basis for positive reinforcement when they indicated that behavior had not been disruptive.

TRAINING

There were three major phases in this study:

1. *Baseline Phase:* when no changes were made
2. *Intervention Phase:* when the children were trained in self-evaluation
3. *Self-Management Phase:* when the children were on their own

In the baseline phase of the study, teachers were told to operate as usual in the conduct of classroom lectures and playground sessions, using their regular verbal comments in response to inappropriate behavior.

The intervention phase of the study was designed to train the children to evaluate their own behavior. It had two components. The first part was the introduction of a *token economy,* a term meaning that behavior was shaped with some kind of reward, or token. The token economy in this study consisted of a reward system designed to shape the behavior of the student, but also to make the student familiar with the rating system that would later be used in self-evaluation. The rules, the nature of the desired behavior, and the rewards were described to both the teachers and the students.

During the token phase the teacher would indicate the beginning of a 5-minute observation period to the student. During the subsequent 5 minutes, the teacher would rate the students' behavior from 0 to 5 using the following scale:

5 = Excellent, all student behavior is appropriate

4 = Very good, only minor rule infraction such as "talk out" or "off task"

3 = Average, followed rules 80 percent of the time, no major infractions

2 = Below average, some rule following but other behavior not acceptable

1 = Most of the interval spent in inappropriate behavior

0 = Entire 5-minute interval spent in inappropriate behavior

At the end of the 5-minute rating period, the teacher showed the student his or her rating. The procedure was repeated for two more consecutive 5-minute periods. At the end of the total 15 minutes of rating, the teacher gave overall feedback and an explanation so that the child could understand the ratings. The children understood that the ratings could be converted to points or tokens earning them rewards. In this way, good behavior earned attractive outcomes. These positive reinforcers were things such as extra computer time, a "free homework pass," and pencils.

This token economy was the first part of the intervention phase. The second part was *teacher matching*. This phase consisted of the students using the scale to self-rate their behavior at the same time the teacher was rating it. The goal for the students was to have their rating match the rating of the teacher as closely as possible. Teacher and student ratings were compared at the end of the 15-minute observation interval. The students got a bonus point added to points earned for appropriate behavior if their rating matched the teacher's rating. If the child was within 1 point of the teacher's ratings no points were gained or lost. If there was a 2-point difference or more in the ratings, children lost any points they might have earned through good behavior during the interval. The ratings were always compared but there was only discussion if there was a mismatch of more than 1 point.

A goal was to get the students to rate themselves without having a parallel rating from the teacher. In order to accomplish this, the frequency of observation periods during which the teacher rating actually counted for awarding points was faded from 100 percent to 0 percent in 25-percent increments. In the first fade to 75 percent, the teacher would approach the student following the 15-minute observation interval and ask the students to blindly select one of four squares of paper from a container. Three of the paper squares were red and one was black. If the black square was the one selected, then the students would get the points they had assigned themselves and no matching of teacher ratings was required. However, if they selected a red square, they would have to actually match their ratings with those of the teacher.

As you can see, this technique would have the effect of keeping the students honest in trying to rate their behavior. They never knew if the teacher ratings would be used until the 15 minutes were up and the paper was selected. If they had been very dishonest and wildly exaggerated the points they gave themselves, there was a 75 percent chance that the teacher ratings would be matched to theirs and they would be caught in the lie. While all this seems procedurally complex, it is conceptually quite simple. Over the course of the fading out of teacher matching, the children engaged more frequently in the process of evaluating themselves. Fading continued to 50 percent and 25 percent by changing the proportion of red and black squares in the drawing.

When matching reached 0 percent, the students had entered the third phase of the study, *self-evaluation.* They continued to observe their own behavior and kept the points they awarded themselves to exchange for rewards. Over time, some of the students occasionally awarded higher points than they should have given themselves. To deal with this false appraisal, a "surprise match" with the teacher's rating was introduced, on the average, once every 6 days. Points were lost or gained during surprise matches as previously established in the original rules for teacher matching.

OUTCOME MEASURES

Though we have spent considerable time discussing the teacher and student ratings of behavior, it is important to understand that the results of the study are not a quantification of those ratings. The hypothesis of this study was that the process of self-evaluation would lower levels of disruptive behavior. The measure of disruptive behavior came from observations made by trained observers other than the teachers.

Throughout the three phases of the study, the behavior of the children was observed and recorded on the playground and in the classroom. These observations were made by graduate student researchers who were unaware of the purpose of the study. The observers were given about 12 hours of training using videotapes of behavior. Before they were permitted to do any actual data collection, they had to achieve an interrater reliability of at least 85 percent. Once this criterion was reached, the raters made two observations with the primary investigator to check reliability in the real situation and to help the observer adjust to actual observation conditions before the real data collections started.

The observers used a partial interval recording system for collecting the data. The observation periods were divided into 15-second intervals. The observer listened to a prerecorded audiotape through headphones. The tape announced the beginning and end of a 15-second interval. This was followed by a short period for data recording, then another 15-second observation interval would be announced, and so on. This was a partial interval system because if a specific behavior occurred at any point during the interval, it was recorded as having taken place. This is in contrast to a whole interval recording system in which the behavior would have to occur across the whole 15-second interval in order to be counted. Partial interval systems are good for detecting short bursts of behavior that might be missed by a whole-interval system (G. DuPaul, personal communication, October 3, 2000).

The observers recorded six categories of behavior using the partial interval recording system:

1. Positive interactions (e.g., sharing, friendly, compliant)
2. Negative non-aggressive interactions (e.g., noncompliance with requests)
3. Verbal aggression (e.g., name calling)
4. Physical aggression (e.g., hitting, kicking)
5. Noninteractive behavior (e.g., not participating in a group activity)
6. On- and off-task behavior (e.g., doing or not doing what is supposed to be done)

In addition to the trained raters' observations of these behaviors teachers also rated the behavior of the children about twice during each phase of the study using the aggression subscale of the Iowa Conners Teacher Rating Scale (Loney & Milich, 1982). This subscale has five items measuring the traits: quarrelsome, acts "smart," temper outbursts, defiant, and uncooperative. The complete IOWA scale has a high test-retest reliability.

Consistent with the ideas of Freud, some contemporary theorists who call themselves *psychodynamic* theorists believe that psychological disorders have deep unconscious roots. Freud believed that these roots revolved around underlying sexual tension. The corollary of this belief is that behavior is only a symptom of the "real" problem. Psychodynamic theorists believe that eliminating behavior only treats symptoms, but leaves the real disorder unchanged. In contrast, behavioral theorists feel that the behavior is the disorder: Eliminate the problem behavior and the disorder is eliminated. A Freudian or psychodynamic theorist would predict that if one symptom is eliminated, another will take its place because the repressed "psychic energy" or libido is still present and will express itself in some other way. This is called *symptom substitution.* In order to detect symptom substitution the investigators also created a scale to measure side effects. This was a Likert scale running from 0 (absent) to 9 (serious) that recorded the presence of 11 disruptive behaviors such as arguing, temper outbursts, fighting, and noncompliance with assigned work. Ratings using this scale were taken an average of two times in each phase of the study. Outcomes from this scale could be considered a test, albeit not a very direct one, of psychodynamic notions.

At the conclusion of the study, both teachers and student participants completed either the adult or the children's version of an intervention rating profile that rated the acceptability of the behavior modification intervention (Witt & Martens, 1983; Witt & Elliot, 1985). The adult version had 20 items and the child version had 7 items.

RESULTS AND DISCUSSION

Treatment integrity is the name given to the extent to which the teachers actually adhered to the procedures and rules of the intervention. The primary investigator, Hoff, observed the teacher's management of the study protocols during 20 percent of the intervention sessions. She worked with an 11-item list of steps that were supposed to be part of the intervention. The outcome was that mean treatment integrity was observed to be 98.2 percent. Any time it became apparent that actual procedures were deviating from the rules, a meeting was arranged so that researchers could review the protocols for the teachers.

The percentages of disruptive behavior decreased dramatically as a result of intervention, as can be seen from Figure 16.1. In each case, baseline levels are about three times as high as those seen during the intervention phases. The intervention phases themselves— token, matching, and self-evaluation—do not appear to be very different from one another in terms of their effects on disruptive behavior. The apparent lack of differences among the intervention phases is one of the cases in psychology where finding no difference is, nevertheless, a very important outcome. Another was discussed in Chapter 6. The token and matching phases of the study are both labor-intensive for a busy teacher. Indeed, it was during a matching phase that the lowest level of treatment integrity was observed: 81.8 percent. The power of the self-evaluation strategy is that diminutions in disruptive behavior were maintained. During self-evaluation, the only role of the teacher was to signal the start of the 15-minute

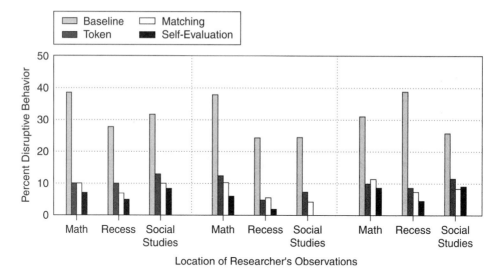

FIGURE 16.1   Percent Disruptive Behavior for Joey, Brandon, and Megan. Percentage of disruptive behavior observed by the researchers using the partial interval recording system to collect data from Joey (left), Brandon (center), and Megan (right) in two classes and during recess for each phase of the study.

Note: Owing to time constraints, Brandon only entered self-evaluation in two of the settings: math and recess. In addition, Brandon's data for *recess* reflects a single observation session.

Source: From Hoff, K. E., & DuPaul, G. J. (1998). Reducing disruptive behavior in general education classrooms: The use of self-management strategies. *School Psychology Review, 27,* 290–303.

self-evaluation period, issue rewards based on self-evaluated behavior, and initiate the surprise match about once every 6 days. Once the children completed the token and matching phases, they maintained appropriate behavior with very little attention from the teacher.

In order to appreciate fully the spectacular changes that resulted, you should also remember that the behavior outcomes for the children shown in Figure 16.1 were measured by graduate student observers outside of the 15-minute self-evaluation periods and in different school settings. It would seem that learning to pay attention to disruptive behavior during 15-minute self-evaluation periods generalized widely to the child's overall behavior in school.

Figure 16.2, taken from the original study by Hoff and DuPaul (1998) shows the data, over observation sessions, for one of the children, the boy called Joey. This type of data display is typical of studies that use behavior modification. In spite of the saw-toothed appearance, one can see from the dotted summary lines that the intervention made a striking difference and that gains in controlling disruptive behavior were maintained under self-evaluation. Although we have not presented them, the parallel data sets for the other two children were quite similar to Joey's. Figure 16.2 also shows the data for a control peer child who, as far as is known, did not have any kind of behavior disorder. In the baseline condition, there were no overlapping points: Joey's level of disruptive behavior was always higher than the level for the peer. Once intervention commenced, the disruptive behaviors of the two children appear to be at similar levels.

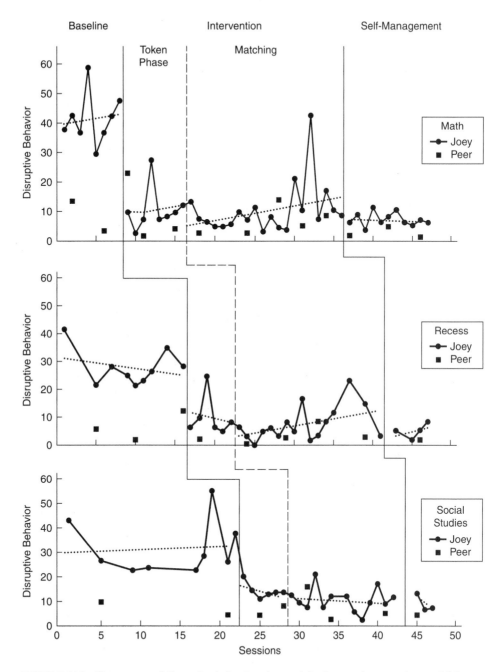

FIGURE 16.2   Percentage of disruptive behavior observed for Joey and a control peer child across all three settings and all phases of the study. Dotted lines show average trends. Note that peer data are shown as unconnected square dots.

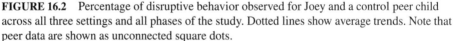

Source: From "Reducing Disruptive Behavior in General Education Classrooms: The Use of Self-Management Strategies," by K. E. Hoff and G. J. DuPaul, 1998, *School Psychology Review, 27,* pp. 299, 290–303. Copyright © 1998 by the National Association of School Psychologists. Reprinted by permission of the publisher.

Figure 16.3 shows the teacher's total side effects ratings for each child in each phase of the study. This scale consisted of 11 items that could be scored from 0 to 9, so the highest possible total score would be 99. An examination of these data gives no indication that the intervention produced increased side effects of undesirable behavior. If anything, the intervention phases are associated with lower levels of these behaviors.

Figure 16.4 shows the outcome of the aggression index from the Iowa Conners Rating Scale. The same process can be used to interpret these data as was used for the side effects outcomes in Figure 16.3. Figure 16.4 presents no evidence that the intervention was associated with increased levels of aggression when comparisons are made with baseline data. As noted above, the absence of side effects can be considered a negation of psychodynamic notions of symptom substitution. The possible range of outcomes is from 0 to 15 on this instrument. To help you to evaluate Figure 16.4, you should know that a clinic sample of hyperactive boys had a mean of 6.18 on this scale ($SD = 4.6$) while unselected ordinary elementary school boys had a mean of 2.29 ($SD = 2.89$) (Loney & Milich, 1982). Because of our own bias, it is possible that we are being unfair to psychodynamic notions. It seems to us that they are rarely tested because they are so difficult to operationally define. In our view, operationally defining Freudian concepts presents the same challenge as trying to nail a piece of Jell-O to the wall.

According to the ratings on the Intervention Rating Profile (IRP-20), the teachers' opinions of treatment acceptability were very favorable. Both teachers strongly agreed that the treatment was beneficial to the children. The children's IRP showed that they also approved of the intervention. All three children strongly agreed that they "liked the intervention, thought it would help them do better in school, and did not think there were better ways to help their behavior" (Hoff & DuPaul, 1998, p. 300). A problem noted by child participant Megan was that she felt the intervention might interfere with peer friendships because the other students could see the teacher repeatedly coming to her desk during the intervention.

In summary, this approach seems to have been effective. It supports the findings of other studies in which self-management was shown to be an efficacious treatment for disruptive behavior (Rhode, Morgan, & Young, 1983; Smith, Young, Nelson, & West, 1992; Smith, Young, West, Morgan, & Rhode, 1988). This study extended past findings because it

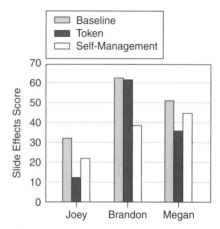

FIGURE 16.3   Total Side Effects Behavior Score. Total score for side effects measured with a scale developed by the investigators. Data are shown for each child in each phase of the study.

Source: From Hoff, K. E., & DuPaul, G. J. (1998). Reducing disruptive behavior in general education classrooms: The use of self-management strategies. *School Psychology Review, 27,* 300.

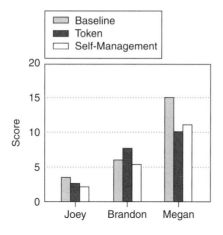

FIGURE 16.4   Iowa Conners Rating Scale Scores. Scores for the aggression subscale of the Iowa Conners Teacher Rating Scale. Data are shown for each child in each phase of the study.

Source: From Hoff, K. E., & DuPaul, G. J. (1998). Reducing disruptive behavior in general education classrooms: The use of self-management strategies. *School Psychology Review, 27,* 300.

examined young children in ordinary classroom and playground settings. The program did not introduce side effects and it was found to be acceptable to both teachers and students.

Hoff and DuPaul (1998) provided a very thoughtful section at the end of their report describing the limitations of the study. Because the authors know their study better than anyone else, it is very helpful to those trying to evaluate the study when limitations are openly discussed. Hoff and DePaul note that the treatment integrity measure may not have been accurate because it could only be assessed when the teachers knew they were being observed. One of the teachers reported that, occasionally, she did not have time to conduct the protocols of the study. Overall, time limitations always exist and, in this case, the researchers had insufficient time to fully implement the self-management phase with the child called Brandon. Beyond this, it would have been interesting to have some long-term follow-up data about the persistence of behavior change.

Another limitation of this study is important to understand for your critical thinking about many different studies. The phases of this intervention occurred in a specific order: baseline, token, matching, and self-evaluation. Because of this, it is not possible to say that the final low levels of disruptive behavior were a result of the self-management procedure. Using the terms we have used before, this study was not an experiment and self-management was not an independent variable. Although the focus of this study was the self-management intervention, Hoff & DuPaul (1998) pointed out that "the statement cannot be made that self-management in isolation was responsible for students' low levels of disruption." In our view, this does not detract from the study, but we want you to understand that the evidence here supports the value of the entire intervention procedure, not specific parts of it.

CRITICAL THINKING TOOLKIT ITEMS

In intervention programs when a number of steps are presented in the same order for all participants, it is not possible to attribute behavior change to the last step in the program. In order to do this it would be necessary to manipulate the last step independently of the other steps.

REFERENCES

Achenbach, T. M. (1991). *Manual for the Teacher's Report Form and 1991 Profile.* Burlington: University of Vermont, Department of Psychiatry.

American Psychiatric Association. (1994). *Diagnostic and statistical manual of mental disorders* (4th ed.). Washington DC: Author.

DuPaul, G. J., Eckert, T. L., & McGoey, K. E. (1997). Interventions for students with attention-deficit/hyperactivity disorder: One size does not fit all. *School Psychology Review,* 26, 369–381.

Hoff, K. E., & DuPaul, G. J. (1998). Reducing disruptive behavior in general education classrooms: The use of self-management strategies. *School Psychology Review,* 27, 290–303.

Loney, J., & Milich, R., (1982). Hyperactivity, inattention, and aggression in clinical practice. In D. Routh & M. Eolraich (Eds.), *Advances in developmental and behavioral pediatrics* (Vol. 3, pp. 113–147). Greenwich, CT: JAI.

Pelham, W. E., Wheeler, T., & Chronis, A. (1998). Empirically supported psychosocial treatments for attention deficit hyperactivity disorder. *Journal of Clinical Child Psychology,* 27, 190–205.

Rhode, G., Morgan, D. P., & Young, K. R. (1983). Generalization and maintenance of treatment gains of behaviorally handicapped students from resource rooms to regular classrooms using self-evaluation procedures. *Journal of Applied Behavior Analysis,* 16, 171–188.

Skinner, B. F. (1953). *Science and human behavior.* New York: Macmillan.

Skinner, B. F. (1956). A case history in scientific method. *American Psychologist, 11,* 221–233.

Smith, D. J., Young, K. R., Nelson, J. R., & West, R. P. (1992). The effect of a self-management procedure on the classroom academic behavior of students with mild handicaps. *School Psychology Review, 21,* 59–72.

Smith, D. J., Young, K. R., West, R. P., Morgan, D. P., & Rhode, G. (1988). Reducing the disruptive behavior of junior high school students: A classroom self-management procedure. *Behavioral Disorders, 13,* 231–239.

Walker, H. M., & Severson, H. (1990). *Systematic screening for behavior disorders.* Longmont, CO: Sopris West.

Watson, J. B. (1930). *Behaviorism.* (Rev. ed.). Chicago: University of Chicago Press.

Witt, J. C., & Elliot, S. N. (1985). Acceptability of classroom management strategies. In T. R. Kratochwill (Ed.), *Advances in school psychology* (Vol. 4, pp. 251–288). Hillsdale, NJ: Erlbaum.

Witt, J. C., & Martens, B. K. (1983). Assessing the acceptability of behavioral interventions used in classrooms. *Psychology in the Schools, 20,* 510–517.

CHAPTER 17

AT A LOSS FOR WORDS

If a person grows up without being exposed to language, will he or she ever be able to acquire ordinary language skills? In this chapter we discuss the research method called the *case study,* which provides insight into this question. In developmental psychology, a case study is usually a narrative description of the changes in one or a few individuals over some period of the life span. In addition to narrative, there may be quantitative measures of behavior, such as test scores, that help to illustrate development. Case studies usually follow individuals in their normal working or living situations. The confidence that should be placed in case study data will vary depending on the quality of the observations and data collection, often more so than other research methods. Accordingly, one should carefully evaluate case studies with regard to these criteria. The validity of case studies can be challenged if they depend primarily on an individual's memories of events that are long past. The generalizability of case studies may be challenged if they are set in unique contexts.

The difference between a narrative case study as a scientific method and a literary biographical sketch is that the case study is a test of a hypothesis, even if it is not a very rigorous test. A case study has little power to exclude rival hypotheses. Case studies are best used to investigate situations that cannot be addressed by other research methods. In developmental psychology, this usually means that the participants face some highly unusual situation or rare circumstances affecting their development.

With more standard developmental topics, larger numbers of participants can be found, which permits correlational tactics or other research methods to be used. We believe that case studies are usually inappropriate when the behavior under study is commonplace. For example, when we searched bookshelves for topics addressed by what might be considered case studies, we found a book that described an ordinary child having a bad day. We do not want to seem cold and unfeeling, but from the standpoint of scientific psychology this information is trivial.

LANGUAGE DEVELOPMENT

Language is essential for much of our daily functioning, so it should not be a surprise that the development of language has long been an important research topic within

Incorporating the research of G. M. Grimshaw, A. Adelstein, M. P. Bryden, and G. E. MacKinnon, "First Language Aquisition in Adolescence: Evidence for a Critical Period for Verbal Language Development," 1998, *Brain and Language, 63,* pp. 237–255.

developmental psychology. Research has suggested that there are some intriguing sensitive periods in language development. Chapter 3 described a *critical* or *sensitive period* as a short period of time during which some experience occurs that results in irreversible developmental differences.

Werker (1989) demonstrated that early experience with the sounds of a particular language can have long-lasting effects. She and her colleagues studied the ability to recognize speech sounds that occur in the Hindi language but do not occur in English. Typically, native speakers of English cannot tell the difference between a few particular Hindi speech sounds that are superficially similar, while a native speaker of Hindi would have little difficulty making this discrimination. Werker tested a group of English-speaking adults who had been exposed to Hindi in the first years of life, but who had little subsequent experience of that language and could not speak it. Compared to English speakers with no early experience of Hindi, they were much better at making discriminations among Hindi speech sounds; in fact, they were almost as good as native speakers of Hindi.

Johnson and Newport (1989) studied Korean and Chinese immigrants who learned English as a second language, some of whom began learning English when they were 3 years old and others who began at age 17 or older. Interestingly, the researchers found that the amount of formal instruction in English did not account for English proficiency. The length of experience living in an English-speaking environment also had no impact. Age of first learning was the most important factor. Those who were older when they started learning did more poorly. A recent study found that people who acquired English after age 4 showed different brain wave patterns when listening to English compared to people who had learned English before age 4 (Weber-Fox and Neville, 1996). These findings point to a sensitive period for language development that results in permanent neurological changes.

THE WILD BOY OF AVEYRON

While research with bilingual individuals has pointed the way to an understanding of the role of early experience in language, researchers have long been interested in what happens when an individual is not exposed to any language in the early years of life. One of the earliest detailed accounts of such an event was Jean Itard's description, published in 1801, of the individual called the "wild boy of Aveyron." This boy, about 12 years old, had been sighted running naked around the outskirts of a small village in France. He was eventually captured, and observations showed him to have no ability to understand or produce language. Although nothing was known about his past, the remarkably unlikely presumption was made that he had been raised by wolves or, at least, that he had experienced no significant human contact. He ate in the style normally associated with monkeys and, at first, he refused to wear clothes. Itard, a talented teacher of the deaf, worked patiently with this boy, whom he named Victor. Despite Itard's concentrated efforts, Victor developed hardly any language. Victor died when he was thought to be in his early 40s (Lane, 1976).

GENIE

A more recent case is that of the individual called Genie (Curtiss, 1977). A great deal has been written about this woman who was horribly deprived of stimulation in childhood.

Locked in a small room, she was restrained in a harness-like device for most of her early life by her father. She had almost no exposure to language and was beaten when she made noises. When she was discovered at age 13, her language was very primitive. Even after years of training starting in adolescence, her language only resembled that of a 4-year-old (Rymer, 1993).

TWINS STUDIED BY KOLUCHOVÁ

Koluchová (1972) described a similar case involving twin boys, whose mother died not long after they were born. Shortly after birth, they were placed in a children's home where they spent much of their first year. During that time, they were judged to be developing normally. Their father brought them home when they were 18 months old. His new wife hated the twins and deprived them of almost all stimulation, including exposure to language. When they were examined by a pediatrician at age 7, their physical development was so far behind that the doctor thought they were poorly developed 3-year-olds. Their motor skills were seriously deficient and their language ability was almost nonexistent. They were placed in a children's home and subsequently adopted into a loving home. By age 11, they had caught up to their peers in most aspects of development, including language development.

This is an interesting case because evidence provided when the twins were 18 months old, while they were in the first children's home, indicated that they were developing normally. They showed no language deficits after recovery from deprivation, but they had been exposed to normal language during their first stay in a children's home. This exposure occurred during the first year of life, which research has suggested is a sensitive period for language development.

THE CASE OF E. M.

Grimshaw, Adelstein, Bryden, and MacKinnon (1998) presented an interesting case study of a 19-year-old male called E. M., who had been diagnosed with Waardenburg syndrome. This disorder results from the inheritance of a single dominant gene and is characterized by skin pigmentation abnormalities and, occasionally, deafness. E. M.'s aunt and his sister were also deaf, perhaps from the same disorder. Although his family reported that he had been deaf from birth, the first formal record of this condition was made as part of a medical examination when he was 3 years old.

E. M.'s hearing was tested again at ages 6, 8, 16, and 18. The findings of those evaluations consistently showed that he had hearing loss for sounds below about 90 dB to 100 dB. The maximum level of sound for normal conversation is about 60 dB. Perceived loudness approximately doubles for every measured increase of 10 dB (Stevens, 1955). This means that E. M.'s hearing loss was so profound that he would not have been able to hear speech, though he could hear sounds as loud as a subway train roaring through a station. E. M. was fitted for hearing aids in childhood, but this intervention was unsuccessful and he did not continue to wear the aids.

E. M. grew up in rural Mexico. He had very little formal education. He spent a year in school at age 9 when "an attempt was made to teach him to read" (Grimshaw et al., 1998, p. 242). When he was 12 years old he spent some months in a day school for the deaf where learning focused on oral training, but he did not seem to benefit much from this experience.

HOMESIGN

In the absence of any significant formal education, E. M.'s need to communicate was met with what is called a *homesign.* Unlike some of the standard sign languages that E. M. might have been taught, this was a personal communication system that evolved to fulfill his needs in his restricted environment. A disadvantage of homesign was that because it was not standardized, it was not fully understood by people other than those in the immediate home environment. Nevertheless, it is not unusual for deaf children to develop a homesign that is understood by family members and others in the rearing context (Golden-Meadow, Butcher, Mylander, & Dodge, 1994). In homesign, objects may be identified by pointing to them or by making hand movements that physically resemble the objects themselves. For example, if E. M. wanted to refer to a dog, he would hold up his hand with four fingers pointed downward, in imitation of the legs of a dog.

E. M.'s homesign was somewhat more elaborate than homesigns usually associated with younger children, which tend to have one sign for one object or action (Golden-Meadow and Mylander, 1990). E. M.'s signs included some *classifiers,* that is, single signs that denote large classes of objects. For example, his sign for any flat object was his left hand held out flat with the palm down. If he wanted to sign that the dog had jumped over the bed, he would hold out his left hand in the flat-object gesture and move his right hand, fingers down, over it to show the iconic dog jumping over the bed. Presumably, the flat-object classifier would have to be used in a context where it was obvious that the intended flat object was a bed. While this homesign may have allowed E. M. to communicate with those around him, it had much less flexibility than other language systems, including standardized systems of signing, such as American Sign Language (ASL). The homesign could not, for example, combine its signs to create new words nor did it include noniconic symbols.

When E. M. was almost 16 years old, he traveled to Canada to spend time with relatives. There, he was examined and given hearing aids for both ears that permitted him to hear sounds at volumes as low as 35 dB, well within the range of all but the most softly spoken normal conversation. When Grimshaw et al. (1998) reported their findings, E. M. was 19 years old and had not yet attended school or undertaken any formal language training. Nevertheless, from age 15 onward, E. M. was first exposed to ordinary spoken language, much in the same way a prelinguistic child might be exposed. This late exposure to conventional language was one of the characteristics of E. M.'s situation that made for such an intriguing and important case study.

Another characteristic that made his case extraordinarily important was that E. M. had been tested for cognitive ability at ages 8, 10, and 16, and found to be only slightly below average intelligence. His IQ test results at ages 8 and 10 were 82 and 92 respectively. At age 16, the Nonverbal Test of Intelligence (TONI-II) measured his IQ at 83, while he scored 88 on the performance scale of the Wechsler Intelligence Scale for Children-Revised (WISC-R). This performance scale is supposed to measure nonverbal intelligence. At age 19, his performance IQ was retested with the Wechsler Adult Intelligence Scale (WAIS), producing a score of 85. Grimshaw et al. (1998) suggested that these estimates might have been low because E. M. could not receive verbal instructions for the test. Further, not having been in school, he was unused to standardized testing procedures and this may have had an adverse effect on his scores.

The cognitive testing in this case study was crucial to the hypothesis that a lack of early language experience during a sensitive period leads to irreversible language deficits. If it were found that the individual also had a lack of cognitive ability, the study would have a major confound: It would not be possible to know if poor language performance was the result of a lack of early exposure, a lack of cognitive ability, some of each, or some other factor. This problem is instantiated by the case of the wild boy of Aveyron. Although the findings for the wild boy might seem to support the existence of a sensitive period in language development, we know nothing about Victor's cognitive abilities. His lack of progress in other domains, such as learning to eat with utensils, suggests that he might have been well below normal intelligence. The same situation exists for the case of Genie; there is no evidence about her cognitive functioning before deprivation. The twins studied by Koluchová seemed to be normal before deprivation and recovered from language deficits, but the extent of their isolation was different. They were with each other and they were exposed to language early in life.

RESULTS OF LANGUAGE PRODUCTION ASSESSMENT

It is fortunate that E. M. was willing to undergo repeated testing. Without his cooperation and the hard work of the investigators, the details of this important case might have been lost. Three tests of E. M.'s language production were reported by Grimshaw et al. (1998). Sixteen months after the restoration of hearing, he was given the Verbs of Motion Morphology Production subtest of the Test Battery for American Sign Language Morphology and Syntax (Supalla et al., in press). This test consists of 40 video segments, each 3 seconds long, depicting the movement of an object, sometimes compared to another object. The test was originally designed to examine the adequacy of an individual's sign language to describe the object(s) and action in each video clip. With E. M. the test was used to elicit and examine his sign language as well as his spoken language.

When first tested, E. M. produced signs for all the events. The gestures were consistent with his homesign, usually involving movement of one of his classifier hand positions. For a video clip showing a boy jumping into a circle he used the *person* sign—two fingers walking—and had the two fingers jump into a circle made by touching the ends of the thumb and index finger on the other hand.

At 34 months following hearing restoration, E. M. was asked to describe a Tweety and Sylvester cartoon. At this period in his life, his speech production was extremely under-developed and he rarely produced utterances without prompting. In response to the cartoon, he was only able to speak one word, *gato* (cat). In order to ensure that his difficulties with the articulation of spoken language were not masking better language skills, he was given an opportunity to watch the cartoon with a remote control and a pad of paper, so that he could stop the tape and write a description. He wrote the words for *cat, coins, monkey,* and *telephone* in Spanish. These words described things that appeared in the story, but E. M. made no attempt to tell a story with them. Grimshaw et al. (1998) believed that E. M.

understood the task and he understood the story of the cartoon. He was able to convey the narrative of the story in sign, but not verbally.

At 48 months, E. M. was again tested with the video clips from the Test Battery for American Sign Language Morphology and Syntax. He still depended heavily on gestures and used signs as part of his description for each video. However, in contrast to the 16-month test result, at 48 months he used a combination of speech and sign for 18 of the video segments. For 16 of these, the speech component consisted of a verbal label for the subject of the action. For example, boy jumping into a circle was signed in the same way as earlier, but now E. M. also produced the word *niño* (boy) in order to be more specific about the signed classifier *person*. This was the way the single words were typically used: to modify homesign classifiers, adding clarification.

In a few cases, the spoken word seemed to have resulted in modification to the homesign. In the original homesign, *airplane* was signed by holding up a hand, sticking out the thumb and the little finger. With spoken language, this changed to a more generalized sign, an open hand, coupled with the word *airplane* at 48 months. E. M. also produced the phrase *airplane stop* which was the only recorded instance in which E. M. used more than one word at a time. (For comparison purposes E. M. was 19 years old at this achievement and two word phrases usually appear at about 20 months of age.)

RESULTS OF LANGUAGE COMPREHENSION ASSESSMENT

E. M. was examined for language comprehension at 8, 12, 16, 20, 24, and 34 months after restoration of hearing. In case he had not heard the spoken instructions, at 34 months he was tested twice, once with oral instructions and once with written instructions. A number of comprehension tasks were used as tests. These had originally been developed for working with Genie (Curtiss, 1977). Each of these required indicating the correct solution manually. First, E. M. was administered a vocabulary check to be sure he understood the words, for example, *point to the circle*. Next the type of sentence structure was checked, as in, *point to the big blue circle*. Briefly described, examples of the tasks were:

Simple Modification. From a group of objects of two sizes: "Show me the small square."

Complex Modification. From a group of objects of two sizes, three colors: "Show me the small blue square."

Singular vs. Plural. From pairs of singular and plural objects: "Show me the flowers."

Possessives. From his own body, the experimenter's body, or pictures of a boy and girl: "Show me your nose."

Comparative and Superlative. From buttons and strips of paper of different sizes: "Which button is smaller?"

Conjunctions. From a series of common objects: "Show me the watch and the button."

Verb Tense. From a series of pictures showing children cooking, eating, and holding full stomachs: "The boys are going to eat sausages."

Before/After Word Order. Instructions such as: "Touch your nose after you touch your head."

Some/One/All. Presented with buttons and coins: "Place some of the buttons in the cup."

Pronouns. Pictures of children feeding themselves or others: "Show me, she is feeding him."

Spatial Prepositions. Four stacking boxes of different colors: "Put the green box in the blue box."

Simple Negation. Pictures showing presence-absence relationship: "The rabbit does not have a carrot."

Some months, E. M. was not able to complete all tests in the language comprehension evaluation battery. Even when he did complete the tasks, his score was not always above the chance level; that is, he did not exceed the number correct that could be achieved by pure guessing. The percentage of comprehension tasks on which he scored above the chance level at each test opportunity is shown in Figure 17.1.

The data are difficult to describe except to say that there is no obvious trend. It does not appear that E. M. improved in comprehension over time. Rather, it appears that language comprehension demonstrated at one test session may be gone in a later session. The session procedures were slightly different. At the 24- and 34-month evaluations, all items were administered regardless of accuracy, whereas at the first four evaluations (8, 12, 16, and 20 months) the particular test was discontinued if E. M. was unsuccessful on four items in a row. As a result, fatigue and lack of motivation may account for part of the seeming depression of scores in the 24- and 34-month evaluations. It is important to remember that these data do not represent the percentage of comprehension tasks accurately completed. Rather they show those completed above the chance level. Even those above the chance level usually contained many errors.

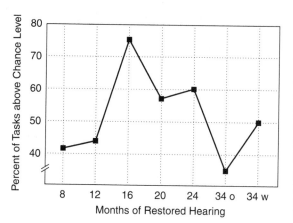

FIGURE 17.1   Percent Comprehension Tasks above Chance Level. Percentage of tasks undertaken in the verbal comprehension evaluation that resulted in performance above the chance level for correctness. The 34-month evaluations were performed twice; once with orally spoken instructions (34 o) and once with written instructions (34 w).

Source: From Grimshaw, G. M., Adelstein, A., Bryden, M. P., & MacKinnon, G. E. (1998). First language acquisition in adolescence: Evidence for a critical period for verbal language development. *Brain and Language, 63,* 237–255.

Figure 17.2 shows the percentage of specific tasks undertaken which were above the chance level. E. M. performed well on some, such as simple and complex modification but was unable to score above chance on before/after and simple negation. The other tasks fell between these extremes.

DISCUSSION AND CONCLUSIONS

Grimshaw et al. (1998) pointed out that it is difficult to know what group would represent a reasonable control group for the observations they reported on E. M. If comparison is made to other individuals of his chronological age, he consistently shows massive language deficits. It may be that a more fair comparison can be made by using 3- or 4-year-olds, thus comparing E. M. to people with the same amount of exposure to spoken language. This is a conservative comparison, because E. M. had years of homesign and other experience with the world that might have given him an advantage compared to 3- or 4-year-olds.

Yet, even when compared to young children, the language ability of E. M. can be seen as delayed. Except for their use with Genie, there were no norms for the tests of language comprehension that were used with E. M. Nevertheless, the specific skills that were measured

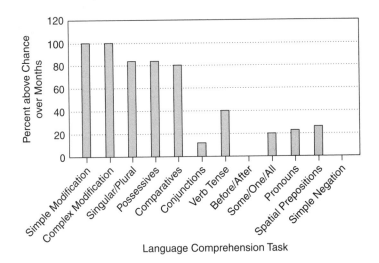

FIGURE 17.2   Percent above Chance over Seven Different Evaluations. Percentage of evaluations on which E. M. scored above chance considering total performances collapsed over time for each task. Each task was performed a maximum of seven times over the months of the study, but a few were performed less often because some tests were stopped following a series of failures at a single task.

Note: Two of the seven evaluations were at 34 months.

Source: From Grimshaw, G. M., Adelstein, A., Bryden, M. P., & MacKinnon, G. E. (1998). First language acquisition in adolescence: Evidence for a critical period for verbal language development. *Brain and Language, 63,* 237–255.

can be compared with the expectations for ordinary children. While 8 months of language exposure was sufficient for E. M. to be successful on some tasks, such as singular vs. plural, even at 34 months he did not understand verb tenses, negation, pronouns, or prepositions. Ordinary 3-year-old children produce simple negation by 26 months and comprehend it before then (Brown, 1973). Even for singular vs. plural, E. M.'s performance was never perfect. His performance in all aspects of language comprehension was highly variable within sessions. This highlights the extent to which his language development was unlike that of small children. Grimshaw et al. (1998) summed it up by saying: "Most notably, E. M. did not demonstrate significant improvement on a single subtest over the 2-year period of our assessment."

Even after 4 years of language exposure, E. M. rarely produced more than one word at a time. By the time an ordinary child is 4 years old, typical mean utterance length (MLU) is 4.4 (Brown, 1973). E. M. did not show some behaviors that are typical of language learning in young children. He never babbled and never tried out phrases with word forms or arrangements. He did not mimic more skilled speakers. His homesign may have been adequate for his needs in Mexico, but during the part of the year when he was in Canada, his relatives persistently encouraged verbal communication.

The highly unusual case of E. M. suggests that there may be a sensitive period for language development. However, few specific details about this sensitive period can be gleaned from this case. Lennenberg (1967) suggested that the sensitive period for language ended by adolescence. This assertion was not contradicted by the observations of E. M. reported by Grimshaw et al. (1998). While this study could not attempt to discover the nature of possible neurological changes or factors other than lack of exposure that might be components of the sensitive period, it was, nevertheless, a groundbreaking study. Perhaps future research will assess the permanence of language deficits. We hope that E. M. will continue to cooperate in future studies so that more can be learned about this important case.

CRITICAL THINKING TOOLKIT ITEMS

Case studies may be trivial and misleading if they do not focus on appropriate problems. These problems should be rare, important happenings to a group, or significant events involving only one or a few individuals. If the topic of a case study is a behavior that occurs frequently, other research methods can be used to achieve a more representative sample of participants.

REFERENCES

Brown, R. (1973). *A first language: The early stages.* Cambridge, MA: Harvard University Press.

Curtiss, S. (1977). *Genie: A psycholingusitic study of a modern-day "wild child."* New York: Academic.

Golden-Meadow, S., & Mylander, C. (1990). Beyond the input given: The child's role in the acquisition of language. *Language, 66,* 323–355.

Golden-Meadow, S., Butcher, C., Mylander, C., & Dodge, M. (1994). Nouns and verbs in a self-styled gesture system: What's in a name? *Cognitive Psychology, 27,* 259–319.

Grimshaw, G. M., Adelstein, A., Bryden, M. P., & Mac-Kinnon, G. E. (1998). First language acquisition in adolescence: Evidence for a critical period for verbal language development. *Brain and Language, 63,* 237–255.

Johnson, J., & Newport, E. (1989). Critical period effects in second language learning: The influence of maturational state on the acquisition of English as a second language. *Cognitive Psychology, 21,* 60–99.

Koluchová, J. (1972). Severe deprivation in twins: A case study. *Journal of Child Psychology and Psychiatry, 13,* 107–114.

Lane, H. (1976). *The wild boy of Aveyron.* Cambridge, MA: Harvard University Press.

Lennenberg, E. H. (1967). *Biological foundations of language.* New York: Wiley.

Rymer, R. (1993). *Genie: A scientific tragedy.* New York: HarperCollins.

Stevens, S. S. (1955). The measurement of loudness. *Journal of the Acoustical Society of America, 27,* 815–819.

Supalla, T., Newport, E., Singleton, J., Supalla, S., Coulter, G., & Metlay, D. (in press). *Test battery for American Sign Language morphology and syntax.* San Diego, CA: Dawnsign.

Weber-Fox, C. M., & Neville, H. J. (1996). Maturational constraints on functional specializations for language processing: ERP and behavioral evidence in bilingual speakers. *Journal of Cognitive Neuroscience, 8,* 231–256.

Werker, J. F. (1989). Becoming a native listener. *American Scientist, 77,* 54–59.

CHAPTER 18

COMING OF AGE

Think back to your high school years. Were the kids who seemed more physically mature also more popular? The need to cope with the extreme body changes that accompany physical maturation is among the challenges of adolescence. Unlike the relatively slow and continuous body growth that is experienced early in life, growth in adolescence is accompanied by rapid changes. These changes include the development of sexual maturity. Sexual maturity, or puberty, is a qualitative change in development that takes place at the same time as rapid quantitative changes in the body, such as height. Considerable research has been devoted to studying the onset or timing of puberty. The hallmarks of puberty can appear at different ages in different individuals. Some research has shown that pubertal timing is associated with personality differences that persist into later life, particularly if maturity appears very early or very late.

Early maturing in males has been shown to be correlated with initial advantages in social status. In a society that values a mesomorphic, muscular appearance in males, early-maturing boys may be treated more favorably than their less-mature counterparts by important adults, such as parents and teachers. Early-maturing boys seemingly respond to this new treatment by being more self-confident, behaviorally appropriate, and competent. Their peers also respond differently to them, and they are more likely to be chosen for leadership positions than their less mature age mates (Tobin-Richards, Boxer, & Peterson, 1983). However, there are disadvantages to early maturation. Some early-maturing boys have been shown to be less flexible, less open to new experiences, less creative, less spontaneous, and more conforming to adult values (Brooks-Gunn, 1987).

Late-maturing boys may be seen as more child-like because of their physical appearance. They may be treated less favorably by teachers and others, including their own peers. Because of the emphasis on athletics that pervades many schools, delayed physical development may affect the popularity of these boys. However, delayed maturity may function to protect these adolescents from the pressure to adopt adult social roles before they are sufficiently experienced to be successful. Because our culture is less likely to expect sterling performance in athletic and social domains from late-maturing boys, they may be better at allowing their own interests to develop in unique ways.

Incorporating the research of D. J. Flannery, D. C. Rowe, and B. L. Gulley, "Impact of Pubertal Status, Timing, and Age on Adolescent Sexual Experience and Delinquency," 1993, *Journal of Adolescent Research, 8,* pp. 21–40.

Early-maturing girls do not seem to have the same initial advantages associated with early maturing in boys. Quantitative changes, such as being tall, muscular, and perhaps heavyset, may put the early-maturing girl outside of the cultural standards for beauty. As her sexual maturity advances, she may be placed in sexual situations where her psychological judgment is inadequate. Early maturation in girls has been associated with problem behaviors, such as drug and alcohol use and absence from school. However, after the initial growth spurt, early-maturing girls are likely to realize the benefits of their increased maturity—they are likely to become more popular. The problems of rapid growth are behind them and there are many options available to them in social arenas and other domains requiring maturity (Statton & Magnusson, 1990).

Late-maturing girls show a less predictable pattern than is seen with late-maturing boys. The girls often command social and leadership advantages through much of adolescence. In long-term studies, 30-year-old adults who had been late-maturing girls as adolescents were shown to have more poise and self-direction. Although most research has focused on early and late maturation, it has been found that boys who matured on time believe they are at a disadvantage compared to earlier maturing males, while on-time females seem to have more positive body images and feel more socially attractive than either early- or late-maturing girls (Tobin-Richards et al., 1983).

Because peer groups of boys and girls are usually age-graded, or composed of people about the same age, and because girls are generally ahead of boys in physical development by as much as a year or two, at first, the early-maturing girl is likely to be alone in her peer group in the experience of accelerating development. Within an age group, the earliest boys will be next to experience the changes associated with puberty, followed by the late-maturing girls. The late-maturing boys may be at a particular disadvantage because they are the last in their age group to experience puberty.

Flannery, Rowe, and Gulley (1993) did a study examining the effects of timing of pubertal status and chronological age on sexual experience and delinquency. Their goal was to try to untangle some effects of age and puberty. Adolescents are likely to be influenced by both; they often attend age-graded schools and are exposed to age-graded peers. On the other hand, they are likely to respond to biological processes, such as hormonal influences, even though their peers may be experiencing different stages of biological maturation.

PARTICIPANTS

A list of phone numbers in a Southwestern city was the original source of participants for Flannery et al. (1993). This list contained 7,014 working numbers that had been compiled by a marketing firm from commercially available lists such as school registrations, drivers license records, and product and service purchase lists. The numbers on the list included those that were listed in the ordinary phone directory and some additional numbers that were not. A local commercial data collection company used these phone numbers to identify potential participants. The adolescent participants selected for further scrutiny were all English-speaking pairs of siblings between 10 and 16 years old. They were offered $50 for their participation.

Only a few (7.5 percent) of the families contacted by phone qualified, but 95 percent of these qualified families agreed to participate ($N = 499$). Of the 499 original families, 418 of them actually provided interview data for the study. The others had either moved away or had some other problem that prevented them from being included. For 33 boys and 30 girls, no data on physical maturation could be collected so they had to be dropped from the study. These 63 individuals did not appear to be different on the main measures of the study: self-reported delinquency and sexual behavior. They were, however, more likely to belong to either the Mormon religion or to a charismatic Christian religion. It seems likely that members of these groups objected to the assessment of physical maturation status that was part of this study.

The characteristics of the final sample for the study are shown in Table 18.1. Two interviewers went to the homes of the adolescents, one for each participant sibling. Wherever possible, adolescents were interviewed by a same-sex interviewer, but most of the interviewers were female and it was not always possible to match sex of adolescent and sex of interviewer. The adolescents were taken to a part of the home where they could not be overheard by other members of the household during the interview. The adolescents and at least one parent gave permission to participate in the study before any data collection began. The family members were assured that their responses would be kept confidential and no families dropped out of the study at this point.

The survey instrument was presented to the participants on a portable computer that had the questions and answer choices encoded on a database program (D-Base III+). Adolescents were given a choice as to whether they wanted to use the computer to enter their own choices or if they preferred to have the interviewer read the questions and enter the answers. Flannery et al. (1993) reported that the procedures used to collect the data "held most subjects' [participants'] attention well." Although the data were self-reported

TABLE 18.1   Characteristics of the Final Sample

CHARACTERISTIC	PERCENT
Mother's education	
Less than high school	3
High school	28
Some post high school	24
College graduate	44
Living with both birth parents	89
One or two Hispanic parents	15
Caucasian parents	78
Used illicit drug at least once	11
Used alcohol in past year	39
Smoked	18
Committed at least one delinquent act	78
Had dating or intimate experience	60

Source: From Flannery, D. J., Rowe, D. C., & Gulley, B. L. (1993). Impact of pubertal status, timing and age on adolescent sexual experience and delinquency. *Journal of Adolescent Research, 8,* 25.

and therefore open to the usual questions about validity, the researchers found predictable intercorrelations between adolescents' accounts of their own behavior and the accounts of their siblings (Rowe & Gulley, 1992). This was taken to be evidence supporting the validity of the data collection procedure.

MEASURING DELINQUENCY

Delinquency was measured with a scale that was a modification of that used by Rowe (1985). The instrument comprised 20 questions that were scored as 0 for never; 1, one time; 2, several times; and 3, very often. The statements referred to different kinds of delinquency:

NUMBER OF ITEMS	TYPE OF BEHAVIOR
6	Vandalism and trespassing
4	Shoplifting and theft
1	Lying
7	Aggression
1	Speeding in a car
1	Failure to obey an adult

The items on this scale had an alpha of .81, suggesting that the scale had adequate internal consistency. Other statistical analysis suggested that the separate items were reasonable measures of delinquency. The Likert scale used here is believed to be reliable and valid for self-report measures of delinquency (Hindelang, Hirschi, & Weiss, 1981).

MEASURING SEXUAL EXPERIENCE

The adolescents were also scored on the Sexual Experience Scale, consisting of five items that ranged from low to high intimacy in heterosexual behaviors (1 = kissed or held hands, 2 = dated, 3 = made out, 4 = petted heavily [touched under clothes], and 5 = sexual intercourse). The instrument was scored by having the adolescents choose the descriptor representing the highest level of intimacy achieved in their lifetimes. For example, if the individual had performed all of these behaviors, the score would be 5. If only the first two on the list had been performed, the score reported to the researchers would be 2.

MEASURING MATURATION

Chronological age was one index of maturation. The age ranges of the adolescents in three clusters were 10 or 11 years old (24 percent), 12 through 14 years old (50 percent), and 15 through 16 years old (26 percent). Chronological age is not a very accurate measure of physical maturity, particularly at this stage in the life span. Some individuals will be well advanced in physical development and some will be behind. Figure 18.1 shows diagrams illustrating this phenomenon from the classic work of Tanner (1973, 1978).

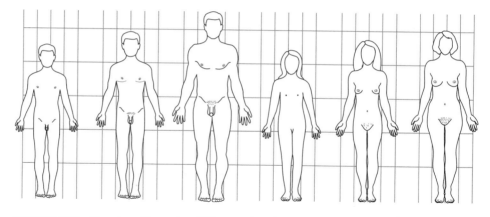

FIGURE 18.1   Drawings illustrating differences in pubertal timing among same-age adolescents. The boys are all 14.75 years old and the girls are all 12.75 years old.

Source: From "Growing Up," by J. M. Tanner, 1973, *Scientific American, 229,* p. 38.

        The boys in this figure are all 14.75 years old and the girls are all 12.75 years old. While these are cases chosen to represent the extremes, they do illustrate the potential problems that may occur if chronological age alone is used as a measure of physical maturation. The authors used line drawings made from photographs taken by Tanner (1978) illustrating five distinct stages of physical maturation for males and for females. These drawings identify five distinct stages of puberty, called *Tanner stages,* that are frequently used to assess or describe maturation during puberty. Tanner stages are scaled from 1, least mature and clearly prepubescent, to 5, physically mature. The researchers showed two separate sets of line drawings to each participant. For females, one set of drawings showed five stages of breast development, while the second set showed five stages of pubic hair development. For males, the first set of drawings illustrated five stages of genital development and the second set depicted five stages of pubic hair development.

        Once the questionnaires had been administered, the researchers showed the drawings of the appropriate sex to each adolescent, calling his or her attention to the details that represented important characteristics of each of the five stages. The adolescents selected the drawings that most closely represented their own stage of maturational development. The sum of the stage numbers represented in each of the two pictures selected was the individual's score, resulting in scores from 2 to 10. That is, if a boy rated himself as a 3 for genital development and a 3 for pubic hair development, he would be assigned a score of 6. It is important to realize that this measure assesses the adolescents' perception of their maturational level, which may not exactly correspond to more objective measures. Nevertheless, as a method of rating this has been shown to have some validity; in other research, this form of self-rating has correlated with ratings by health care providers at levels from $r = .77$ to $r = .91$ (Dorn, Susman, Nottelmann, Inoff-Germain, & Chrousos, 1990). We should note that in the study of Dorn et al. (1990) accurate rating was the primary goal and adolescents knew that their ratings would be correlated with those of a health care professional.

        In assessing their own Tanner stage, about 20 percent of the adolescents rated themselves in Stage 1 or 2 on both of the pictures they chose, 34 percent placed themselves in

Stages 2, 3, or 4 on their two picture choices, and 46 percent placed themselves in Stage 4 or 5 on both pictures.

RESULTS

The main interest of this study was the timing of puberty, not merely the adolescents' Tanner stage. It would be expected that the older adolescents would be in higher Tanner stages and the younger adolescents would be in lower Tanner stages. Therefore, the researchers needed a measure where adolescents were compared to expectations for their age group to see if they were ahead or behind expected levels of maturity. In order to get this kind of comparative measure, the adolescents' data were placed in groups representing a 12-month age span, as might happen if those born between January and December of a given year were considered together. The researchers then used the Tanner scale ratings of group members to calculate a set of *standard scores* or Z scores.

Standard Scores (Z scores)

The researchers were interested in showing the way an individual's raw score compared to other scores of fellow group members and to the mean of the group. They wanted to know if an individual had matured earlier or later than others in his or her age group. Comparisons like this are often made simply by comparing an individual's raw score to the average, or mean, of the group scores; an individual is thus said to be above or below the group average. A measure of the location of an individual score above or below the mean, which also takes into account the rest of the scores in the group, is called a *standard deviation* or *SD*, as you will remember from earlier chapters.

In order to find out how the individual's raw maturity score compares to the group of scores, the score can be expressed in terms of standard deviation units or how far this score deviates from the mean. When scores are expressed in the latter fashion, they are known as standard scores, or Z scores. In a distribution of standard scores, the mean of the group is set at 0. A rating that is one standard deviation above the mean becomes a Z score of +1. A score that is one standard deviation below the mean becomes a Z score of –1. The higher or lower the Z score, the more extreme the individual case is compared to the rest of the group. As you can see by looking at Figure 18.2, if the distribution of scores is bell-shaped, or "normal"; a Z score that is greater than 2 or less than –2 is different than 97 percent of the scores in the group.

IQ, for example, has a mean of 100 and an *SD* of 15. From this information you can make an evaluation of an individual IQ score. An IQ of 145 would have a standard score of 3 and would be higher than 99 percent of the population of IQ scores, a very high score indeed. We have also put SAT scores on Figure 18.2 so you can see where an individual score might fall within the population. Returning to maturity scores, an adolescent who had a standard score of 2 for pubertal status would be included in the top 3 percent of adolescents in his or her age group with respect to maturity; clearly more mature than most of the others. Notice that the standard score is important only when comparing an individual's Tanner score to the Tanner scores of others who are the same age.

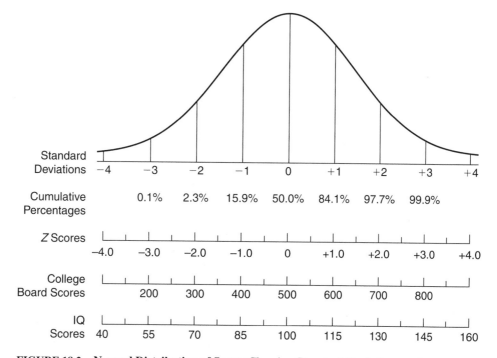

FIGURE 18.2   Normal Distribution of Scores Showing Standard Deviations and Cumulative Percentages Represented by Z Scores, College Board (SAT) Scores, and IQ Scores.

We hope you can see how the standard score improves upon saying that a 12-year-old adolescent has a Tanner maturity score of 5. From age information alone, it is not possible to know if this is unusual or not. However, if we say that this adolescent's standard score for Tanner maturity is 2.3 when compared to others the same age, we know that this individual is more mature than almost the entire age cohort. This discussion of standard scores is important because standard scores for maturity were the basis for correlational results reported. The Z scores for maturity are called *pubertal status* and were used as outcomes in correlations with other measures.

Correlations

The correlations that were found between pubertal status, chronological age, delinquency, and sexual experience are shown in Table 18.2. The predictor variables of pubertal status and chronological age were each positively related to delinquent behavior and sexual experience. In general, the correlations between the predictors were stronger for sexual experience than for delinquency. All the correlations in Table 18.2 were statistically significant, but you should remember that this means they were significantly different from 0. The relationships between the predictors and delinquency, while well within the range expected for

TABLE 18.2   Correlations among Age, Delinquency, Pubertal Status, and Sexual Activity Measures for Boys and Girls

	AGE	PUBERTAL STATUS	DELINQUENT BEHAVIOR	SEXUAL EXPERIENCE
Age	—	.79	.29	.62
Pubertal status	.75	—	.28	.51
Delinquent behavior	.24	.26	—	.43
Sexual experience	.64	.53	.46	—

Note: Correlations above the imaginary diagonal (where no numbers appear) refer to males and correlations below the diagonal line refer to females.

Source: From Flannery, D. J., Rowe, D. C., & Gulley, B. L. (1993). Impact of pubertal status, timing and age on adolescent sexual experience and delinquency. *Journal of Adolescent Research, 8,* 31.

complex social science data, account for between 5 percent and 8 percent of the variance, as described earlier in Chapter 2.

Flannery et al. (1993) also used pubertal status to determine if early maturing was associated with delinquency or sexual experience. In this arrangement of the data, males and females had to be divided into groups of early, on time, and late maturers. Standard deviations were used as boundaries. Individuals within plus or minus one standard deviation of the mean were considered to be on time. As you can see in Figure 18.2, this would include the middle 68 percent of the distribution of maturity. Above one *SD,* individuals were considered to be early-maturing while being below one *SD* assigned individuals to the late-maturing group. The data from this analysis are found in Figure 18.3.

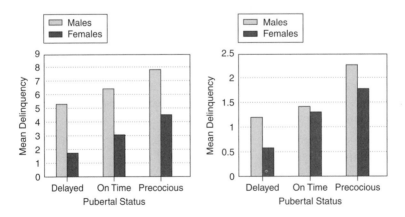

FIGURE 18.3   Delinquency and Sexual Experience. Self-reports of delinquency and sexual experience in males and females who were ahead, behind, or similar to their age mates in terms of sexual maturity.

Source: From Flannery, D. J., Rowe, D. C., & Gulley, B. L. (1993). Impact of pubertal status, timing, and age on adolescent sexual experience and delinquency. *Journal of Adolescent Research, 8,* 35.

Girls who matured earlier than their age cohort reported that they engaged in more intimate sexual behavior and more delinquent behavior ($p < .001$). Early-maturing males also reported that they had been involved in more intimate sexual behavior ($p < .001$) and more delinquent behavior ($p < .05$). Early-maturing males were making out and engaging in under-the-clothes touching, while late-maturing males had just started having dating relationships. The same pattern was found for girls, but the girls reported being slightly behind the boys in the extent of delinquency and sexual intimacy. In thinking about this finding, it may be important to understand that a number of studies have suggested that males may overreport sexual activity and females may underreport it (Roche & Ramsbey, 1983).

Tanner Stage and Outcomes

The sexual experience and delinquency outcome measures of all individuals at a particular Tanner stage of maturity, without reference to chronological age, are plotted in Figure 18.4. These graphs can give us a rough idea of the timing of behavioral change in relation to maturity. Sexual experience is probably the most clear-cut in showing an obvious change in rate about half way through Tanner Stage 3. Although we phrase the interpretation in this way, you should remember that these are not longitudinal data. Behavioral change is inferred from cross-sectional evidence. Menarche, the beginning of menstrual periods in females, is associated with the level of maturity found in Tanner Stage 4. For males, Tanner Stage 4 is the first of the stages with adult-like sexual maturity. Although Stage 4 may be reached at chronological ages ranging from about age 12.5 to age 14.75 in females and age 13.25 to 14.75 in males (Tanner, 1978), it is associated with an increase in sexual experience, though not necessarily sexual intercourse. Sexual experience may depend more on the Tanner stage than on chronological age, putting the early maturers at risk for involvement in sexual behavior before they have the adult cognitive skills to deal with the problems that may arise from sexual activity.

Perhaps the most obvious thing about delinquency across the Tanner stages is the persistent difference between boys and girls, with boys appearing to be more delinquent at all Tanner stages. Overall, in reporting Tanner stages, females reported themselves to be more mature than males but the differences were not statistically significant. This lack of significance would

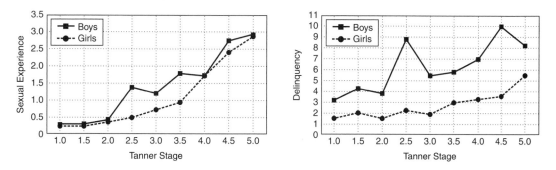

FIGURE 18.4   Sexual Experience and Delinquency in Adolescents by Tanner Stages.

Note: Chronological age is not considered.

Source: From Flannery, D. J., Rowe, D. C., & Gulley, B. L. (1993). Impact of pubertal status, timing and age on adolescent sexual experience and delinquency. *Journal of Adolescent Research, 8,* 33.

seem to contradict the evidence that during adolescence girls are a year or two ahead of boys in physical maturity. It will not surprise you to hear that adolescent males have been known to overestimate their own levels of physical maturity (Frankowski et al., 1987). Although this would have altered the absolute level of the Tanner stage data, it would not necessarily have altered the rank ordering of individuals: the earliest and latest maturing males would still be the same individuals; however, they might not be as mature as their ratings suggested.

DISCUSSION

The effects of pubertal status and chronological age are intertwined. It probably would make no sense for one to speak of them as if they were independent. The correlation between age and pubertal status in males was $r = .79$ and in females it was $r = .75$. Clearly these two influences are closely related. Although they are not independent influences, they are not identical. Differences that were found between early and late maturers speak to the disparate influences of age and physical maturity. Early maturers were found to be different than late maturers. In this instance, rate of maturity was implicated and age was not.

Early-maturing adolescents were shown to have higher levels of sexual experience and delinquency in this study. For girls, Caspi and Moffitt (1991) found that this may be because the early maturers associated with older peers who are, themselves, more involved in this kind of behavior. Males engage in more frequent delinquent behavior with increasing age, to an extent not seen in females. Peer pressure is almost certainly a component of this and, as Brown (1982) has found, female adolescents are likely to be encouraged to form steady relationships, whereas males are more encouraged by their peers to engage in sex and to become involved with drugs and alcohol. They are also more likely to participate in other problem behavior (Berndt, 1979).

Flannery et al. (1993) stated that their findings "reinforce the need to disentangle the influence of pubertal status from the timing of puberty and chronological age" (p. 37). This developmental issue also has practical facets that might be applied to the real world. First, early-maturing adolescents may receive less supervision from their parents (Moore, Peterson, & Furstenberg, 1986). These adolescents appear to be more like adults and they may be treated accordingly by parents and others. The evidence from the work of Flannery et al. (1993) and other researchers suggests that adults should be cautious about using the appearance of maturity in adolescents as an indication of cognitive or social development. Second, for the adolescents, better understanding of their situation might help them to understand and cope with the temporary nature of pubertal timing, particularly in the most problematic cases—the early-maturing girl and the late-maturing boy.

CRITICAL THINKING TOOLKIT ITEMS

Validity of a measure can be clearly established in one situation but this may not ensure that the measure will be valid in other uses. As was seen with the assessment of physical maturity, self-assessment was valid when participants knew it would also be rated by professionals. This does not necessarily mean that self-assessment is valid when it is not going to be confirmed by others.

REFERENCES

Berndt, T. J. (1979). Developmental changes in conformity to peers and parents. *Developmental Psychology, 15,* 608–616.

Brooks-Gunn, J. (1987). Pubertal pressures: Their relevance for developmental research. In V. B. Van Hasselt & M. Hersen (Eds.), *Handbook of adolescent psychology* (pp. 111–130). New York: Pergamen Press.

Brown, B. (1982). The extent and effects of peer pressure among high school students: A retrospective analysis. *Journal of Youth and Adolescence, 11,* 121–133.

Caspi, A., & Moffitt, T. (1991). Individual differences are accentuated during periods of social change: The sample case of girls at puberty. *Journal of Personality and Social Psychology, 61,* 157–168.

Dorn, L., Susman, E., Nottelmann, E. D., Inoff-Germain, G., & Chrousos, G. P. (1990). Perceptions of puberty: Adolescent, parent, and health care personnel. *Developmental Psychology, 26,* 322–329.

Flannery, D. J., Rowe, D. C., & Gulley, B. L. (1993). Impact of pubertal status, timing, and age on adolescent sexual experience and delinquency. *Journal of Adolescent Research, 8,* 21–40.

Frankowski, B., Duke-Duncan, P., Guillot, A., McDougal, D., Wasserman, R., & Young, P. (1987). Young adolescents' self-assessment of sexual maturation. *American Journal of Diseases of Children, 141,* 385–386.

Hindelang, M. E., Hirschi, T., & Weiss, J. G. (1981). *Measuring delinquency.* Beverly Hills, CA: Sage.

Moore, K., Peterson, J., & Furstenberg, F. (1986). Parental attitudes and the occurrence of early sexual activity. *Journal of Marriage and the Family, 48,* 777–782.

Roche, J., & Ramsbey, T. (1983). Premarital sexuality: A five-year follow-up study of attitudes and behavior by dating stage. *Adolescence, 28,* 67–80.

Rowe, D. C. (1985). Sibling interactions and self-reported delinquent behavior. A study of 265 twin pairs. *Criminology, 23,* 223–240.

Rowe, D. C., & Gulley, B. (1992). Sibling effects on substance abuse and delinquency. *Criminology, 30,* 217–233.

Statton, H., & Magnusson, D. (1990). *Pubertal maturation in female development.* Hillsdale, NJ: Erlbaum.

Tanner, J. M. (1973). Growing up. *Scientific American, 229,* 38.

Tanner, J. M. (1978). *Fetus into man.* Cambridge, MA: Harvard University Press.

Tobin-Richards, M. H., Boxer, A. M., & Peterson, A. C. (1983). The psychological significance of pubertal change: Sex differences in perceptions of self in early adolescence. In J. Brooks-Gunn & A. C. Peterson (Eds.), *Girls at Puberty: Biological and psychological perspectives* (pp. 127–154). New York: Plenum.

CHAPTER 19

APPARENT FROM THE PARENTS

After being exposed to headlines in the media regarding acts of adolescent violence, such as the school shootings during the last few years, we are eager to ask the question: To what extent do parents affect the behavior and personality of their children? Drawing on a large body of research, developmental psychologist Sandra Scarr (1992), for example, proposed a view that questions the role of parents in the creation of individual differences among children. In order to follow her argument, you must first understand that she is talking about a group of parents whom she has labeled *good enough parents.* Of course, she understood that if parents abuse or deprive their children, the development of the children will be altered. However, if children are brought up by good enough parents, by definition the parents have provided adequate stimulation, warmth, love, security, and limits. Scarr called this the *average expectable environment,* and believed that parents who provide it may contribute little to the differences that are found among groups of normal children. Scarr stated:

> How can it be that different parents have few differential effects on the intellectual or personality development of their children? For parents who care, it is impossible to believe that this could be the case. This is not to say that parents may not have effects on children's self-esteem, motivation, ambitiousness, and other important characteristics. It is to say that parental *differences* in rearing styles, social class, and income have small effects on the measurable *differences* in intelligence, interests and personality among their children. (p. 10)

Scarr's ideas are sometimes misunderstood by those who do not know that a goal of psychology is to understand the variability within groups of people. One measure of that variability is the statistic called the *variance.* Psychology often seeks to account for, or explain, the variance within a group. Why are some children very ambitious while others are not? Why do some children have high self-esteem and others low self-esteem? These questions seek explanations for the variance in particular traits. If there is a wide range of differences, the variance will be large. Scarr's argument is that for good enough parents, the variability in parenting styles does not account for much of the variance in the traits of their children. However, this does not mean that bad parents cannot negatively influence

Incorporating the research of L. Steinberg, S. D. Lamborn, N. Darling, N. S. Mounts, and S. M. Dornbusch. "Over-Time Changes in Adjustment and Competence among Adolescents from Authoritative, Authoritarian, Indulgent, and Neglectful Families," 1994, *Child Development, 65,* pp. 754–770.

their children in measurable ways. Bad parenting may explain some of the variance in child traits. When considering only good enough parents, on the other hand, different parenting styles do not make much difference when their kids are compared to other children, also from good enough parents. Rowe (1990) has shown that parents defined by our culture as "super-parents" may not positively affect their children's development to a greater extent than the more usual, run-of-the-mill, good enough parents.

Scarr's assertions echo the work of researchers who have studied genetic factors in personality, as you have seen in earlier chapters. The common finding in these studies is that about 50 percent of the variance in personality is explained by genetic factors. Scarr believes the remaining percentage of the variance is idiosyncratic. She proposed that one possible source of idiosyncratic variance is the different contexts in which an individual spends time. The more an individual becomes different from others, the more differently that individual is treated, and this spiraling change would increasingly become a source of some of the variance observed.

In contrast to Scarr's formulations, many developmental psychologists have stressed the role of parents in influencing personality development. While these two bodies of thought seem to be in conflict, it may be that even good enough parents are more important in the development of some characteristics and less important for others. For example, Steinberg, Lamborn, Dornbusch, and Darling (1992) reported that parents might play a role in their children's long-term goal setting, while peers and contexts may exert a greater influence in their actual day-to-day behavior.

SURVEYS

This chapter presents a study that is an excellent example of using a survey as the research method. There are many studies that employ the survey method to answer questions. Unfortunately, many surveys are not very thoroughly or carefully designed. There are at least two characteristics you should consider when evaluating a study that has used survey methodology. First, of course, there are the usual questions about reliability, validity, and some measure of internal consistency, such as the alpha statistic, described in Chapter 11. Second, surveys should have adequate samples.

There are at least two aspects that should be considered in the assessment of samples: *size* and *representativeness*. There are many studies in the literature that present survey data collected from very small samples. We have gone out of our way to exclude such studies from this book, but you can easily find them in psychological journals. One of the problems with small samples is that they are likely to be unrepresentative. Large samples may also be unrepresentative, but this is less likely to be the case. A great deal is known about sampling and it is possible to construct highly representative modest-sized samples from which findings can be generalized to large populations. This is the manner in which the best national polls are constructed. Whether the sample of a survey is representative is to some extent a value judgment that you will need to make for yourself. One way to approach this judgment is to ask yourself about the population to which you would like to apply the findings of the survey. If no attempt has been made to represent this population—or people like them—in the research sample, this sample will be unrepresentative of the particular group.

A STUDY OF PARENTING STYLE

A team of researchers including Laurence Steinberg (Steinberg, Lamborn, Darling, Mounts, & Dornbusch, 1994) has been studying adolescent personality for a number of years using survey methodology (see also Lamborn, Mounts, Steinberg, & Dornbusch, 1991; Steinberg, Dornbusch, & Brown, 1992; Steinberg, Lamborn, Dornbusch, & Darling, 1992). This team conducted a very large, 1-year longitudinal survey, first collecting data in 1987–1988 (Lamborn et al., 1991) and again in 1988–1989 (Steinberg et al., 1994). While the data from these surveys have been used to answer a number of different questions, the primary focus of this particular chapter will be the survey findings pertaining to parenting style and adolescent adjustment.

One of the first research-based classifications of parenting style was formulated by Diana Baumrind (1967, 1971). Baumrind proposed three different types of parenting; these categories were later expanded by other researchers to four (Maccoby & Martin, 1983; Lamborn et al., 1991). The four types of parenting identified by previous research were subject variables in the study discussed in this chapter: authoritative, authoritarian, indulgent, and neglectful. We did not design the language that is used to describe the parenting styles in this chapter, but if we had, we would not have chosen to classify parents as either *authoritative* or *authoritarian* because the similarity of the words invites confusion. Nevertheless, these are the accepted terms, so we advise you to pay careful attention when reading about them.

The characteristics of the four parenting styles are shown in Table 19.1. Authoritative parenting is usually defined by three hallmarks known as the authoritative trinity: warmth, democracy, and firm limits. As you can see from Table 19.1, authoritative parents are high in acceptance and involvement, the dimension that includes warmth and democracy. These parents are also high in strictness and supervision. They set firm limits but are open to democratic reasoning about these limits. Authoritarian parents are strict and controlling, without the warmth and involvement that is part of authoritative parenting. Indulgent parents love and accept their children but do not set limits. Neglectful parents have little involvement or interest in their children and do not give them adequate supervision or rules.

Studies such as the one in this chapter report correlations among various subject variables. Parental style is seen to be correlated with various outcomes in adolescent offspring. Chapter 2, "Deep Roots," provided an introduction to correlational thinking. By this point in your reading, you are certainly aware that correlations are not solid evidence for a causal relationship. In the case of parenting styles, one often carelessly assumes the parental type

TABLE 19.1   Characteristics of Parenting Styles

		ACCEPTANCE AND INVOLVEMENT	
		High	*Low*
STRICTNESS AND SUPERVISION	*High*	Authoritative Parenting	Authoritarian Parenting
	Low	Indulgent Parenting	Neglectful Parenting

Note: Acceptance and involvement and strictness and supervision are parenting styles that can occur at high or low levels, as shown in the table.

has caused the adolescent outcome. However, the reverse is also possible: Parental style may be a reaction to the personality of the child. For example, the research discussed in this chapter has shown that well-adjusted children tend to have authoritative parents. Yet, it could be that parents whose children are well adjusted respond to their children's behavior by becoming authoritative parents.

PARTICIPANTS

The participants were part of a larger survey study conducted in two consecutive years in nine high schools located in Wisconsin and Northern California. In the first school year, 1987–1988, a total of 11,669 students filled out questionnaires; the next year, 11,248 students participated. Because the study was longitudinal, only individuals who filled out questionnaires in both years could be included. A total of 6,357 students met this requirement. The largest group of students who did not fill out questionnaires in the second year was the group of seniors who had graduated. Other reasons for not persisting in the study included dropping out of school, moving from the district, and being absent from school on a day when survey data were collected. In spite of this loss of participants over the year of the study, the final sample appeared to be quite similar demographically to the initial sample. About 40 percent of the students identified themselves as ethnic minorities. About one third of them were not living with both biological parents in one household. Also, about a third of the students had parents with no schooling beyond 12th grade.

The researchers used a strategy called *passive* parental consent to get permission for students to participate in the study. Permission for this procedure had to be obtained from the grant agency that funded the study, the U.S. Department of Education, and from the educational institutions to which the authors belonged. Passive consent meant that the parents were sent a letter explaining the study and asking them to notify the school if they did not want their child to participate. Because one of the parenting styles of interest was neglectful parents, the researchers were concerned that an active consent procedure might remove children of neglectful parents from the study because neglectful parents might not bother to return a form giving permission for their child to participate in the study. Active consent was obtained from the students themselves. About 5 percent of the students did not participate owing either to objections from parents or because the students themselves would not give consent.

PARENTAL STYLE MEASURES

The survey instrument collected demographic data such as ethnicity, sex, parent education, family constellation (number of parents, siblings, and others), and year in school. Parental style measures included questions that had been adapted from a variety of earlier research projects, but included some questions designed specifically for use in this study. The parental style measures were requested only in the first year of this study, because previous research indicated that parenting style is very stable from one year to the next (Hetherington et al., 1992). Looking across the surveys, the researchers found that many of the individual items could be seen as measures of larger, more general factors. The factors that were found for parenting included two we have previously described: *acceptance/involvement* and *strictness/supervision*.

The parenting scale that measured acceptance/involvement consisted of 10 items ($\alpha = .72$) including things such as "He helps me with my school work if there is something I don't understand" and "I can count on her to help me out if I have some kind of problem." (The gender reference was changed appropriately for questions about mothers and fathers.) The scale that measured strictness/supervision was composed of nine items ($\alpha = .76$). The items asked questions such as "How much do your parents try to know about where you are most afternoons after school?" and "In a typical week, what is the latest you can stay out on school nights?" From these items, Steinberg et al. (1994) created a *typology* of parenting types. This means that the researchers grouped the parents into one of the specifically defined categories shown in Table 19.1.

Another approach that might have been used to describe parent styles is called a *dimensional* approach, which assumes that parenting styles occur along a continuum. A dimensionally classified parenting style might be given a score reflecting the extent to which the style was, for example, strict. The higher the score, the stricter the parent. Parents could be scored anywhere from very lenient to very strict. We mention this to expose you to the two kinds of thinking that are common in this area of study. Steinberg et al. (1994) adopted the typological approach because they wished to extend the theoretical framework established by Baumrind (1971), which also used a typology system. They note, however, that each approach to classification "has its merits and a decision to use one versus the other should be made on theoretical grounds" (p. 758).

In order to put parents into parenting style categories, the researchers divided the scores on the acceptance/involvement and strictness/supervision scales into thirds, called *tertiles,* cutting off the top and the bottom third of scorers. High scores were operationally defined as being in the top tertile on each variable, while low scores were defined as being in the bottom tertile on each variable. These high and low scores were used to define parent type in Table 19.1. This division resulted in the inclusion of 2,353 families. The number of families assigned to each parenting style is shown in Table 19.2.

People scoring in the middle tertile on *acceptance/involvement* and on *strictness/ supervision* were removed from this study by the typological definitions of the variables. Researchers quite commonly form groups using only the extreme cases. As a critical thinker you should be aware that selection process impacts the representativeness of the sample. You will remember that in Chapter 14, "Boldface Letters," a somewhat similar sampling problem presented itself. In that study, the researchers randomly assigned children who scored close to the mean on a personality test to one or another experimental group. That was one approach; dropping them out is another.

OUTCOME MEASURES

The outcome variables consisted of four sets of adolescent characteristics:

1. *Psychosocial Development:* included 5 items from a social competence scale ($\alpha = .78$) asking about popularity and friends, 10 items measuring work orientation ($\alpha = .73$) asking about motivation to complete tasks, and 10 items measuring self-reliance ($\alpha = .81$) considering attitudes about ability to control events or the extent to which events are a matter of luck.

**TABLE 19.2   Family Group Sizes
Categorized by Parenting Style**

GROUP	N
Authoritative	817
Authoritarian	451
Indulgent	251
Neglectful	838

Source: From Steinberg, L., Lamborn, S. D., Darling, N., Mounts, N. S., & Dornbusch, S. M. (1994). Over-time changes in adjustment and competence among adolescents from authoritative, authoritarian, indulgent, and neglectful families. *Child Development, 65,* 759.

2. *Academic Competence:* included grade point average, 5 items asking about speed of homework completion and brightness compared to peers ($\alpha = .73$), and 6 items assessing satisfaction toward school ($\alpha = .69$).
3. *Internalized Distress:* measured depression and also included 7 items assessing somatic symptoms such as headaches and colds ($\alpha = .67$), and 6 items measuring psychological problems such as anxiety and tension ($\alpha = .88$).
4. *Problem Behavior:* included a 5-item measure of alcohol and drug use ($\alpha = .86$), 4 items measuring school problems such as tardiness and cheating ($\alpha = .68$), and a delinquency measure asking about serious problems such as trouble with the police and weapon carrying ($\alpha = .86$).

With the exception of grade point average, all of the outcomes were measured by 4-point Likert scales, where the high ratings indicated the extent to which the statement was a good description of the adolescent. Grade point average was converted to the usual scale in which A = 4.0, so that it could be numerically scaled from 0 to 4.

The questionnaires containing these questions were massive. You will recognize from the numbers of students that this research project was a serious attempt to collect data on a large number of participants. The survey itself was so long that it was divided in half and given over two school days.

RESULTS

From the data reported in the original journal article, it was not always possible to determine if a specific difference was statistically significant and at what level. Owing to the nature of this study, we are willing to relax our usual vigilance about statistical significance because the number of participants, also called *sample size,* is so large that statistical significance may not mean very much. As we have mentioned before, most statistical tests are designed to be sensitive to the number of data points, or number of participants. Very large numbers of participants can render these statistical tests less sensitive. When samples are very large, almost any differences, even very small and apparently trivial ones, may come out to be statistically significant. In this study, for example, correlations that accounted for a minuscule one tenth of 1 percent of the variance were found to be statistically significant. In cases such as these, we believe that statistical significance becomes meaningless. In order to evaluate the importance of the outcomes it can be useful to determine if the differences reported are large enough to make any difference in the real world. Statistical approaches to this are discussed in Chapter 2 (squaring correlations) and in later chapters. This is also where a little common sense can help. For example, imagine that a study skills program at a large university was found to make a significant difference in the GPA of students in the program. One of the first questions to ask concerns the actual value of the GPA difference. If students who took the program have a mean GPA of 2.89 and students who did not have a mean GPA of 2.87, the program is not having much real impact, even if the difference is significant. In this study of parenting the number of participants was so large that all correlations above .04 were statistically significant.

To check for longitudinal stability, correlations were calculated for each of the outcome measures showing the relationship between the level of these measures in the first year of the study and the level reported a year later. These correlations ranged from $r = .35$ to $r = .56$, with the exception of three outliers. These three outlying high scores represented the relationship between psychological symptoms from one year to the next ($r = .60$), the relationship between GPAs in each year ($r = .72$), and the relationship between reports of drug use over a year ($r = .71$).

A few other correlations suggested a cluster of traits associated with success in school. School orientation and work orientation in the first year correlated, $r = .46$. In the second year, this relationship was $r = .44$. Furthermore, in the second year, academic competence was correlated with self-reliance (r) = .42 and with work orientation (r) = .48. In the first year, these relationships were a bit weaker. Another cluster could be found, with correlations in the .40s, between school misconduct, drug use, and delinquency. All of the intercorrelations for these outcome measures are reported in the original article, if you have any interest in other specific relationships.

The mean scores for each of the outcome measures, for each parenting-style group, are found in Figure 19.1. The means shown in Figure 19.1 only reflect the first year of data collection. It is important to understand that although these data are not correlation coefficients, these quasi-experimental data are what we might call *conceptually correlational* in the sense that they display relationships between parenting style and adolescent outcomes that may or may not be causal. Nevertheless, some of these relationships are quite interesting. Looking at the profile presented for the adolescents from authoritative homes, there is an obvious decline at the boundary along the *x* axis between traits that might be considered "good," such as academic competence, and traits that might be considered "bad," such as adverse psychological symptoms.

Figure 19.2 presents the longitudinal data in the form of difference scores—the score for the first year subtracted from the second year score. Because these are difference scores, the bars above the line show that there was an increase in the outcome measure from the first to the second year. The bars hanging below the line show that the mean score for the outcome measure was lower in the second year than in the first. In order to interpret these data, you must also remember that these items were scaled from 0 to 4. Although the

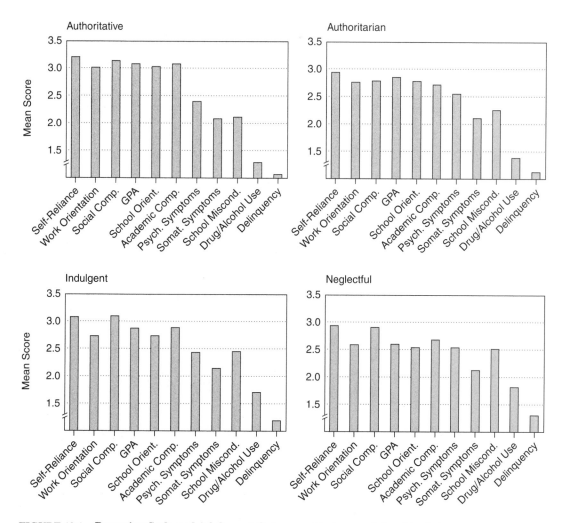

FIGURE 19.1   Parenting Style and Adolescent Outcomes. First-year relationships between four types of parenting and the mean scores for various outcome measures. Outcome measures were scaled from 0 to 4 with 4 reflecting the highest level of the trait.

Source: From Steinberg, L., Lamborn, S. D., Darling, N. Mounts, N. S., & Dornsbusch, S. M. (1994). Over-time changes in adjustment and comptenece among adoloescents from authoritative, authoritarian, indulgent, and neglectful families. *Child Development, 65,* 763.

changes may not seem particularly sigificant in their absolute magnitudes, some of them represent a substantial percentage of change, particularly over one year.

There are a number of interpretative statements that one could make when referring to these data; the following are a few of our favorites. When comparing the authoritative group with the neglectful group on the first six measures that represent beneficial changes, only social competence and GPA are not significantly better in the authoritative group ($p < .05$).

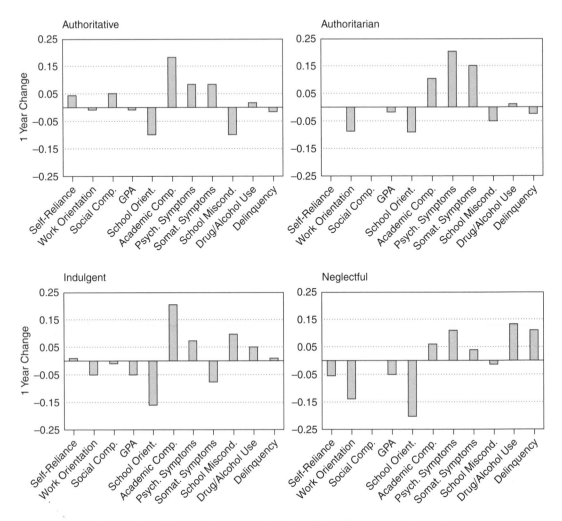

FIGURE 19.2   Change in Adolescent Outcomes Over One Year. Change scores in various outcome measures cover one year of high school for adolescents who reported four different types of parenting style. Scores above the axis indicate an increase in the particular trait over the year. Scores below the axis indicate a decrease in the trait over the year.

Source: From Steinberg, L., Lamborn, S. D., Darling, N. Mounts, N. S., & Dornsbusch, S. M. (1994). Over-time changes in adjustment and comptenece among adoloescents from authoritative, authoritarian, indulgent, and neglectful families. *Child Development, 65,* 763.

Of the last five measures, only psychological symptoms is not statistically different (at the $p < .05$ level or better) when the authoritative group is compared to the neglectful group.

DISCUSSION

The first-year results suggest a tendency toward more beneficial outcomes and lower levels of problem outcomes for the authoritative group of adolescents. Authoritative parenting is associated with better adjustment in adolescents. Both authoritative and authoritarian group students seem to have lower levels of drug or alcohol use than the indulgent group or neglectful group of students. This suggests that strict homes with supervision from parents may inoculate against drug use. In a related finding from a large-scale longitudinal study, Shedler and Block (1990) found that abstaining from drugs was associated with strict parenting from fathers, even though parenting was observed when the children were age 5, and drug use was assessed at age 18. Further, the results presented by Steinberg et al. (1994) indicate that merely being an accepting and involved parent does not inoculate children against drug use; drug use levels were nearly the same in indulgent families, which were involved and accepting, compared to neglectful families which were not.

Looking at the change data, it is tempting to conclude that academic competence thrives in an atmosphere of acceptance and involvement. This finding might seem to be contradicted by the literature about ethnic differences in school achievement and parenting styles which has shown that in Asian-American homes, parents tend to be more authoritarian and children do better in school (Steinberg et al., 1992). In order to resolve this seeming contradiction, it is important to know that this link between authoritarian parenting and school success may only apply to the Asian-Americans and that there are other confounding differences which correlate with ethnicity. Some of these were discussed earlier in Chapter 15. As seen in Figure 19.2, when ethnic groups are not considered separately, it would be difficult to say that authoritarian parenting is associated with any particular advantages. Indeed, among the four groups, it shows a first-year level of reported psychological symptoms similar to neglectful parenting.

Other aspects of the one-year change data are even more striking. If we assume that parenting style has not changed over the year, we can see that the authoritarian group adolescents continue on a behavior trajectory of increasing psychological symptoms during that year. This may be a result of the stress associated with strict parenting that is not mediated by involvement and warmth.

A visual scan of the one-year change data for neglectful parenting implies that the adolescents in this group are continuing to decrease in beneficial outcomes and increase in problem outcomes, perhaps as a result of parental neglect. Of the desirable outcomes, only academic competence increased during the year. However, this increase is smaller than in the other groups. Also, for the neglectful group, problem behaviors all show increases except for school misconduct, which, you will remember, includes tardiness, cheating, and other offenses that might result in a visit to the principal's office. School misconduct, if anything, shows a little improvement. If the adolescents were evaluating their school misconduct based on the number of actual incidents with school officials, this apparent improvement might really only be a matter of undetected malfeasance owing to better covering of tracks.

It is important to remember that in this study parenting styles preceded the data changes shown in Figure 19.2. Because of this, it would be difficult to believe that behavior changes during the year caused the parents to adopt a style such as authoritarian or neglectful. In speculating about these longitudinal outcomes being causally linked to parenting styles, we can probably say that the outcomes are not causing the parenting. Other speculations about cause are impossible to confirm because one cannot perform a true experiment on this topic. However, because there are so many divorces in which children may be assigned, albeit not randomly, to a new parent who may have a different style, there may be an opportunity for future research to collect additional information to clarify the relationship between parenting style and the behavior of offspring.

CRITICAL THINKING TOOLKIT ITEMS

Surveys should report alpha levels or some other statistic, such as a correlation coefficient, to demonstrate internal consistency.

Representativeness of a sample is, to some extent, a judgment that you must make. Some samples may be very carefully chosen to represent a particular population. Even in these cases, your judgment is involved because you may want to generalize the study's findings to people other than the target population under study. This study, for example, looks at adolescents in Wisconsin and Northern California. You might want to tread carefully in generalizing its findings to adolescents living in the South Bronx.

When groups in studies are formed by taking the extreme cases, representativeness is compromised.

Reliability may sometimes be used as an indication of validity in psychological studies, but they are not the same things. For example, politicians may send out highly biased surveys that have questions beginning "Do you want your legislator to help cut wasted expenditures in government by voting for [some specific piece of legislation]." Most people want to cut waste, so the survey might be very internally consistent. It might not be a valid measure of what people really want because of the biased wording of the questions.

Beware of statistically significant differences when sample sizes are very large. Many statistical tests were designed to critically examine small numbers of data points and when confronted with large numbers the tests readily find significant differences, even when the actual difference is so small that it is unimportant. Sometimes the terms *social significance* or *clinical significance* are used to describe the applied, real-world importance of findings when, for whatever reason, statistical tests are not dependable.

REFERENCES

Baumrind, D. (1967). Child care practices anteceding three patterns of preschool behavior. *Genetic Psychology Monographs, 75,* 43–88.

Baumrind, D. (1971). Current patterns of parental authority. *Developmental Psychology Monograph, 4* (1), part 2.

Hetherington, E. M., Clingempeel, W., Anderson, E., Hagan, J., Hollier, E., & Lindner, M. (1992). Coping with marital transitions: A family perspective. *Monographs of the Society for Research in Child Development, 57* (2–3, Serial No. 227).

Lamborn, S., Mounts, N., Steinberg, L., & Dornbusch, S. (1991). Patterns of competence and adjustment among adolescents from authoritative, authoritarian, indulgent, and neglectful homes. *Child Development, 62,* 1049–1065.

Maccoby, E., & Martin, J. (1983) Socialization in the context for the family: Parent-child interaction. In E. M. Hetherington (Ed.) & P. H. Mussen (Series Ed.), *Handbook of child psychology: Vol. 4. Socialization, personality and social development* (pp. 1–101). New York: Wiley.

Rowe, D. C. (1990). As the twig is bent? The myth of child-rearing influences on personality development. *Journal of Counseling & Development, 68,* 606–611.

Scarr, S. (1992). Developmental theories for the 1990s: Development and individual differences. *Child Development, 63,* 1–19.

Shedler, J., & Block, J. (1990). Adolescent drug use and psychological health: A longitudinal inquiry. *American Psychologist, 45,* 612–630.

Steinberg, L., Dornbusch, S., & Brown, B. (1992). Ethnic differences in adolescent achievement: An ecological perspective. *American Psychologist, 47,* 723–729.

Steinberg, L., Lamborn, S. D., Darling, N., Mounts, N. S., & Dornsbusch, S. M. (1994). Over-time charges in adjustment and competence among adolescents from authoritative, authoritarian, indulgent, and neglectful families. *Child Development, 65,* 754–770.

Steinberg, L., Lamborn, S., Dornbusch, S., & Darling, N. (1992). Impact of parenting practices on adolescent achievement: Authoritative parenting, school achievement, and encouragement to succeed. *Child Development, 63,* 1266–1281.

CHAPTER 20

MAKING THE GRADE

Chances are, the last time you heard the words *intervention program* mentioned, it was election time for local, state, or federal policy makers. Recently, the funding of intervention programs has become a hot topic in the political arena. On occasion we even hear these policy makers attempting to sell an intervention program as a panacea for a particular societal problem. (It is usually at this point that we click off C-SPAN and go back to watching *The Simpsons.*) The growth of intervention programs during the past 40 years or so makes the careful and systematic evaluation of these programs all the more relevant. Clearly, people have the right to know if the programs funded by their tax dollars provide a beneficial service to those they are designed to help.

A large percentage of intervention programs are child focused. Although these programs tend to vary considerably in terms of scope and methodology, they can be classified into two major categories: primary preventative or remedial. Primary preventative programs are designed to prevent or buffer such things as the onset of normally occurring deficits in cognitive performance among children from impoverished families. They often are implemented very early in a child's life, usually within the first few months, and continue until the child is ready for formal schooling. Remedial programs are designed to assist school-age children who already have learning deficiencies to overcome these problems. They often focus on the establishment of intellectual skills such as vocabulary building, number learning, and basic problem solving. In contrast, other remedial programs have attempted to enhance children's self-concepts and motivations for academic success.

PROJECT HEAD START

One of the best-known federally funded intervention programs, Project Head Start was designed as primary prevention to prepare impoverished preschool children for later school-age learning. The program, which began in 1965, has attempted to foster impoverished children's social and cognitive development by incorporating several basic elements into their early preschooling. These elements usually include necessities one normally takes for

Incorporating the research of F. Campbell, and C. Ramey, "Effects of Early Intervention on Intellectual and Academic Achievement: A Follow-Up Study of Children from Low-Income Families," 1994, *Child Development, 65,* pp. 684–698.

granted: the involvement of parents in their child's learning experiences, basic needs such as medical care and nutritional supplements, and qualified and competent teachers. Sadly, children from impoverished backgrounds who do not receive early interventions have been shown to possess cognitive, social, and academic achievement deficits (Blair, Ramey, & Hardin 1995; Patterson, Kupersmidt, & Vaden, 1990). In contrast, a variety of studies have shown that children enrolled in Head Start programs experienced some short-term social and intellectual gains which they maintained through the first grade (Brooks-Gunn, 1995; Lee, Brooks-Gunn, & Schnur, 1988; Lee, Brooks-Gunn, Schnur, & Liaw, 1990). Similarly, there have been some positive long-term outcomes associated with these types of intervention programs. For instance, the Consortium for Longitudinal Studies, a group established to evaluate the long-term effects of several different intervention programs, found that children in programs that included early intervention had a lower incidence of being held back in school, and were not assigned to special education classes as frequently as their peers (Lazar, Darlington, Murray, Royce, & Snipper, 1982). However, some of the early cognitive advantages shown by children enrolled in intervention programs have been found to fade over time. In the consortium effort, it was shown that the IQ gains of children in intervention programs persisted for only 3 years, while superior measures of academic achievement were sustained for only 5 to 6 years (Lazar et al., 1982).

Given the fact that long-term intellectual and achievement gains resulting from some intervention programs have not been shown to be consistently maintained over time, it is reasonable for us to question what types of intervention programs increase the probability that these early developmental gains will be long-lasting. Some research has identified important standards for effective early intervention programs. These include early timing of treatment (usually within the first two years of life); long-term intervention with intensive contact hours devoted to intense treatment; the offer of direct care for the child; inclusion of a broad range of social services; recognition of individual differences and an effort to meet varying needs during treatment; support within multiple domains such as parental aid and academic support; and culturally relevant intervention methods (Ramey, Ramey, Gaines, & Blair, 1995).

THE CAROLINA ABECEDARIAN PROJECT

Campbell and Ramey (1994) organized a follow-up study to a longitudinal intervention program known as the Carolina Abecedarian Project. The purpose of the project was to see if active intervention techniques, beginning at infancy, would boost IQ scores and school performance measures in children from impoverished families (Ramey & Campbell, 1984, 1991; Ramey & Haskins, 1981; Ramey, Yeates, & Short, 1984).

Method and Design

Children who were considered to be at high risk for cognitive deficits were selected as participants for the study based on sociodemographic data obtained from social services agencies and public health clinics. Initially, 120 families with mothers who had recently given birth to full-term infants with no preexisting developmental deficits agreed to participate in the study. The total attrition rate throughout the 8-year period of the original study was

18.9 percent. Ninety-eight percent of the participants in the study were African American. The authors state that this trend "reflects both the confounding of poverty and race generally found in the United States and the history of the study site, a university town without many disadvantaged white families" (p. 686). The mean IQ of the mothers was 85 (range 49–124), while their mean maternal age was 19.9 years (range 13–44). The mothers' mean level of education was 10.62 years. The average reported income for the families was none. Only about 25 percent of the children in the study lived with both biological parents; most resided with their mothers, other extended family members, or both.

The newborns were randomly assigned to either a preschool experimental group (E) or a preschool control group (C). Treatment intervention was implemented for participants assigned to the experimental group from early infancy until the end of preschool. The control group received no treatment intervention during this period. Of the original 120 families participating in the study, 8 families (7 E and 1 C) dropped out of the study after learning of their group assignment. Two other children from the control group were excluded from the study due to interference by local authorities, and an additional child was not included after being diagnosed as having biological reasons for developmental delay. A second randomization of the children who remained in the sample took place after the children in both the experimental and control groups had completed preschool. Half of the children in each group were assigned to either a school-age intervention or school-age control group. Thus, four groups were created from the original two following the preschool years:

1. *Experimental-Experimental Group (EE):* children who received both the preschool and school-age interventions.
2. *Experimental-Control Group (EC):* children who received only the preschool intervention.
3. *Control-Experimental Group (CE):* children who received only the school-age intervention.
4. *Control-Control Group (CC):* children who received neither preschool nor school-age interventions.

Children in the preschool experimental group (E) were enrolled in a day-care facility as infants (mean age of enrollment = 4.4 months). The day-care center was open 5 days a week, 8 hours day, for 50 weeks of the year. These children received a treatment intervention that consisted of infant programs designed to boost cognitive, perceptual-motor, language, and social skills (Sparling & Lewis, 1979). When the children were old enough for preschool, the intervention program changed, focusing more on the development of language and preparing children for literacy tasks (Ramey, McGinness, Cross, Collier, & Barrie-Blackley, 1982). The day-care center also provided the children with primary medical care. Efforts were made to involve the children's parents in activities during the preschool program. Family social events were held at the center and parents were encouraged to participate in programs where they received advice on a number of issues including legal matters, nutrition, and behavior management. Social services were available to those parents facing trouble with food, transportation, housing, and so on.

Children in the preschool control group (C) were placed on diets of iron-fortified formula from birth until their 15th week of life. This was done to eliminate early nutritional differences as a potential confound. The researchers also provided parents of the preschool control group with free disposable diapers until the children were toilet-trained. Social work services were also made available to these parents.

When children were old enough to enter kindergarten, school-age treatment was either administered or withheld. Children who received the school-age treatment had a home school resource teacher give them activities designed to increase specific learning skills, usually in reading and math. The children's classroom teachers identified the learning needs to be addressed by these supplemental activities. Parents were visited twice a week and were shown how to use the learning activities with their children. Parents were also encouraged to participate in school events and conferences.

Previous Findings

Numerous IQ tests and measures of school performance were administered to the children over the course of the Carolina Abecedarian Project's 8-year time span. Because we are mainly interested in the follow-up data to this project, our discussion of the early findings of the project will be brief. However, as always, we encourage you to look at the sources yourself (see Martin, Ramey & Ramey, 1990; Ramey and Campbell, 1984, 1991; Ramey, Yeates, & Short, 1984).

At 3 months, the preschool experimental group (E) and the preschool control group (C) showed no significant differences in IQ scores. However, from 18 months until age 8, the E group maintained significantly higher IQ scores than the C group. The E group also scored higher on measures of math ($p < .01$) and reading performance ($p < .001$) than the C group after attending school for 8 years (Ramey & Campbell, 1984, 1991). Finally, there was a significant negative correlation ($r = -.27, p < .01$) between the amount of treatment intervention received by children and how likely they were to be held back in school (Horacek, Ramey, Campbell, Hoffman & Fletcher, 1987), but no significant relationship between treatment intervention and whether a child was viewed as needing special education (Campbell & Ramey, 1994).

Follow-Up Study

Campbell and Ramey (1994) were interested in seeing if the early advantage held by the E group in IQ testing and measures of school performance at age 8 would be maintained following an additional 4 years of school. Accordingly, the children were retested as 12-year-olds on measures of IQ, scholastic achievement, grade retention, and assignment to special education classes.

Ninety participants were involved in the 12-year follow-up, 81 percent of these children had been in the study since its outset. The follow-up also included 93.4 percent of the participants in the EE group who had been assigned to both the preschool and school-age interventions. An additional sample of new 12-year-olds was measured to serve as a comparison for the high-risk longitudinal sample. This additional group was referred to as the local population sample (LPS) and was composed of 56 children randomly selected from the local testing area. This comparison sample was 73 percent white, 19.6 percent African American, and 4 percent Asian American. They came from families with parents who had mostly professional or academic jobs. The same battery of tests was administered to both the longitudinal and LPS samples.

Both samples of 12-year-olds were tested on the Wechsler Intelligence Scale for Children-Revised (WISC-R; Wechsler 1974). As discussed in previous chapters, this test provides a measure of IQ and has been shown to have good reliability and validity. Scholastic achievement was assessed using the Woodcock-Johnson Psychoeducational Battery Part 2: Tests of Academic Achievement (Woodcock & Johnson, 1977). This test provides scores for reading, math, written language, and general knowledge. Measures of grade retention and assignment to special education were taken by examining students' school records using the School Archival Records System (Walker, Block, Todis, Barkley, & Severson, 1988). Placement in special education was coded as follows:

Children were coded 0 if they had not received any form of special education or resource help during their 7 years in school.

Children were coded 1 if they had received a resource service such as a special reading program or had met with the school counselor.

Children were coded 2 if they had been placed into a special education program or had qualified as needing some special resource assistance.

During all testing procedures, the researchers were unaware of the group or groups to which the 12-year-olds had been assigned. Tests were conducted at two different times at a research center during the children's summer break. Parents were also interviewed and they filled out questionnaires about their child and family. All participants were paid for their participation in this follow-up study. Some of the participants' school records could not be located, including 12 of the LPS group members. Records were complete for members of the longitudinal group for all 7 years in school.

RESULTS AND DISCUSSION

IQ scores for all of the children participating in the longitudinal sample from infancy until the 12-year-follow-up are shown in Figure 20.1. When averaged across ages, a significant relationship was found between schooling and children's IQ scores. Children who had been in the preschool treatment had significantly higher IQs ($p < .05$). One of the conclusions suggested by these remarkable data is that school-age interventions may be too late to do much good. You can see this if you look at the results for the preschool control group that was given the intervention at school age. Table 20.1 displays the data for normal, borderline, and mildly retarded individuals in the longitudinal sample.

The 12-year-old longitudinal sample possessed a significantly higher percentage of mildly retarded individuals (IQ < 70) than would be found in the same number of individuals randomly selected from the general population, 2.9 percent compared to 1.15 percent (Robinson & Robinson, 1976). Three individuals were classified as mildly retarded and all of them were members of the preschool control group. There was also a large proportion of individuals who were classified as having borderline IQ scores. In particular, the preschool control group possessed a significantly higher percentage of these borderline cases than the preschool experimental group ($p < .0001$).

A statistical test known as *factor analysis* was performed using the 12-year-olds' IQ test data. The test essentially locates factors that are mathematically similar and clusters

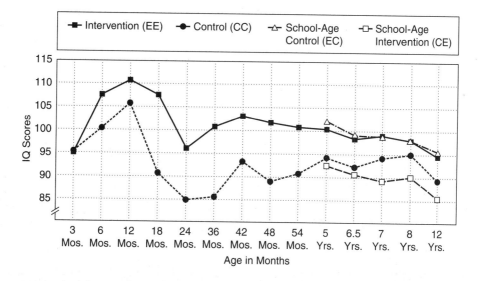

FIGURE 20.1   Longitudinal IQ Results from 3 Months through 12 Years.

Source: From "Effects of Early Intervention on Intellectual and Academic Achievement: A Follow-Up Study of Children from Low Income Families," by F. Campbell and C. Ramey, 1994, *Child Development, 65,* pp. 690–698.

them together in distinct categories. It then seeks out the categories that explain or account for the largest percentage of the variance on any given measure. The statistic called the *variance* was discussed in Chapter 19. It is probably easiest to understand how factor analysis works by imagining that you have to sort a large and diverse sample of fruit into two or three categories based on a few characteristics of your sample. For example, you probably would not end up with a category for fruits with elongated bodies and yellow color because it is unlikely that many different fruits in your sample have these characteristics. In statistical phrasing, not much of the variance in your fruit sample is accounted for by yellow elongation. There is probably only one fruit in the whole pile that varies from the group

TABLE 20.1   Abecedarian Preschool Experimental and Control Groups at Age 12

	IQ Level					
	MILDLY RETARDED (IQ < 70)		BORDERLINE (IQ = 70–85)		NORMAL IQ (IQ ≥ 86)	
	N	%	N	%	N	%
Preschool Group						
Experimental (N = 47)	0	0	6	12.8	41	87.2
Control (N = 43)	3	7.0	16	37.2	24	55.8

Source: From Campbell, F., & Ramey, C. (1994). Effects of early intervention on intellectual and academic achievement: A follow-up study of children from low income families. *Child Development, 65,* 690.

along this dimension. However, you might end up with better, more inclusive, factors such as grows on trees, red, or tropical, which might account for a larger portion of the variance in your sample.

Sixty-eight percent of the variance of the IQ score in the longitudinal sample at age 12 was accounted for by the factor of verbal achievement. This measure included verbal IQ of the longitudinal sample as well as all of the Woodcock and Johnson achievement tests. An additional 13 percent of the variance was explained by the performance IQ score of the longitudinal sample. Performance IQ is the part of the IQ that is supposed to be less dependent on verbal factors.

The researchers conducted a complex statistical analysis on the IQ and achievement test data belonging to the four groups in the longitudinal sample. They found that the intensity and duration of the treatment intervention program significantly impacted how well a child performed across all tests ($p < .02$). Specifically, one can describe this effect as a hierarchy of benefits: (EE > EC > CE > CC). Thus, the EE group, who received both the preschool and school-age interventions outperformed all other groups within the longitudinal sample on measures of IQ and test performance, followed by the EC, CE, and CC groups. This effect was not generalizable to each of the individual subtests on the IQ and achievement tests—it was an overall trend that could be seen only when looking across all test scores of all groups within the longitudinal sample.

We have refrained from presenting the achievement test data for the 12-year-olds because the outcomes were similar to the IQ data. The researchers also tested the extent to which maternal IQ made a difference to the success of the intervention. Past literature has indicated that for families living in poverty, the education and verbal ability of the mother has an impact on the IQ of the child (Brooks-Gunn, Klebanov, & Duncan, 1996). However, in this intervention study Campbell and Ramey (1994) found that although the IQ of mothers is usually a good predictor of the children's IQ, it had little impact on the effects of the treatment intervention. This is important because it suggests that this kind of intervention can be successful regardless of the mother's intellectual level.

Campbell and Ramey (1994) reported that "the intellectual and academic gains from the Abecedarian program persisted through 7 years in school" (p. 694). Perhaps most importantly, the preschool experimental group (E) continued to exceed the preschool control group (C) on measures of intelligence at 12 years of age. This finding suggests that attempts to foster intellectual growth for impoverished children within the first few months of life may lead to longer lasting and more pronounced intellectual gains. Campbell and Ramey (1994) are quick to point out that these results "do not permit a definitive test of the degree to which having intervention during the sensorimotor period might have been critical to the maintenance of an IQ advantage. Only a study with a staggered age at entry could definitively address that question" (p. 694). Nevertheless, these findings have interesting implications for local, state, and federal policies designed to help impoverished families; specifically, that early intervention programs providing quality day care and preschool education are associated with long-term cognitive benefits. Policies that advocate for these forms of early treatment may yield effective outcomes. It may be argued that long-term intervention programs such as the Abecedarian project are expensive to implement; however, if one considers the greater cost of addressing the problems associated with later academic failure, it is easy to see how this primary preventative care would yield long-term savings.

CRITICAL THINKING TOOLKIT ITEMS

It is possible to conduct true experiments designed to investigate socially important problems on people in real-life settings. This type of study is likely to be an immense amount of work but the result is an ability to detect very important cause-and-effect relationships. In the critical evaluation of studies using other research methods it can be useful to ask if an experiment would be possible, given the research question.

REFERENCES

Blair, C., Ramey, C. T., & Hardin, M. (1995). Early intervention for low birthweight premature infants: Participation and intellectual development. *American Journal of Mental Retardation, 99,* 542–554.

Brooks-Gunn, J., Klebanov, P., & Duncan, G. (1996). Ethnic differences in children's intelligence test scores: Role of economic deprivation, home environment, and maternal characteristics. *Child Development, 67,* 396–408.

Brooks-Gunn, J. (1995). Children in families in communities: Risk and intervention in the Bronfenbrenner tradition. In P. Moen, G. H. Edler, & K. Lüscher (Eds.), *Examining lives in context* (pp. 467–519). Washington, DC: American Psychological Association.

Campbell, F., & Ramey, C. (1994). Effects of early intervention on intellectual and academic achievement: A follow-up study of children from low-income families. *Child Development, 65,* 684–698.

Horacek, H. J., Ramey, C. T., Campbell, F. A., Hoffman, K. P., & Fletcher, R. H. (1987). Predicting school failure and assessing early intervention with high-risk children. *American Academy of Child and Adolescent Psychiatry, 26,* 758–763.

Lazar, I., Darlington, R., Murray, H., Royce, J., & Snipper, A. (1982). Lasting effects of early education: A report from the Consortium for Longitudinal Studies. *Monographs of the Society for Research in Child Development, 47* (2–3, Serial No. 195).

Lee, V. E., Brooks-Gunn, J., & Schnur, E. (1988). Does Head Start work? A 1-year follow-up comparison of disadvantaged children attending Head Start, no preschool, and other preschool programs. *Developmental Psychology, 24,* 210–222.

Lee, V. E., Brooks-Gunn, J., Schnur, E., & Liaw, F. (1990). Are Head Start effects sustained? A longitudinal follow-up comparison of disadvantaged children attending Head Start, no preschool, and other preschool programs. *Child Development, 61,* 495–507.

Martin, S. L., Ramey, C. T., & Ramey, S. L. (1990). The prevention of intellectual impairment in children of impoverished families: Findings of a randomized trial of educational day care. *American Journal of Public Health, 80(7),* 844–847.

Patterson, C. J., Kupersmidt, J. B., & Vaden, N. A. (1990). Income level, gender, ethnicity, and household composition as predictors of children's school-based competence. *Child Development, 61,* 485–494.

Ramey, C. T., & Campbell, F. A. (1984). Preventive education for high-risk children: Cognitive consequences of the Carolina Abecedarian Project. *American Journal of Mental Deficiency, 88,* 515–523.

Ramey, C. T., & Campbell, F. A. (1991). Poverty, early childhood education, and academic competence: The Abecedarian experiment. In A. Huston, (Ed.), *Children reared in poverty* (pp. 190–221). New York: Cambridge University Press.

Ramey, C. T., & Haskins, R. (1981). The causes and treatment of social failure: Insights from the California Abecedarian Project. In M. Begab, H. Garber, & H. C. Haywood (Eds.), *Causes and prevention of retarded development in psychosocially disadvantaged children* (pp. 89–112). Baltimore: University Park Press.

Ramey, C. T., McGinness, G. D., Cross, L., Collier, A. M., & Barrie-Blackley, S. (1982). The Abecedarian approach to social competence: Cognitive and linguistic intervention for disadvantaged preschoolers. In K. Borman (Ed.), *The social life of children in a changing society* (pp. 145–174). Hillsdale, NJ: Erlbaum.

Ramey, C. T., Ramey, S. L., Gaines, K. R., & Blair, C. (1995). Two-generation early intervention programs: A child development perspective. In S. Smith, (Ed.), *Two-generation programs for families in poverty: A new intervention strategy* (pp. 202–215). Norwood, NJ: Ablex.

Ramey, C. T., Yeates, K. O., & Short, E. J. (1984). The plasticity of intellectual development: Insights from early intervention. *Child Development, 55,* 1913–1925.

Robinson, N. M., & Robinson, H. B. (1976). *The mentally retarded child: A psychological approach* (2nd ed.). New York: McGraw-Hill.

Sparling, J. J., & Lewis, I. (1979). *Learning games for the first three years: A guide to parental child play.* New York: Walker.

Walker, H., Block, A., Todis, B., Barkley, M., & Severson, H. (1988). *The school archival records search* (SARS). Eugene: Oregon Research Institute.

Wechsler, D. (1974). *Wechsler Intelligence Scale for Children—Revised.* New York: Psychological Corp.

Woodcock, R. W., & Johnson, M. B. (1977). *Woodcock-Johnson Psychoeducational Battery Part 2: Tests of Academic Achievement.* Hingham, MA: Teaching Resources Corp.

CHAPTER 21

WHO'S OLD FIRST?

In comparison to the study of children and elderly persons, the study of normal free-living adults has presented a considerable challenge to developmental psychologists. Often, it is hard to find populations of adults who are available and willing to participate in time-consuming psychological research. In contrast, at both extremes of the life span, participants are easier to find. Populations of young people are generally concentrated in some sort of school system while elderly adults may be institutionalized or, at least, have sufficient leisure time to volunteer as participants in psychological studies. For the purposes of some studies, college students are used to represent young adults. In Chapter 10, "Reach for the Sky," college students were compared to younger people in ability to estimate affordances. In that study, college students may have been a reasonable comparison group of adults for the cross-sectional prediction of ability estimation. We see no particular reason why being a college student would make one better or worse at affordance judging than any other group of young adults.

COLLEGE STUDENTS AS PARTICIPANTS

Because college students are so commonly used as participants in psychological studies, it should be part of your critical thinking toolkit to seek this information. You should assess for yourself if this sampling technique is likely to have affected the results in some important way. There are a number of criteria that you can use in making this decision, but one way to approach it is to ask yourself how much difference would it make to your evaluation of the study if the participants were randomly selected young adults rather than college students. In some studies it might make little difference; in others it might make quite a bit.

Probably no one would make the general assertion that college students are representative of the general population of young American adults. The age range of college students distributes in an unusual way. According to the Website of the U.S. Department of Education, the distribution of four-year college student ages is bimodal, with about the same number of 18- to 19-year-old students as students age 35 and older. Also, many college

Incorporating the research of R. Schulz, D. Musa, J. Staszewski, & R. S. Siegler, "The Relationship Between Age and Major League Baseball Performance: Implications for Development," 1994, *Psychology and Aging, 9,* pp. 274–286.

students are probably unrepresentative young adults because they tend to come from moderate to high socioeconomic status (SES) backgrounds and are often financially secure. They can find the money for college and, in many cases, they can afford to forestall entry into the world of work while they study. On the other hand, students who must study and work full-time, sometimes while also meeting family responsibilities, are heroes in managing multiple pursuits. The motivation they demonstrate sets them apart from their age mates in another way. As a group, college students also have higher IQs than the population at large.

Of course, college students may be the participants of choice if the reason for the study is some aspect of student behavior such as academic attributions (Peterson & Barrett, 1987; Jones, Slate, Marini, & DeWater, 1993), student alcohol consumption (Gross, 1993), fraternity membership (Montgomery & Haemmerlie, 1993), student sexuality (Roche & Ramsbey, 1993; Hays & Hays, 1992), or student stress (Engelmann, Krupka, & Vener, 1993). We raise this issue to present you with one more avenue for critical thinking, particularly when studies purport to investigate adulthood.

GETTING OLD

When do we start to get old? This question might be easier to address if *getting old* is defined as "showing declines in measurable physical or cognitive domains." The notion of disability or decline is, unfortunately, what is popularly and stereotypically understood as the experience of growing old. Physical and cognitive performance do become more limited as people age, but the extent of these changes is often overstated. Many research studies indicate that, for most people, measurable declines begin somewhere between age 20 and 30. Often, these decrements begin so slowly that they are difficult to detect at first. Not surprisingly, early physical deficits are more noticeable in top athletes because their performances may be measured for strength or time and to tolerances as close as hundredths of a second. For example, the strength and flexibility of female gymnasts peaks very early in life, and many of them seem to be already well past this peak by the time they are 18 years old.

A number of physiological factors contribute to the changes that can be observed in early adulthood. After about age 30, basal metabolic rate begins to fall, as does maximum breathing capacity. These declines influence the amount of nutrients and oxygen that are available for vigorous activity. Falling metabolic rate may mean that appetite for food decreases, making it very important for adults to be sure that the calories they consume contain adequately balanced nutrition. Also, the reduction in metabolic rate can pose an added risk for adults. Unless they lower their caloric intake while in their 20s, they are likely to put on weight, and perhaps become obese. Cardiac output typically peaks a little later than age 20, decreasing the rate of blood circulation and, consequently, limiting the transport of nutrients and oxygen to muscles. Beginning at about age 40, the brain begins to show decreases in weight. Further, the conduction velocity of the neurons in the body begins to decrease. All of these trends will continue across the life span. By about age 75, the average person may have experienced a 10 percent decrease in brain weight, a 15 percent decrease in nerve conduction velocity, a 20 percent decrease in basal metabolic rate, a 30 percent decrease in cardiac output, and a 50 percent decrease in maximum breathing capacity (Leaf, 1973).

There are a number of theories about why these changes happen. These theories are not mutually exclusive: Confirming one of them does not have any bearing on the correctness of the others. It is likely that many factors contribute to the changes that occur as adults get older (Schneider, 1993). These factors represent different levels of influence. They range in size from things as small as molecules to things as large as the sun. One of the molecules that has been implicated is DNA. The role of genetic material was discussed earlier in Chapter 12. An amazing set of instructions, DNA is actually a molecule 6 feet long and 250 millionths of an inch wide (L. Hayflick cited in Schaie & Willis, 1996). One idea about its role in aging is that DNA gradually becomes damaged, either spontaneously or owing to externally caused mutations. DNA contains instructions for body maintenance and frequently makes copies of itself. Errors in copying, called *mutations,* accumulate, affecting cell replacement and repair (Kanugo, 1994).

Based on what we know about DNA, it is not surprising that the composition of body tissue changes as people get older. One of the ways this happens is that normally separate fibers become connected, or *cross-linked,* making the entire tissue less elastic or flexible (Arking, 1991). Regular exercise and good diet will postpone, but not eliminate, these effects. It is easy to imagine the role of cross-linkage in the decrements of aging if you consider how important it is for the heart and lungs to retain flexibility. Unless they can stretch adequately, they cannot work well. Recently, considerable attention has focused on changes in endocrine function. These changes are believed to be key factors in the declines associated with aging because hormones affect the body in so many ways. For example, it has been found that age-related decreases in growth hormones are associated with increases in body fat and muscle loss (Corpas, Harman, & Blackman, 1993).

A considerable amount of literature in developmental psychology has focused on the effects of aging (see, for example, Schaie & Willis, 1996). Physical declines are evident and have been well documented in elderly people (Holliday, 1995), but little is known about the age at which these declines start to appear. If you were to study the beginning of age-related declines you would have to confront the difficulties of trying to recruit young adults and middle-aged adults willing to cooperate. If practical constraints did not exist, imagine your ideal population for a study of this nature. For instance, it would be nice to have individuals who are all physically fit so that the variance owing to illness or "couch potatoism" would not disrupt your study. Further, these ideal participants should undertake a variety of measurable physical tasks and you should keep meticulous records of their performances across a substantial portion of the life span. This would enable you to make both cross-sectional and longitudinal comparisons. Also, you would probably want some assurance that each individual was trying very hard to achieve peak output in the tasks being measured, so that variance due to motivational factors would be minimal.

We have previously noted that part of the fun of psychological research is in finding research methodologies that provide stunningly clever approaches to important questions. We believe that research reported by Schulz, Musa, Staszewski, and Siegler (1994) falls in this category. They managed to collect data on a sample of people who meet all the constraints for our ideal study of physical performance. Schulz et al. used the extensive and detailed records that are kept on the game performances of major league baseball players. Their source for all the data in this study was *The Baseball Encyclopedia* (Macmillan, 1990). Depending on exactly what is done in a particular study, there might be a number of ways to describe this type of research method. Nevertheless, the primary methodology seen here is usually described as an *archival study*.

We are aware that some of our readers will know the game of baseball very well and that others will have less knowledge of the rules and terms used in the game. We assume that you know something about the general way in which baseball is played. For those who know little about the sport, there are many sources for general information. If you know little and want to know more, we suggest you ask a friend who understands the game. We have found that it is very easy to find people who are eager to talk about baseball, but be careful because it can be a bit difficult to get some of them to stop talking about it.

For our purposes, we have minimized definitions of baseball procedures and statistics. As a contribution to developmental psychology, most of the behaviors, and the statistics that describe them, can be viewed as indicators of performance at a particular age. We will focus on the patterns of change, rather than on the definitional nuances. For example, there may be a number of reasons why a player might "walk," that is, get on base without having to hit the ball and run. In some circumstances, it may be to the benefit of the pitcher to allow this to happen. Nevertheless, the more usual goal of a pitcher should be to keep batters from getting on base. Overall, we might expect good pitchers to allow few batters to walk, although we understand that a superior hitter might sometimes be walked to get him out of the way.

THE SAMPLE

In other chapters we have used the term *participants* to describe the individuals who were being studied. In this case, the term *sample* seems more apt because their contribution to the study was a statistical description of behavior in a public setting. The sample was drawn from men who were playing in the major leagues of baseball in the year 1965. This year was chosen as a defining characteristic because the players who were active at that time had not been playing through previous disruptive events such as World War II. In addition, this sample avoided major changes in the rules and procedures of the game. There were 699 such players active in 1965. The sample was further restricted to players who had at least 10 years of play in the major leagues; a little over half of the active players met the 10-year criterion. The final sample included 153 pitchers and 235 hitters.

RESULTS AND DISCUSSION

The statistics kept for hitters largely reflect the performance of the hitters themselves. In contrast, pitchers' performances were most often operationally defined by recording the batters' responses to pitches. As the pitchers' performances get better, the batters facing them do worse: They strike out more and they get fewer hits and runs. They are, after all, on different teams competing to win the game. Performance measures for pitchers include striking out batters, pitching balls that were hit by batters, and pitching in such a way that batters were able to walk.

The hitters' peak annual number of at bats and hits and the pitchers' peak number of games pitched all occurred at age 27. We would expect a baseball team to use its best players the most, so this cross-sectional analysis suggested that in an overall sense the skills important to the game are best in 27-year-old players.

Twenty-seven was also the median age among hitters for peak performance in hits, batting average, slugging average, home runs, and stolen bases. These are measures that require physical strength and agility. Hits measures what you would expect: hits. Batting average divides hits by times at bat, slugging average assesses the power of the hit because it takes account of how many bases can be traveled on a single hit. Home runs is another assessment of hitting power and stolen bases measures running speed with an additional component of risk taking. Figure 21.1 shows cross-sectional data for the peak ages of three hitter performance measures: batting average, home runs, and stolen bases. It is likely that these players were working very hard to play to the best of their ability. If so, then the decline seen after age 27 may be a valid indication of the zenith of physical ability in adulthood, at least for the kinds of activity represented by the measures depicted.

In contrast, the number of times a hitter gets on base without hitting, or walks, peaks at an average age of 30. In order to walk, the hitter must avoid swinging at four pitches that did not travel directly over the small area of home plate. It is possible that the older hitter is more likely to walk because he is more cautious and restrained in swinging as well as more skilled in determining which pitches are to one side or the other of the plate. Caution and judgment of pitch trajectory are different kinds of skills than the sheer physical prowess involved in hitting a home run or slugging.

The quality of the hitters' work on the field in helping his team to achieve outs against the other team also peaks at an average of 30 years of age. This measure involves a number of skills such as running to catch a hit ball, catching it, and throwing it over long distances, as well as considerable judgment under pressure. It should be noted that many of the measures of hitter behavior were quite strongly correlated with each other; for example, strikeouts were negatively correlated with hits ($r = -.41$) because if a player hit the ball, he usually did not strike out. However, among all hitters, the measures of hitting were uncorrelated with fielding; these were independent assessments of

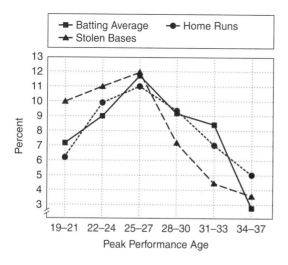

FIGURE 21.1   Percent of Hitters Peaking by Age. Cross-sectional depiction of peak performance for 235 baseball hitters on the skill measures of batting average, home runs, and stolen bases. Each data point represents the percent of hitters whose peak performance in a particular skill occurred at the ages shown on the x axis.

Source: From Schulz, R., Musa, D., Staszewski, J., & Siegler, R. S. (1994). The relationship between age and major league baseball performance: Implications for development. *Psychology and Aging 9*, 274–286.

performance. In other words, good hitters were not necessarily good fielders. Independence is important because it suggests that the skills did not all depend on a single factor, such as physical strength. Data for walking, also called base on balls, and fielding are found in Figure 21.2.

You can see that although the mean age is 30, some players continue to get better after that age. We have graphed these together because although they are distinct aspects of the game of baseball, the patterns of peak years appear quite similar. The contrasting shape of the data distributions in Figure 21.1 and Figure 21.2 suggests that baseball is composed of skills that peak at different points in adulthood. The data in these two figures are, after all, from the same group of hitters.

For pitchers, 27 was the median age for strikeouts. In order to strike a batter out, we presume that pitches must be fast and precise. In hits allowed and walks allowed, where low numbers mean better pitching, the pitchers' best performances were later at age 30 and 31 respectively. This may be a result of the mastery that comes with repeated practice of a skill. Eventually mastery from practice begins to be moderated by the effects of aging. It is important to note that these data described the best performance for players. Mastery from practice does not continue to increase beyond age 31 for most of the skills measured in this study. Earned run average, or ERA, is a measure of runs scored by batters against a pitcher. Effectively, it is a measure of pitching quality: the lower, the better. The cross-sectional pattern peaks in ERAs among pitchers is quite similar to hits allowed and strikeouts. Ages at which the pitchers peaked for these skills are shown in Figure 21.3.

In another cross-sectional analysis, the authors divided the entire sample of players into thirds based on ability groupings derived from the hitters' lifetime batting averages and the pitchers' ERAs. For the skills of hitters, trends were difficult to detect. In general, the best players achieved their peak hitting skills a bit later in their lives than less skilled players. This trend was more pronounced for the pitcher's skills where the least skilled players hit their performance peak at an earlier age for all of the pitching skills examined. A further analysis was undertaken by examining the small group (hitters, $N = 18$; pitchers, $N = 12$) who had been inducted into the Baseball Hall of Fame as a separate group. These players

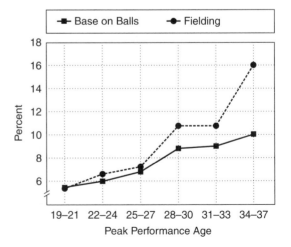

FIGURE 21.2   Percent of Hitters Peaking by Age. Cross-sectional depiction of peak performance for 235 baseball hitters on the skill measures of base on balls (walks) and fielding. Each data point represents the percent of hitters whose peak performance in a particular skill occurred at the ages shown on the *x* axis.

Source: From Schulz, R., Musa, D., Staszewski, J., & Siegler, R. S. (1994). The relationship between age and major league baseball performance: Implications for development. *Psychology and Aging 9,* 274–286.

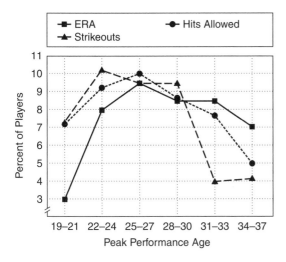

FIGURE 21.3 Percent of Pitchers Peaking by Age. Cross-sectional depiction of peak performance for 153 baseball pitchers on the skill measures of earned run averages (ERAs), hits allowed to batters while pitching, and strikeouts. Each data point represents the percent of hitters whose peak performance in a particular skill occurred at the ages shown on the *x* axis.

Source: From Schulz, R., Musa, D., Staszewski, J., & Siegler, R. S. (1994). The relationship between age and major league baseball performance: Implications for development. *Psychology and Aging 9,* 274–286.

probably represented the best players in the sample. In most performance categories, these select players were at their skill peaks later than the other players.

Because of the nature of the data set, it was also possible to see longitudinal trends in the data. These were particularly important because beyond this kind of sample it is quite difficult to collect longitudinal measures of adult physical development on most groups of people. Imagine trying to collect good data on tasks that involve considerable physical effort for a large longitudinal sample of ordinary adults over a span of 20 years.

The longitudinal data showing that the better players had longer careers can be seen in Figure 21.4. In career length, the bottom, middle, and top groups of hitters were significantly different from each other ($p < .05$), and the Hall of Fame hitters were significantly different from all other players combined ($p < .05$). For the Hall of Famers, there was a slight tendency to begin major league play earlier, but most of the differences seen in career length were the result of better players playing longer. For pitchers, the bottom group was significantly different from both the middle and the top groups ($p < .05$) but the latter two

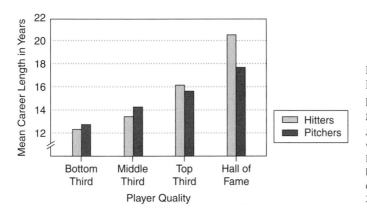

FIGURE 21.4 Mean Career Length. Mean career length of 153 pitchers and 235 hitters shown in groups of different player quality.

Source: From Schulz, R., Musa, D., Staszewski, J., & Siegler, R. S. (1994). The relationship between age and major league baseball performance: Implications for development. *Psychology and Aging 9,* 274–286.

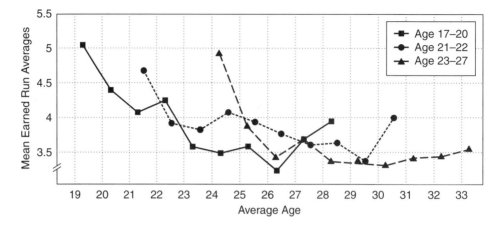

FIGURE 21.5 Mean Earned Run Average by Age. Longitudinal analysis of earned run average (ERA) for 153 baseball pitchers divided into groups based on age of starting play in the major leagues.

Source: From Schulz, R., Musa, D., Staszewski, J., & Siegler, R. S. (1994). The relationship between age and major league baseball performance: Implications for development. *Psychology and Aging 9*, 274–286.

groups were not significantly different from each other. Again, as with hitters, the Hall of Fame pitchers had significantly longer careers than the group of all other players combined ($p < .05$).

Another longitudinal analysis undertaken by Schulz et al. (1994) examined career performance for pitchers and hitters. When the pitcher sample was divided into three age cohorts based on the age at which they started in the major leagues, it can be seen in Figure 21.5 that ERAs started quite high for all groups. (If you are not a baseball fan, remember that this is a negative statement about early pitching skill: ERA refers to the number of runs scored by the other team while a particular pitcher was pitching). The pitchers improved quite a bit in the first year or two of play, compared to the amount of improvement seen across the rest of the career. Following this initial burst of improvement, there were slower gains through most of the rest of the career. The two younger starting cohorts showed worsening ERAs in the last year of the career and the oldest starting cohort showed a reversal in the final 3 years.

Starting age cohort data using batting averages from the hitters are shown in Figure 21.6. The hitters also showed improvement in the first years of their careers. As with the pitchers, this was followed by a period of comparatively stable skill performance. At the end of the career, there is a small decline. It is not possible to determine if the small declines at the ends of both hitters' and pitchers' careers would have become larger if these athletes had remained in play for a few more years. It is reasonable to assume that the slips in performance signaled the end of the career and were one of the reasons for retirement from the game.

The hitters' data in Figure 21.6 might be more interesting to those who follow baseball than to developmental psychologists if it were not so well mirrored by the ERA statistics from the pitchers found in Figure 21.5. Batting average and ERAs are composed

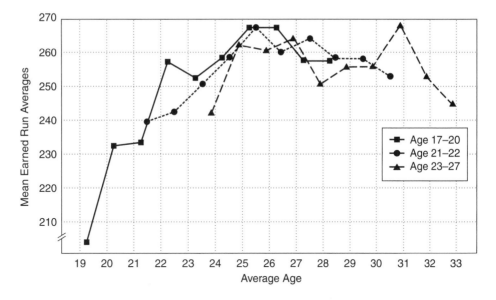

FIGURE 21.6   Mean Batting Average by Age. Longitudinal analysis of batting average for 235 baseball hitters divided into groups based on age of starting play in the major leagues.

Source: From Schulz, R., Musa, D., Staszewski, J., & Siegler, R. S. (1994). The relationship between age and major league baseball performance: Implications for development. *Psychology and Aging 9,* 274–286.

of two quite different sets of skills and they were collected from players with different primary roles in the game. Nevertheless, both of them show improvements until players are in their mid-20s, followed by more stable performance for a few years and declines when the players are in their 30s.

The declines that were found by Schulz et al. (1994) for baseball players correspond to those found in other research on early adults. Although declines can be seen when careful measurements are taken, they probably do not have much or any influence on the daily lives of most people around 30 years old. Psychologists make a distinction between primary and secondary aging. *Primary aging* refers to the universal and nonreversible changes that occur to all organisms as they get older. *Secondary aging* describes illnesses or other disabling conditions that are commonly a part of aging, but which vary from person to person owing to different individual histories of factors such as health habits and genetics. In the baseball players, we have seen the beginning of primary aging. The onset and course of secondary aging would be expected in people older than this group.

In thinking about aging, it is important not to fall into ageism, the prejudice in which people are presumed to have certain characteristics simply because of their age. Ageism can be applied to people of any age. The *terrible twos* is ageist in making the suggestion that all two-year olds are difficult. Likewise, beliefs that teenagers are irresponsible or hormone-driven are ageist. Ageist stereotypes may be more harmful to adults, particularly when the adults themselves adopt prejudices about aging. Ageism may lead younger adults to give up on physical challenges with excuses such as "I'm not a kid any more." In older adults, ageism may include erroneous assumptions about the effects of primary and secondary aging. Physical declines start in early adulthood and continue through life, but there is no reason why most people should expect this trend to be the beginning of illness and disability that threaten an active and independent life in later adulthood.

CRITICAL THINKING TOOLKIT ITEMS

When participants are adults or young adults, determine if they were college students. If they were, assess the extent to which this may limit the generalizability of study findings to adults who are not college students.

REFERENCES

Arking, R. (1991). *Biology of aging.* Englewood Cliffs, N.J.: Prentice-Hall.

Corpas, E., Harman, S. M., & Blackman, M. R. (1993). Human growth hormone and human aging. *Endocrine Reviews, 14,* 20–39.

Engelmann, M., Krupka, L., & Vener, A. (1993). Health-related behavior and somatic stress among college students. *College Student Journal, 27,* 274–283.

Gross, W. (1993). Gender and age differences in college students' alcohol consumption. *Psychological Reports, 72,* 211–216.

Hays, H., & Hays, J. (1992). Students' knowledge of AIDS and sexual risk behavior. *Psychological Reports, 71,* 649–650.

Holliday, R. (1995). *Understanding aging.* Cambridge, England: Cambridge University Press.

Jones, C., Slate, J., Marini, I., & DeWater, B. (1993). Academic skills and attitudes towards intelligence. *Journal of College Student Development, 34,* 422–424.

Kanugo, M. S. (1994). *Genes and aging.* New York: Cambridge University Press.

Leaf, A. (1973). Growing old. *Scientific American, 229,* 44–52.

Macmillian Publishing Co. (1990). *The baseball encyclopedia* (8th ed.). New York: Author.

Montgomery, R., & Haemmerlie, F. (1993). Undergraduate adjustment to college drinking behavior and fraternity membership. *Psychological Reports, 73,* 801–802.

Peterson, C., & Barrett, L. (1987). Explanatory style and academic performance among university freshmen. *Journal of Personality and Social Psychology, 53,* 603–607.

Roche, J., & Ramsbey, T. (1993). Premarital sexuality: A five-year follow-up study of attitudes and behavior by dating stage. *Adolescence, 28,* 67–80.

Schaie, W. K., & Willis, S. L. (1996). *Adult development and aging* (4th ed.). New York: HarperCollins.

Schneider, E. L. (1993). Biological theories of aging. In R. L. Sprott, R. W. Huber, & T. F. Williams (Eds.), *The biology of aging* (pp. 3–12). New York: Springer.

Schulz, R., Musa, D., Staszewski, J., & Siegler, R. S. (1994). The relationship between age and major league baseball performance: Implications for development. *Psychology and Aging, 9,* 274–286.

CHAPTER 22

LET'S SEE WHAT THIS BABY CAN DO

The primary research we discuss in this chapter involves the impact of a new baby on the relationship of the parents. In addition to this topic, we want to provide some context about the institution of marriage. Some version of marriage is found in all societies. Nevertheless, the cultural phrasing of marriage is highly variable in different societies. Americans and members of other developed Western cultures are likely to believe that love is essential for a good marriage. These industrialized cultures have been labeled *individualistic cultures* because the main concern is with one's own interests and those of the immediate family. In contrast, *collective societies* are those in which people conform more to the expectations of larger groups, such as extended families, tribes, or clans. These larger groups look after the welfare of the individual in return for loyalty. In collective societies, love is considered to be less important than the opinions of family members, often based on the economic or social advantages of the marriage (Levine, Sato, Hashimoto, & Verma, 1995).

Almost 90 percent of Americans get married at least once during their lives, typically before age 30 (Michael, Gagnon, Laumann, & Kolata, 1994). While this percentage has remained high over time, there have been a number of changes in other statistics about marriage. In the past 50 years, there has been a trend toward people waiting longer to get married. In 1950, the average age of first marriage for women and men, respectively, was 20.3 years and 22.8 years. By the mid-1990s these ages had increased to 24.5 and 26.5 (U.S. Bureau of the Census, 1996).

Longitudinal research has shown that compared to unmarried individuals, married people are more likely to live longer, are less likely to be ill, are less prone to mental illness, and are likely to score high on measures of general psychological well-being (Friedman et al., 1995). As a group, people with the least favorable levels of these variables are those who were formerly married; that is, people who are widowed or divorced. Never married people have intermediate scores on well-being, falling between the scores for formerly married and those for married people (Ross, Mirowsky & Goldsteen, 1990).

Incorporating the research of T. H. Monk, M. J. Essex, N. A. Smider, M. H. Klein, K. K. Lowe, and D. J. Kupfer, "The Impact of the Birth of a Baby on the Time Structure and Social Mixture of a Couple's Daily Life and Its Consequences for Well-Being," 1996, *Journal of Applied Psychology, 26,* pp. 1237–1258.

Recently, what might be called the *happiness gap* between never married and married people is closing. Today, young adults are happier being never married than young adults decades ago. In contrast, young married people have become less happy over the decades. Part of the reason for this latter trend may be that women enter marriage with an increased expectation that they will be equal partners, only to discover the reality of a more traditional relationship in marriage (Lee, Seccombe, & Shehan, 1991). More men than women report that they are happily married (Levenson, Carstenson, & Gottman, 1993). This may be because wives still do most of the housework. Even in dual earner households, husbands spend only about a third as many hours doing housework as wives (Starrels, 1994).

Because people are getting married later, there are more single persons among young adults and this may help to account for the increased satisfaction of never married people. They are less likely to see themselves as unusual. The reasons commonly given for singlehood are occupational goals, disappointing past relationships, and failure to meet "the right person" (Dalton, 1992).

There are also a variety of lifestyles available to contemporary adults. Cohabitation of opposite sex individuals in America has increased dramatically. Overall, the estimates have changed from 500,000 cohabiting couples in 1970 to 3.5 million in 1994. The biggest percentage increase in cohabitation has been among adults in the 25-to-44 age range. The 1994 frequency of cohabitation was 15 times greater than in 1970 (U.S. Bureau of the Census, 1994). Even though cohabitants say that getting used to living with each other provides a firm foundation for subsequent marriage, the data collected over past decades indicates that higher quality marriages are not associated with previous cohabitation. However, as the number of cohabitants has increased in recent years, the quality of subsequent marriages among them has increased.

Young adults may have other lifestyles, for example, cohabiting as gay or lesbian couples. At the time of this writing, legal marriage is not possible for these couples, even though their relationships may be very long-lasting. Blumstein and Schwartz (1983) found that married couples were less likely to break up in the first 10 years of the relationship, but beyond 10 years the percentage of breakups was about the same for gay couples as for married couples. These researchers also attempted to compare gay couples with heterosexual cohabitants. While they had difficulty in finding long-lasting heterosexual cohabitants, they experienced no difficulty in finding numbers of gay couples who had been together more than 10 years.

Of course, it is not only the cohabitation relationships that break up. Divorce is also common. The United States has the highest rate of divorce of any major country; about half of the new marriages in the United States break up. In industrialized countries such as Canada, Sweden, Great Britain, and Australia about one third of marriages end in divorce. Others countries such as Japan, Spain, Israel, and Italy have divorce rates of less than one in five (U.S. Bureau of the Census, 1996). A number of researchers have studied the reasons why the United States has so many troubled marriages. Chapter 28 explores cognitive similarity between partners in long-term relationships.

Young people, represented by college students, have a number of beliefs about marriage, some of which have been found to be apochryphal (Bernard, 1981). Among these mistaken ideas are the notions that

> quality of sex life is the best predictor of marital satisfaction
>
> marital satisfaction is likely to increase during the first year
>
> a spouse should be able to detect unspoken unhappiness in a partner
>
> a spouse should love a marriage partner regardless of behavior

If couples expect these statements to be true, they may be in for disappointments.

Because marriage is by far the modal pattern for Americans, considerable research has investigated factors associated with marital satisfaction in young people (Levenson et al., 1993; McGoldrick, Heiman & Carter, 1993, Russell & Wells, 1994; Skolnick, 1981). Satisfied marriage partners are likely to be

> similar in religion, education, socioeconomic status (SES) and age
>
> at least 20 years old
>
> thoroughly acquainted and seeing each other for at least 6 months
>
> warm and positive in relationships with in-laws
>
> from families with stable marital patterns
>
> secure financially
>
> good at conflict resolution and nonimpulsive
>
> childless for a while with no pregnancy until after first year of marriage

As suggested by the last item, a new baby may be a delightful diversion, but it can also be a source of strain and change in a marriage. Many young people have no experience in child rearing before they become parents themselves. Most of the other important roles of early adulthood, such as those associated with employment, are accompanied by substantial training. For some people there may be no formal training at all for parenthood; for most others, the training is far less than in other life domains, for example, in job-related tasks (Rossi, 1982). We doubt that any adults, married or not, are fully prepared for all the changes that are associated with the birth of a new baby.

Past research has typically surveyed new parents, usually first-time parents, and collected their perceptions about postnatal side effects such as loss of sleep, decrease in leisure activities, and lack of time alone with spouse. Typically, such studies have considered mothers and ignored fathers. In general, research on stress has pointed to the problems associated with sudden changes in daily routines and the extent to which such disruptions may affect emotional well-being. Problems are particularly likely if the stress is long-term, as it would be for the birth of a child (Lazarus, 1990).

Studies in the past have tended to rely on retrospective memories that may well be inaccurate. In an attempt to overcome this and other problems of past studies, Monk, Essex, et al., (1996) used a different technique to collect information. They used an instrument called the Social Rhythm Metric (SRM; Monk, Kupfer, Frank, & Ritenour, 1991). The SRM is a diary-like psychological data collection device that has been used for studies of depression, bereavement, and advancing age (Monk, Essex, et al., 1996). Records are kept by the participant of daily events for a total of 7 or 14 days. The instrument lists 17 events that are likely to happen in a day. The time of each event is recorded, as is the presence of any other people who might be included in the activity. These events are shown in Table 22.1.

TABLE 22.1   List of Activities from the Wisconsin SRM

Out of bed	Take an afternoon nap
First contact (in person or by phone) with another person	Have dinner
	Physical exercise
First contact with new baby	Have an evening snack/drink
Have morning beverage	Watch TV news program
Have breakfast	Watch another TV program
Go outside for the first time	Activity A (_____)
Start work, school, housework, volunteer activities, child or family care	Activity B (_____)
	Return home (last time)
Have lunch	Go to bed

Source: From Monk, T. H., Essex, M. J., Smider, N. A., Klein, M. H., Lowe, K. K., & Kupfer, D. J. (1996). The impact of the birth of a baby on the time structure and social mixture of a couple's daily life and its consequences for well being. *Journal of Applied Psychology, 26,* 1237–1258.

The activities appear on a checklist with a column to check if the activity did not occur, a column for time, and some columns to record other people actively involved, or merely present, during the activity.

HYPOTHESES

Monk, Essex, et al. (1996) had six hypotheses about the effects of a new baby on a family:

Hypothesis 1. The birth of a child would change the habitual times with which parents performed various activities of daily life.

Hypothesis 2. The daily lives of mothers and fathers would be differentially affected by the birth, leading to a separation between them in habitual activity times.

Hypothesis 3. The birth would result in fewer activities being done completely alone by either parent.

Hypothesis 4. The birth would result in fewer activities being done by the couple together, on their own.

Hypothesis 5. The birth would result in fewer activities involving the presence of nonfamily persons.

Hypothesis 6. The birth would have, on average, greater impact on mothers than on fathers, and on first-time parents than on experienced parents. (p. 1240)

PARTICIPANTS

The participants were recruited through five clinics. One was a clinic designed to assist low-income parents, two clinics were at a university hospital, and two were health maintenance organization clinics. All participants were part of a larger study, the Wisconsin Maternity Leave and Health Project (WMLH). In order to be included, at the beginning of the study all female participants had to be over the age of 18 and between 12 and 21 weeks pregnant. Disabled females were not included and all participants had to be living with the baby's father, married or not. The women had to be employed, on leave from work, or career homemakers, but they could not classify themselves as unemployed and looking for work. Students were excluded from the study as well. The male participants were the partners of the female participants who claimed to be the fathers of the babies born in the study.

Eighty-three couples from the WMLH were willing to participate in the diary study using the SRM. Ten of these were screened out because of events such as change in employment status. By the end of the data collection, 37 couples were left who had remained eligible throughout the study and who had completed all of the diary SRM checklists required by the study.

Three of the couples in the study were other than Caucasian and three were unmarried. Mean age for the women was 29.5 years (range = 20 to 40 years), while for the men it was 32 years (range = 21 to 45 years). Slightly more than half of the men and women had attended some college and the mean income was $46,041 (range = $15,000 to $104,000)

PROCEDURE

Participants were asked to complete a 14-day SRM at each of four different times surrounding the birth of their child. They were given an initial training session in how to use the SRM and a few refresher instructions about its use at each subsequent measurement time. Diary entries were made for a 2-week prebirth period during the second trimester and for 2-week stretches at 1, 4, and 12 months postpartum. At each of these four assessment times participants were also interviewed, females in the home, and males over the telephone. Each interviewer was the same sex as the participant.

Outcomes were measured as an activity level index, which was part of the score of the SRM. These activity levels were calculated by comparing the frequency of a given activity to a measure of total activities for that individual. In this particular study, the analysis was applied to habitual times, solitude ratio, couple only ratio, and nonfamily person present ratio:

> *Habitual Time:* the average time each activity occurred after obvious outliers were eliminated
>
> *Solitude Ratio:* number of activities done alone divided by total activities
>
> *Couple Only Ratio:* number of activities done with spouse alone divided by total activities
>
> *Nonfamily Person Present Ratio:* number of activities for which other persons were present divided by total activities

Each of these measures was calculated using the SRM diary data for a week. The two weekly scores from each observation period were averaged to produce an overall score for each of the four observation periods. The reason ratios were used is that some families were more active and some were less so. The overall number of events did not affect the ratio data because the ratios were a comparison of frequencies within a family. Both inactive persons and active persons might have reported that one tenth of their activities were done alone with their spouse. The absolute number of activities for the active persons might have been much higher than for the inactive persons, but the ratio ignores this difference.

Anger and depression were also assessed. Anger was measured with a 10-item psychological instrument called the Anger Inventory (Spielberger, Jacobs, Russell, & Crane, 1983). Depression was measured with a version of the CES-D scale (Radloff, 1977). Several items were dropped from the full scale to make this version. Items that were dropped were somatic complaints that, along with being measures of depression, are also common outcomes of pregnancy; these items measured such things as "restless sleep" and the extent to which "everything seemed to be an effort." These two instruments were completed three times during each 2-week observation period: on the day before starting SRM diary recording, at the end of the 1st week, and at the end of the 2nd week.

An additional measure was given to assess marital quality. Eight items were selected from a scale developed by Barnett, Marshall, Raudenbush, & Brennan (1993). These items were chosen to measure communication and intimacy in the relationship. The items were scaled from 1 to 4 with higher numbers reflecting better relationships. The alpha levels for these items across sex and observation period exceeded .90.

RESULTS

The data from the SRM that addressed time of day of habitual activities were divided into morning, midday, and evening activities. The most disruption to daily schedules occurred in the events of the morning, such as time of getting out of bed, time of eating breakfast, and first time of going outside. The data for several of the morning measures are shown in Figure 22.1.

As you can see, the birth of a new baby seems to be associated with changes in the daily schedule, particularly for the mothers. Statistical analysis of these data revealed that the change in time of daily schedules for the three events shown was significant when both parents were considered together (all $p < .001$). Mothers were significantly later on the measures out of bed ($p < .005$) and go outside ($p < .001$) but not for breakfast ($p < .078$, NS) when all four observation periods were considered together. The findings for midday and evening disruption to schedule were less striking and did not show the large gender differences, so we will not consider them in detail.

Figure 22.2 shows the solitude ratio for mothers and fathers. These data have been divided into two groups based on whether the parents were first-time parents or experienced parents. The solitude ratio consisted of the number of events done alone divided by the total number of events reported on the SRM. Therefore, if the solitude ratio were equal to 1, all events would have been experienced alone. To interpret these ratio values remember that smaller numbers mean that fewer events happened alone.

Following the birth, mothers were less likely to have time alone than fathers ($p < .001$). Mothers had approximately half as many events alone as fathers. The changes over time across the four observation periods were also significant ($p < .001$) and the first-time parents experienced more change than the experienced parents ($p < .001$).

Anger, as measured by the Anger Inventory, also changed following the birth of a child as can be seen in Figure 22.3. When all three variables—gender, time, and experience—were considered by a statistical analysis that could examine all three at once,

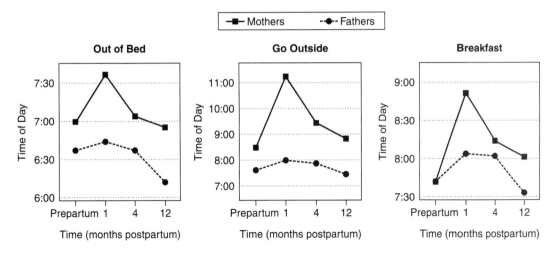

FIGURE 22.1   Morning Events. Data from SRM diary assessment for the three activities of mothers and fathers from before birth to 1 year following birth.

Source: From Monk, T. H., Essex, M. J., Smider, N. A., Klein, M. H., Lowe, K. K., & Kupfer, D. J. (1996). The impact of the birth of a baby on the time structure and social mixture of a couple's daily life and its consequences for well being. *Journal of Applied Psychology, 26,* 1245.

the differences resulting from them were significant ($p < .01$). First-time fathers seem to have problems with anger immediately following the birth, but these are not seen in first-time mothers. The trend is for experienced parents to have less anger as the birth takes place and subsequent time passes.

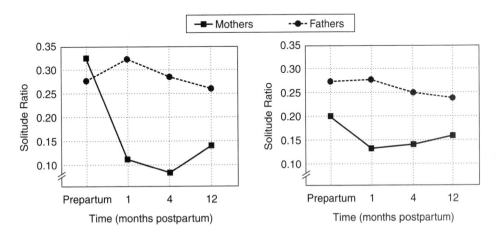

FIGURE 22.2   Solitude Ratio. Events alone divided by total events from SRM diary assessments of inexperienced (left) and experienced (right) parents.

Source: From Monk, T. H., Essex, M. J., Smider, N. A., Klein, M. H., Lowe, K. K., & Kupfer, D. J. (1996). The impact of the birth of a baby on the time structure and social mixture of a couple's daily life and its consequences for well being. *Journal of Applied Psychology, 26,* 1248.

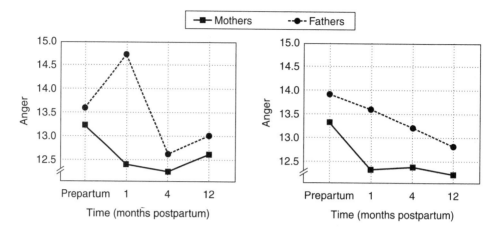

FIGURE 22.3   Anger. Measured by the Anger Inventory for inexperienced (left) and experienced (right) parents.

Source: From Monk, T. H., Essex, M. J., Smider, N. A., Klein, M. H., Lowe, K. K., & Kupfer, D. J. (1996). The impact of the birth of a baby on the time structure and social mixture of a couple's daily life and its consequences for well being. *Journal of Applied Psychology, 26,* 1251.

The results are less clear for depressive symptoms, as shown if Figure 22.4. The changes shown across time were significant ($p < .001$), as were the gender differences considered over time ($p < .03$). When gender, time, and experience were all analyzed at once, the interrelationships among them were found to be different from chance at the $p < .053$ level. Inexperienced fathers had a peak of depression immediately following the birth; experienced fathers did not appear to be particularly depressed compared to the other adults in the study.

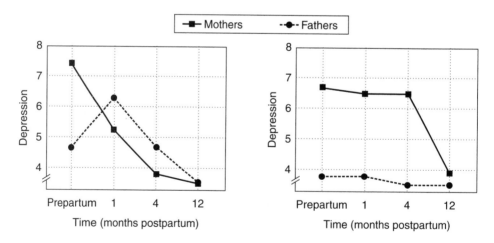

FIGURE 22.4   Depression. Depressive symptoms as measured by the modified CES-D scale for inexperienced (left) and experienced (right) parents.

Source: From Monk, T. H., Essex, M. J., Smider, N. A., Klein, M. H., Lowe, K. K., & Kupfer, D. J. (1996). The impact of the birth of a baby on the time structure and social mixture of a couple's daily life and its consequences for well being. *Journal of Applied Psychology, 26,* 1252.

First-time mothers peaked in depression before birth compared to experienced mothers, for whom the depression lasted longer, finally returning to baseline at 1 year following birth.

Marital quality, as measured by the scale developed by Barnett et al. (1993), is shown in Figure 22.5. The statistical analyses of these data were not reported separately by Monk, Essex, et al. (1996), but they are interesting to look at in any event. The trend for first-time parents seems to be that overall marital quality falls immediately following the birth and continues to fall. The experienced parents may be starting at lower levels of quality, and the fathers seem to be showing more decrease in overall quality across time.

DISCUSSION

We have presented some details of the data that bear on several hypotheses proposed by the authors. Support was found for Hypothesis 1 that habitual times would be changed; Hypothesis 2 that parents would be differentially affected; Hypothesis 3 that time spent alone would decrease; and Hypothesis 6 that mothers and first-time parents would feel the greatest impact. We did not present data that supported Hypothesis 4 that less time would be spent as a couple and Hypothesis 5 that there would be fewer activities with nonfamily members. Both parents experienced decreased time as a couple. Particularly for inexperienced parents, birth was associated with dramatic decreases in time together. For the mother, it is likely that this time was replaced with time spent caring for the baby. For fathers, especially new fathers, more time was spent alone. Before the birth, couples also spent about twice as much time with nonfamily members compared to after the birth. It is likely that this activity represented socialization with other friends and that it was curtailed by the responsibilities of the new baby.

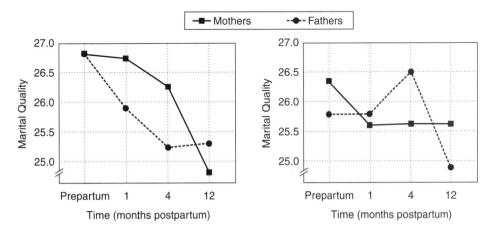

FIGURE 22.5   Overall Marital Quality. Reported by inexperienced (left) and experienced (right) parents.

Source: From Monk, T. H., Essex, M. J., Smider, N. A., Klein, M. H., Lowe, K. K., & Kupfer, D. J. (1996). The impact of the birth of a baby on the time structure and social mixture of a couple's daily life and its consequences for well being. *Journal of Applied Psychology, 26,* 1250.

The birth of a new baby is disruptive of daily schedules and of parental mood. This is particularly the case with first-time parents and may have overall effects for them that show in their perceptions of marital quality. Experience with previous children appears to inoculate parents against some of the marital difficulty that besets inexperienced parents. While this may seem like common sense, it pays to remember that the experienced parents are already dealing with at least one child when a new baby is added to the family. A rival view might suggest that it would be more difficult to look after two children than one, although the data presented here do not support this assertion.

One of the trends in diary data that we did not present in detail was that fathers of new babies stay up later and get up earlier. It is also probably safe to assume that both father and mother lose sleep by being awakened during the night. A great deal is known about the effects of sleep loss and of shifting the times of daily activity. The bulk of this information comes from research about jet lag and shift work. Sudden shifts in the time of daily activity have been associated with sleeplessness, digestive disturbances, and general malaise, as well as decrements in cognitive and motor functioning. Many college students are similar to new parents in that they are chronically sleep deprived. If you have difficulty concentrating and find that your attention wanders while you are reading, this can be a symptom. One of the best things you can do to remedy this is to go to sleep about the same time every night and get up about the same time every day. This permits your body to establish a sleep pattern that is more efficient because it maps over a routine biological circadian rhythm. This type of scheduled lifestyle is socially difficult for many college students, and it is impossible for new parents (Winget, DeRosha, Markley, & Holley, 1984).

Caution must always be urged in generalizing from the findings of one study, but if the findings for this study are valid, they would seriously question the belief that a troubled marriage can be repaired by having a child, particularly a first child. In the introduction, we noted that the birth of a child in the first year of marriage was a risk factor for the survival of the marriage. Financial insecurity was also seen as a risk, as was parental age of less than 20 years. It is easy to imagine that these three risks are likely to occur together all too frequently in our society. When they do, marriage will probably be severely strained.

CRITICAL THINKING TOOLKIT ITEMS

Studies that rely on recollections from the past may suffer in validity owing to faulty memory. Self-report field data may be improved with some sort of more immediate data collection tactic.

REFERENCES

Barnett, R. C., Marshall, N. L., Raudenbush, S. W., & Brennan, R. T. (1993). Gender and the relationship between job experiences and psychological distress: A study of dual-earner couples. *Journal of Personality and Social Psychology, 64,* 794–806.

Bernard, J. (1981). The good provider role: Its rise and fall. *American Psychologist, 36,* 1–12.

Blumstein, P., & Schwartz, P. (1983). *American couples: Money, work, sex.* New York: Morrow.

Dalton, S. T. (1992). Lived experience of never-married women. *Issues in Mental Health Nursing, 13,* 69–80.

Friedman, H. S., Tucker, J. S., Schwartz, J. E., Tomlinson-Keasy, C., Martin, L. R., Wingard, D. L., & Cirqui, M. H. (1995). Psychosocial and behavioral predic-

233

tors of longevity: The aging and death of the "Termites." *American Psychologist, 50,* 69–78.

Lazarus, R. S. (1990). Theory-based stress management. *Psychological Inquiry, 1,* 3–13.

Lee, G. R., Seccombe, K., & Shehan, C. L. (1991). Marital status and personal happiness: An analysis of trend data. *Journal of Marriage and the Family, 53,* 839–844.

Levenson, R. W., Carstenson, L. L., & Gottman, J. M. (1993). The influence of age and gender on affect, physiology, and their interrelations: A study of long-term marriages. *Journal of Personality and Social Psychology, 67,* 56–68.

Levine, R., Sato, S., Hashimoto, T., & Verma, J. (1995). Love and marriage in eleven cultures. *Journal of Cross-Cultural Psychology, 26,* 554–571.

McGoldrick, M., Heiman, M., & Carter, B. (1993). The changing family life cycle: A perspective on normalcy. In F. Walsh (Ed.), *Normal family processes* (pp. 405–443). New York: Guilford.

Michael, R. T., Gagnon, J. H., Laumann, E. O., & Kolata, G. (1994). *Sex in America: A definitive survey.* Boston: Little Brown.

Monk, T. H., Essex, M. J., Smider, N. A., Klein, M. H., Lowe, K. K., & Kupfer, D. J. (1996). The impact of the birth of a baby on the time structure and social mixture of a couple's daily life and its consequences for well-being. *Journal of Applied Psychology, 26,* 1237–1258.

Monk, T. H., Kupfer, D. J., Frank, E., & Ritenour, A. M. (1991). The social rhythm metric (SRM): Measuring daily social rhythms over a 12-week period. *Psychiatry Research, 36,* 195–207.

Radloff, L. S. (1977). The CES-D Scale: A self-report depression scale for research in the general population. *Applied Psychological Measurement, 1,* 385–401.

Ross, C. E., Mirowsky, J., & Goldsteen, K. (1990). The impact of the family on health: A decade in review. *Journal of Marriage and the Family, 52,* 1059–1078.

Rossi, A. S. (1982). Transition to parenthood. In L. R. Allman & D. T. Jaffe (Eds.), *Readings in adult psychology: Contemporary perspectives* (2nd ed., pp. 263–275). New York: Harper & Row.

Russell, R. J. H., & Wells, P. A. (1994). Predictors of happiness in married couples. *Personality and Individual Differences, 17,* 313–321.

Skolnick, A. (1981). Married lives: Longitudinal perspectives on marriage. In D. Eichorn, J. Clausen, N. Haan, M. Honzig, & P. Mussen (Eds.), *Present and past in middle age* (pp. 270–300). New York: Academic.

Spielberger, C. D., Jacobs, G., Russell, S., & Crane, R. S. (1983). Assessment of anger: The State-Trait Anger Scale. In J. N. Butcher & C. D. Spielberger (Eds.), *Advances in personality assessment* (Vol. 2, pp. 159–187). Hillsdale, NJ: Erlbaum.

Starrels, M. E. (1994). Husband's involvement in female gender-typed household chores. *Sex Roles, 31,* 473–491.

U.S. Bureau of the Census. (1996). *Statistical abstract of the United States* (118th ed.). Washington, DC: U.S. Government Printing Office.

Winget, C. M., DeRosha, C. W., Markley, C. L., & Holley, D. C. (1984). A review of human physiological and performance changes associated with desynchronosis of biological rhythms. *Aviation, Space and Environmental Medicine, 55,* 1085–1096.

CHAPTER 23

LOVE MAKES THE
WORLD GO 'ROUND

Some people may look at this book and ask "Where are the theories?" As we have mentioned several times, we have tried to present current research and, as a result, we have only included theories that have empirical support. We freely admit that we have ignored some of the absurd old fluff that passes for theory in some developmental texts. Make no mistake however; this book contains quite a few theories. Several chapters have contained tests of Piagetian theory and, while Piaget's original notions have generally failed these tests, a new theory of cognition emerges in which competence is seen early in life and experience makes a difference. In Chapter 12, we discussed a theoretical approach to human psychological development that assigns a larger importance to genetic factors than was the case with outdated theories. You will remember from that chapter that the empirical support was robust. A number of chapters presented tests of theories regarding sensitive periods: Chapter 3, "Drinking without Thinking"; Chapter 6, "Attachment in Separation"; Chapter 11, "Some Restrictions May Apply"; and Chapter 17, "At a Loss for Words" all fell into this category. The theoretical outcomes of these studies and of other contemporary research indicate that sensitive periods exist, but they may be less pervasive than older theories assumed. Classical learning theory is presented in Chapter 16 and classical attribution theory is presented in Chapter 14. Sandra Scarr's groundbreaking developmental theory about the role of good enough parents was presented in Chapter 19. You may be happy to learn that more theories will be reported in the remainder of this book.

We hope we have made our point: This is a book full of theories. They are all part of the overarching theory that behavior is multidetermined and that no one big statement can possibly account for the diversity observed when development is studied scientifically. However, if any theory can be said to apply to all behavior, we believe that it is the theory of evolution by natural selection.

The notion of evolution by natural selection has been around a long time and has been the topic of intensive research. Though it is called the "theory" of evolution, we would not want you to believe that biologists are still tentative in their acceptance of it. Science does not

Incorporating the research of D. M. Buss, T. K. Shackelford, L. A. Kirkpatrick, J. C. Choe, H. K. Lim, M. Hasegawa, T. Hasegawa, and K. Bennett, "Jealousy and the Nature of Beliefs about Infidelity: Tests of Competing Hypotheses about Sex Differences in the United States, Korea, and Japan," 1999, *Personal Relationships, 6,* pp. 125–150.

find absolute proof for anything and decisions about correctness of a theory usually rest on the weight of evidence. In the case of evolution by natural selection, the weight of evidence is enormous. The main tenets of evolution by natural selection have been so thoroughly confirmed that, in our view, they may be considered to be facts—whatever that means.

WHAT DID DARWIN PROPOSE?

There are many ways to approach a description of evolution by natural selection but one of the clearest ways is to simplify Darwin's notions into four related propositions.

1. *Each organism has enormous reproductive potential* The emphasis here should be on the word *potential.* Some organisms can produce millions of offspring. For example, a single starfish (*Pisaster ocraceus*) can lay well in excess of 1 million eggs. In areas where these animals are dense, it would not be surprising to find 100 of them in an area the size of a normal parking space. If half of them were females, they would produce a total of 50 million eggs. If half of these eggs were females and all of them lived, that would mean that from the original 100 starfish, we would have 50 million starfish. If all offspring of all these animals survived for 15 generations, there would be 10^{79} starfish. This is more starfish than there are electrons in the visible universe. They would easily fill the entire sea and be crowded out onto land (Dodson & Dodson, 1985). While this seems like rather a lot of starfish, the reproductive potential of starfish is small compared to many other organisms.

In case you are wondering about the reproductive potential for humans, the *Guinness Book of World Records* claims that the record for a woman is the 69 offspring born to a Russian peasant in the mid-1700s. We might question the quality of record keeping for a case that was so long in the past. However, the most prolific living mother is Leontina Albina who produced her 55th and last child in 1981 (Guinness Publishing Co., 1997). The *Guinness Book of World Records* does not, apparently, consider it worth publishing records for fathers. This is probably because few fathers could produce good evidence—such as a DNA test—to confirm paternity for very many children. If we could collect the confirmatory evidence, it is likely that the actual record for the number of children born to a father would be much higher than Leontina's mere 55. For men, regardless of the actual number of children produced, the biological potential is virtually unlimited.

2. *Not all offspring survive and breed* This point was presaged in our description of the starfish. For most organisms, most of the individuals do not survive to breed. If they did, we would be up to our necks in things like starfish.

3. *Mortality occurring among organisms is **not** random* Most of the offspring of most organisms do not manage to survive very long. Those who do survive long enough to breed are those who are the best adapted to the environment in which they live. It is in this sense that mortality is not random. Some organisms are better than others at finding food and shelter and avoiding predators. Because those individuals are superior at solving their ecological problems, they are more likely than other members of their own species, called *conspecifics,* to survive. Notice that adaptation, as it is described here, is not merely equivalent to traits of an organism. Adaptation is also a function of the circumstances in the environment. Mice living in a desert may be well adapted to avoid predators if the mice are only active after dark, when predators cannot see them. However, they may be considered to be less well adapted when a rattlesnake evolves because rattlesnakes can hunt in the dark by sensing the warmth of their prey. In this example, the mice themselves have not changed, but there has been a change in the extent to which nocturnal activity would be considered adaptive. If some of the mice were able in turn to detect the rattlesnake, then those individuals would be the best adapted mice in the mouse population and would be more likely to survive.

4. *Some individuals within a species survive and have more offspring than others* The individuals who survive and reproduce are, by definition, the best adapted. They will pass on to their offspring some of the characteristics that made them successful. Inasmuch as these offspring are also more successful than offspring of unrelated conspecific individuals, they will also be more likely to survive and reproduce. What happens, then, is that within a group of conspecifics, certain genetic lineages end up better adapted than others. One way to measure this is to assess the number of copies of genes that are passed on. Some individuals will reproduce more successfully and, therefore, make more gene copies. Some individuals will be less successful. Over time, the less successful genes will disappear as the individuals who carry them fail to reproduce. This is why *survival of the fittest* is a poor description of evolution by natural selection: Survival is important, but reproduction is more important. An organism may seem to be very fit, or adapted, but if that organism does not breed, it is an evolutionary dead end. Over generations, successful adaptations may make certain organisms within a group so different from their original conspecifics that they can no longer successfully breed with them. At this point the rapidly changing and adapting branch of the family would be considered a new species.

EVOLUTIONARY PSYCHOLOGY

We believe that our evolutionary heritage, acting through our genes, is a component of every behavior and every psychological event. The new discipline that has grown up around this idea is called *evolutionary psychology.* Some people view this discipline as the brash new kid on the block. That is an odd thing to say about a theory that was launched in 1859. Nevertheless, evolutionary psychology is branching in all directions, formulating and testing hypotheses. In this chapter and the next, we will provide you with examples of new research that has tested predictions made by evolutionary psychology.

One of the areas in which evolutionary psychology has had particular success in making predictions has been sexual behavior. In particular, evolutionary psychologists have predicted that there ought to be striking differences between men and women in their sexual psychology—the way they think and act when it comes to mate choice, mate infidelity, and parental investment. Evolutionary psychologists propose that this is because males and females have confronted very different sets of adaptive problems over millions of years of evolution. The successful survivors, currently represented by all of us, found winning solutions to these challenges. Our ancestors survived and reproduced, passing on the genetic package that was a component of their success.

DEFINING MALE AND FEMALE

The situations facing males and females were fundamentally different right from the beginning and it should be no surprise that the sexes end up being quite different in psychological characteristics. No matter what species we are talking about, the female is defined as the member of a sexually reproducing pair who contributes the largest sex cell. In species where members of a pair contribute sex cells of equal size, no distinction is made between male and female. In humans this initial male-female asymmetry is quite large: The human egg is about 85,000 times larger than the human sperm. As you can see from this ratio, right from fertilization, the human female is making a much larger investment in an offspring than the male. This investment is rapidly compounded as the human embryo and fetus grow inside the woman's body for about 9 months. For most of human history, it was a necessity for women to breast-feed their offspring for a period of time following birth, perhaps as long as a few years. While males can now help bottle feed a baby, over millions of years of evolution this was not possible. Our ancestral females had no choice but to be committed to a considerable amount of child care, also called *parental investment*. The situation for ancestral males was different, continuing the situation we have called the male-female asymmetry.

Another asymmetry that occurs when we compare males to females exists because fertilization is internal in humans and other mammals. The male can never be sure that the offspring are actually his. This is different in some fish, for example, where the female lays eggs on the bottom of a pond and the male, following directly behind her, deposits his sperm over them. In that situation, if the male guards the eggs while fertilization occurs, he can be certain of paternity. In mammals such as humans it is not possible to watch fertilization (except in the case of in vitro fertilization). A direct result of fertilization being hidden within the female is that males can never be certain of paternity. In contrast, human females are always certain of maternity. In the words of an old saying, "Mama's baby, Papa's maybe."

In summary, for thousands of years, males did not have to contribute much parental investment and were always uncertain of paternity, while females made a large initial parental investment and were always sure the children were theirs. This situation set the stage for psychological sex differences to emerge. Both males and females should act as if reproduction is an ultimate goal. Being consciously aware of this goal is not necessary. If the ultimate goal is to maximize reproductive success, then the best strategy for males is not necessarily the best for females and visa versa. Males may be able to increase their reproductive success by mating with multiple fertile females. Biologically, human males are almost unlimited in the number of offspring they can produce—there are enough sperm in one ejaculation to fertilize all the fertile women in America.

Females are much more limited in potential fertility. As a result, females ought to be very concerned about finding quality mates because this choice is the key to maximizing their reproductive success. Females will have few offspring, so reproductive success is increased by a focus on quality mates. Merely mating with a number of different males in quick succession will not increase the reproductive success of a female the way it might for a male. Females should choose mates carefully and one of the things they should be looking for is a male who has the resources and willingness to undertake some parental investment. As Symonds (1992) pointed out, given that these differences have existed for males and females over a very long expanse of human evolutionary history, there is a probability of about zero that males and females are identical in their psychological responses to sexual matters.

In one compelling demonstration of the prediction that females choose mates carefully and males do not, Clark and Hatfield (1989) sent reasonably attractive students out to approach complete strangers of the opposite sex and to suggest going somewhere to have sexual intercourse. Seventy-five percent of the men approached in this way consented, while 0 percent of the women agreed to this request. In another study, men stated on a survey that they would ideally like to have an average of about 18 sex partners in a lifetime, whereas women stated that they only wanted 4 or 5 (Buss & Schmidt, 1993).

If men are uncertain of their paternity and women are very concerned about parental investment, the men should be more jealous of sexual infidelity than of a partner forming a purely emotional bond with another male. This is because if a male's mate is in a sexual relationship with another male, the first male can end up raising children fathered by someone else. Women, in contrast, should be more jealous of a mate who forms a new extra-pair emotional bond than of a mate who becomes involved in a purely sexual relationship with no emotional ties. The new emotional bond can mean a lack of support and investment. In other words, women should be more likely than men to forgive one-night stands.

FALSIFICATION

Perhaps one of the most interesting aspects of evolutionary theory applied to psychology is the extent to which it produces testable hypotheses. In order to be testable, a theory should predict what will happen. Most people do not realize that embedded in the predictions of good theories there should also be some statements about what should not be observed if the theory is to be considered correct. This is precisely the problem with some of the older so-called theories in psychology. While they offered explanations for everything, there was no way to show that they were wrong. Whatever could possibly be observed was considered to be support for the theory. In Freudian thinking, if someone likes to smoke cigarettes, it might be said that they are fixated at the oral stage in development. If they do not smoke, they are supposed to be fixated at some other stage. Either way, the Freudian notion of fixation at psychosexual stages is confirmed. Contrast this with the Piagetian theory covered in several earlier chapters. Piaget made specific predictions that were subject to empirical validation. For instance, he proposed that object permanence would not appear until 9 months of age. When object permanence was observed at 5 months of age, this aspect of Piaget's theory was found to be wrong. As we noted at the end of Chapter 3, the usual way to phrase this in science is to say that Piaget's theory had been *falsified.*

If, in the evolutionary example cited previously, Clark and Hatfield (1989) had found that females would happily run off with strange men to have sex but men were reluctant to do so, evolutionary psychology would have been falsified. It would also have been falsified if women had claimed that ideally they would like to have many sex partners while men had expressed interest in having only a few. So far, thousands of such falsifiable predictions have been made by the theory of evolution and hundreds have been made by evolutionary psychology (e.g., see Buss, 1999). In all this testing, evolutionary theory has not yet been falsified.

CULTURAL EXPLANATIONS

Often culture is used as a rival hypothesis to evolutionary theory. For example, one might say that the attention females give to cosmetics and clothes is cultural, which we suppose means that it is dictated by the surrounding society. In contrast, the evolutionary thinker would say that females who appear younger are judged by males to be more fertile and therefore are more likely to achieve a stable relationship with a male. Makeup and clothes seem to be a way of making a person look young.

There are at least two difficulties with the cultural explanation for behavior. One difficulty is that it appeals to a naive nature-nurture dichotomy and we think the evidence is overwhelming that behavior is multidetermined. The evolutionary approach does not assert causation from genes—it does not take the stance that use of wrinkle cream is caused by the wrinkle cream gene. Rather it says that attempts to appear younger have had particular selective value for women in the past. The specifics of contemporary attempts to appear youthful will be phrased by current contextual factors. A second problem with saying that women use cosmetics "because of culture" is that it does not explain why they do so. One might equally well expect men to make the majority of cosmetic purchases because of culture. The explanatory phrase "because of culture" is not falsifiable because it can be applied to everything observed. In contrast, evolutionary theory would predict that women would be more eager than men to appear young because in an ancestral context youth equals fertility.

A CROSS-CULTURAL STUDY

Basic predictions from evolutionary psychology ought to apply to different cultures. One of the hallmarks of evolutionary psychology research has been the attempt to demonstrate the predictive power of the theory in a variety of different cultures. The rival explanation "because of culture" might even seem to suggest that cross-cultural comparisons should yield differences, not similarities, unless it is argued that different cultures just happen to have prescribed the same behaviors.

Leading evolutionary theorist David Buss and his colleagues conducted a cross-cultural study that included an examination of the prediction that men would exhibit more sexual jealousy than women and that women would be more jealous of emotional infidelity than men (Buss, Shackelford, et al., 1999). The data we will report were a subset taken from this large cross-cultural study of sex differences.

PARTICIPANTS

Two samples of American students were among the participants. Both groups were students in introductory psychology classes at a liberal arts college in the southeast United States. The first sample consisted of 173 men and 323 women; the other sample contained 201 men and 425 women. Participation was voluntary and was not rewarded. We presume that the task was of such short duration that it was presented for a few minutes before, after, or during class. Two other groups of students also participated: 100 men and 90 women from Seoul National University in Korea, as well as 213 men and 103 women at a large university in Japan. Participation for these international samples was also voluntary and was not rewarded.

PROCEDURE

We are going to report on the results from two of the questions that were posed to the participants. These questions had previously been asked by Buss, Larsen, Westen, and Semmelroth (1992). The main scenario was the same for each of the two questions:

> Please think of a serious committed romantic relationship that you have had in the past, that you currently have, or that you would like to have. Imagine that you discover that the person with whom you've been seriously involved became interested in someone else. What would upset or distress you more:
>
> Question 1:
> (A) Imagining your partner forming a deep emotional attachment to that other person
> or
> (B) Imagining your partner enjoying passionate sexual intercourse with that other person.
>
> Question 2:
> (A) Imagining your partner falling in love with that other person
> or
> (B) Imagining your partner trying different sexual positions with that other person.
>   (p. 132)

Participants were asked to circle only one choice, A or B, from each question.

RESULTS

In each of the three cultures, men were more upset by sexual infidelity than were women. This difference persisted across both versions of the question. For all three cultures, and for each question, a statistical analysis found the difference between men and women to be significant at the $p < .001$ level. The data for the two American samples, combined, are shown in Figure 23.1 along with the data from the Korean and Japanese samples.

The outcomes shown in Figure 23.1 were in the direction predicted by evolutionary psychology. Men reported being more sexually jealous and women said they were more emotionally jealous. After the first study containing these questions was published in 1992, DeSteno and Salovey (1996) published an article that criticized the research design. This article suggested that the findings of Buss, Larsen, et al. (1992) could have been confounded because people might assume that a deep emotional relationship would include sex or that a passionate sexual relationship would necessarily include some emotional attachment. If a linkage between these two cognitions was more common in participants of one or the other sex, the results might not merely reflect females being more emotionally jealous or men being more sexually jealous. For example, imagine that males as a group assumed that sexual infidelity always involved emotional infidelity too, but that they did not think emo-

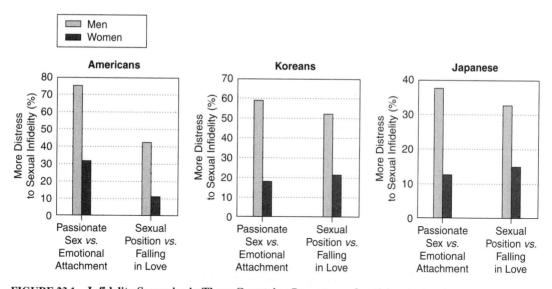

FIGURE 23.1   Infidelity Scenarios in Three Countries. Percentage of participants showing more distress to sexual infidelity on each of two questions: passionate sexual intercourse vs. deep emotional attachment and different sexual positions vs. falling in love.

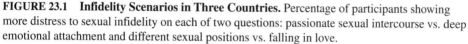

Source: From Buss, D. M., Shackelford, T. K., Kirkpatrick, L. A., Choe, J. C., Lim, H. K., Hasegawa, M., Hasegawa, T., & Bennett, K. (1999). Jealousy and the nature of beliefs about infidelity: Tests of competing hypotheses about sex differences in the United States, Korea and Japan. *Personal Relationships, 6,* 125–150.

tional infidelity was always accompanied by sexual infidelity. If this happened, males might consider sexual infidelity to be a larger problem than emotional infidelity because they believe emotional infidelity can occur by itself. This is called the *double shot* hypothesis.

In response to this problem, Buss, Shackelford, et al. (1999) presented other scenarios that involved forced choices designed to eliminate the double shot explanation:

> Imagine that your partner <u>both</u> formed an emotional attachment to another person <u>and</u> had sexual intercourse with that other person. <u>Which aspect</u> of your partner's involvement would upset you more?:
> (A) the sexual intercourse with that other person.
> (B) the emotional attachment to that other person. (p. 132)

The results of the presentation of this scenario to the three different national samples are shown in Figure 23.2.

Even when the double shot hypothesis was ruled out as an explanation of sex differences because the instructions insisted that both types of infidelity occurred together, males reported being more upset by the sexual infidelity in the United States ($p < .001$), Korea ($p < .006$), and Japan ($p = .019$).

Three other scenarios were also used to test the double shot hypothesis. Two stressed that the imagined relationship was only emotional or only sexual. The third asked which of the following situations would be more distressing on finding out that a partner is reinvolved with a former lover: the partner's pure sexual interest in this person or the partner's

FIGURE 23.2   Most Upsetting Aspect of Infidelity. Percentage of men reporting most upset to sexual infidelity when instructions clearly stated that both sexual and emotional infidelity were taking place at the same time.

Source: From Buss, D. M., Shackelford, T. K., Kirkpatrick, L. A., Choe, J. C., Lim, H. K., Hasegawa, M., Hasegawa, T., & Bennett, K. (1999). Jealousy and the nature of beliefs about infidelity: Tests of competing hypotheses about sex differences in the United States, Korea and Japan. *Personal Relationships, 6,* 125–150.

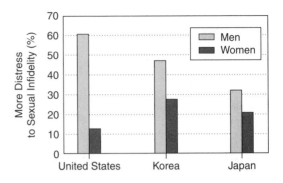

pure emotional interest in this person. Of the data for all three additional scenarios in each of the three countries, only one comparison failed to show a significant difference between men and women—a single scenario with the Japanese participants. Of all 18 scenarios (6 scenarios in each of three countries) presented, only one failed to support the evolutionary psychological prediction. It is not obvious why Japanese men and women responded similarly to one scenario but this can be a topic for future research. It would seem that the overwhelming bulk of evidence from the other data in this study support evolutionary interpretations.

DISCUSSION

Not everyone in psychology has as much confidence in the value of evolutionary psychology as we do. One of the reasons for this is that many studies have relied upon conclusions drawn from the interpretation of quickly administered surveys. The lively debate between some opponents and the evolutionary psychologists has been carried on in popular media, such as the *New York Times* and the Internet, as well as in scientific journals. For a spirited, but otherwise unconvincing, attack on evolutionary psychology, see the *New York Times Magazine* article by Angier (1999). In keeping with the main theme of this book, we are more impressed by the outcomes of scientific studies than by the war of words in other publications.

The center of the public media controversy is that evolutionary psychology is thought by some to sentence women to a life of monogamous drudgery raising children while males are empowered to flit from woman to woman, having sex with reckless abandon. This caricature would not be accepted by any evolutionary psychologist. Among the many reasons why this stereotype is wrong are findings from research suggesting that human women were not designed to be monogamous. Remember, in an evolutionary system, each individual is ultimately interested in his or her own self-benefit, and while individual interests may sometimes overlap, it is probably more common that what maximizes reproductive potential for one partner does not do so for the other.

One line of evidence regarding female mating strategies comes from a comparison of humans with other great apes. Among many species, including apes, the size of the male's testes in comparison to the rest of his body size indicates the extent to which his sperm might be expected to compete with the sperm of other males in the fertilization of eggs within females. The reason should be obvious: Larger testes produce more sperm and more sperm are required when there is more competition. Chimpanzees, for instance, have relatively large testes by this measure and female chimps are quite promiscuous when they are ovulating. In gorillas, the testes are quite small compared to body size and females are carefully guarded by a male, having little chance to wander off and mate with other males. The human ratio for this measure falls somewhere between gorillas and chimps. If female humans evolved to be monogamous, the human testes–body size ratio would be more like the gorilla's. Rather, it appears that the best strategy for a female has been to mate with a few other males, perhaps to acquire the best genes, and then draw on the parental investment and resources from some other unwitting male who is best able to provide support. It even appears as if males produce several kinds of sperm, some of which are dedicated to the role of soldiers, fighting off sperm from other males while their genetic brothers swim for the egg. This mechanism would be unlikely to exist in males if females had evolved to be monogamous (Bellis & Baker, 1995).

In addition to this, it is likely that a human male strategy of mating with as many females as possible is not the optimal means to maximize reproductive potential and never has been. Female ovulation is hidden. Mating with many women in short-term liaisons results in a low probability of fertilizing any eggs at all. Evolutionary psychologists recognize that more permanent associations between males and females should be highly desirable for males because of the increased likelihood of reproduction. If a male is able to continue to mate with a fertile female over a period of months, he becomes quite likely to sire her offspring. The mathematics of the situation, particularly when sperm competition from other males is taken into account, favors exclusive long-term relationships for men over a series of one-night stands.

It is very important to remember that the evolutionarily successful animal is probably somewhat flexible when it comes to day-to-day behavior. To be successful, the animal must survive to reproduce and pass on genes and adaptations. However, the details of the animal's survival strategy may be more subject to change than previously expected within the context of evolutionary thought. For example, the animal that hunts by running down prey might miss a great deal of food by not lurking and waiting for some prey while trying to run down others. Inasmuch as genes influence this strategy, the genes should promote the best hunting strategies, even though the specific behaviors that are best for hunting one prey may not be the best for another.

Earlier, in Chapter 12, evidence from the Colorado Adoption Project was presented to show that cognitive ability has a major genetic component. That chapter also cited the Minnesota Twin Study that had similar findings concerning personality. If you consider these findings in the light of evolution by natural selection, it would be surprising if this were not the case. Surely intellect and personality are too important to survival to be left totally to the vagaries of haphazard rearing conditions and idiosyncratic factors. The idiosyncratic factors are there, but they are underpinned by some genetic components that ensure considerable similarity between parents and offspring in general behavioral dispositions. The parent who is quick to solve new problems is likely to have offspring who can also solve problems rapidly. Although this may have less survival value now than it did throughout most of our heritage, the evolutionary benefit of psychological systems that have major genetic components should be obvious.

It is important to remember that we are not talking about behaviors that are caused by genes. Rather, we are talking about psychological architecture that influences behaviors in ways that help to ensure survival and reproductive success in constantly changing environments. The term *psychological architecture* refers to the way our brain is structured, or wired. Some of the structure of the brain is certainly influenced by genes. Some of the ways we think about the world are influenced by the actual structure of our brains. If the evolutionary psychologists are correct, some of our behavior should give evidence of a psychological architecture that has been influenced by our evolutionary heritage.

CRITICAL THINKING TOOLKIT ITEMS

Unless a theory specifies some events that will not happen, everything that is observed can be taken as evidence for the thory. In such a case, the theory is not falsifiable. If it is not falsifiable, it cannot be tested because the nature of a scientific test is that one of two outcomes will be observed. If the outcome denied by the theory is, in fact, observed during the test, then the theory has not been supported and needs to be modified or discarded.

REFERENCES

Angier, N. (1999, February 21). Men, women, sex, and Darwin. *New York Times Magazine, CXLVIII,* 48–53.

Bellis, M. A., & Baker, R. R. (1995). *Human sperm competition: Copulation, masturbation, and infidelity.* London: Chapman and Hall.

Buss, D. M. (1999). *Evolutionary psychology: The new science of the mind.* New York: Allyn & Bacon.

Buss, D. M., Larsen, R. J., Westen, D., & Semmelroth, J. (1992). Sex differences in jealousy: Evolution, physiology, and psychology. *Psychological Science, 3,* 251–255.

Buss, D. M., & Schmidt, D. P. (1993). Sexual strategies theory: An evolutionary perspective on human mating. *Psychological Review, 100,* 204–232.

Buss, D. M., Shackelford, T. K., Kirkpatrick, L. A., Choe, J. C., Lim, H. K., Hasegawa, M., Hasegawa, T., & Bennett, K. (1999). Jealousy and the nature of beliefs about infidelity: Tests of competing hypotheses about sex differences in the United States, Korea, and Japan. *Personal relationships, 6,* 125–150.

Clark, R. D., & Hatfield, E. (1989). Gender differences in receptivity to sexual offers. *Journal of Psychology and Human Sexuality, 2,* 39–55.

DeSteno, D. A., & Salovey, P. (1996). Evolutionary origins of sex differences in jealousy: Questioning the "fitness" of the model. *Psychological Science, 7,* 367–372.

Dodson, E. O., & Dodson, P. (1985). *Evolution: Process and product.* Boston: Prindle, Weber & Schmidt.

Guinness book of world records (36th ed.). (1997). Stanford, CT: Guinness Media.

Symonds, D. (1992). On the use and misuse of Darwinism in the study of human behavior. In J. Barkow, L. Cosmides, & J. Tooby (Eds.), *The adapted mind: Evolutionary psychology and the generation of culture* (pp. 137–159). New York: Oxford University Press.

CHAPTER 24

TAKE A WHIFF

PROXIMATE AND ULTIMATE
EXPLANATIONS OF BEHAVIOR

In order to understand the workings of evolution in psychology, there is an important distinction that must be made between *proximate factors* and *ultimate factors*. Proximate factors are the reasons we give for our behavior. We are fully aware of them and if someone asks you why you do certain behaviors, proximate factors are the reasons you are likely to give. Ultimate factors, on the other hand, are the evolutionary reasons behind our behavior. We do not have to be aware of them and frequently we have no conscious recognition of these ultimate factors. Some examples will help to illustrate the distinction between proximate and ultimate reasons for behavior.

Most people enjoy foods such as hot, crispy French fries or cold, creamy ice cream. If you ask people why they like these things, they are likely to say that these foods taste good. That is a proximate reason for eating fries or ice cream. The ultimate reason addresses the question of why these things taste great. The ultimate evolutionary reason is likely to be that they contain substances that were essential but rare in the diet of our ancestors over the course of our evolution. One of these substances is saturated fat. Saturated fat occurs only in animal products. For our hunter-gatherer ancestors, saturated fat was difficult to obtain because it meant successfully hunting some animal. Even then, the animals hunted did not contain much saturated fat because the prey animals themselves had diets that were low in fat compared to the farm animals of today. Despite the bad press these substances receive today, saturated fat and the accompanying cholesterol are critical for life. They are essential components of our cell walls and of the myelin sheaths that surround many of our nerve cells, enhancing transmission of neural impulses throughout the body.

In an evolutionary situation in which saturated fat was difficult to obtain, it is not surprising that organisms evolved a preference for the mouth-feel and taste of foods high in saturated fat. When asked why we are eating ice cream, we do not say: "Because it contains essential saturated fat and cholesterol without which we would not have cell walls or functioning neurons. Without these structures we could not survive and reproduce." That would be the ultimate reason and most of us are not aware of that as we

Incorporating the research of C. Wedekind, & S. Füri, "Body Odour Preferences in Men and Women: Do They Aim for Specific MHC Combinations or Simple Heterozygosity?" 1997, *Proceedings of the Royal Society of London Series B, 264*, pp. 1471–1479.

pull the lid off that premium brand of ice cream. We say, instead, "It tastes great," or, "I just can't resist it." These are proximal reasons. In contrast, we do not like the smell of food that has spoiled. That is the proximate reason why we would not drink sour milk—it smells and tastes bad. The ultimate reason is that it would be bad for us, perhaps making us sick. Nevertheless, we operate with a proximate rule—do not eat things that smell bad—and this enhances the probability of our survival.

Saturated fat forms an interesting example because we seem to have a persistent built-in taste preference for it which, now that food processing has made it plentiful, would seem to be a threat to our cardiovascular health. While those individuals who cannot resist the taste of saturated fat may end up as heart attack victims, this will only play a role in natural selection if it affects reproductive success. Most heart attacks occur after people have finished reproducing. There may be subtle natural selection anyway because if parents are not around to invest in older offspring, those offspring may be at a selective disadvantage. Nevertheless, the effects of missing later parental investment would seem to be small compared to the selection which would take place if poor diet commonly resulted in heart attacks in prepubescent individuals, eliminating them before they could breed.

Evolutionary thinkers believe that the ultimate reason for much of our behavior is survival and reproduction. Remember, you do not have to be aware of this reason, any more than you have to be aware of it when you eat ice cream. When you eat ice cream, you do not usually think of the necessity of fat in the fat-deficient diets of our distant ancestors. Likewise, when you study for an exam, you probably do not think of the role a good education can play in attracting mates. The most usual route to this attraction is probably in the ability of people with a good education to control resources. In today's world controlling resources probably more or less means getting money. Studying hard may be one way to succeed in the competition for the best mates, but students are likely to say that they study carefully to achieve a particular grade. The grade is the proximate reason and the mate is the ultimate reason.

Even when people are having sex, they are likely to be more aware of the proximate reason—that it feels good—than the ultimate reason of making gene copies in subsequent generations. While most of us do not spend all day thinking about reproductive success, the proximate reasons for our behavior are usually consistent with survival and reproductive success as ultimate goals. We have also seen in the previous chapter, "Love Makes the World Go 'Round," that each of us appears to have a specialized genetic package leading to psychological architecture that helped our ancestors solve adaptive problems and reproduce successfully.

Developments in genetic research have allowed scientists to isolate some specific components of our genetic makeup. One component of this package that is currently being investigated is the group of genes called the *major histocompatibility complex* (MHC). One current hypothesis suggests that MHC might help human immune systems respond to foreign invaders, such as viruses and bacteria, by producing substances that adhere these invaders to the surfaces of body cells. Certain white blood cells, which make up your body's own SWAT team, are then able to easily locate and destroy invading diseases (Klein, 1986). Hence, it would be evolutionarily advantageous for a person to possess the best possible combination of MHC genes because an effective and speedy immune response is essential for survival and reproduction. Individuals with immune systems that responded poorly to foreign substances are not our ancestors; they did not survive long enough to have a chance at reproduction and their unsuccessful genes were selected out of the population.

We presented a brief discussion of genetics that described human chromosomes at the beginning of Chapter 12. Chromosomes contain the chemical messages that are called genes. Because chromosomes occur in pairs, so do genes. Genes are arranged along chromosomes with one member of each gene pair on each of the paired chromosomes. Each single member of a gene pair is called an *allele*. It is important to understand that the alleles do not have to be identical to be members of a pair. However, there are a limited number of possible alleles an organism can possess for any one location on the chromosome. Because one chromosome has come from the mother and the other from the father, any particular pair of alleles may, by chance, be the same or they may not. If these alleles are the same, the individual is said to be *homozygous* for that particular trait. If the alleles are not the same, the individual is said to be *heterozygous* for the trait. A plant may carry the allele for red flowers on one chromosome and the allele for white flowers on the other. The plant would be heterozygous and might be pink, or red with white stripes. As you may remember from biology classes, heterozygosity does not have to be expressed. If one gene is dominant and one is recessive, the dominant one will influence some bodily characteristic while the recessive allele will sit, waiting for its chance to be passed on to the next generation where it might be expressed as a result of a pairing with a nondominant allele. If the red allele is dominant, parents possessing at least one copy of it will be red in color. Humans with brown eyes may be homozygous or heterozygous. If these people carry the allele for blue eyes they will not have blue eyes but their offspring may, if the offspring inherits a blue-eyed allele from both parents.

Heterozygosity is often advantageous. New gene combinations within a species are likely to introduce small yet meaningful amounts of variation in individuals that carry these new combinations. If these variant individuals survive and reproduce at greater rates than others, the genes that underlie the variation will become more frequent. If enough of this selection happens, the result can be the evolution of a new species. Of course, it is also possible that new gene combinations will put some individuals at risk by disrupting an existing adaptation. Because the environment of most organisms is constantly changing, the best strategy for many organisms is to introduce some small amounts of variation within the gene pool of their descendents. By occasionally giving their gene pool a little stir, these organisms create new combinations of alleles. Sexual reproduction is one of the mechanisms that creates new combinations of alleles. There are, however, some organisms that do not sexually reproduce. Rather, these organisms can clone themselves; that is, they produce offspring that are genetically identical to the parent organism. Not surprisingly, cloning is more common in sentient organisms living in highly stable environments and less common in organisms that travel around and live in changing environments. Organisms that move around are more likely to face changes that require new adaptations.

As we mentioned in Chapter 3, a function of our immune system is to make a discrimination between what is "us" and what is some other organism. Once other organisms from outside our system have been identified, our body activates a number of defenses to keep them under control. These outside organisms might be things such as unfriendly viruses or bacteria. These and other organisms may invade our bodies and take up residence, using our resources to facilitate their own reproduction. This situation is called *parasitism.*

We have evolved defenses to repel parasites and the *parasites* have counterevolved ways to get around these defenses in an ongoing contest called *coevolution*. Given this context, it is not surprising that heterozygosity is advantageous for animals that are exposed to pathogenic parasites (Doherty & Zinkernagel, 1975; Hughes & Nei, 1988; Brown, 1997). As parasites adapt to the existing defenses of the immune system, new defenses must be developed to ensure continued protection. Heterozygosity, the introduction of varied alleles, is one way to mount these new defenses.

The MHC is a group of genes that is an important determinant of the structure of the immune system. If it is correct that a slightly changing immune system might be better at dealing with evolving parasites, an organism would be at an evolutionary advantage if it mated with members of its species that have MHC alleles different from its own. This is because any offspring that result from such unions might inherit alleles that are dissimilar. Some of these alleles would be inherited from the father and others would be inherited from the mother. If the mother and father had different alleles to donate, the offspring would be heterozygous. If parents produce MHC-heterozygous offspring, these new organisms might be better able to resist certain parasites or diseases, making it more likely that the offspring will reproduce and pass on some of their beneficial MHC alleles to future generations. However, you will notice that we said only *some* of these alleles will be passed on. Each time an organism chooses a mate, it cannot guarantee that its offspring will be heterozygous. To increase the probability of heterozygous offspring, any mechanism an organism might evolve for detecting mates with dissimilar MHC genes might be of significant benefit.

It is most usual among animals that males propose mating and females choose. This is really another way of saying that males choose females and propose mating, but females choose males and mate with them. Clearly, the female choice is the more crucial one for evolution because reproduction is the direct outcome of that choice. Nevertheless, it is possible that both males and females might benefit from being able to detect MHCs that are different from their own and so might produce heterozygous offspring. The evolutionary prediction would be that if they can detect this difference, they should prefer to mate with individuals unlike themselves.

The number of different alleles for a single gene are not unlimited. For any single characteristic influenced by a gene locus, there may be a handful of possible alleles within the gene pool of the species. One study suggested the advantage of heterozygosity is based on the evidence that human populations have more heterozgosity for MHC than would be expected if genes were distributed randomly (Hedrick & Thompson, 1983). This is only indirect evidence for heterozygote advantage and it is based on the argument that a frequently occurring genetic combination is also likely to be an adaptive combination. Perhaps more importantly, this finding carried the implication that humans may be able to manipulate the frequency of MHC heterozygosity through selective mating. Corollary to this finding is the assertion that humans possess some ability to detect MHC genes and use that information in mate selection.

Using odors, humans have been shown to be able to detect MHC differences in strains of mice that are otherwise virtually identical in genotype, that is, in overall genetic architecture (Gilbert, Yamazaki, Beauchamp, & Thomas, 1986). Also from the rodent world, rats seem to be able to make discriminations among human urine samples that differ in MHC (Ferstl, Eggert, Westphal, Zavazava, & Müller-Ruchholtz, 1992). While this cross-species evidence for MHC detection is interesting, research more directly relevant to humans has shown that humans may be able to discriminate between certain combinations of human MHC through their preferences for certain body odors (see Wedekind, Seebeck, Bettens & Paepke, 1995). For example, females have been shown to prefer the body odors of males who have fewer MHC alleles in common with them; however, this effect was not found for women taking birth control pills (Wedekind et al., 1995).

As we have noted, the female choice may be the most important one: Females will have fewer offspring and therefore should be concerned with the quality of their mate. However, it might be useful for males to be able to detect MHC heterozygosity because they also make choices, even if the final reproductive outcome depends on female acceptance. Claus Wedekind and Sandra Füri conducted a study examining male and female perceptions of body odors and their relationship with MHC-type.

PARTICIPANTS

The sample was composed of 121 college students and lab assistants who were affiliated with a Swiss university. Each participant's MHC type was assessed through sophisticated genetic tests on blood components. The participants were divided into smellers and T-shirt wearers. Six of the participants, four males and two females, were asked to be T-shirt wearers. The rest of the participants were smellers.

PROCEDURE

The T-shirt wearers, who did not have shaved armpits, wore 100 percent cotton T-shirts for two consecutive nights. They were given fragrance-free soap for showering or bathing. They were also provided with fragrance-free detergent, which they were to use to wash their bedding and other clothes. The T-shirt wearers stored the T-shirts in open plastic bags during the times they were not required to wear them. They were asked to avoid situations that could transmit odors, other than their own body odors, onto the T-shirt. For example, they were asked to avoid several situations and behaviors such as entering rooms with strong odors, smoking, drinking alcohol, having sex, sharing a bed, eating certain foods, and wearing perfume or deodorant. After the T-shirt wearers had completed their duties, the T-shirts were collected and placed in individual cardboard boxes that were lined with plastic wrap. A triangular hole was cut in the top of each box so smellers could sniff the odor emanating from the T-shirt inside. Smellers were unaware of the T-shirt wearer's gender and MHC type.

Before each test trial a layer of plastic wrap was placed on top of the cardboard box and the researcher used a scalpel to cut the wrap where the triangular hole was positioned. This was done to make the smelling situation as sanitary as possible for participants and was always conducted in front of them so they could be assured of the hygienic preparation of the box. The smellers were asked to rate each of the T-shirts for degree of odor intensity and pleasantness on separate 10-point Likert scales, with higher numbers indicating more intensity or pleasantness. One of the cardboard boxes contained an unworn T-shirt. Participants were allowed to smell this box to get a sense of what the shirt smelled like minus any body odor. Additionally, for each T-shirt odor, smellers were asked to indicate on a 10-point scale the suspected gender of the T-shirt wearer (0 = definitely female, 5 = ambiguous,

10 = definitely male). Smellers were then asked to free associate and record any memories the T-shirt odor conjured, especially if it reminded them of someone they knew (e.g., past or present partners, family members, friends, etc.). They were also asked to record if the T-shirts smelled of perfume or tobacco smoke.

Female smellers were asked to indicate if they were currently taking birth control pills because this was shown to be a confounding variable in past research (Wedekind et al., 1995). An attempt was made to have females smell the T-shirts during the second week after the beginning of menstruation. Research has indicated that females may experience heightened sensitivity to smells during this time (e.g., see Doty, Snyder, Huggins, & Lowry, 1981). Forty of the smellers had already participated in the first author's previous study where they rated T-shirt odors in a manner similar to this research. Likewise, two participants who had been T-shirt wearers in the previous study were also T-shirt wearers in this study. The researchers examined the data to see if there was a relationship between these former smellers' ratings of intensity and pleasantness for the two veteran T-shirt wearers in both the previous and current studies. No significant relationships were found (pleasantness, $r = .06$, ns; intensity, $r = .16$, ns). The authors interpret this lack of a significant relationship as evidence that experience in the previous study did not confound the results of the present study.

RESULTS

The means for intensity and pleasantness of the T-shirt odors are presented in Table 24.1. Sex of the T-shirt wearer and a significance rating for gender discrimination are also shown in this table. As you can see from this table, three of the T-shirt wearers did not completely avoid contact with tobacco smoke or perfume; one of them seems to have ignored the instructions altogether. This lack of caution on the part of the participants clearly hurts the internal validity of the study, yet can be a practical limitation in this type of research.

TABLE 24.1   Mean Ratings of Odor Intensity and Pleasantness as a Function of Sex of T-Shirt Wearer

T-SHIRT WEARER	ASSOCIATIONS TO TOBACCO SMOKE OR PERFUME	AVERAGE INTENSITY	AVERAGE PLEASANTNESS	GENDER DISCRIMINATION
M1	<1%	5.7	4.4	$t = 0.989$, ns
M2	0	7.2	3.5	$t = 9.80, p < .001$
M3	0	6.1	4.5	$t = 0.47$, ns
M4	21%	6.2	6.3	$t = 3.17, p < .01$
F1	0	4.2	5.4	$t = 3.10, p < .01$
F2	<1%	4.6	5.3	$t = 4.16, p < .001$

Note: M 1–4 = male T-shirt wearers; F1, F2 = female T-shirt wearers. Negative *t* values indicate incorrect sex.

Source: From Wedekind, C., & Füri, S. (1997). Body odour preferences in men and women: do they aim for specific MHC combinations or simple heterozygosity? *Proceedings of the Royal Society of London Series B.,* 264, 1472.

Although not shown in this table, the smellers' intensity ratings were found to be significantly different from one another ($p < .001$). Some of the variance for this effect was explained by smellers' age, with older smellers rating the odors as less intense than younger smellers. Smellers tended to rate the odors of the three T-shirts that were contaminated by tobacco smoke or perfume as more pleasant, particularly the most contaminated T-shirt, which achieved a pleasantness rating of 6.3. Furthermore, the smellers tended to rate more intense body odors as less pleasant. Correlations between pleasantness and intensity were $r = -.22$ for men and $r = -.26$ for women (both $p < .05$).

You can see from Table 24.1 that smellers were able to identify the gender of three of the T-shirt wearers significantly above the chance level. Females were more likely than males to correctly indicate the gender of these T-shirt wearers ($p < .001$). However, smellers were more likely than chance to incorrectly guess the gender of the T-shirt wearers when the T-shirt had been contaminated by smoke/perfume. None of the smellers correctly identified the gender of T-shirt wearers with 100 percent accuracy. The smellers were significantly more likely to assign the male gender to more unpleasant smells and the female gender to more pleasant ones, regardless of the actual gender of the T-shirt wearer ($p < .02$). This method of gender discrimination was more frequently used by men than women ($p = .03$).

ODOR PERCEPTION AND DEGREE OF MHC SIMILARITY

Figure 24.1 presents the relationship between smeller's perceptions of odor and degree of MHC similarity to T-shirt wearers when a particular odor reminded them of a relative, usually someone in their immediate family. The average MHC similarity between all smellers and T-shirt wearers is also shown in the figure.

Because family members are closely related, they should have more MHC alleles in common, on average, than unrelated individuals. Thus, if the smellers think that a T-shirt smells like a family member, the wearer of the T-shirt may share more MHC alleles with the smellers. If this were the case, we would expect smellers who were reminded of a relative to share more MHC genes with that wearer than was found for other smellers, who were not

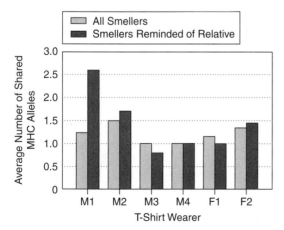

FIGURE 24.1 Average number of shared alleles among all smellers and those who believe T-shirt smells like relative.

Source: From Wedekind, C., & Füri, S. (1997). Body odour preferences in men and women: do they aim for specific MHC combinations or simple heterozygosity? *Proceedings of the Royal Society of London Series B, 264,* 1475.

particularly reminded of relatives. While this may have happened for wearer M1 in Figure 24.1, the finding does not appear for other wearers. An analysis of the overall data also did not lend support to the notion that MHC similarity reminds smellers of relatives. However, only 49 percent of these smellers ($n = 22$) were found to have more MHC alleles in common with the T-shirt wearers than would be expected by chance. If a few of the T-shirt wearers had shared most of their MHC alleles with large numbers of participants, the hypothesis might have been given a more robust test. As it was, these results were not strong enough to lend support to the MHC relatedness hypothesis. An additional problem for this research strategy is the reconstructive nature of human memory: The smellers may have formed an association between the odor of the T-shirt wearer and a family member that was reconstructed and invalid.

Figure 24.2 shows the relationship between odor perception and MHC similarity for all smellers and for those reminded of a mate. The dark bars show 28 smellers who indicated that a T-shirt's odor had reminded them of a current or past mate. For 71 percent ($n = 20$) of the 28 cases, more MHC differences were found between the T-shirt wearer and the smeller who was reminded of a mate than would be expected by chance ($p = .02$). You can see this in Figure 24.2 because in most cases the average number of shared alleles is lower for people who are reminded of a mate (dark bars) as compared to all smellers together (light bars). This finding lends support to the contention that individuals may seek mates whose MHC differs from their own. There were no significant differences for gender: Males did not differ from females in recalling past or present mates after smelling the T-shirt odors. In the analysis, six men and two women indicated that the odors of T-shirts belonging to T-shirt wearers who were of the same gender reminded them of a past mate. However, this finding does not hinder the MHC hypothesis since this hypothesis does not make specific assertions about gender; it only states that MHC among mates should differ more than chance. Furthermore, participants were not asked about possible homosexual preferences prior to the start of the study. This might be a threat to the internal validity of the study.

Correlations were computed between the smeller's rating of pleasantness for each of the six T-shirt odors and the degree of MHC similarity between the smeller and the T-shirt wearer. Women who were not currently taking birth control pills and men tended to rate the odors of T-shirt wearers as significantly more pleasant if the T-shirt wearer had more MHC alleles unlike their own. In men and non-pill women combined, the correlation between pleas-

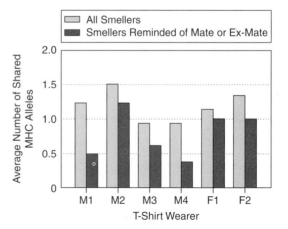

FIGURE 24.2 Average number of shared alleles among all smellers and those who believe T-shirt smells like mate or ex-mate.

Source: Wedekind, C., & Füri, S. (1997). Body odour preferences in men and women: do they aim for specific MHC combinations or simple heterozygosity? *Proceedings of the Royal Society of London Series B, 264,* 1475.

antness and MHC similarity was low but significant ($r = -.04$, $p = .02$). In contrast, women smellers on birth control pills tended to rate MHC-similar T-shirt odors as more pleasant but this correlation failed to reach significance. Individual correlations between pleasantness and MHC type varied considerably. Scores for pleasantness accounted for 2 percent to 12 percent of the variance in MHC similarity across all smellers and T-shirt wearers.

DISCUSSION

It is not clear exactly how the genes involved in the MHC are actually linked to mammalian body odors. Secretions of the apocrine glands, which are found in the axillary areas of the body (and elsewhere on the body in smaller numbers), may contain molecules that reveal the particular nature of these genes. It is also possible that human odor is largely a result of bacteria. Bacteria live on the human skin and different people have different bacterial flora. It may be that the specific MHC combinations create an environment suited for one kind of bacteria on one person and another kind on another person. In this case, body odors may be related to the components of the MHC through the bacterial environment permitted by MHC.

The effects in this study are small. Even though these percentages might not seem like very much, we think it is an important finding that any of the variance for MHC type is accounted for by odor pleasantness. There have been many social psychology studies that have studied attractiveness. Physical proximity, such as living in the same building or working for the same organization, has been shown to play a role in judgments of attractiveness (Moreland & Beach, 1992). Social similarity has also been found to be a component of attractiveness (Park & Fink, 1989). Social similarity refers to things such as attitudes, beliefs, and personal habits. We have been careful to call this *social* similarity because, in contrast, genetic dissimilarity may also be a basis for attraction.

The findings in this study provide an excellent example of the difference between proximate and ultimate factors in evolution. When a person is physically or sexually attracted to another, the attraction is likely to be based on some aspect of appearance, a proximate factor. It is, of course, also possible that people might be attracted to partners because they smell good, another proximate cue. We doubt that very many people would say, "I am attracted to my mate because our offspring would be likely to be heterozygous for MHC and they would be more likely than MHC homozygous offspring to survive and reproduce." Perhaps greeting card companies should try to raise consciousness on this matter by creating a line of ultimate reason cards with sayings such as:

> I love you my dear,
> our love is fine,
> Your MHC
> smells quite different from mine.

An alternative hypothesis for the role of MHC that was not tested separately by this study is that individuals prefer MHC-dissimilar mates because it reduces their chances for inbreeding. This explanation is not mutually exclusive of the hypothesis that heterozygosity assists the immune system. Either or both may be correct.

These two explanations are both examples of sexual selection. Sexual selection is the name given to the type of natural selection in which mate choice plays a role. Sexual selection can remove an animal from the breeding population just as surely as other forms of natural selection, such as death through failing to avoid a predator. In sexual selection, the pressure is on males to choose fertile females, while the pressure is on females to choose the best males. In many species, a few males fertilize most of the females, leaving the rest of the males selected out. Their genes will not continue in the next generation because no female chose to mate with them. The odors associated with MHC may be one means by which males and females choose each other. In this context, it is interesting that in some societies, such as ours, a great deal of time and money is spent covering up body odors. In the face of the evolutionary evidence, the reasons for this are a matter of speculation and we encourage you to ponder this issue.

CRITICAL THINKING TOOLKIT ITEMS

In the domain of evolutionary psychology, it is important to remember that conscious awareness of motives does not make any difference. Natural selection has acted on what organisms do, not on what they think about what they do. This reality is more obvious if you are considering the selection pressures on a carrot as opposed to a human, but it holds for both organisms.

REFERENCES

Brown, J. L. (1997). A theory of mate choice based on heterozygosity. *Behavior Ecology, 8,* 60–65.

Doherty, P. C., & Zinkernagel, R. M. (1975). Enhanced immunological surveillance in mice heterozygous at the H-2 gene complex. *Nature, 256,* 50–52.

Doty, R. L., Snyder, P. J., Huggins, G. R., & Lowry, L. D. (1981). Endocrine, cardiovascular, and psychological correlates of olfactory sensitivity changes during the human menstrual cycle. *Journal of Comparative Physiological Psychology, 95,* 45–60.

Ferstl, R., Eggert, F., Westphal, E., Zavazava, N., & Müller-Ruchholtz, W. (1992). MHC-related odors in humans. In R. L. Doty (Ed.), *Chemical signals in vertebrates VI* (pp. 205–211). New York: Plenum.

Gilbert, A. N., Yamazaki, K., Beauchamp, G. K., & Thomas, L. (1986). Olfactory discrimination of mouse strains (*M. musculus*) and major histocompatibilty types by humans (Homo sapiens). *Journal of Comparative Psychology, 100,* 262–265.

Hedrick, P. W., & Thompson, G. (1983). Evidence for balancing selection at HLA. *Genetics, 104,* 449–456.

Hughes, A. L., & Nei, M. (1988). Pattern of nucleotide substitution at major histocompatibility complex class I loci reveals overdominant selection. *Nature, 335,* 167–170.

Klein, J. (1986). *Natural history of the major histocompatibility complex.* New York: Wiley.

Moreland, R. L., & Beach, S. R. (1992). Exposure effects in the classroom: The development of affinity among students. *Journal of Experimental Social Psychology, 28,* 255–276.

Park, B., & Fink, C. (1989). A social relations analysis of agreement in liking judgments. *Journal of Personality and Social Psychology, 56,* 506–518.

Wedekind, C., & Füri, S. (1997). Body odour preferences in men and women: Do they aim for specific MHC combinations or simple heterozygosity? *Proceedings of the Royal Society of London Series B, 264,* 1471–1479.

Wedekind, C., Seebeck, T., Bettens, F., & Paepke, A. J. (1995). MHC-dependent mate preferences in humans. *Proceedings of the Royal Society of London Series B, 260,* 245–249.

CHAPTER 25

WORK IT OUT

Our species evolved in a situation in which there was no alternative to a low-fat diet and regular physical exercise. These constraints were imposed by the inflexible demands of the hunter-gatherer lifestyle of our distant ancestors, including long walks to collect food alternating with bursts of more vigorous physical activity during hunts. Our forbears gathered fruits and vegetables, which contain no saturated fat, and hunted animals whose meat was very lean compared to that found in the supermarkets of today. As you will have noticed, the environment we currently inhabit is much different than the one in which our ancestors dwelled for millions of years. If you are hungry, fast-food restaurants and grocery stores are found in almost every town in America (no spear required).

In the Western world, technological progress has also led to a decline in the number of people performing real manual labor as part of their jobs. It is more often the case that backhoes dig holes, trucks carry goods, and forklifts move heavy objects. One result of this departure from manual activity has been that people do not get the exercise required to maintain good health. In the past few decades, however, more awareness has been focused on the need for good diet and regular exercise throughout the adult years. We have included this topic as a chapter because it highlights a problem faced by many ordinary adults. It also is a problem with a large psychological component because although many adults know they should be exercising regularly, they do not do so.

EXERCISE

An early start may be important. Trudeau, Laurencelle, Tremblay, Rajic, and Shepherd (1999) studied 147 adults who, as children, had been in schools where they were exposed to regular physical education (PE) sessions during their first six years. They were compared to a large number of control people who did not have this experience, but who were otherwise similar in demographic factors. Questionnaire responses suggested that as adults, the women in the PE group engaged in more physical activity than control women. Fewer men from the PE group were smokers as adults. Admittedly, this study was retrospective and

Incorporating the research of J. J. Annesi, "Effects of Computer Feedback on Adherence to Exercise,"1998, *Perceptual and Motor Skills, 87,* pp. 723–730.

suffers in the manner typical of that kind of investigation, but it is an intriguing finding, even if not very robust.

Another recent study found that 87 previously inactive older adults benefited from participation in a year-long exercise program (Hill, Storandt, and Malley, 1993). Heart function improved and participants also experienced a positive change in self-reported morale. Although this research also sought evidence of cognitive changes, particularly in memory, exercise training was not shown to confer obvious benefits in the cognitive domains in this group.

PSYCHOLOGY AND EXERCISE

Psychological side effects of exercise were also investigated by Maroulakis and Zervas (1993). They studied adults exercising in a fitness club at different times of the day. Although time of day did not make much difference, overall the people who exercised had more positive ratings on a scale designed to rate mood than did nonexercising control individuals. Lee (1993) reported that the reason why some adults did not exercise was that they expected few psychological benefits. Some people were unaware of obvious health benefits, such as better sleep. In Lee's study, people were apt to believe that exercise was less important than, for example, quitting smoking as a way of achieving improved health. The nonexercisers in Lee's sample also managed to find practical barriers that they felt prevented them from working out. This suggested that attitudes might be the first hurdle in changing the amount of exercise an adult will undertake.

You may know someone who seems to be obsessed with exercise. While the evidence suggests that exercise is a good thing, some people have wondered if an overly zealous commitment to regular exercise is somehow a sign of a psychological problem. In a study by Iannos and Tiggeman (1997), 205 male and female regular exercisers were given measures that estimated the amount of exercise and a variety of personality traits. Contrary to what may be popular belief, those exercisers judged to be excessive did not seem different from others in measures of self-esteem, locus of control, or obsessive-compulsive behavior. The evidence from this study does not support the contention that commitment to exercise is an indication of a personality disorder. This might make sense if we reconsider the evolutionary roots of exercise in our lives. For most of the history of humankind, exercise was the rule, not the exception. Based on this, we might expect lack of exercise to be associated with psychological disorders, not the reverse.

Indeed, in an exciting study by Hatch, Levin, Shu, and Susser (1998) 557 pregnant women were followed through their pregnancies until delivery. Low and moderate levels of exercise did not have an effect on gestational length—the overall duration of the pregnancy. More vigorous exercise however, appeared to reduce the risk of preterm birth. This happened in spite of the common belief that such exercise might be harmful, or that it might somehow bring on birth prematurely. From the child's expected date of birth onward, vigorous exercisers also delivered sooner than nonexercisers, reducing the risk factors that accompany seriously delayed births. One such complication is that the fetus overdevelops in utero and grows too large for the birth canal. A delivery that happens about on time, not early or late, is associated with the least risk and vigorous exercise was associated with timely deliveries.

Exercise has been studied extensively for its role in rehabilitation from disease, particularly heart disease. Although many adults are more active than in past decades, more than half of the adult population is sedentary, a lifestyle that doubles the risk of coronary artery disease. Primary prevention of heart disease includes regular exercise for all adults. Secondary prevention programs, those designed for treating existing heart disease, have shown that exercise is an important component in the recuperation process (Miller, Balady, & Fletcher, 1997). Amigo, Gonzalez, and Herrera (1997) conducted an experimental study in which both relaxation and exercise were found to lower blood pressure to a greater extent than a placebo treatment. In a follow-up study neither the participants who received relaxation training nor those who performed exercise routines required medication to control high blood pressure. Regular exercise may lead to relaxation but both appear to help reduce high blood pressure, a recognized cardiovascular risk factor.

POVERTY AND MEDICAL ADVICE ABOUT EXERCISE

Poverty and education, common components of socioeconomic status (SES), also play a role in the risk of disease related to lifestyle factors such as exercise. In a sample of poor women from Philadelphia, about 85 percent of survey participants did not meet the minimum requirement for exercise set by the American Heart Association. They had little awareness that diet, smoking, and exercise were factors influencing cardiovascular disease risk (Poduri & Grisso, 1998). Poduri and Grisso (1998) also addressed the question of how people can learn about the value of exercise, particularly those people with few resources. Among the Philadelphia participants, only 34 percent said that their health care provider had ever discussed measures that might prevent heart disease. The lack of professional advice is one reason why so many studies have shown SES to be linked to health.

People with the least money are also the least healthy. In a large survey of 2,791 adults, 59 percent reported themselves to be sedentary, and only 15 percent of that group said that their health care provider had told them to increase their exercise levels (Friedman, Brownson, Peterson, & Wilkerson, 1994). The main focus of this study was replicated in a study by Kreuter, Scharff, Brennan, and Lukwago (1997) where questionnaire responses from 915 adult patients indicated no relationship between the actual content of their diet or activity level and advice on maintaining a healthy lifestyle given by a family medical practitioner. Among a group of elderly women (70–98 years old), 40 percent were not sure that their physician would approve of exercise and 25 percent felt that their physician would strongly disapprove of exercise. However, about half of this group indicated approval for exercise from their family and friends (Cousins, 1995).

The advice of physicians and, presumably, other health care providers is important. When medical providers take the time to counsel patients about exercise, levels of physical activity have been shown to increase (Calfas, Long, Sallis, & Wooten, 1996; Bull & Jamrozik, 1998).

PROGRAM EFFICACY

A number of studies have evaluated the efficacy of programs designed to promote fitness through exercise. Changes in intrinsic motivation have been shown to take place following tactics that increase involvement in exercise programs. For instance, women age 60 to 70 years were encouraged to walk on their own as part of membership in a health education group. Not only did they walk, but also they came to value the effects of exercise (Caserta & Gillett, 1998). In a similar population of retired women, active participation in exercise promoted increased knowledge of the benefits of exercise and the development of reasonable expectations regarding these benefits (Rowland, Dickinson, Newman, & Ford, 1994).

Attitudes are very important because if exercise can change attitudes, a change in attitudes toward exercise may, in turn, make exercise more likely. Attitudes have been shown to be related to intention to exercise (Theodorakis, 1994). It is easy to make excuses about lack of exercise and it has been found, for example, that some women see the consuming tasks of motherhood as being one of these barriers (Verhoef & Love, 1994). In other samples, such as seniors living in a retirement center, the timing of and access to an exercise program were cited as reasons why participation was low (Richter, Macera, Williams, & Koerber, 1993).

Incentives to maintain exercise have also been studied. Music has been shown to help in maintaining positive affect, particularly for untrained runners (Brownley, McMurray, & Hackney, 1995). Group cohesion helped to maintain attendance at workout sessions in 37 women taking fitness classes among a university setting (Spink & Carron, 1994). Adherence to programs is very important because the motivation to continue to exercise, either for rehabilitation or for general health, wanes for many adults (Dishman, 1994; Willis & Campbell, 1992).

Much of the literature in this area has concentrated on people working out in fitness centers and clubs. This is probably because people are easier to study at these locations than in their own homes. However, it seems clear that motivation to exercise can fade, regardless of whether the exercise program occurs in a fitness club or a home. The plethora of exercise equipment described as "almost new" that is available through newspaper classified advertisements and at garage sales would seem to testify to the lack of commitment to exercise at home. Most of the methods that have been found to attack the persistence problems faced by fitness center members are costly because they consume significant staff time and resources. These approaches usually involve detailed feedback of performance with suggestions for adjustments to exercise plans as fitness levels increase. Yet, while a consultation is being given to one member, other members may also want the staff to help with machines, give advice on maneuvers, or provide a personal feedback session.

SCIENCE AND COMMERCIALISM

Annesi (1998) described a research project that evaluated a device called the FitLinxx Interactive Fitness Network designed to overcome the problem of expensive staff feedback. One of the reasons why we chose to include this study is that, although it presents evidence for the efficacy of a commercial product, it was published in a psychology journal, *Perceptual and Motor Skills*. The research was conducted by Dr. James Annesi, who, according to the information in the original journal article, has an appointment at Rutgers, the State University of New Jersey, and also works for Enhanced Performance Technologies. This presents an interesting issue. One extreme view might be that the research is being used as an infomercial to sell the product. A less extreme stance, though still somewhat accusatory, would be that the prestige of the journal is somehow being prostituted if the article is seen as an endorsement of the product. Another negative allegation which could be made is that the research was only done to provide "scientific evidence" of the effectiveness of this device. At least at the time of this writing, the Fitlinxx Website did not specifically mention the publication of the article (check for yourself at http://www.fitlinxx.com). We are not suggesting the correctness of any of these views; we are only describing them.

While it may be easy to think that science should not dirty its hands with commercial bias, it is important to remember that science is a very biased enterprise. Sometimes beginning students think that scientists rise above bias, have no strong opinions, and would be happy with any research outcome in a quest to discover the unknown. While this might be a cheerful and charming view of the world, it is probably not very accurate. Scientists are highly biased individuals. Their biases are called *theories* or *hypotheses* and scientists are always trying to convince other scientists of the correctness of their views. The nature of convincing evidence in science is the presentation of a robust study that supports its hypothesis. Studies must be convincing demonstrations; if they are not, they will be criticized by other researchers. The objectivity in science comes from this process, not from any lack of strongly biased beliefs on the part of individual scientists. In this context, we do not see why there should be any particular problem with a scientific study being done to promote a bias that is commercial rather than theoretical. Studies promote strongly held beliefs of one sort or another, commercial or otherwise. If a study does not effectively exclude other hypotheses, it will be criticized.

PARTICIPANTS

The participants in the treatment group of the Fitlinxx study were 93 adult members of a large fitness center in the northeastern United States, with a total of around 2,700 members. It was a multisport facility but only the exercise area of the center was used for the investigation. Participants were all between 20 and 60 years old and had undertaken no regular exercise in the 6 months preceding the study. They were selected from people who joined the fitness center with new, unrestricted memberships in April and May of 1996. As far as could be determined, they were in good health. The treatment group consisted of 44 males and 49 females ($M = 0.4$, $SD = 10.7$). The control group was composed of 31 males and 40 females and had a mean age of 37.4 ($SD = 10.1$). The age difference between groups was not significant.

After joining the fitness center, all participants were given a physical assessment consisting of a body fat measurement, a flexibility evaluation, and a blood pressure reading. Their health histories were recorded and they were each given a personalized exercise regime. At intervals during the study, they received encouragement from the staff and modifications were made to their exercise plans. These procedures were administered by the fitness center professional staff to all clients, including the participants, as part of the routine of the fitness center. The individually prescribed exercise plans suggested a variety of types of workouts in keeping with recommendations from the American College of Sports Medicine (1991). Clients were told that they should exercise three times a week.

PROCEDURE

An electronic check-in device recorded each time a participant entered the exercise area. Manual and automatic systems confirmed that these electronic check-in events were valid indications that a participant was actually exercising. Beginning with the first visit to the facility, the exercise sessions of all participants were followed for 32 weeks.

The data for the treatment group were collected electronically by the Fitlinxx system installed in the fitness center. The treatment group used the Fitlinxx electronic system to record their exercise and get feedback. This device supplied feedback on exercise form, number of repetitions, and completed exercise. This was displayed on a small 9 × 6 inch computer screen on each of the machines used in the workout. When the treatment group clients arrived to check in, their exercise record would be displayed on a larger screen in numbers and, additionally, plotted as graphic presentations. The staff professionals could also access this electronic information. The staff could leave comments about adjustments to the exercise routine for review the next time the client accessed the main screen.

In the control condition, participants kept track of their exercise routines using standard exercise tracking cards. The participants noted exercises performed on various machines for each workout date. This type of pencil-and-paper recording is very common in fitness centers.

The exercise equipment, staff professionals, and policies for interaction with staff were matched for treatment and control groups. The only difference was supposed to be the electronic exercise feedback given to the treatment group.

OUTCOME MEASURES

Three types of outcome measures were used in this study: attendance, adherence, and dropout rate. Because the American College of Sports Medicine (1991) considers three workouts per week to be ideal, attendance recording was based on this number. Three or more sessions per week were counted as 3, for the purpose of attendance. A person who attended two sessions was given a score of 2 and one session per week was scored as 1. Because there were 32 weeks in the study and a maximum attendance score of 3 was allowed, the total possible attendance score was 96.

Adherence was defined as the number of weeks passing before a participant had an average score of fewer than the three sessions per week that were considered to be optimal. A dropout was a person who went for 30 days in a row with no exercise at all in the fitness center. Dropout data were reported as the number of days, counted from the beginning of the study, before the individual dropped out. The actual day of dropping out was identified as the last day of exercise before the start of a 30-day period of absence from exercise.

RESULTS

The attendance was significantly greater for the treatment group than for the control group ($p < .001$). Length of adherence to the exercise program was also longer for the treatment group ($p < .05$). Sixteen percent of the treatment group adhered 10 weeks or longer, whereas only 6 percent of the control group were still working out regularly at 10 weeks. The treatment group also went longer than the control group before dropping out altogether ($p < .001$). The means are presented in Figure 25.1.

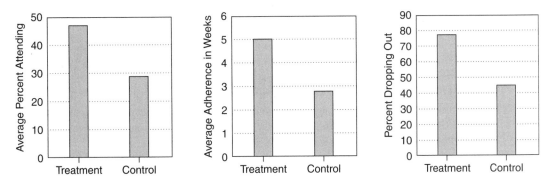

FIGURE 25.1   Outcome Measures for Treatment and Control Groups.

Source: From Annesi, J. J. (1998). Effects of computer feedback on adherence to exercise. *Perceptual and Motor Skills, 87,* 727.

Both the standard pencil-and-paper feedback and the Fitlinxx electronic feedback were associated with dropouts, but the Fitlinxx system had fewer at any given time. The data for dropouts across the 32-week span of the study are presented in Figure 25.2. By the end of the 8-month study, twice as many participants in the treatment group persisted in the exercise program compared to the control group (54 percent vs. 23 percent).

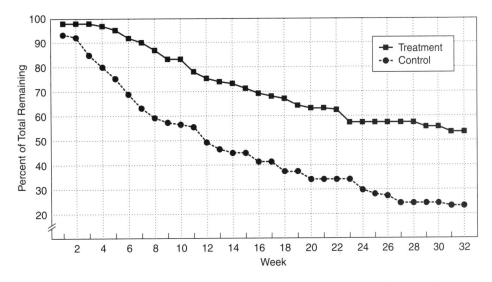

FIGURE 25.2   Participants Remaining by Week. Dropouts over the entire 8 months of the study. Because dropping out was defined as 30 consecutive days of no exercise at the center, it could not be known who was dropping out until at least 30 days passed. This graph shows the percentage of people who began their drop out during each week of the study, calculated after the study was finished.

Source: From Annesi, J. J. (1998). Effects of computer feedback on adherence to exercise. *Perceptual and Motor Skills, 87,* 727.

DISCUSSION

Annesi (1998) pointed out that the participants gave positive self-reports of the motivating qualities of the Fitlinxx. A strength of this study is that the researcher went beyond self-report and included a number of behavioral measures. Annesi also noted that this study was a short-term intervention. While 8 months may seem to be a long time, it is important to remember that adults should undertake regular physical exercise week after week, year after year. Given the trend shown in Figure 25.2, it is an open question whether the effects of Fitlinxx will last across the adult years for many participants.

One of the main uses of exercise programs with adults is in rehabilitation, and caution should be used before the findings of this study are generalized to that population. The participants in this study were all healthy adults. Motivational factors and physical difficulties might be quite different for adults requiring exercise for a problem such as cardiovascular disease.

A use of the system that was not tested in this research but that was proposed by Annesi (1998) was to use the automated feedback system to try to flag people who are in the process of dropping out. The outcome measure of adherence could be an early indicator because it reflects a decreasing number of visits to the fitness center. It would be interesting to know if staff intervention, triggered by growing adherence problems, could be a preventative for dropouts.

In the original research article and on the Website, the Fitlinxx system is advertised as a device to cut costs in the fitness business by keeping clients from dropping out while, at the same time, being able to avoid the expense of additional personalized staff time. This sales pitch is, of course, typical of a business venture. At the time of this writing the Website also featured quotes from frustrated fitness club managers such as: "We are fighting for the same 10 percent of the market as everyone else. How can we attract seniors or the 'ready to stay fit' and get them to stay?" The presumption seems to be that Fitlinxx is the answer. While there may be answers to these questions, they are not found in this research because the issues of attracting people to fitness were not addressed.

What this article does make clear is that there is a place for psychological research in business applications. It also illustrates the role that applied psychology can have in helping organizations evaluate products and services. All organizations need to do this, and skills obtained in this domain, which come from taking scientifically oriented psychology courses such as this one, should be attractive to employers in many fields.

CRITICAL THINKING TOOLKIT ITEMS

Science is not the work of unbiased people seeking to discover the unknown. Scientists are biased but they state their biases openly as hypotheses. Scientists usually know what they are hoping to find. They engineer situations to convince others of the correctness of their views. The research design of the situation so engineered should take care to eliminate as much bias as possible or it will be criticized by others. This is the nature of objectivity in science.

REFERENCES

American College of Sports Medicine. (1991). *Guidelines for testing and prescription* (4th ed.). Philadelphia: Lea & Febiger.

Amigo, I., Gonzalez, A., & Herrera, J. (1997). Comparison of physical exercise and muscle relaxation training in the treatment of mild essential hypertension. *Stress Medicine, 13,* 59–65.

Annesi, J. J. (1998). Effects of computer feedback on adherence to exercise. *Perceptual and Motor Skills, 87,* 723–730.

Brownley, K. A., McMurray, R. G., & Hackney, A. C. (1995). Effects of music on physiological and affective responses to graded treadmill exercise in trained and untrained runners. *International Journal of Psychophysiology, 19,* 193–201.

Bull, F. C., & Jamrozik, K. (1998). Advice on exercise from a family physician can help sedentary patients to become active. *American Journal of Preventive Medicine, 15,* 85–94.

Calfas, K. J., Long, B. J., Sallis, J. F., & Wooten, W. J. (1996). A controlled trial of physician counseling to promote the adoption of physical activity. *Preventive Medicine, 25,* 225–233.

Caserta, M. S., & Gillett, P. A. (1998). Older women's feelings about exercise and their adherence to an aerobic regimen over time. *Gerontologist, 38,* 602–609.

Cousins, S. O. (1995). Social support for exercise among elderly women in Canada. *Health Promotion International, 10,* 273–282.

Dishman, R. K. (Ed.). (1994). *Advances in exercise adherence.* Champaign, IL: Human Kinetics.

Friedman, C., Brownson, R. C., Peterson, D. E., & Wilkerson, J. C. (1994). Physician advice to reduce chronic disease risk factors. *American Journal of Preventive Medicine, 10,* 367–371.

Hatch, M., Levin, B., Shu, X., & Susser, M. (1998). Maternal leisure-time exercise and timely delivery. *American Journal of Public Health, 88,* 1528–1533.

Hill, R. D., Storandt, M., & Malley, M. (1993). The impact of long-term exercise training on psychological function in older adults. *Journals of Gerontology, 48,* 12–17.

Iannos, M., & Tiggeman, M. (1997). Personality of the excessive exerciser. *Personality & Individual Differences, 22,* 775–778.

Kreuter, M. W., Scharff, D. P., Brennan, L. K., & Lukwago, S. N. (1997). Physician recommendations for diet and physical activity: Which patients get advised to change? *Preventive Medicine, 26,* 825–833.

Lee, C. (1993). Attitudes, knowledge, and stages of change: A survey of exercise patterns in older Australian women. *Health Psychology, 12,* 476–480.

Maroulakis, E., & Zervas, Y. (1993). Effects of aerobic exercise on mood of adult women. *Perceptual & Motor Skills, 76,* 795–801.

Miller, T. D., Balady, G. J., & Fletcher, G. F. (1997). Exercise and its role in the prevention and rehabilitation of cardiovascular disease. *Annals of Behavioral Medicine, 19,* 220–229.

Poduri, A., & Grisso, J. A. (1998). Cardiovascular risk factors in economically disadvantaged women: A study of prevalence and awareness. *Journal of the National Medical Association, 90,* 531–536.

Richter, D. L., Macera, C. A., Williams, H., & Koerber, M. (1993). Disincentives to participation in planned exercise activities among older adults. *Health Values, 17,* 51–55.

Rowland, L., Dickinson, E. J., Newman, P., & Ford, D. (1994). Look after your heart programme: Impact on health status, exercise knowledge, attitudes, and behavior of retired women in England. *Journal of Epidemiology & Community Health, 48,* 123–128.

Spink, K. S., & Carron, A. V. (1994). Group cohesion effects in exercise classes. *Small Group Research, 25,* 26–42.

Trudeau, F., Laurencelle, L., Tremblay, J., Rajic, M., & Shepherd, R. J. (1999). Daily primary school physical education: Effects on physical activity during adult life. *Medicine & Science in Sports & Exercise, 31,* 111–117.

Theodorakis, Y. (1994). Planned behavior, attitude strength, role identity, and the prediction of exercise behavior. *Sport Psychologist, 8,* 149–165.

Verhoef, M. J., & Love, E. J. (1994). Women and exercise participation: The mixed blessings of motherhood. *Health Care for Women International, 15,* 297–306.

Willis, J. D., & Campbell, L. F. (1992). *Exercise psychology.* Champaign, IL: Human Kinetics.

CHAPTER 26

BLOWING IN THE WIND

Most people are exposed to at least one traumatic event during the course of their lifetime. Traumatic events can be defined as unusual, potentially life-threatening circumstances, which are not faced on a daily basis. This could be as private as being the victim of a physical assault or experiencing a death in the family. It could be as public as witnessing the horror of war. Sometimes people who have been exposed to traumatic events experience negative psychological symptoms that are collectively defined as post-traumatic stress disorder (PTSD). According to the *Diagnostic and Statistical Manual,* 4th edition, (*DSM-IV;* American Psychiatric Association, 1994), symptoms of PTSD include uncontrollable fear, nightmares, anxiety, depression, intrusive recollections or flashbacks, avoidance of stimuli associated with past trauma, emotional numbing, and increased restlessness. Substance abuse problems are recognized as a complication that can accompany this disorder. To qualify for diagnosis, symptoms must persist for at least one month. *DSM-IV* specifically excludes common experiences such as common bereavements, chronic illness, business problems, and marital disruption.

SHELL SHOCK

PTSD has existed throughout known history, and was particularly evident in soldiers returning from combat. For instance, during World War I and World War II this disorder was often referred to as *shell shock* or *combat fatigue* and was manifested by increasing irritability and a tendency to be startled by minor noises. Many American GIs returning from Vietnam experienced symptoms of PTSD. In fact, Vietnam vets were approximately 25 times as likely to commit suicide as the average person who had not been involved in the Vietnam conflict (Pollock, Rhodes, Boyle, Decoufle, & McGee 1990; Peterson, Prout, & Schwarz, 1991). It is important to keep in mind that a person suffering from PTSD did not necessarily possess any negative psychological symptoms before the traumatic event occurred. In serious cases of PTSD a person can seemingly reexperience the traumatic event at any time, without warning. For example, a person who fought in the Vietnam War might hear the backfiring of car exhaust and duck for cover, thinking a grenade or land mine has just exploded.

Incorporating the research of M. P. Thompson, F. H. Norris, and B. Hanacek, "Age Differences in the Psychological Consequences of Hurricane Hugo," 1993, *Psychology and Aging, 8,* pp. 606–616.

PTSD may be very long lasting. World War II concentration camp survivors who developed PTSD continued to show the symptom of emotional numbing many years after the event. The emotional responses of these individuals were flat and they avoided any discussion of the event. When asked about the experience, one survivor said with no obvious emotion: "What is there to say? There was just killing and death" (Kinzie, Frederickson, Ben, Fleck, & Karls, 1984, p. 646).

AGE AND PTSD

Not everyone who experiences a traumatic event develops PTSD. Little is known about why some people experience PTSD while others do not. The cognitive component—meaning the way the person views the event—has been shown to make a difference in one's susceptibility to this disorder (Janoff-Bullman, 1985). This suggests that it may not be the event itself that predisposes individuals to PTSD. The seriousness of PTSD symptoms have also been known in some cases to increase with advancing age, contrary to the common sense notion that time will heal the wounds (Leopold & Dillon, 1963).

Age has been found to have another role in recovery from trauma. The age at which disaster is experienced has been found to be a variable in the probability of recovery. Notice that this is a different finding than the age-related increase in symptoms mentioned in the previous paragraph. Huerta and Horton (1978) found that flood survivors over 65 years old expressed less emotional burden than survivors under 65. Among the older group, 29 percent responded to a survey that they believed they would never fully recover from the experience. Among the younger participants, 42 percent felt they would not recover. Similar age trends have been reported for hurricane victims (Bolin & Klenow, 1985–1986) and tornado victims (Bell, 1978). In these and other studies of the response to traumatic events at different ages, there has been no standard for age categories such as young or old people. When finer distinctions have been made, some research has found a curvilinear trend in which middle-age people have the most negative reactions to disaster (Gleser, Green, & Winget, 1981; Shore, Tatum, & Vollmer, 1986; Price, 1978).

EXPLANATORY MODELS

Thompson, Norris, and Hanacek (1993) used a longitudinal design to examine how people of different ages cope with the trauma of living in an area hit by a severe hurricane. They were primarily concerned with the question: "What age group is most likely to experience negative psychological symptoms after being exposed to a natural disaster?" They presented four perspectives, or hypotheses, about age effects, each of which had received some support from previous literature:

1. The *exposure perspective* suggests that elderly people will suffer more from disasters because they are less likely to receive warnings and less likely to heed warnings to evacuate. In addition, they are more exposed to consequences because they have highly stable patterns of life and so may feel disruption more acutely (Friedsam, 1962).
2. The *resource perspective* suggests that older people should do less well following disaster because they have fewer physical or economic resources. Being less robust

physically might make them more vulnerable to extreme stress. Having less money might make it more difficult for them to rebuild their predisaster lifestyles (Philfer, 1990; Kaniasty, Norris, & Murrell, 1990).

3. The *inoculation perspective* suggests that the ability to cope with traumatic events should increase with age. Over the life span, people are repeatedly exposed to varying levels of stress. This viewpoint assumes that repeated exposure desensitizes people to disaster, making them better able to adjust because of past exposure to stressors (Eysenck, 1983).

4. The *burden perspective* suggests that the worst effects of disaster will fall on individuals who are in the roles of providing for others. This notion fits best with the findings that middle-age people are most affected by the stress of disaster. In middle age, people are most likely to have responsibility for children and perhaps also have parents, or other elderly relatives, who require social or economic support. Middle adults have been called "the sandwich generation" because they are sandwiched between provider roles for younger and older people. In the face of disaster, it is one thing to worry about your own well-being; having to also worry about the daily lives of others in emergency conditions is likely to compound stress.

The disaster that provided the stress studied by Thompson et al. (1993) was Hurricane Hugo, which lasted from 10 to 22 September 1989. It came across the West Indies and hit the U.S. coast at South Carolina. A search of Internet sources revealed slightly different damage figures, but Hugo caused approximately $7 billion in damage, $5 billion of this in South Carolina alone. For example, about 30 supposedly well-constructed buildings in downtown Charleston were completely flattened. Hugo caused about 60 deaths, 28 of which were in the United States. The bulk of the deaths were in Puerto Rico, where the storm was followed by mass looting and riots. Many people in North and South Carolina were without homes, food, or electricity for weeks following the storm.

PARTICIPANTS

The participants were 1,000 economically and racially diverse adults whose ages ranged from 18 to 89 years old. In order to attain 1,000 participants, a total of 1,404 people were approached to participate. Four hundred four people declined to participate in the study; most of them cited lack of interest as their primary reason for nonparticipation. Two hundred fifty participants were selected from each of four cities along the East Coast: Charleston, South Carolina; Charlotte, North Carolina; Greenville, South Carolina; and Savannah, Georgia. Charleston and Charlotte were considered target cities because both had sustained heavy storm damage from Hugo. In order to be selected as a participant in these two cities, a person had to live in a neighborhood that had sustained hurricane damage and continued to show signs of this damage for several weeks following Hugo's breach of the mainland. Correspondingly, neighborhoods in Greenville and Savannah were used as comparison sites because they were undamaged. Participants in all cities were placed into one of the following age categories: young adults (18–39 years); middle-age adults (40–59 years); and elderly adults (60+ years). Restrictions were placed on the number of participants who could be selected from each residential block, and only one member of a given household was allowed to supply data for the study.

PROCEDURE

Participants were interviewed in their own neighborhoods one year after Hugo. In addition, two follow-up interviews were conducted at 6 and 12 months after the initial interview had taken place.

Measurement Instruments

Levels of depression, anxiety, and somatic complaints were assessed using the Brief Symptom Inventory (BSI; Derogatis & Spencer, 1982). The BSI measured overall symptoms, depression, anxiety, and somatic complaints. The BSI has alpha levels ranging from .77 to .90. This means that the measurements are quite internally consistent, as you will remember from Chapter 4. Questionnaire measures were also obtained on the participant's level of general life stress using a version of the Perceived Stress Scale (PSS; Cohen, Kamarck, & Mermelstein, 1983). This instrument was not particularly oriented to disaster survivors. Levels of traumatic stress (TS) were measured with a scale developed by Norris (1990) that assessed symptoms similar to those of PTSD, such as being easily startled. Alpha levels for these two instruments were .84 and .76, respectively. A separate pilot study was conducted to confirm the reliability of the measures (Norris & Kaniasty, 1992). For each of these instruments, the participants' responses were scored on 5-point scales with 0 indicating that they had not experienced any negative psychological symptoms owing to the disaster in the past 4 weeks, and 4 indicating that over the past 4 weeks they had experienced, or were currently experiencing, extreme levels of psychological symptoms.

Finally, data were collected on four disaster strain measures to assess the extent to which Hurricane Hugo had disturbed the participants' lives. The measures were rated on a 2-point scale, as either present or absent, and consisted of questions about the following issues:

Injury: Were either you or someone who lives with you physically injured as a direct result of the hurricane?

Life-Threat: Did you believe at any time during the hurricane that your life was in danger?

Financial Loss: Have you lost more than one thousand dollars in mostly uninsured items?

Personal Loss: Did you experience the loss of important sentimental objects?

RESULTS

Symptoms over Time

A complex statistical analysis called a *curvilinear regression* was used to analyze the data. The details of this statistical process are beyond the scope of this book but it will be sufficient for our purposes to say that it sought significant relationships between the outcome measures—overall symptoms, depression, anxiety, and somatic complaints from the BSI, as well as general stress from the PSS and traumatic stress from the Norris instrument—and each of the four disaster strain measures.

The statistically significant relationships that were found for the assessments at 12, 18, and 24 months are shown in Table 26.1. Each of the relationships shown in Table 26.1 was based only on those participants who reported a particular disaster strain. For example, the strain called *injury* only shows the symptom reports for people who actually reported having been injured.

As you can see, each of the outcomes was significantly related to each of the six symptom outcome measures a year after the hurricane. An overall scan of Table 26.1 further indicates that these significant relationships tend to fade away as time passed. However, even 2 years after the event, a significant relationship continues to exist between reports of injury from the hurricane and stress, both general and traumatic. This attests to the long-lasting nature of symptoms similar to classic PTSD. Perhaps unsurprisingly, there was a strong relationship between the report of symptoms and the feeling that Hugo had been a personal life threat. Only anxiety has ceased to have a significant relationship to life threat 2 years after the hurricane. Financial loss seems to be the disaster strain that is most quickly overcome with respect to specific physical symptoms, although there is some evidence of associated long-term stress. Personal loss was the destruction of potentially irreplaceable

TABLE 26.1   Significant Relationships between Type of Disaster Strain Experienced and Psychological Outcomes at 12 Months, 18 Months, and 24 Months Following the Hurricane

INJURY N = 630				LIFE THREAT N = 769			
	12 Mos.	*18 Mos.*	*24 Mos.*		*12 Mos.*	*18 Mos.*	*24 Mos.*
overall symptoms	***	**	ns	overall symptoms	***	***	**
depression	***	***	ns	depression	***	***	*
anxiety	***	***	ns	anxiety	***	***	ns
somatic complaints	***	ns	***	somatic complaints	***	**	***
general stress	***	***	**	general stress	***	**	***
traumatic stress	***	***	***	traumatic stress	***	**	***
FINANCIAL LOSS N = 669				**PERSONAL LOSS N = 646**			
overall symptoms	***	ns	ns	overall symptoms	***	ns	*
depression	*	ns	ns	depression	***	ns	ns
anxiety	***	ns	ns	anxiety	***	ns	***
somatic complaints	***	ns	ns	somatic complaints	***	ns	***
general stress	*	ns	*	general stress	***	*	ns
traumatic stress	*	ns	**	traumatic stress	***	*	ns

ns = not significant.
* = $p < .05$.
** = $p < .01$.
*** = $p < .001$.

Source: From Thompson, M. P., Norris, F. H. & Hanacek, B. (1993). Age differences in the psychological consequences of Hurricane Hugo. *Psychology and Aging, 8*, 606–616.

sentimental objects, such as family photographs, and this was also strongly associated with symptoms 1 year after Hugo. This relationship also faded with time.

In summary, injury and life threat seem to have a more lasting association with symptom outcomes than loss of money or objects. These findings appear to make sense if you remember that these people experienced the awesome power of a hurricane in their own neighborhoods. They really had been at risk. You can get a sense of this if you imagine yourself living in an area where a natural disaster has just taken place. Any efforts that can be made to control the situation, to prevent injury, and stop damage seem puny in the face of natural forces (McPhee, 1989). It seems logical to assume that you would score high on many different psychological symptom measures if you, or one of your family members, had been injured during a natural disaster. Conversely, you might not score as high on all psychological symptom measures if you had lost a few material objects, some of which you might even be able to replace.

Age and Symptoms

The researchers also examined the relationships between age of participant, number of symptoms, and a measure called disaster strain exposure. Disaster strain exposure was operationally defined by the number of disaster strains people experienced as the result of Hurricane Hugo. Each participant's data were examined to determine if a person was considered to be exposed or not. In order for a person to be considered exposed they had to have experienced 3 to 4 disaster-related strains. Unexposed participants were those who indicated experiencing no strains, mostly those people who lived in the comparison cities where the hurricane had not caused damage.

It is common in psychological research that the researchers will choose participants who represent the extreme cases in order to illustrate the effects of an event that is being studied. In this analysis participants were only considered if they belonged to one of two groups: exposed or unexposed. As you can see in the operational definitions, these groups represented the extremes: the exposed group was not merely "exposed," they experienced multiple stressors as a result of the hurricane. By assigning participants to these two groups, and dropping out those who fell in between, the effects of the hurricane can be seen more clearly. What is most important is that the researchers have told us how participants were assigned to groups. When considering the results as a critical thinker, you should remember that the comparison was between people who had no experience of the hurricane in their city and people who not only experienced it, but who were exposed to considerable strain as a result. Scientific reports are obliged to describe the operational definitions of terms such as "exposed to disaster strain." Unfortunately, media reports are not constrained in this way. In order to question a media report of a scientific study, you should ask yourself what might have been done to assign participants to groups. In order to critically evaluate a scientific study, you should remember to pay attention to operational definitions as they bear on group assignment. The results for the strain exposure measures, taken 12 months following the hurricane, are presented in Figure 26.1.

The measure of total symptoms in Figure 26.1 is a transformed score showing the standard deviations for the total symptoms. You will remember our discussion about standard deviations from Chapter 10. The standard deviation (*SD*) indicates the location of a single score with respect to the other scores in the group. A score that falls at plus one

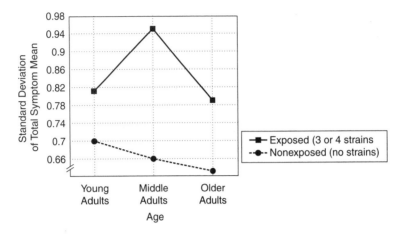

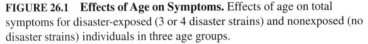

FIGURE 26.1   Effects of Age on Symptoms. Effects of age on total symptoms for disaster-exposed (3 or 4 disaster strains) and nonexposed (no disaster strains) individuals in three age groups.

Source: From Thompson, M. P., Norris, F. H. & Hanacek, B. (1993). Age differences in the psychological consequences of Hurricane Hugo. *Psychology and Aging, 8,* 612.

standard deviation is higher than about 84 percent of all the scores in the group. The total symptom scores for the exposed middle adults are quite close to this value, highlighting the effects of the disaster on this group. They have quite a few symptoms compared to older and younger exposed adults.

Looking at Figure 26.1, you can see that in the exposed condition, middle-age adults possessed the highest levels of psychological symptoms, followed by young adults and older adults. In contrast, younger adults possessed the highest number of psychological symptoms in the unexposed condition, followed by middle-age and older adults.

As with the data from Table 26.1, the researchers also used a regression analysis procedure to evaluate the effects of disaster strain on psychological outcomes within the age groups at the 12-month data collection. For this analysis, the researchers re-divided the participants into four age groupings: young adults (18–34 years), early-middle-age adults (35–49 years), late-middle-age adult (50–64 years) and older adults (65+ year). The results of these findings are presented in Figure 26.2. The data presented here are regression coefficients, which are similar to correlation coefficients. Scaled within a range of +1.00 to −1.00, they show the strength of relationship between symptoms and disaster strain for each age group.

The findings indicated that late-middle-age adults experienced the greatest psychological symptomatology across all disaster strains ($p < .001$,) followed by early-middle-age adults (at least $p < .05$ for all except financial loss, which was *ns*) and older adults (also at least $p < .05$, except for financial loss). The findings for the young adults across all disaster strains were nonsignificant. The findings for young adults are particularly interesting because, as shown in Figure 26.1, young adults possessed the greatest level of psychological symptoms among those people who were not exposed to the hurricane. The authors stated that the reason older adults did not experience significant negative outcomes for financial

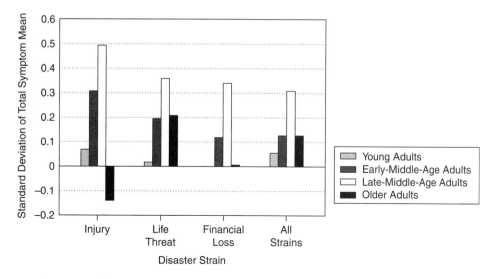

FIGURE 26.2   Effects of Disaster Strain on Overall Psychological Symptoms.

Source: From Thompson, M. P., Norris, F. H. & Hanacek, B. (1993). Age differences in the psychological consequences of Hurricane Hugo. *Psychology and Aging, 8,* 606–616 .

loss was because they were more likely than other age groups to have insurance that sufficiently covered many damages to their property. Even though younger adults had less insurance, the youngest may have had less financial investment in objects and, therefore, less to lose.

TESTS OF HYPOTHESES

You will remember that Thompson et al. (1993) offered four perspectives, or hypotheses, about the effects of disaster on different age groups. The exposure perspective predicted that the elderly would suffer the most from disaster because they would not follow warnings that might disrupt their usual daily habits. The data did not support this contention. The resource perspective, stating that fragile physical and financial conditions might make elderly people more susceptible to harm from disaster, was also not supported. The inoculation perspective, that experience with the problems of life should increase the ability to deal with disasters over the life span, was also inconsistent with the data at least for those exposed to the hurricane. In nonexposed individuals, as shown in Figure 26.1, something like this might be seen in the downward trend for symptoms across the life span but it is important to note that these data are cross-sectional. There is always a possibility of cohort effects in this kind of data collection. Thompson et al. (1993) collected data on the most obvious cohort effects by asking how many previous disasters each age group had experienced. No differences were found in frequency of previous disaster experience when early- and late-middle-age and elderly people were compared. This finding undermined the basic premise of the inoculation perspective: that the experience accumulates over the adult life span.

The burden perspective, that those who are responsible for the welfare of other people will be most affected by disaster, was the most congruent with the data. The striking difference between middle adults who had been exposed and those who had not been exposed shown in Figure 26.1 might be taken as support of this hypothesis. Likewise, the differences in the relationships between age and total symptoms across disaster strains found in Figure 26.2 also seems to support this hypothesis. Early- and late-middle-age adults reporting injury, life threat, and total disaster strains showed significant levels of stress. In a detailed analysis of separate questionnaire items, all daily stresses were greater for the middle-age adults except marital stress, which was greatest for the young adults ($p < .001$), and physical stress, which was greatest for older adults ($p < .001$).

The authors point out that the symptoms in this study were not at a level that would qualify them for PTSD or other psychopathology. However, the effects were serious and, in some cases, were long lasting. It is important to note that the first measurement in this study was taken a year after the disaster. Reasonable ethical concerns would limit the desirability of trying to collect data on participants who had experienced a hurricane a few days earlier, but it seems almost certain that the amounts of distress and symptoms would have been much greater immediately following the event. Nevertheless, psychological symptoms were common even 1 or 2 years later, particularly for people who had been injured or experienced a life threat.

NEEDING AND GIVING SUPPORT

One of the scales given to the exposed group assessed the extent to which people had provided support to others and the extent to which they had received it. Young people provided a great deal of support, but also received considerable support in return. Elderly people received relatively little social support but also gave little. Social support, in this context, goes beyond looking after physical well-being. It includes things such as offers of help with children, procurement of supplies, cooking, and other daily life tasks in a disaster area. In any event, both the young and the old maintained a balance between support received and support provided. In contrast, the middle-age people received considerable support, but they provided more than they received. Individual questionnaire items indicated that middle adults have heavy burdens without the intervention of natural disaster. Separate analysis of questionnaire items showed the middle adults to be experiencing more problems with children and more concern over money and jobs, as well as concern for issues of neighborhoods and schools, such as drugs, crime, and noise. Adding the stress of a disaster to these daily worries was likely to result in psychological symptoms.

With a certain amount of diffidence, Thompson et al. (1993) suggested that one resource available in disaster situations might be the elderly. No one is suggesting that elderly people should be clambering over the rubble of collapsed buildings swinging pickaxes, but given their life experience there are a number of things that they could do. Certainly, the healthy and educated elderly could help with relief program administration and could be useful in child care, house sitting, and meal preparation if they had the required skills. In this way some of the extraordinary burden brought on by an emergency might be borne by older people, relieving some of the pressure on the middle adult providers. The results of this study "are certainly compatible with this view" (p. 615).

CRITICAL THINKING TOOLKIT ITEMS

Pay attention to operational definitions of group membership when these groups are compared in a study. They may represent extreme cases or be unrepresentative in other ways. The nature of operational definitions is one of the first questions to ask in evaluating assertions about behavior. Media reports rarely give this essential information.

REFERENCES

American Psychiatric Association. (1994). *Diagnostic and statistical manual of mental disorders* (4th ed.). Washington DC: Author.

Bell, B. (1978). Disaster impact and response: Overcoming the thousand natural shocks. *The Gerontologist, 18,* 531–540.

Bolin, R., & Klenow, D. (1982–1983). Response of the elderly to disaster: An age-stratified analysis. *International Journal of Aging and Human Development, 16,* 283–296.

Cohen, S., Kamarck, T., & Mermelstein, R. (1983). A global measure of perceived stress. *Journal of Health and Social Behavior, 24,* 385–396.

Derogatis, L., & Spencer, L. M. (1982). *The Brief Symptom Inventory (BSI): Administration, scoring, and procedures manual-I.* Baltimore: Author.

Eysenck, H. J. (1983). Stress, disease, and personality: "The inoculation effect." In C. L. Cooper (Ed.), *Stress research* (pp. 121–146). New York: Wiley.

Friedsam, H. (1962). Older persons in disaster. In G. W. Baker & D. W. Chapman (Eds.), *Man and society in disaster* (pp. 151–182). New York: Basic.

Gleser, G., Green, B. L., & Winget, C. M. (1981). *Prolonged psychosocial effects of disaster: A study of Buffalo Creek.* San Diego, CA: Academic Press.

Huerta, F., & Horton, R. (1978). Coping behavior of elderly flood victims. *The Gerontologist, 18,* 541–546.

Janoff-Bullman, R. (1985). Aftermath of victimization: Rebuilding shattered assumptions. In C. R. Figley (Ed.), *Trauma and its wake* (pp. 15–31). New York: Brunner/Mazel.

Kaniasty, K., Norris, F., & Murrell, S. (1990). Received and perceived social support following natural disaster. *Journal of Applied Psychology, 20,* 85–114.

Kinzie, J. D., Frederickson, R. H., Ben, R., Fleck, J., & Karls, W. (1984). Posttraumatic stress disorder. *American Journal of Psychiatry, 141,* 645–650.

Leopold, R. L., & Dillon, H. (1963). Psychoanatomy of a disaster: A long-term study of post-traumatic neuroses in survivors of a marine explosion. *American Journal of Psychiatry, 119,* 913–921.

McPhee, J. (1989). *The Control of Nature.* New York: Farrar, Straus & Giroux.

Norris, F. (1990). Screening for traumatic stress: A scale for use in the general population. *Journal of Applied Social Psychology, 20,* 1704–1718.

Norris, F., & Kaniasty, K. (1992). Reliability of delayed self-reports in disaster research. *Journal of Traumatic Stress, 5,* 575–588.

Peterson, K. C., Prout, M. F., & Schwarz, R. A. (1991). *Post-traumatic stress disorder: A clinician's guide.* New York: Plenum.

Philfer, J. (1990). Psychological distress and somatic symptoms after natural disaster: Differential vulnerability among older adults. *Psychology and Aging, 5,* 412–420.

Pollock, D. A., Rhodes, P., Boyle, C. A., Decoufle, P., & McGee, D. L. (1990). Estimating the number of suicides among Vietnam veterans. *American Journal of Psychiatry, 147,* 772–776.

Price, J. (1978). Some age-related effects of the 1974 Brisbane floods. *Australian and New Zealand Journal of Psychiatry, 12,* 55–58.

Shore, J., Tatum, E., & Vollmer, W. (1986). Evaluation of mental effects of disaster, Mount St. Helens eruption. *American Journal of Public Health, 76,* 76–83.

Thompson, M. P., Norris, F. H., & Hanacek, B. (1993). Age differences in the psychological consequences of Hurricane Hugo. *Psychology and Aging, 8,* 606–616.

CHAPTER 27

BACK TO WORK

For most adults, work is not only a source of income; it is the primary way in which waking time is spent. Some people are defined by their work, and take great pride in it, while for others work can be a boring and dreary necessity. Perhaps in contrast to common sense notions, high pay is not the most important consideration in job satisfaction; challenge and creativity have been shown to be more important (Wickler & August, 1995).

Overall, research has shown that regardless of occupational level, job satisfaction tends to increase with age. This is particularly true for contentment with the specific tasks of work. Other aspects of employment, such as quality of supervision and pay, do not change as much over the career (Warr, 1994). Some of the older and more simplistic stage notions of career development, such as those proposed by Super (1974) and Ginzberg (Minor, 1992), failed to include a phenomenon called *mid-career assessment.* This is a period of time in which work is reexamined and workers may feel less positive about their jobs (Warr, 1992). There are a number of reasons for this reassessment, including lack of promotion and the fading challenge associated with doing the same job for years. Women are more likely than men to take a break from a career to assume family responsibilities and, for them, returning to the workforce can be associated with reevaluation of employment.

JOB MOBILITY

Although people entering the workforce should now expect periodic changes in employment, this has not always been the case. Previous generations were more likely to find a job and stay in it for life. Adult workers used to be less likely to have to change jobs (Rhodes, 1983) but the change, if it happened, was more traumatic for middle adults. One of the reasons behind the changes experienced by many employees has been the extent to which the day-to-day value of company stock has become a force in corporate management. Investors may be much more concerned with short-term profitability than with the long-term good of a company. CEOs who are not able to produce ever-increasing profits may soon find themselves unemployed. The personal feelings of loyal workers may be the last factor

Incorporating the research of J. C. Rife, and J. R. Belcher, "Assisting Unemployed Older Workers to Become Reemployed: An Experiment Evaluation," 1994, *Research on Social Work Practice, 4,* pp. 3–13.

considered as companies are realigned, downsized, moved, sold, or closed. Unemployment, particularly when not chosen by the worker, can be difficult. It is accompanied by a sudden drop in income that presents practical problems. Parallel to these problems are the difficulties faced by workers for whom work provides the major definition of their identity. They lose more than money when they are thrown out of work; they may also have feelings of personal worthlessness (Voydanoff, 1983).

Job loss is probably more difficult for the middle adult than for the younger person. The financial loss in middle age can threaten family lifestyle, college plans for offspring, and retirement options. It is also likely that a middle-age person will have more commitment to a job, stemming from years of hard work and close relationships with colleagues. If a middle-age person has been with the same company since entering the workforce, it is probable that many of the skills acquired over the years are specific to that company and will not easily transfer to other job situations (DuBrin, 1978). Although laws forbid age discrimination in many hiring decisions, it is likely that older job candidates face prejudice anyway (Kelvin & Jarrett, 1985; Sinfeld, 1985).

WORKER PRODUCTIVITY

Older workers are productive. They are less likely to be absent from work, less likely to quit a job suddenly, have fewer accidents, and show reliable levels of productivity (Warr, 1994). In spite of this, when older adults lose a job, it may be a challenge to find another job that pays as well or is as satisfying as the original position. Shamir and Arthur (1989) reported that even a mediocre job is better than having no job but this stance is controversial, at least according to researchers studying young people. Winefield, Winefield, Tiggeman, and Goldney (1991) found that both depression and negative mood improved in people after satisfactory employment was obtained. In contrast, increased depression and mood problems were found for both unemployed and dissatisfied-employed comparison groups.

Wanberg (1995) studied various aspects of job satisfaction in young and middle adults ($M = 35.7$ years). She found that previously unemployed people who found satisfactory employment reported increases in mental health measured by standard instruments. Similar to the findings of Winefield et al. (1991), she found that unemployed individuals were similar on these measures to people who had found employment in unsatisfactory positions. Liem (1992) also addressed this issue, suggesting that in taking an unsatisfactory job and being unhappily reemployed, the person has given up the search in comparison to the unemployed person who may be seen as holding out for a good job. The latter may experience feelings of being in control, even though unemployed. Leana and Feldman (1995) did a prospective study of workers who faced a plant closing both before they were actually unemployed and after. The researchers found that reemployment was negatively correlated with factors such as depression and lack of satisfaction with life. They also found that dissatisfied reemployed people were less satisfied with life than individuals who remained unemployed.

The problems of unemployment are magnified in older workers. As the baby boomers get older, there are likely to be many more people impacted by unemployment. Rife and Kilty (1989) found that unemployed older people felt socially isolated and had problems with depression. In addition, these individuals worried about personal finances. In a review of the literature, Couch (1998) pointed out that although the national rates of workers becoming unemployed have not changed since the early 1980s, in the last decade, workers age 55 to 64 have moved from being the least likely to be unemployed to being the most likely. Not only are older workers the most likely to be displaced from work, they are the least likely to be reemployed. It should be noted that these older workers are not yet eligible for Social Security benefits or, in some cases, other pension income.

Levels of job-displaced older workers are about the same for blue- and white-collar jobs but, of course, the immediate economic impact on lower income workers will be greater. Household income for all displaced workers, unemployed plus reemployed, is estimated to drop by about 39 percent. At this lower income level, it is likely to be substantially difficult to meet even minimal life expenses.

AN INTERVENTION

Professors of social work Rife and Belcher (1994) conducted an intervention with unemployed adults. We decided to discuss this particular research partially because the project was designed as an experiment to evaluate the efficacy of a particular approach to helping older unemployed people. There are many tactics that might be used to help unemployed adults, but this is one of the only studies we have found that presents credible evidence to suggest a particular approach is any good at all. Because a great deal is known about designing research to properly evaluate programs, we are puzzled as to why adequate program assessment is so rare. Two alternatives occur to us. Either the people who promulgate specific programs are unaware of the need for sound evaluation, or perhaps they are afraid that proper assessment will show their work to be less than satisfactory. Of course it is also possible that designers of programs do not have the resources to build in evaluation. We feel that the situation should be the same as it is for bridges. If there is no evidence that it will work, it should not be built.

One strategy for assisting with job hunting is called a job club. The central focus of a job club is to train a group of unemployed people in job-hunting skills and encourage them to work together. This eases feelings of social isolation and, at the same time, permits members to monitor job-searching behavior of others in the group. The job club is not a new idea. It grew out of the behavioristic philosophy of John Watson and the technology called *behavior modification,* mentioned earlier in Chapter 16. At the very least, the behaviorist heritage of this program encourages measurable outcomes. In 1975, Azrin, Flores, and Kaplan used this approach and found that within 2 months, 90 percent of job club participants had found employment compared to the 55 percent success rate among job seekers using traditional methods. After 3 months, 40 percent of the job seekers were still unemployed. Job club members also achieved higher starting salaries. Gray (1983) randomly assigned unemployed workers to job club participation or standard job-seeking tactics. Twelve weeks later, employment was 74 percent for job club participants and 22 percent for control participants. Gray's participants were older workers. Rife and Belcher (1994) conducted a more recent replication of Gray's 1983 study. This was felt to be a timely issue because in the years to come there are going to be more older workers and, actuarially, that means more unemployed older workers.

PARTICIPANTS

The participants were all adults who had applied for assistance from a nonprofit community agency that offered employment services. Four of the initial participants did not complete the program owing to poor health, relocation, or finding a job. All participants were over 50 years of age. Other participant characteristics are found in Table 27.1.

PROCEDURE

The job club participants attended an initial meeting lasting half a day that presented an overview of job-hunting tactics. In addition, the participants met in a job club for two afternoons each week. These club meetings encouraged each participant to publicly set reasonable job goals. Technical skills such as preparing a résumé, behavior during interviews, and filling out job applications were covered. For example, members had a chance to observe and critique clothing and demeanor of the other members during a practice interview. Members helped each other with these tasks, reviewing other member's materials and making comments. Knowing the goals of the other members of the club, they were able to alert club members to appropriate job leads they uncovered. Telephones were available so that they could phone prospective employers about job openings. Members were taught that not all job openings are advertised, and the support and advice of club members was sought to help identify potential employers who could be contacted about positions that might become vacant. Members continued to attend job club meetings until they found a job. Being in an atmosphere where members could observe others getting jobs and leaving the club probably acted to encourage continued seeking.

Control group participants were only alerted to the ordinary services available from the agency to anyone in the community who was unemployed. They could register as unemployed, get information about job openings, and receive job referrals. There was no social component, other than meeting with agency representatives. This lack of social support was probably the most striking difference between the experimental and control groups.

TABLE 27.1   Characteristics of Participants in Rife and Belcher (1994)

Number	52
Gender	56% male, 44% female
Age	m = 58 years old
Race	94% white, 6% nonwhite
Past employment	24% managerial/professional
	30% skilled/clerical
	46% manual, unskilled

Source: From Rife, J. C., & Belcher, J. R. (1994). Assisting unemployed older workers to become reemployed: An experimental evaluation. *Research on Social Work Practice, 4,* 7.

OUTCOME MEASURES

The dependent variables in this study were collected in a series of interviews. Both job club and control participants in the study were interviewed 1 week before any intervention, then again at 4-week intervals until the end of the 12-week program. Needless to say, the most important outcome was whether the participants found a job. With the permission of the participants, this was verified by checking with the employer. Believe it or not, there are studies of programs designed to help the unemployed that omit actual employment as an outcome measure. For example, Donohue and Patton (1998) published a study entitled "The Effectiveness of a Career Guidance Program with Long-Term Unemployed Individuals" in which the outcome was the extent to which participants reported that they *believed* the intervention had helped them. No evidence was presented about the success of these people in the job market.

In the study by Rife and Belcher (1994), participants were asked to report their income and their work hours (if any) during each of the four interview sessions. Specifically, they were asked to report income and hours for the week preceding the interview. As another outcome, depression was measured at the first interview, which occurred before intervention, and at the final interview. The short version of the Geriatric Depression Scale (GDS; Sheikh & Yesavage, 1986) was the instrument used to measure depression. At both interviews, the alpha of the GDS was at least .80.

RESULTS

The intervention was successful, as is shown in Table 27.2. The participants who were in the job club had a higher frequency of employment at the end of the 12-week study than the control participants. Seventeen (65.4 percent) of those in the experimental group were

TABLE 27.2   Employment, Income, and Hours Worked for Job Club and Control Participants at 4, 8, and 12 Weeks

DEPENDENT VARIABLE	GROUP	4-WEEK MEAN SCORE	8-WEEK MEAN SCORE	12-WEEK MEAN SCORE
Employment	Job Club	.27	.46	.57
	Control	.07	.07	.15
Income	Job Club	$23.85	$99.46	$154.27
	Control	$ 5.85	$19.04	$ 28.65
Hours Worked	Job Club	5.04	21.46	35.96
	Control	1.15	2.92	6.23

Note: Employment was analyzed by coding it 0 = unemployed, 1 = employed. Hours and income are totals for the week preceding the interview.

Source: From Rife, J. C., & Belcher, J. R. (1994). Assisting uemployed older workers to become reemployed: An experimental evaluation. *Research on Social Work Practice, 4,* 10.

employed at 12 weeks, while only seven (26.9 percent) of the control participants had jobs ($p < .01$).

A statistical analysis called an *analysis of variance* (ANOVA) was conducted on the data in this table. Commonly used in psychological research, the ANOVA is able to assess the significance of differences for more than one variable at a time. The ANOVA mathematically compares the amount of variance within different groups—such as the variance in 4-week earnings for individuals within the job club group with the variance between groups, for example the variance in job club members' mean 4-week earnings compared to the variance in the control group's income at 4 weeks. If the within-group variance is small and the between group variance is large, the difference is likely to be statistically significant. In that case, the ANOVA is telling us that while the groups are fairly similar within themselves, they are quite distinct from one another. If the study is a true experiment, the difference is attributable to the action of the independent variable. As is true for many statistical analyses, the ANOVA is sensitive to the number of scores. Because of the conservative design of the ANOVA, if the number of scores is small, it is more difficult to achieve statistical significance.

In the case of the ANOVA for the data in Table 27.2, the differences between groups were significant ($p < .05$) and so were the differences seen across time ($p < .05$). When we speak of the differences across time, we mean that for all groups of participants, the scores in Table 27.2 changed significantly as the study progressed over weeks. You can see these changes as increases in the values looking along horizontal rows in the table. This finding is probably what you would expect from common sense: that both groups are more likely to be employed, work more hours, and make more money as time passes. As we have seen in other studies, however, psychological findings do not always align with common sense predictions. Although it did not happen, it is imaginable that the job club might have had strong immediate effects of getting people into jobs but that, over time, these people would not have persisted, ending up at the levels of the control group by the final Week 12 interview. Had this happened, an obvious conclusion would be that the job club experience helped people to get jobs for which they were not otherwise prepared. Because this scenario was possible, even though not actualized, it was important to include the analysis of differences across time as part of the results. You will have noticed from looking at Table 27.2 that, as a group, job club participants did not become fabulously wealthy even though they were employed. In the early weeks, many of the participants worked part-time. Rife and Belcher (1994) commented that many of the participants sought only part-time work and were satisfied with that. The research site was a small town with a population of about 40,000 where the economy was slow. Many of the jobs were in service positions, such as clerking in convenience stores and food service in restaurants. Also, this study was published in 1994, which means that it was conducted even earlier, probably in the early 1990s. In looking at any study of employment it is important to remember that even a few years can change the wage expectations of participants.

Depression was also measured as a dependent outcome in a pretest and at 12 weeks. The instrument used for this, the GDS, was scaled from 0 to 15. Mean depression is shown in Figure 27.1. Before the intervention there was no significant difference between groups in depression. At the 12-week assessment, the job club group measured significantly lower depression than they had in the pretest ($p < .05$). The control group actually showed an increase in measured depression over the course of the study, but the change was not significant.

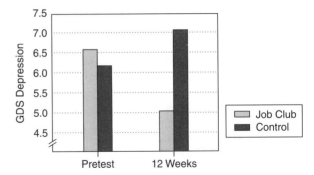

FIGURE 27.1   Depression among Job Club and Control Participants.

Source: From Rife, J. C., & Belcher, J. R. (1994). Assisting unemployed older workers to become re-employed: An experimental evaluation. *Research on Social Work Practice, 4,* 3–13.

DISCUSSION

The absence of improvement in the controls would be unremarkable if the controls had received nothing. However, you will remember that they received standard or traditional vocational services of the sort typically available in many communities. While the results of this study may be taken as an indication of the efficacy of the job club approach, they may also be construed as an exposé of traditional services.

The outcomes for the job club were positive despite the fact that this study was conducted in an economically depressed area. The earlier study reported by Azrin et al. (1975) was in a site that may have been even less promising, a "sparsely populated community in Illinois with no public transportation and a long history of unemployment" (p. 18). Even with these disadvantages, this study by Azrin et al. was able to demonstrate the benefits of the job club approach. It is also noteworthy that the job club was successful with older adults in this study. Gray (1983) also demonstrated success with older workers in Job Clubs. Earlier studies, such as Azrin et al. (1975), used younger workers as participants. Taken together, these findings suggest that the success of the job club does not depend on worker age.

Rife and Belcher (1994) limited the procedures in their study to those used by Gray (1983) because their goal was to replicate Gray's work. Rife and Belcher note, however, that if the replication had not constrained them to twice-weekly meetings, the intervention may have been even more successful. Their participants reported that they would have preferred to meet more frequently because the new job leads that they were sharing did not remain current for very long. Rife and Belcher suggest that future users of the job club may want to consider meetings as frequently as three or four times each week. An additional suggestion that came out of Rife and Belcher's experience was that an event such as an employment-sharing fair be organized where groups of unemployed workers could contact a number of employers. This contact could be less formal and threatening than the one-on-one interview and it could make economic use of the time of busy employers.

The findings presented here suggest that the job club should be considered as a replacement for traditional employment services, at least until some evidence appears that traditional services are superior. Future decades are likely to have more unemployed older workers because there will be more older people as the baby boomers age. Additionally, because people are living longer, older people may need to remain in the workforce out of economic necessity. Some older people will also choose to continue to work as a way to make productive use of their time. In any event, the job club seems to offer hope for the older worker.

CRITICAL THINKING TOOLKIT ITEM

When you read accounts of programs designed to facilitate behavior change, it is reasonable to expect that some evidence will be presented that the program accomplishes its goals. Merely asking participants if they intend to change their behavior is not a valid outcome measure. Because program evaluation is complicated and can be expensive it is often left undone. Failure to evaluate does not mean that the program itself is flawed. The program may be working perfectly, but there is no way to know this. Even if there is some evidence that the program was an agent of behavior change, it would be more important to know that the changes were permanent. This is probably the ultimate hurdle in program evaluation because of the expense and difficulties inherent in longitudinal designs.

REFERENCES

Azrin, N. H., Flores, T., & Kaplan, S. J. (1975). Job-finding club: A group-assisted program for obtaining employment. *Behavior Research and Therapy, 13,* 17–27.

Couch, K. A. (1998). Late life job displacement. *The Gerontologist, 38,* 7–17.

Donohue, R., & Patton, W. (1998). The effectiveness of a career guidance program with long-term unemployed individuals. *Journal of Employment Counseling, 35,* 179–194.

DuBrin, A. (1978). *Fundamentals of organizational behavior: An applied perspective* (2nd ed.). New York: Pergamon Press.

Gray, D. (1983). A job club for older job seekers: An experimental evaluation. *Journal of Gerontology, 38,* 363–368.

Kelvin, P., & Jarrett, J. (1985). *Unemployment: Its social psychological effects.* Cambridge, England: Cambridge University Press.

Leana, C. R., & Feldman, D. C. (1995). Finding new jobs after a plant closing: Antecedents and outcomes of the occurrence and quality of reemployment. *Human Relations, 48,* 1381–1401.

Liem, R. (1992). Unemployed workers and their families: Social victims or social critics? In P. Voydanoff & L. C. Majka (Eds.), *Families and economic distress* (pp. 135–151). Beverly Hills, CA: Sage.

Minor, C. W. (1992). Career development theories and models. In D. H. Montross, *Career development:*

Theory and practice (pp. 7–34). Springfield, IL: Charles C. Thomas.

Rhodes, S. (1983). Age-related differences in work attitudes and behavior: A review and conceptual analysis. *Psychological Bulletin, 93,* 328–367.

Rife, J. C., & Belcher, J. R. (1994). Assisting unemployed older workers to become reemployed: An experimental evaluation. *Research on Social Work Practice, 4,* 3–13.

Rife, J. C., & Kilty, K. (1989). Job search discouragement and the older worker: Implications for social work practice. *Journal of Applied Social Sciences, 14,* 71–94.

Shamir, B., & Arthur, M. N. (1989). An exploratory study of perceived career change and job attitudes among job changers. *Journal of Applied Social Psychology, 19,* 701–716.

Sheikh, J., & Yesavage, J. (1986). Geriatric Depression Scale (GDS): Recent evidence and development of a shorter version. In T. L. Brink (Ed.), *Clinical gerontologist: A guide to assessment and intervention* (pp. 165–173). New York: Haworth.

Sinfeld, A. (1985). Being out of work. In C. Littler (Ed.), *The experience of work* (pp. 190–208). New York: St. Martin's.

Super, D. E. (1974). Vocational maturity theory. In D. E. Super (Ed.), *Measuring vocational maturity for counseling.* Washington DC: American Personnel and Guidance Association.

Voydanoff, P. (1983). Unemployment: Family strategies for adaptation. In C. R. Figley & H. I. McCubbin (Eds.), *Stress and the family: Vol. II. Coping with catastrophe.* New York: Brunner/Mazel.

Wanberg, C. R. (1995). A longitudinal study of the effects of unemployment and quality of reemployment. *Journal of Vocational Behavior, 46,* 40–54.

Warr, P. B. (1992). Age and occupational well-being. *Psychology and Aging, 7,* 37–45.

Warr, P. B. (1994). Age and employment. In M. Dunnette, L. Hough, & H. Triandis (Eds.), *Handbook of industrial and organizational psychology* (pp. 485–550). Palo Alto, CA: Consulting Psychologists Press.

Wickler, A. W., & August, R. A. (1995). How far should we generalize? The case of a workload model. *Psychological Science, 6,* 39–44.

Winefield, A. H., Winefield, H. R., Tiggeman, M., and Goldney, R. D. (1991). A longitudinal study of the psychological effects of unemployment and unsatisfactory employment on young adults. *Journal of Applied Psychology, 76,* 424–431.

CHAPTER 28

FOR BETTER OR WORSE

We wonder how many couples on their wedding day really listen to themselves when they repeat words similar to those in the title of this chapter. Some of the other promises made include maintaining the relationship "for richer or poorer, in sickness and in health…" These promises are generally phrased in such a way as to indicate that the couple will stay together through adversity. It is interesting to note, however, that people do not generally promise they will enjoy keeping these promises if, indeed, they keep them at all.

Early marriages can be unstable, as we noted earlier in Chapter 22, "Let's See What This Baby Can Do." Even though marriages of longer duration become less likely to dissolve as the years go by, there has been considerable research interest in the components of satisfaction that accompany long-term marriages.

Effective communication between partners has long been thought to be very important in marital satisfaction. Communication difficulties are a primary reason given by couples seeking therapy (Giess & O'Leary, 1981). Community surveys have confirmed this problem (Cunningham, Braiker, & Kelley, 1982). Burleson & Denton (1997) questioned the assumption that couples having problems were lacking in communication skills. Their research closely examined specific communication skills and indicated that communication skill levels did not differ when distressed couples were compared to nondistressed couples. The individuals in distressed couples did express more negative intentions toward their partners, suggesting that negative communication behaviors might result more from dislike of the partner than lack of skill in communication. They also found that in distressed couples the ability to perceive the partner's thoughts accurately did not predict marital satisfaction. In nondistressed couples, however, more accurate perception of the spouse's thoughts was related to more satisfaction with the marriage. This finding further suggested that distressed couples might have problems that go beyond mere skill differences, in this case, perceptual skills. Although it is only an interpretation of the data, these results suggest that mere remediation of inadequate communication skills may not be enough to repair failing marriages.

Nevertheless, marriages that are not particularly distressed may owe some of their success and satisfaction to the ability of partners to acquire information about each other's intentions. This can lead to better understanding of the partner's sensitivities, needs, and

Incorporating the research of P. L. Camp and L. H. Ganong, "Locus of Control and Marital Satisfaction in Long-Term Marriages," 1997, *Families in Society: The Journal of Contemporary Human Services, 78,* pp. 624–631.

goals (Applegate, 1990). One of the ways couples in long-term marriages might manage to be successful is through the nature of the attributional style that is a component of each partner's thinking style.

As you will remember from Chapter 14, the ways in which individuals interpret events, particularly the ideas they have about the causes of events, are called *attributions*. The attributions studied in that chapter concerned entity and incremental views of intelligence. One of the longest standing attributional schemes is that of internal and external locus of control (Rotter, 1966). You may remember learning about this in other courses you have taken. The phrase *locus of control* refers to where a person believes the control in life is located. People with an external locus of control—so-called externals—think that control of life events is beyond the individual, while people with an internal locus of control—internals—believe that they are responsible for actions and events that affect their lives. Externals are likely to see reinforcements or outcomes as being controlled by fate, luck, or other people. Internals believe that their own skill or ability can be applied to their circumstances to ensure adequate levels of successes.

Rotter (1966) developed an instrument for measuring locus of control, the Internal-External Control Scale, or I-E Scale. This scale consists of 23 paired statements such as

>   a. Becoming a success is a matter of hard work; luck has little or nothing to do with it.
>   b. Getting a good job depends mainly upon being in the right place at the right time (p. 12).
>   and
>   a. Many times I feel that I have little influence over the things that happen to me.
>   b. It is impossible for me to believe that chance or luck plays an important role in my life (p. 12).

A person's total score for these items is tabulated by recording the number of pairs in which the individual chooses the external phrase. In the examples listed, choice a is the internal choice for the first pair and choice b is the internal choice for the second pair. Because the I-E Scale is scored this way, a high score indicates an external orientation and a low score suggests internal locus of control. Other less transparent instruments have been developed to measure locus of control, such as the 40-item questionnaire by Nowicki and Strickland (1973).

In literally hundreds of studies, locus of control has been found to correlate with a variety of psychological characteristics. In school settings, internals do better than externals on standardized tests measuring achievement (Findley & Cooper, 1983). In stressful situations, externals are likely to be most concerned with their own feelings and emotions, rather than with finding solutions to threatening situations causing the stress. As a result, internals are likely to deal with stress in ways that improve psychological adjustment (Lefcourt & Davidson-Katz, 1991). Culture can also make a difference. People in Western countries tend to be more internal than people in Asian countries such as Japan (Berry, Poortinga, Segall, & Dasen, 1992). Black students who became the most involved in the civil rights activities of the 1960s, such as voter registration efforts and demonstrations, were more likely to be internal compared to less involved students (Strickland, 1965). Locus of control has also shown strong associations with both mental and physical well-being. In general, in our society, outcomes have been shown to be better when locus of control is internal (Lefcourt, 1982).

A number of studies during the past 20 years have investigated the relationship between locus of control and marital satisfaction (Doherty, 1981; Miller, Lefcourt, Holmes, Ware, & Saleh, 1986; Miller, Lefcourt, & Ware, 1983; Sabatelli, 1986). In keeping with past research about the value of internality, studies have demonstrated that internal locus of control usually is associated with higher levels of marital satisfaction. It was thought that people who feel more control over their own lives might be more prepared to make the effort to maintain the marriage relationship. Without a certain amount of maintenance, marriages easily slide into misunderstandings that start small and grow. If people believe that they can control these misunderstanding and the problems that result, they seem to be more satisfied with their marriages.

Past research has not always found such a positive or direct relationship between extent of internal locus of control and marital satisfaction. A few studies have found no particular relationship (Doherty, 1981; Sabatelli, 1986). Smolen & Spiegel (1987) found that internality was important for husbands but not for wives with respect to marital satisfaction. The seeming contradictions in research outcomes may result from the use of different instruments to measure locus of control. The more global instruments, such as Rotter's I-E Scale, may not be sufficiently sensitive to ensure validity when the domain of interest is the marriage relationship. The questions on the I-E Scale refer to internality and externality in broad global terms, as you can see from the sample questions on page 284, and people might make different attributions when it comes to the behavior required to maintain a marriage.

In addition, past studies have tended to investigate the locus of control and marital satisfaction for only one marriage partner. It is possible, however, that marital satisfaction does not depend only on the internality or externality of one person. Perhaps the attributional style of both partners makes a difference.

Paul Camp and Lawrence Ganong (1997) designed a study to address some of the problems of these previous studies. It considered two rival hypotheses. A rival hypothesis is one that is in competition with another in its explanation of certain events. Rival hypotheses are competitors in that they cannot both be correct. The first of Camp's and Ganong's hypotheses, the similarity hypothesis, posited that husbands and wives with the same locus of control would be more satisfied in marriages than those who were different. For example, internals may want to take a hands-on approach to solving marital problems, while externals may fail in attempts to engineer and manage behavior. Externals may become irritated because internals may always want to talk about, or work on, small problems. Externals may prefer to let the problems go, believing that if the relationship is "meant to last," it will whether one works on improving the quality of this relationship or not. In this case, the similarity hypothesis suggested that as long as both spouses were externals, they would be satisfied with explanations such as luck or fate.

The rival hypothesis was that similarity was less important than being internal. This internality hypothesis predicted that more internal locus of control within a couple meant more satisfaction. This hypothesis predicted that couples who are both internals would be the most satisfied, couples consisting of two externals would be the least satisfied, and couples in which only one member was an internal would fall in between those two groups.

PARTICIPANTS

The participants were 137 married couples. The mean duration of marriage among the group was 26.2 years (*SD* = 4.5, range = 20 to 48). Mean age for husbands was 49.5 years (*SD* = 5.9, range = 39 to 76) and for wives it was 47.4 years (*SD* = 5.1, range = 38–69). The couples had an average of 2.8 children (*SD* = 1.2, range = 1 to 8). About half of the participants had a college degree and around 20 percent had a graduate degree. Thirty-eight percent of them had incomes over $75,000 per year.

Participants were recruited by their sons or daughters, all of whom were students taking introductory courses in marriage and family relations at a large university in the Midwest. Students who reported that their parents had been married for at least 18 years were asked to provide the addresses of their parents. The students were told that if their parents returned the study surveys, the students would earn 5 points of credit toward their grade in the course. Students who were not eligible because their parents did not fit the criteria were given other opportunities to earn extra credit.

PROCEDURE

The parent participants were sent two questionnaire booklets and a set of instructions about the use of these materials. The instructions asked the individual members of the couple to each fill out a copy of the survey material without discussing the material with their spouse. The return rate for survey materials was 89 percent.

A return envelope was provided for each individual and each return envelope was coded to enable the researchers to give the students their 5 points when the questionnaire material was returned by the parents. The code number did not appear on any of the survey materials in order to ensure anonymity of participants. Once the surveys were returned and students had received credit, the list of student names and code numbers as well as all return envelopes were destroyed.

PSYCHOLOGICAL INSTRUMENTS

Two psychological scales were sent to the participants in their information packets: the Miller Marital Locus of Control Scale (MMLOC; Miller, Lefcourt, & Ware, 1983) and the Marital Comparison Level Index (MCLI; Sabatelli, 1984). The MMLOC is a 44-item questionnaire containing statements suggesting either an internal or an external locus of control in marital situations. For example, two items are "Misunderstandings between my spouse and me are generally purely circumstantial" and "My spouse and I can get along happily in spite of the most trying circumstances, if we decide to." Respondents code each of these items on a 6-point Likert scale from 0 to 5, with higher scores indicating more agreement. Possible total scores range from 0 to 220. When respondents were finished, researchers reversed the scoring scale on the items reflecting an internal locus of control so that for all questions, the final outcome was that higher scores indicated more externality. This *reverse scoring* of some items is a common procedure in questionnaire design because it helps to avoid what is called an *acquiescence response,* in which the participant merely agrees with all statements without having read them carefully. Norms developed for this instrument indicate that there are no significant gender differences (males, $M = 133.42$, $SD = 19.83$; females, $M = 131.43$, $SD = 19.59$). Alpha for the MMLOC according to Miller, Lefcourt, and Ware (1983) is .83, and for the Camp and Ganong (1997) sample it was calculated at .84.

The MCLI operationally defined the outcome variable satisfaction in this study. This instrument is designed to assess marital satisfaction—the extent to which a marriage "either exceeds or falls short of expectations" (Camp & Ganong, 1997, p. 627). The MCLI consists of 32 characteristics of a marriage, such as "the amount of affection your partner displays," "the fairness with which money is spent," and "the amount of time you spend together." Participants' ratings with the MCLI involve a 7-point Likert scale on which 1 means that their experience of the stated characteristic is much worse than they expected, a rating of 4 indicates that the characteristic is at their expected level, and a rating of 7 means that their marital experience for that characteristic is much better than expected. Final scoring is accomplished by adding together all the ratings for individual items. Final scores can fall between 32 and 224. If a respondent were to mark each item as 4, indicating the expected level of experience, the total score would be 128. Sabatelli (1988) collected norms for this instrument (males, $M = 144.7$, $SD = 23.5$, range = 46 to 218; females, $M = 149.7$, $SD = 24.2$, range = 80 to 217) and found that the outcomes were normally distributed, with alpha at .93. Alpha for the MCLI in this study was .90.

GROUP ASSIGNMENT

Because the antecedent variable was locus of control, and locus of control on the MMLOC could theoretically fall between 0 (completely internal) and 220 (completely external), it was necessary to adopt some method of deciding which participants would be considered internal and which would be external. To accomplish this, the median scores were derived for each gender. Individuals above the median were classified as externals and those below it were considered to be internals. Couples could then be placed in one of the four following categories (arbitrarily, the first letter refers to the husband's locus of control orientation):

1. *E/E*: both individuals in the couple were externals, scoring above the median
2. *I/I*: both individuals in the couple were internals, scoring below the median
3. *I/E*: husband was internal, wife was external based on comparison with median
4. *E/I*: husband was external, wife was internal based on comparison with median

The standardization population used by Miller, Lefcourt, and Ware (1983) were married college students. The older married couples studied by Camp and Ganong (1997) were more internal as a group: males at $M = 99.5$ ($SD = 16.7$) and females at $M = 98.9$ ($SD = 15.4$).

These means were almost 40 points below the means of the married students in the data from Miller, Lefcourt, and Ware (1983) but the standard deviation was roughly similar.

RESULTS

Satisfaction scores as measured by the MCLI for each of the four categories of couples, broken out by husband and wife, are shown in Table 28.1. Table 28.1 employs a convention often found in research articles where superscripted letters are used to denote significant differences. You have already seen a fairly simple version of this in Chapter 15, "It All Adds Up." The way to interpret these is to begin with the hypotheses that were tested and look, usually across rows or down columns, to see if patterns of significant differences support a particular hypothesis. In this study, the similarity hypothesis suggested that having similar locus of control orientations would be associated with increased satisfaction. If that hypothesis was supported, groups I/I and E/E would both have to be significantly higher than the other two groups in satisfaction. Looking down the columns, you can see that this did not happen. The men in group E/E were significantly less satisfied than the men in the other groups; you can see this because the superscript attached to the E/E men score is different than that of the men in other groups. There is no support for the similarity hypothesis among the women either. Although the I/E and E/I women do not differ significantly (they share the superscript [c]), the I/I group women were significantly higher in satisfaction than these mixed groups and the E/E women were significantly less satisfied.

   These findings are more consistent with the internality hypothesis that having an internal locus of control is advantageous. For both men and women, the I/I group, in which both spouses were internals, was significantly more satisfied with their marriage than the other groups. A few other comparisons also suggest benefits of internality. At least in the I/E group the internal husbands were more satisfied than the wives, although internality was not found to associate with higher satisfaction in the E/I group, where the women and men did not differ significantly. With that exception, internals were more satisfied than externals, regardless of gender.

TABLE 28.1   Mean Marital Satisfaction Scores from the Marital Comparison Level Index

COUPLE CATEGORY	MEAN HUSBANDS' SATISFACTION	MEAN WIVES' SATISFACTION
I/I—Husband internal/wife internal ($n = 41$)	166.71[a]	162.20[a]
I/E—Husband internal/wife external ($n = 25$)	157.60[a,b]	140.97[c]
E/I—Husband external/wife internal ($n = 25$)	143.17[c]	150.50[b,c]
E/E—Husband external/wife external ($n = 41$)	138.15[d]	135.27[d]
Total	151.34	147.70

Note: Superscripts denote scores that differ significantly at least at the $p < .05$ level. Scores with different superscripts differ significantly from each other.

Source: From Camp, P. L., & Ganong, L. H. (1997). Locus of control and marital satisfaction in long-term marriages. *Families in Society: The Journal of Contemporary Human Services, 78,* 628.

DISCUSSION

If you look back at the demographic characteristics of this sample, you should be able to find a number of reasons why caution should be urged in generalizing these findings to a large and diverse population of married couples. These were not average married people.

The participants may also have been unusual because of the method used to recruit them. We would guess that the students applied considerable pressure on their parents to fill out the questionnaire. While this resulted in a high return rate, it also may have affected the validity of the findings. We might speculate that busy parents being nagged by students might hastily fill out the questionnaires in order to get their children off their backs. The converse is also possible: parents may have wanted to do the best job they could because the project had links to their children's professors and grade. We also have some questions about the ethics of using student course credit as a way of rounding up a group of cooperative, middle-age participants. Not all students were eligible for course credit from parent participation. The authors stated that other credit-giving options were available for the ineligible students, but a fairness issue arises because the task for the study-eligible students was relatively easy. All they had to do was convince their parents to help. It would seem that any other credit option might have been more time-consuming, giving the eligible students the benefit of easy credits.

Aside from the unusual demographics or motivations of the participants, there are several other reasons why it might be important to be cautious in interpretating these results. People were placed in locus of control groups based on a median split of scores on the MMLOC. The MMLOC normative means were slightly above 130, the means for the sample in this study were about 99, indicating that this group was quite internal. Because the standard deviation was about 16 for the study sample, even those classified as externals in the study would probably have been internals if a scoring had been based on a median split of the normative population of Miller, Lefcourt, and Ware (1983). Camp and Ganong (1997) acknowledge and discuss this problem. They point out that one of the founders of locus of control research, Julian Rotter, warned that internal and external should not be used as rigid personality types, but were rather best used to compare groups of people to each other.

While this study was carefully conducted, a great deal of confidence rides on the validity of the measurement scales. The alphas are high enough to indicate that the internal consistency was adequate. You will remember that this is really a measure of reliability that is used as evidence for validity. Aside from this approach, we find it difficult to imagine how else validity might be assessed. In this case, there is some evidence for concurrent validity in that the original Rotter I-E Scale was said to correlate quite strongly with the MMLOC.

CRITICAL THINKING TOOLKIT ITEMS

Part of a critical evaluation of a study should include the question: "Why were the participants willing to participate?" There is no single answer to this question that indicates the quality of the investigation but, at least, external validity may be compromised if the participants were a special group that had something in particular to gain by being in the study.

REFERENCES

Applegate, J. L. (1990). Constructs and communication: A pragmatic integration. In G. Neimeyer (Ed.), *Advances in personal construct psychology* (Vol. 1, pp. 203–230). Greenwich, CT: JAI.

Berry, J. W., Poortinga, Y. H., Segall, M. H., & Dasen, P. R. (1992). *Cross-cultural psychology: Research and applications.* New York: Cambridge University Press.

Burleson, B. R., & Denton, W. H. (1997). The relationship between communication skill and marital satisfaction: Some moderating effects. *Journal of Marriage and the Family, 59,* 884–902.

Camp, P. L., & Ganong, L. H. (1997). Locus of control and marital satisfaction in long-term marriages. *Families in Society: The Journal of Contemporary Human Services, 78,* 624–631.

Cunningham, J. D., Braiker, H., & Kelley, H. (1982). Marital status and sex differences in problems reported by married and cohabiting couples. *Psychology of Women Quarterly, 6,* 415–427.

Doherty, W. (1981). Locus of control differences and marital dissatisfaction. *Journal of Marriage and the Family, 43,* 369–377.

Findley, M. J., & Cooper, H. M. (1983). Locus of control and academic achievement: A literature review. *Journal of Personality and Social Psychology, 44,* 419–427.

Giess, S. K., & O'Leary, K. D. (1981). Therapist ratings of frequency and severity of marital problems: Implications for research. *Journal of Marriage and Family Therapy, 7,* 515–520.

Lefcourt, H. M. (1982). *Locus of control: Current trends in theory and research.* Hillsdale, NJ: Erlbaum.

Lefcourt, H. M., & Davidson-Katz, K. (1991). Locus of control and health. In C. R. Snyder & D. R. Forsyth (Eds.), *Handbook of social and clinical psychology* (pp. 246–266). New York: Pergamon.

Miller, P., Lefcourt, H., Holmes, J., Ware, E., & Saleh, W. (1986). Marital locus of control and marital problem solving. *Journal of Personality and Social Psychology, 51,* 161–169.

Miller, P., Lefcourt, H., & Ware, E. (1983). The construction and development of the Miller Marital Locus of Control Scale. *Canadian Journal of Behavioral Science, 15,* 266–278.

Nowicki, S., & Strickland, B. R. (1973). A locus of control scale for children. *Journal of Consulting & Clinical Psychology, 40,* 148–154.

Rotter, J. (1966). Generalized expectancies for internal versus external control of reinforcement. *Psychological Monographs, 80,* 1–28.

Sabatelli, R. (1984). The marital comparison level index: A measure for assessing outcomes relative to expectations. *Journal of Marriage and the Family, 46,* 651–662.

Sabatelli, R. (1986). Locus of control, locus of control differences, and quality of relationship in married dyads. *Psychological Reports, 58,* 939–945.

Sabatelli, R. (1988). Measurement issues in marital research: A review and critique of contemporary survey instruments. *Journal of Marriage and the Family, 50,* 891–915.

Smolen, R., & Spiegel, D. (1987). Marital locus of control as a modifier of the relationship between the frequency of provocation by spouse and marital satisfaction. *Journal of Research in Personality, 21,* 70–80.

Strickland, B. R. (1965). The prediction of social action from a dimension of internal-external control. *Journal of Social Psychology, 66,* 353–358.

CHAPTER 29

OLD FOLKS AT HOME

The structure of our population is going to change dramatically in the years ahead (U.S. Bureau of the Census, 1996). As the baby boomer generation—starting with those people born following the end of World War II—continues to age, the proportion of elderly people in our country's population will shift. This phenomenon has been called the squaring of the pyramid because for years the age distribution in our society has resembled a pyramid with many young people at the bottom and relatively few elderly people at the top. The growing number of aging baby boomers is certain to change the structure of our society and will present new challenges for the future in terms of such things as living arrangements, transportation, and health care.

Elderly people have begun to attract more attention from developmental researchers owing to their increasing numbers. As we mentioned in Chapter 21, in the past it was widely believed that old age represented a continuous decay of abilities. Old people were expected to sink into physical disability or dementia, becoming dependent on others for daily care. However, even poor quality anecdotal data should challenge the universality of this prescription; most of us know an older person who does not fit this model of declining faculties and abilities. At age 90, Picasso was still producing art works. Actress Ruth Gordon won an Emmy Award at age 83. Jazz singer Alberta Hunter gave regular performances in New York when she was 88. In contrast, most of us know an older person who is disabled and confined to an institution. While there are elderly people who are examples of the limits of functional ability and disability, most older people fall between these two extremes.

Well-known researchers Paul and Margaret Baltes have conducted considerable research on adulthood. They believe that many older adults who have made a good transition to older age have adopted a strategy of selective optimization with compensation (Baltes & Baltes, 1990). The word *optimization* describes the behavior of people who focus on particular activities for which they have the necessary motivation and skills. At the same time, these people cease activities that have become too difficult to perform due to aging. For example, a person may give up playing tennis and start to play more golf as reaction time slows. Golf involves challenge and some exercise but does not require the fast action

Incorporating the research of A. E. Dickerson and A. G. Fisher, "Effects of Familiarity of Task and Choice on the Functional Performance of Younger and Older Adults," 1997, *Psychology and Aging, 12,* pp. 247–254.

of a tennis game. A related term, *compensation,* refers to finding new ways to achieve goals that have become blocked by the effects of aging. The person who formerly drove a car while vacationing gives that up because of poor eyesight and reflexes and compensates by taking a senior citizen bus tour.

Elderly people may attract the concern of family members when they begin to show signs that normal activities of daily living (ADLs) can no longer be performed adequately. These may be activities such as cooking, cleaning, shopping, personal hygiene, managing transport, and telephoning. Because the performance of ADLs can mean the difference between independent living and institutional life, they have been an important topic of study for psychologists interested in aging. Andrew Guccione and coworkers (Guccione et al., 1994) studied functional limitations of elderly people who were part of the Framingham Study, a famous longitudinal study of adult health. They found that community-dwelling elderly people were usually able to perform most of the ADLs required for daily functioning without outside help. Even people with illness-related disabilities could perform most daily tasks except for the heaviest home chores.

Anne Dickerson and Anne Fisher (1997) designed a research project to probe some of the reasons why older people might have difficulty performing household tasks. Previous research suggested that elderly people performed better on familiar tasks (Bosman, 1993) and on tasks they had chosen (Perlmuter & Monty, 1986). Choice gives people a feeling of control that seems to increase their motivation for activities (Langer & Rodin, 1976). One of the reasons why Dickerson and Fisher likely undertook this project was to extend our knowledge of the capabilities of elderly people and to try to refine our understanding of performance declines that accompany old age.

PARTICIPANTS

The participants in this study were noninstitutionalized people. This is important because only about 10 percent of elderly people live in institutions (Moos & Lemke, 1985) and many previous studies have used only institutional residents as participants. This may be fine if the goal of a study is to learn about institutionalized people, but in obvious ways residents of nursing homes and adult care centers are not representative of the general elderly population. Probably one reason why institutional residents are often used as participants in studies of older people is that they are a relatively easy sample of people to locate. They are confined to institutions and may be unable to come and go as they please. Community-dwelling elderly people, as studied by Dickerson and Fisher, may be more difficult to find because they are not confined to a given area, complicating recruitment and testing procedures.

In this study, the behavior of 28 community-dwelling elderly volunteers was compared to the behavior of 31 young adults. Participant volunteers were solicited from a variety of settings including a retirement community, several recreational groups, a student group, and a military base. The elderly people had a mean age of 69.19 years (range = 59 to 81, $SD = 5.17$) and consisted of 9 men and 19 women. The younger adults were 11 men and 20 women whose mean age was 29.90 years (range = 21 to 41, $SD = 5.07$). In order to qualify for the study, participants had to rate their health as being at least an 8 on a scale running from 1 (poor health) to 10 (excellent health). Furthermore, all participants had to be high school graduates to participate in the study. Mean self-reported health scores for the two groups were not significantly different but there was a significant difference ($p < .03$) in educational attainments. The older group had a higher mean education level ($M = 16.14$, $SD = 2.97$) than the younger group ($M = 14.71$, $SD = 1.77$). This is slightly unusual because typically most young adults have had more educational opportunities. We have no particular explanation for this outcome, but there is no reason to think that this difference is responsible for biasing the outcomes of the study.

SKILL ASSESSMENT

A standardized instrument called the Assessment of Motor and Process Skills (AMPS; Fisher, 1995) was used to evaluate the performance of the participants. The AMPS has a scoring scheme that can be used by a trained observer to quantify the skill levels people display while performing basic tasks. The instrument allows for the measurement of two different types of performance: motor skills and process skills. Motor skills are actions performed by individuals such as lifting, gripping, walking, and reaching. In contrast, process skills are observable movements that are indicators of cognitive ability. Examples of process skills include:

> *Sequencing:* the ability to take on subtasks in the correct order to facilitate completion of major tasks
>
> *Accommodating:* performing actions that might help overcome personal deficits
>
> *Choosing:* selecting appropriate actions or objects for task performance

The difference between process skill tasks and motor skill tasks can be seen in the amount of cognitive processing that is required for the behavior. Sequencing, accommodating, and choosing have a large and more obvious cognitive component than motor skills such as lifting, gripping, walking, and reaching, which seem more automatic and do not require much conscious thought.

The AMPS evaluates 16 motor skills and 20 process skills. The use of the AMPS scale requires an individual to undertake two tasks. Task performance is observed and rated by an observer trained in the use of the AMPS. The observer gives a maximum score of 4 for each motor skill and process skill on the instrument. When the task being rated is performed with no obvious problems it is scored as a 4 (competent). If there is even a slight indication of a deficit, the task is rated as 3 (questionable). A score of 2 (ineffective) is given when there is some obvious problem that interferes with the effectiveness of the task, and a 1 (deficit) is the score given when the task cannot be completed, becomes dangerous, or is performed too slowly to be practical. For example, the task undertaken by a participant might be to make a salad using a specific list of ingredients, including red onions. If the onions are left out, he or she would be scored 2 for the AMPS process skill items *chooses* and *heeds*. The participant has failed to choose the correct object and failed to heed the instructions to include red onions. If the participant had tried to grab the onion and it was dropped, a score of 2 would be given for the motor skill item *grips*. If the participant had sliced the onion and accidentally cut a finger, the *grips* score would be 1 because of the demonstrated danger of the skill.

The AMPS is an excellent instrument to use in the assessment of normal people's real-life skills because it can be applied to practical daily tasks. The tasks observed are not artificial and this would seem to increase the ecological validity of the measurement.

RESEARCH DESIGN

A research design called a *2 × 2 × 2 factorial design* was used. This means that there were three variables used, each having two possible levels. The effects of each variable could be examined either independently or in relationship to one or both of the other variables. The three variables and the levels assessed by Dickerson and Fisher were:

VARIABLE	LEVELS
1. Age	Older or younger
2. Task familiarity	Familiar or unfamiliar
3. Task choice	Chosen or assigned without choice

Any one of these variables might have been associated with important outcomes. For example, a study of these three variables might find that only the familiarity of the task had a significant impact on performance, with no effect by age or choice. This would be called a *main effect.* In a 2 × 2 × 2 factorial design it is also possible to see the effects of two or all three variables acting together, rather than separately as in a main effect. For example, imagine that task familiarity might have made a difference in performance, but only for the younger participants—not for the older ones. This kind of relationship between two variables is called an *interaction,* meaning the findings depend on the way two variables interact. Put another way, the effect of one variable depends on the level of another variable. Figure 29.1 contains fictitious data that illustrate a main effect (left) and an interaction (right). These outcomes are only used as examples and do not represent the actual findings of the research under discussion.

PROCEDURE

Six kitchen tasks were identified for use as the familiar tasks in the study. These involved preparing common food items. A detailed written description was developed for each task. Familiar tasks specified the preparation of a green salad, a tuna sandwich, a grilled cheese sandwich, an omelet with toast and beverage, a fruit salad, and two eggs with toast and beverage.

Familiar tasks were quite easy to find. Because previous research had suggested that elderly people might have trouble with unfamiliar tasks, Dickerson and Fisher wanted to include this as a variable. In order to do so, they had to design unfamiliar tasks that were comparable to the familiar tasks. This presented a challenge. Considerable creativity was required to actually design somewhat parallel unfamiliar tasks. The unfamiliar tasks had to be things that ordinary people could do by following instructions, but they had to be tasks none of the participants had ever undertaken before. Dickerson and Fisher created nine such tasks. These unfamiliar tasks were pilot-tested on people other than the actual participants to see if ordinary people could complete them from written instructions. Based on pilot

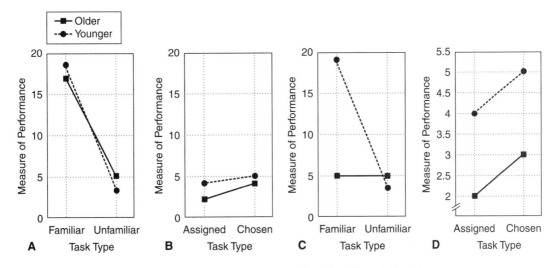

FIGURE 29.1   Fictitious Data Created to Illustrate a Main Effect (A and B) and an Interaction (C and D). We created these data using the variables described in this chapter but these are not real findings, only illustrations. If the data existed for Panels A & B with statistical significances for the large differences in panel A, there would be a main effect for task familiarity. Panel C is a classic interaction. Younger people perform better, but only on the familiar task. Two variables, age and familiarity, interacted to produce these results.

tests, six of the unfamiliar tasks were chosen. Dickerson and Fisher named these tasks and described them as follows:

> *Cheeriopotato:* covering a peeled raw potato with sugar and placing it on a glass of water after piercing it with toothpicks and placing cheerios on the toothpicks
>
> *Canned Tent:* making two flour-and-water dough balls and placing them on top of a sheet placed over two chairs with the four corners held down by a can of food placed on top of a washcloth
>
> *Dark Secret:* cutting strips of newspaper, mixing them with popcorn in a container, then covering the mixture with soil, macaroni, and salt and placing it in a bag, and putting the bag in a dark place
>
> *Hold That Water:* screwing six to eight screws into a precut board and winding string around the screws to make a structure strong enough to hold a cup of water
>
> *PVC Lunch:* putting together pieces of polyvinyl chloride (PVC) pipe into a three-legged structure that has string, which has been boiled, hanging over the pieces and a peeled carrot dangling from the center joint
>
> *Hang Them High:* boiling six clothes pins and hanging them from strings of varying lengths attached to a wire coat hanger that has a ribbon decorating its neck

As you can see, Dickerson and Fisher went to considerable lengths to ensure that the unfamiliar tasks were not familiar. Have you ever buried anything in soil and macaroni?

The participants performed both the familiar and unfamiliar tasks in their homes while being observed and videotaped by a researcher. The researcher brought particular items necessary for the tasks to the homes of the participants. It was felt that participants might feel more comfortable doing the tasks in their own kitchens, using their own stoves, sinks, and other basic equipment. For the familiar food preparation tasks, the participants were instructed to make the object "as they would normally do it." For the unfamiliar tasks, they were instructed to follow the directions and to perform the tasks "as they might expect" them to be done. They were told that the researchers were interested in observing the process of doing the task and in the final product. They were assured that they could have all the time they needed to do each task and that time was not important to the researchers. They were asked to read the directions and to signify that they understood each task.

Each participant, young and old, performed eight tasks as part of the study. Four of these were familiar food preparation tasks and four were unfamiliar tasks. Participants were allowed to choose two of the familiar tasks and two of the unfamiliar tasks. They were randomly assigned two additional familiar tasks and two additional unfamiliar tasks.

Participants were tested in two separate sessions about a week apart. One reason for this might have been to keep single sessions to a reasonable length of time. Dickerson and Fisher also noted that observations were made in two separate sessions to try to ensure that the experience of one session did not influence the other. A session consisted either of assigned tasks or chosen tasks. Half of each group, young and old, were given the tasks they had chosen in their first session. The other half of each group was given the tasks they were assigned as their first session. This procedure is called *counterbalancing,* and it is used as a check, or control, to be sure that previous experience in a research project has not biased the results of later parts of the research. For example, if performing familiar tasks first had made it easier to perform subsequent unfamiliar tasks, the effects could be demonstrated by comparing unfamiliar task outcomes occurring in the first sessions with those in the second sessions.

As a manipulation check, participants were asked to rate the familiarity of the tasks on a 5-point scale from 1 (unfamiliar, never do this activity) to 5 (familiar, do this activity frequently). This is a check of the manipulation because if, for some reason, the unfamiliar tasks were familiar to participants, or vice versa, it would be impossible to interpret the results of task familiarity. The results of these rating scales showed no significant differences in the ratings of young and old people; they agreed about the degree of familiarity of the tasks. The manipulation seemed to be sound because both old and young people rated familiar tasks as significantly different from unfamiliar tasks ($p < .001$).

The data in this study were generated from the ratings of people trained in the use of the AMPS. One of these raters, the primary investigator Anne Dickerson, watched the videotapes and rated all participants. In addition, most of the participants were scored by at least one of five other raters on at least two of the tasks. Dickerson excepted, the AMPS raters were not aware of the hypothesis. In all, 64 percent of all the tasks were scored by one of these other raters. There was a high degree of interrater reliability.

RESULTS

AMPS motor and process scores for each task type at each age are shown in Figure 29.2. Motor and process scales have been shown to measure separate but related abilities. Al-

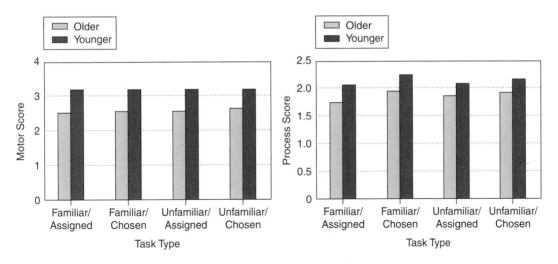

FIGURE 29.2   Outcomes of AMPS Motor (left) and Process (right) Scores for Age, Task Familiarity, and Task Choice. These scores are reported in a unit called a *logit,* which is a type of mathematically transformed mean.

Source: From Dickerson, A. E. & Fisher, A. G. (1997). Effects of familiarity of task and choice on the functional performance of younger and older adults. *Psychology and Aging, 12,* 250.

though they both measure aspects of the functional ability of adults, they focus on different aspects of performance. Scores on the two measures have been shown to be moderately correlated, $r = .50$ (Fisher, 1995). The magnitude of this correlation suggests that knowing one score does not enable a very good prediction of the other score. While these two measures are not completely independent, they are not measuring the same things.

Figure 29.2 suggests that there were important effects of age group on the performance of motor tasks and, indeed, these age differences were statistically significant ($p < .001$). Older people performed less well than younger people. For motor scales shown in Figure 29.2, there were no significant differences for familiarity ($p < .38$) or for choice ($p < .29$).

The process scores shown in Figure 29.2 also suggest a statistically significant age difference ($p < .001$) with older adults doing more poorly, the same direction as was seen on the motor scale. There was no significant difference for task familiarity ($p < .92$) but the difference between chosen and assigned tasks was significant for process skills ($p < .04$). The overall age difference did not interact with these findings. That is, familiarity did not affect performance no matter how old people were. Choice did make a difference, but that difference was not related to age: Older and younger people did better when they could choose the task. Another way to phrase this would be to say that for process skills there were main effects for age and choice but no interactions.

DISCUSSION

At least with these kinds of tasks, age makes a difference. Every attempt was made to see that the tasks used in the study were either part of daily life or abstracted from tasks of daily living. Because these either resembled cooking operations or were cooking operations, we think the study can claim substantial ecological validity. Although some of the unfamiliar tasks were artificial, they were composed of the sorts of actions and cognitive processing that is required for independent living.

The results presented here suggest that older people differ from younger people in the performance of the ADLs. This study does not support the contention that older people perform poorly only because the tasks on which they are examined are artificial or because they cannot choose their tasks. It is further possible to reject the rival hypothesis that older people do less well on manual tasks in research because they are more affected by the laboratory environment than are younger people. All participants here were observed in their own homes. Participants often scheduled the task observations to take place at the same time that they normally worked in the kitchen.

The findings here also do not support the idea that extensive experience or practice on a task will help to inoculate individuals against the declines of old age. The older participants in this study had practiced the skills of these tasks, in part or whole, for many years and they performed more poorly nevertheless. While some studies reported findings that seem to indicate this kind of practice effect (Bosman, 1993; Denny, 1982; Geary, Frensch, & Wiley, 1993; Morrow, Leirer, Alteri, & Fitzsimmons 1994; Salthouse, 1985), this study suggested that the declines of old age may not be completely overcome by years of practice, at least with the types of activities that were studied.

In seeking an explanation for this discrepancy, Dickerson and Fisher pointed out that past studies often evaluated the product resulting from a task, rather than the efficiency of the task itself. Young and old people may both be able to produce a perfectly adequate tuna sandwich as lunch but the AMPS is sensitive to aspects of performance that go beyond the adequacy of the product. The AMPS also measures inefficiency and ineffective attempts to overcome performance problems. Imagine an older person making a salad and forgetting one item, the tomatoes, until after the salad dressing had been applied and the salad had been tossed. This is the type of activity that the AMPS would detect. While the tomatoes might be added at the end and the salad tossed again, this type of inefficiency in process would result in a lower AMPS score.

Who cares when the tomatoes are added, as long as the salad is OK? While you might think that this is a meaningless distinction, there has been considerable interest in the gradual nature of deficit onset associated with old age. These deficits might not show in a finished product such as a salad, but an instrument as sensitive as the AMPS may be able to discover earlier indications of problems in the procedures of making the salad.

Choice of task did not make a difference in the motor scale outcomes. This may not be surprising if you consider that many studies have demonstrated that motor performance fades with advanced age (e.g., see, Meeuwsen, Sawicki, & Stelmach, 1993). Declines in motor performance probably have some neurological and/or muscular components. The impacts of these physiological deficits are not likely to be altered whether a task is chosen or assigned. Choice of task did make a difference in the process measures. Other studies have demonstrated that choosing tasks may be associated with enhanced effectiveness in task performance (Chan, Karbowski, Monty, & Perlmuter, 1986). This may be because perceived control over events increases motivation to do the task efficiently. Motivation may be more likely to increase efficiency than it is to alter the physiological constraints that may underlie motor performance. When we want to do something and feel we have chosen it, we are more likely to do it well. This seems to be the case for older as well as younger people.

Dickerson and Fisher initially expected that choice would have little or no impact on the unfamiliar tasks compared to the familiar tasks. They believed that the unfamiliar tasks, in a way, offered less choice because they were so meaningless. It would be difficult for a participant to give reasons for choosing any particular one of the somewhat bizarre unfamiliar tasks. Their data did not support this contention. Choice did make a difference on the process score of the AMPS. People did better when they chose and this did not interact with task familiarity. There might be two reasons for this outcome. First, the unfamiliar tasks may not have been all that unfamiliar. They were, after all, composed of familiar components but combined in unusual ways. Second, participants may have had reasons for choosing some over others. For example, we could guess that some participants avoided dark secret because they did not want to get soil all over the place or because they saw it as a waste of food. Additionally, the unfamiliar tasks were somewhat humorous and perhaps even fun. This may have increased motivation to undertake them. In any event, it is important to remember that age was not a factor. Both young and older people did better when they had some choice.

As a group, younger participants did better on the tasks in this study than older participants, but there was a great deal of variability within the groups. Some older participants did better than a few of the younger participants. It is important to remember that older people are quite diverse in the things they are able to accomplish. Probably all of us know an old person who is barely able to do anything and, at the same time, some old people who are more active than many 20-year-olds. Some of the diversity of ability seen in this study might be better understood by a longitudinal approach to ADLs. Nevertheless, the variability within the older group observed in this study should act as a caution against stereotyping the functional abilities of older people.

CRITICAL THINKING TOOLKIT ITEMS

It is important to know where a study was conducted and specifically what was measured in order to make judgments about ecological validity. Brief media reports rarely supply this information but often imply that findings are ecologically valid.

REFERENCES

Baltes, P. B., & Baltes, M. M. (1990). Perspectives on successful aging: The model of selective optimization with compensation. In P. B. Baltes & M. M. Baltes (Eds.), *Successful aging: Perspectives from the behavioral sciences* (pp. 1–34). Cambridge: Cambridge University Press.

Bosman, E. A. (1993). Age-related differences in the motoric aspects of transcription typing skill. *Psychology and Aging, 8,* 87–102.

Chan, F., Karbowski, J., Monty, R. A., & Perlmuter, L. C. (1986). Performance as a source of perceived control. *Motivation and Emotion, 10,* 59–70.

Denny, N. W. (1982). Aging in cognitive changes. In B. B. Wohlman (Ed.), *Handbook of developmental psychology* (pp. 807–827). Englewood Cliffs, NJ: Prentice Hall.

Dickerson, A. E., & Fisher, A. G. (1997). Effects of familiarity of task and choice on the functional performance of younger and older adults. *Psychology and Aging, 12,* 247–254.

Fisher, A. G. (1995). *Assessment of motor and process skills.* Fort Collins, CO: Three Star.

Geary, D. C., Frensch, P. A., & Wiley, J. G. (1993). Simple and complex mental subtraction: Strategy choice and speed-of-processing differences in younger and older adults. *Psychology and Aging, 8,* 242–256.

Guccione, A., Felson, D., Anderson, J., Anthony, J., Zhang, Y., Wilson, P., Kelly-Hayes, M., Wolf, P., Kreger, B., & Kannel, W. (1994). The effects of specific medical conditions on the functional limitations of elders in the Framingham Study. *American Journal of Public Health, 84,* 351–358.

Langer, E. J., & Rodin, J. (1976). The effects of choice and enhanced personality for the aged: A field experiment in an institutional setting. *Journal of Personality and Social Psychology, 34,* 191–198.

Meeuwsen, H. J., Sawicki, T. M., & Stelmach, G. E. (1993). Improved foot position sense as a result of repetitions in older adults. *Journal of Gerontology: Psychological Sciences, 48,* P137–P141.

Moos, R. H., & Lemke, S. (1985). Specialized living environments for older people. In J. E. Birren & K. W. Schaie (Eds.), *Handbook of the psychology of aging.* New York: Van Nostrand Reinhold.

Morrow, D. G., Leirer, V. O., Alteri, P. A., & Fitzsimmons, C. (1994). When expertise reduces age differences in performance. *Psychology and Aging, 9,* 134–148.

Perlmuter, L. C., & Monty, R. A. (1986). The importance of perceived control: Fact or fantasy? *American Scientist, 65,* 759–765.

Salthouse, T. A. (1985). *A theory of cognitive aging.* New York: Elsevier Science.

U.S. Bureau of the Census. (1996). *Statistical abstract of the United States, 1996* (115th ed.). Washington DC: U.S. Department of Commerce.

CHAPTER 30

OVER THE HILL

We are sure that you have heard the title of this chapter used in reference to a specific person. Depending on the context, it can be a comic jab or a callous dismissal of an older adult. Much of the literature on aging has focused on declines that appear with age. In Chapter 21, "Who's Old First?" there were indications that physical ability in baseball players begins to decline around age 27 for the tasks of baseball. The previous chapter, "Old Folks at Home," found declines in activities of daily living (ADLs), albeit not very striking ones. While there is a great deal of research being done on older adults, the bulk of it has been devoted to probing cognitive declines. The reasons for this are varied, but one of them is the widespread perception that severe cognitive declines are a normal part of aging if a person lives long enough.

Research has shown that this perception can become a self-fulfilling prophecy. In one study, old and young people were cued with lists of words that contained either positive stereotypes of aging (*sage, accomplished, creative, wise*) or negative stereotypes (*decline, dependent, senile, confused, decrepit*). When this exposure was followed by cognitive tests, older people scored higher after exposure to positive terms than to negative terms. No difference was found for younger people. It seems as if memory capabilities can be damaged by attitudes about aging, but only in older people (Levy, 1996).

There may be a variety of things that older people can do to help with failing cognitive performance. Studies using aged rats have shown that if they live in stimulating environments the rats do not lose an appreciable number of cortical cells and they may gain connections between these neurons. Inactive, unstimulating lifestyles may be a component of the memory loss seen in some elderly individuals (Diamond, 1988).

Anecdotally, old people often feel that their memories are failing: "Now where did I put those car keys?" (Pezdek, 1983). In one study of noninstitutionalized elderly people, only 12 percent thought that they had no memory problems (Smith, Peterson, Ivnik, Malec, & Tangalos, 1996). It appears that elderly people are less efficient at organizing their memories and at encoding information that will be stored for long-term retention. Encoding is the process by which events and information are stored in memory. Older people may have

Incorporating the research of L.-G. Nilsson, L. Bäckman, K. Erngrund, L. Nyberg, R. Adofsson, G. Bucht, S. Karlsson, M. Widing, and B. Winblad, "The Betula Prospective Cohort Study: Memory, Health, and Aging," 1997, *Aging, Neuropsychology and Cognition, 4,* pp. 1–32.

trouble remembering partially because information was never stored in the first place (Hess & Slaughter, 1990).

In the research presented in this book, we have tried to focus on normal behavior, whatever that is. While it can be difficult to define normality, it is less difficult to recognize behavior that appears to be abnormal. In the area of cognitive ability and aging, a distinction should be made between the results of normal aging and disease processes. The old and imprecise term *senile* used to be used to describe any cognitive deficit in elderly people. Cognitive decline was expected and accepted as a part of normal aging. As more has been learned about diseases such as Alzheimer's, it has become more obvious that there is a difference between the profound dementia associated with this disease and the ordinary daily forgetting that is characterized by being unable to find the car keys.

THE PERFECT DEVELOPMENTAL DESIGN

Perfect design? By this point in the book, you recognize that there is no perfect study and no perfect research design. A design that comes closer than most others is sometimes called *Schaie's most efficient design* (Schaie, 1965, 1977). It solves the problems that are usually associated with cross-sectional research and longitudinal research by combining both approaches. The overall model in this design is to do a cross-sectional study at a point we will call Time 1. For example, let us say that there were three groups of people in the study, aged 25, 30, and 35 at Time 1. At some Time 2, such as 5 years later, the members of that cross-sectional study are brought back and assessed again on the same variables. After this second assessment, we have not only a cross-sectional study at each time period, but we also have the beginnings of a longitudinal study if participant's scores from Time 1 are compared to their scores for Time 2. This example is diagrammed in Table 30.1.

In Table 30.1, you can see the longitudinal comparison that can be made along any of the rows. In the columns for each year, you can see three different groups of people at three different ages, representing a cross-sectional study. A third comparison is possible from this design. This is a *time-lag design* in which the comparison is diagonal; that is, the 35-year-

TABLE 30.1   **Example of Schaie's Design for Developmental Research**

	1980 TIME 1	1985 TIME 2	1990 TIME 3
Cohort 1 Born 1945	35	40	45
Cohort 2 Born 1950	30	35	40
Cohort 3 Born 1955	25	30	35

Note: The numbers on the table are the age of participants at testing.

olds from Cohort 1 in 1980 can be compared with people who were 35 years old 5 and 10 years later. In this analysis, age is not a variable—all participants are 35 years old at the time they provide data. The time-lag design is a good way to haul cohort effects out into the daylight for study. In this sense, the time-lag comparison acts as a control for cohort effects because if they are lurking in the cross-sectional comparison, they are likely to be more obvious in the time-lag data (Schaie & Willis, 1996).

For example, if sexual behavior were the topic investigated with the group shown in Table 30.1, it is possible that there would be differences in some measure, such as attitudes about sex, in the 1980 cross-sectional comparison shown in the 1980 column. Cohort 1 was 20 years old in the mid-1960s and may have experienced the dramatic change in sexual mores that was associated with the 1960s and that was somewhat attenuated in later times. A strictly cross-sectional data collection might suggest that older people were more liberal in their views. The time-lag analysis could add additional information by comparing attitudes of different cohorts of 35-year-olds. Table 30.1 shows only a simple version of Schaie's design. More groups could be introduced, increasing the complexity; for example, a new group of 25-year-olds whom we would call Cohort 4 could be started in 1985. The limitations on the possibilities are largely financial and practical. These studies are expensive and difficult.

Now that we have described this method, we probably should tell you that we are not going to detail the findings of a Schaie's most efficient design study in this chapter—not quite. We discussed this research design because the study that we examine more fully in this chapter uses Schaie's method but is still in its early days: cross-sectional analysis is possible, but longitudinal data are not yet available. It is as if the study in Table 30.1 started in 1980 and had only completed the data collection from that year. Researchers using Schaie's design make interim cross-sectional reports while waiting for the longitudinal data. Agencies that give grants to support this type of work want to see some signs of progress and early cross-sectional analyses fulfill that requirement.

Much of this chapter will cover research by Nilsson et al. (1997). If you remain involved in psychology over the next few years and have an interest in aging, we recommend you keep an eye out for future publications about this study as the longitudinal data unfold. As you will see, this one is a blockbuster.

Nilsson et al. (1997) have reported the first phase of a study of cognitive ability and health across the adult life span. It is called the *Betula Study* because it is taking place in the city of Umeå in Sweden. Umeå is known as "the city of birches" because of its many beautiful birch trees and *betula* is Latin for birch tree. There have been other similar studies. One of these, the Seattle longitudinal study by Schaie (Schaie, 1983), was a very thorough study of intelligence in older adulthood. There are several other well-known examples of longitudinal studies through adulthood. The Harvard Grant Study has followed male Harvard graduates since 1940 (e.g., see, Valliant & Valliant, 1993). The Berkeley Older Generation Study has been going on for over 50 years, following a representative sample from Berkeley, California, consisting of every third baby born in Berkeley in 1928. The parents of these babies have been followed, as have the babies themselves (Field & Millsap, 1991). A study that has followed a sample of high-IQ people through most of their lives taking a variety of measurements will be discussed in some detail in Chapter 32. While excellent in unique ways, the Seattle study has focused on intelligence and the Harvard study has followed a clearly unrepresentative sample of people. The Berkeley study has lost many participants, going from 420 to 72, and these people are no longer representative of the population of Berkeley in 1928: They represent the intellectually and financially advantaged because the less advantaged tend to drop out at higher rates. The Betula Study aims to avoid this common problem of long-term studies by doing a shorter term, more intensive study.

PARTICIPANTS

The participants consist of 1,000 people randomly selected from Umeå. Umeå is a city of about 65,000 people surrounded by a rural area inhabited by about 35,000 more people. Participants are from both the urban and the rural areas. Unlike the simple example we presented in Table 30.1, the participants in this study belong to one of 10 different cohorts. In the first sample the participants were 35, 40, 45, 50, 55, 60, 65, 70, 75, and 80 years of age. There were 100 people in each cohort. The study will add what amounts to two new complete sets of participants, bringing the eventual total of participants to 3,000. These additional waves of data collection occurred during 1993–1995 and 1998–2000. Because of the massive amount of data collected, it will probably be a number of years before substantial longitudinal data are published.

Sweden has a long history of maintaining a careful and accurate population registry; this registry was used to recruit participants. Of the 1,976 people who were mailed letters asking them to join the study, 976 did not participate for reasons such as illness, inability to schedule the necessary time, no desire to participate, or death. A total of 106 other participants had to be replaced because they suffered from some condition that precluded cognitive testing (severe visual or auditory handicaps or suspected dementia) or because they did not show up for data collection appointments.

Random sampling produced a group of participants who appear to be demographically similar to population averages for Sweden as a whole, as well as to those who were invited to participate but did not. Slightly more than half of the participants are females and about two thirds of them are married.

METHOD

Nilsson et al. (1997) reported on large amounts of data collected at the first of the three assessments that will be part of the final study. Health was assessed by both self-reported and hard measures. The participants were asked whether they currently felt healthy. Additionally, they were asked about any symptoms they had experienced of a physical or psychological nature. Physical symptoms might be things such as pain. Psychological problems might be things such as depression or anxiety.

The hard measures of health were extensive, including 42 different tests performed on a blood sample and five urine tests. Objective health measures also included blood pressure, heart rate, visits to a health care provider in the previous three months, and current medications. Although these last three items were self-reported, they were still *objective* measures in the way psychologists use the term because the participants provided a specific number, rather than a subjective response such as "I often go to the clinic."

The cognitive testing was also extensive by any standards. Thirty-five individual cognitive tasks were administered to the individuals. These are listed in Table 30.2. As you can see, the tests that were given cover a wide range of different kinds of memory.

TABLE 30.2   Cognitive Tasks Administered in the First Wave of the Betula Study

TASKS ADMINISTERED BY PSYCHOMETRICIAN

1. Instruction about a later test of prospective memory—told to remind researcher to sign paper at end of session

2. Study episode for a later face recognition test—16 color pictures of 10-year-old children

3. Study episode for a later name recognition task—fictitious names presented for photographs in 2

4. Study of lists of short sentences with or without enactment—e.g., "break the match" read or acted out

5. Immediate free recall of list of sentences presented in 4—try to recall eight imperatives read or acted out

6. Study of lists of short sentences with or without enactment—eight imperatives read or acted, whichever not done in 4

7. Immediate free recall of list of sentences presented in 6—try to recall eight imperatives read or acted out

8. Cued recall of nouns in sentences presented in 4 and 6—e.g., a "match" in "break the match; "ball" in "roll the ball"

9. Stem completion of surnames presented in 3—give first two letters of family names in 3, asked to remember name

10. Word fluency—Initial letter *A*: produce as many words as possible within 1 minute

11. Word fluency—Initial letter *M* for five letter words: produce as many words as possible within 1 minute

12. Word fluency—Initial letter *B* for names of professions: produce as many words as possible within 1 minute

13. Word fluency—Initial letter *S* for names of animals: produce as many words as possible within 1 minute

14. Free choice recognition of faces presented in 2—recognize 12 faces seen in 2 from a group of 24 total faces

15. Forced choice recognition of names presented in 3—recognize names from a list for faces presented in 3

16. Block design—arrange blocks with patterns on sides to resemble pictures of patterns

17. Free choice recognition of nouns in sentences presented in 4 and 6—remember as many as possible

18. Cued recall of nouns in sentences presented in 4 and 6—cue with verb from sentence

19. Source recall of sentences (enactment/no enactment) presented in 4 and 6—remember if acted out or not

20. Study word list with or without concurrent task—sort cards by color while hearing list of words

21. Immediate free recall of word list presented in 20, with or without concurrent tasks

22. Study word list with or without concurrent task—counterbalanced other version of 20

23. Immediate free recall of word list presented in 22, with or without concurrent task

24. Study word list with or without concurrent task—counterbalanced other version of 20

25. Immediate free recall of word list presented in 24, with or without concurrent tasks

26. Study word list with or without concurrent task—counterbalanced other version of 20

27. Immediate free recall of word list presented in 26, with or without concurrent tasks

28. Memory of activities in whole session (1–27)—report as many activities as possible from whole session

29. Prospective memory test, with or without cueing—task from 1.

TASKS ADMINISTERED BY NURSE*

1. Word comprehension test—multiple-choice test of word synonyms

2. Study episode for statements of facts—20 little-known facts and 20 well-known facts on cards or spoken

3. Cued recall of facts presented in 2—information presented as question "What is Harrison Ford's hobby?"

4. Source recall of facts presented in 2—asked if 2 was spoken (male or female voice) or written on what color card

5. Mini-Mental state examination**—standardized instrument

6. Draw-a-man test—instrument supposed to measure personality

*These tasks were administered as part of the health examination session.
**MMSE (Folstein, Folstein, & McHugh, 1975).

Source: From "The betula prospective cohort study: Memory, health, and aging," by Nilsson et al., 1997, *Aging, Neuropsychology, and Cognition, 41,* p. 7.

RESULTS AND DISCUSSION

In order to assess the data collected on health, correlations were calculated between each of the health indicators. Combinining all the blood and urine tests and other measures, there are 55 measures. Only four of the objective health indicators had any significant correlation with the participant's subjective reports of health. Two of the blood tests, erythrocyte sedimentation rate and haptoglobin, had significant correlations of $r = -.15$ with subjectively reported health. Erythrocyte sedimentation rate measures things such as autoimmune diseases and acute infections. Haptoglobin is also a measure of infection but may also indicate inflammation, such as that associated with arthritis and cancer. The other two significant correlations were of the same magnitude: $r = -.18$ for visits to doctor and $r = -.19$ for medications taken.

In contrast to self-reported health, there were 13 significant correlations between age and the medical indicators. Nine of these were correlations with blood and urine tests. The magnitude of these was larger than was seen for subjective reports of health. Age correlations with blood and urine tests ranged from $r = -.43$ to $r = .33$. It appears from these data that age makes better predictions about health than do people's self-reported feelings about health.

In order to handle the vast number of cognitive tasks presented in Table 30.2, the researchers undertook a type of factor analysis called *principle components analysis*. Factor analysis was described in Chapter 20. It is a statistical way of taking many small measures and finding those that are sufficiently similar to be considered indicators of some larger, more central factor. It is a way to simplify and summarize the outcomes of many measures, creating larger factors under fewer headings. By this point, you understand that psychologists often seek to explain the variance, or variability, of some kind of scores or outcomes (see Chapters 2 and 12). To explain the variance is to find answers to the question: What accounts for the differences that are observed on memory tasks within this group, that is, why do some people score high while others do not? The results of the factor analysis for memory tasks, expressed as the amount of variance explained by each large factor, are shown in Table 30.3.

TABLE 30.3   Principal Components Analysis of Cognitive Tasks

COMPONENT LABEL	EXAMPLE	PERCENT OF VARIANCE EXPLAINED
Action memory	Recall enacted words	16.5
Sentence memory	Recall sentence noun and verb	14.1
Recall attention	Recall words while attention divided	10.0
Name recognition	Recall people names from pictures	9.5
Word fluency	Produce words beginning with *A*	7.3
General knowledge	Knowledge from MMSE	4.6
Priming	Stem completion task	3.2
Total explained		65.2

Source: From Nilsson, L.-G., Bäckman, L., Erngrund, K., Nyberg, L., Adofsson, R., Bucht, G., Karlsson, S., Widing, M., & Winblad, B. (1997). The betula prospective cohort study: Memory, health and aging. *Aging, Neuropsychology and Cognition, 4,* 19.

The data in Table 30.3 come from the entire sample in the study with all age groups combined. Much of the variance in overall memory ability is explained by the first four items in this table. Collectively, these are called *episodic memory,* which is defined as the memory of personal experiences. The participants experienced the words, actions, and names in the protocol described in Table 30.2 and their memories of those experiences were tested. In contrast, the next two, word fluency and general knowledge, are examples of *semantic memory.* Semantic memory includes concepts ("big cities tend to be rather impersonal"), the meaning of words ("a *cat* is a roughly rectangular furry mammal with a leg at each corner"), and facts ("New York state shares a border with Canada"). These are things that are known by many people and are not the result of a particular individual experience. The last item, *priming,* refers to recollections that appear in response to hints, such as giving the first letter of a word. The hint helps make us aware that we have encountered the material earlier.

While no one factor shown in Table 30.3 seems to explain much of the variance, taken together, 65 percent of the variance in memory is explained by performance on the tasks presented in this study. The bulk of the explained variance is in episodic memory. Simplified almost to the point of inaccuracy, this means that people who did well on episodic memory also did well on overall memory, and people who did poorly on it tended to do poorly on overall memory. Episodic memory, across the life span, is an indicator of the health of the memory processes. General knowledge and word frequency are less indicative as memory benchmarks.

Because the primary purpose of the study was to examine age-related changes in memory, these factors were also examined across age groups. These data are shown in Figure 30.1. The data in this figure are presented as Z scores. You will remember from Chapter 18 that a Z score is a standard score which is used, among other things, to graph data from different psychology instruments in a way that makes them comparable. The

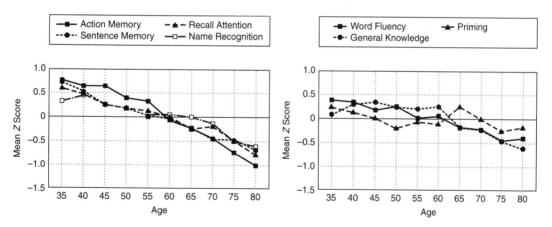

FIGURE 30.1   Performance on Episodic Memory, Semantic Memory, and Priming Tasks as a Function of Age.

Source: From Nilsson, L.-G., Bäckman, L., Erngrund, K., Nyberg, L., Adofsson, R., Bucht, G., Karlsson, S., Widing, M., & Winblad, B. (1997). The betula prospective cohort study: Memory, health, and aging. *Aging, Neuropsychology, and Cognition, 4, 20.*

mean of each data set is defined as a Z score of 0 and the Z scores range in each direction from that mean. A Z score with a value of 1 equals a standard deviation of 1.

As you can see from the graph on the left in Figure 30.1, the cross-sectional data show an almost steady decline in episodic memory across the life span. The drop in all four kinds of episodic memory is a decrease of at least 1 standard deviation. Compared to the rest of the population, the 80-year-old participants scored about 34 percent lower than the 35-year-olds. The decreases shown in the left of Figure 30.1 were analyzed with an analysis of variance and all of them show significant changes with age ($p < .0001$). Although the decline is less pronounced, the data shown on the right in Figure 30.1 also reveal an overall significant effect for age ($p < .0001$).

HEALTH AND MEMORY

A series of correlations were calculated to assess the relationship between heath and memory. Correlations between self-reported health and memory were very low and were not statistically significant. However, among the blood and urine parameters, eight had significant correlations with episodic memory, as did blood pressure and number of visits to the doctor. These significant correlations were not large, ranging from the strongest at $r = -.34$ to the weakest at $r = -.14$. This is the story we have seen before in that no single factor accounts for much of the variance in behavior. A relationship between blood pressure and cognitive ability was found in some earlier studies (Launer, Masaki, Petrovitch, Foley, & Havlik, 1995), but not in others (Wahlin, Bäckman, & Winblad, 1995). There may be little doubt that certain people taking certain medications may suffer negative effects on cognitive performance. The relationship between number of medications and episodic memory found in this study was low but significant, $r = -.27$ ($p < .001$). The correlations of health indicators with semantic memory and priming were not statistically significant.

The results of this study, although cross-sectional at this point, suggested a decline in episodic memory over the end of the adult life span. This decline appeared to be continuous; that is, it did not appear to happen in stages. Age and health indicators were so closely intertwined that it probably makes little sense to talk about them independently. Further research will be required to discover why there is a cognitive decline in old age. Factors such as changes in memory capacity and speed of processing have been proposed (Salthouse, 1991).

A complex statistical analysis was done to control for educational level among participants. Not surprisingly, there was a significant trend in the number of years of education across cohorts ($p < .001$). The youngest cohort had about 14 years of formal education whereas the oldest had about seven years. Obviously, this could be the basis of a classic cohort effect if the amount of education is a major determinant of later cognitive functioning. In order to investigate this, a complex statistical analysis was done to mathematically remove education as a variable. After controlling for education in this way, episodic memory continued to show a pattern of decline across age groups. However, decreases in semantic memory across age groups were reduced or eliminated after controlling for education. Controlling for education also eliminated any age-related decrease in memory associated with priming. It is not surprising that the concepts, words, and facts that made up semantic memory were related to amount of education. Apparently, loss of this cross-sectionally determined semantic memory had less to do with aging than with educational background. It might follow that this type of cognitive impairment would not be a major problem for older people because there was little or no actual decrease with age. The decrease that was seen across age was largely a reflection of differences in education level.

Priming, which may include the giving of hints as well as other memory assists, also seemed to be less affected by age in this cross-sectional analysis. It is more typical that memory studies with elderly people use tasks which do not include priming, probably in order to study memory in some pure sense. Nevertheless, life is rich in priming and the practical conclusion is that if elderly people are allowed to prime by leaving notes, having a standard place to keep the car keys, or by tying a string around a finger, they may remember better than would be indicated by lab tasks where no priming is allowed.

Being aware that we are extrapolating from the cross-sectional data, we see that older people function semantically at about the level they achieved during early adulthood. In contrast, the more personal episodic memories fade away. It is noteworthy that this study largely, but not exclusively, examined episodic memories that had been created in the study. People were asked to remember, for example, sentences they heard or sentences that were acted out earlier in the session. If elderly people have trouble remembering events that happened a short while before, this impairment might make daily functioning considerably more difficult. The distinction between episodic and semantic memory is similar to the long-recognized difference between *fluid intelligence* and *crystallized intelligence*. Fluid intelligence is the ability to make original behavioral responses to new situations and crystallized intelligence is the ability to reuse previously known vocabulary and concepts. Fluid intelligence has been shown to decrease more in later years (Horn & Donaldson, 1977).

It seems likely that reports of the longitudinal findings from this study will appear quite soon and it will be interesting to see the extent to which the cross-sectional trends we have discussed are replicated by longitudinal findings as this research unfolds.

CRITICAL THINKING TOOLKIT ITEMS

While random assignment to groups is common in some sorts of studies, there is almost never true random selection of participants in a study. This is because participants can refuse to be included. True random selection is probably only achieved in archival studies where people do not have to give permission to be included as participants. Random selection can be approached by replacing lost participants with new randomly selected participants.

Cross-sectional research designs are susceptible to cohort effects, in which an experience unique to one age group becomes confounded with ordinary developmental change. Although cohort effects are less often associated with longitudinal studies, you should recognize that longitudinals are also susceptible because they follow one group. When reading studies of these two types you should consider the potential for confounding cohort effects. In contrast, Schaie's design allows cohort effects to be identified. In media and other simplified reports of study findings, it may not always be clear what sort of research method was used. As a critical thinker you will need this information in order to evaluate the findings.

REFERENCES

Diamond, M. C. (1988). *Enriching heredity.* New York: Free Press.

Field, D., & Millsap, R. E. (1991). Personality in advanced old age: Continuity or change? *Journal of Gerontology: Psychological Sciences, 46,* 299–308.

Folstein, M. G., Folstein, S. E., & McHugh, P. R. (1975). "Mini-mental state": A practical method for grading the cognitive state of patients for the clinician. *Journal of Psychiatric Research, 12,* 189–198.

Hess, T. M., & Slaughter, S. J. (1990). Schematic knowledge influences on memory for scene information in younger and older adults. *Developmental Psychology, 26,* 855–865.

Horn, J. L., & Donaldson, G. (1977). Faith is not enough. *American Psychologist, 32,* 369–373.

Launer, L. J., Masaki, K., Petrovitch, H., Foley, D., & Havlik, R. J. (1995). The association between mid-life blood pressure levels and late-life cognitive functioning: The Honolulu Aging Study. *Journal of the American Medical Association, 274,* 1846–1851.

Levy, B. (1996). Improving memory in old age through implicit self-stereotyping. *Journal of Personality and Social Psychology, 71,* 1092–1106.

Nilsson, L.-G., Bläckman, L., Erngrund, K., Nyberg, L., Adofsson, R., Bucht, G., Karlsson, S., Widing, M., & Winblad, B. (1997). The betula prospective cohort study: Memory, health, and aging. *Aging, Neuropsychology, and Cognition, 4,* 1–32.

Pezdek, K. (1983). Memory for items and their spatial locations by young and elderly adults. *Developmental Psychology, 19,* 895–900.

Salthouse, T. A. (1991). *Theoretical perspectives on cognitive aging.* Hillsdale, NJ: Erlbaum.

Schaie, K. W. (1965). A general model for the study of developmental problems. *Psychological Bulletin, 64,* 92–107.

Schaie, K. W. (1977). Quasi-experimental research designs in the psychology of aging. In J. E. Birren & K. W. Schaie (Eds.), *Handbook of the psychology of aging* (pp. 39–58). New York: Gilford.

Schaie, K. W. (1983). The Seattle longitudinal study: A 21-year exploration of psychometric intelligence in adulthood. In K. W. Schaie (Ed.), *Longitudinal studies of adult psychological development* (pp. 64–135). New York: Guilford.

Schaie, K. W., & Willis, S. L. (1996). *Adult development and aging.* New York: HarperCollins.

Smith, G. E., Peterson, R. C., Ivnik, R. J., Malec, J. F., & Tangalos, E. G. (1996). Subjective memory complaints, psychological distress, and longitudinal change in objective memory performance. *Psychology and Aging, 11,* 272–279.

Valliant, G. E., & Valliant, C. O. (1993). Is the U curve of marital satisfaction an illusion? A 40-year study of marriage. *Journal of Marriage and the Family, 55,* 230–239.

Wahlin, Å., Bäckman, L., & Winblad, B. (1995). Free recall and recognition of slowly and rapidly presented words in very old age: A community-based study. *Experimental Aging Research, 21,* 251–271.

CHAPTER 31

PLEASE DON'T DEPEND ON ME

Most of us know elderly people who are no longer able to care for themselves owing to physical deficits, cognitive deficits, or both. When these deficits first begin to appear, family members are likely to be placed under a great deal of stress, usually because they have to make a series of decisions about what is best for the welfare of their elderly loved ones. As the situation progresses, one option is to relocate an elderly person to a nursing home. However, it is often the case that elderly persons are not severely impaired and may resist such a move. Elderly persons also often believe that relocation to a nursing home marks the end of their personal freedom and livelihood. Indeed, some elder-care facilities do establish strict schedules and rules for residents that regulate the types of meals served, bedtimes, and so on, as well as group or interpersonal activities. Sadly, some residents of nursing homes with inflexible environments have demonstrated signs of *learned helplessness,* a concept you will remember from the discussion in Chapter 14, "Boldface Letters." Learned helplessness is a lack of perceived control over the environment that is generalized to subsequent situations and often accompanied by feelings of depression and worthlessness (see Seligman, 1975).

Past research has focused on combating the effects of learned helplessness in elder-care facilities by attempting to increase personal choice among residents. For example, Langer and Rodin (1976) designed a field study to increase the autonomy of residents in a Connecticut nursing home. This would have qualified as a true experiment except that residents were assigned to conditions by residential floor. Even so, if the argument could be made that assignment to floor was random, it might be considered a field experiment. On one floor of the home, residents were told that they would be allowed to make choices about basic living issues, such as viewing a movie and how they wanted their rooms arranged. On a different floor, residents were told that these decisions would be made for them. The researchers found that residents who lived on the floor where autonomy was emphasized indicated greater feelings of happiness, alertness, and activity than residents on the no choice floor. Furthermore, following this manipulation, more residents from the autonomous floor participated in the group activities provided by the nursing home than did residents from the no choice floor. Follow-up of these residents at 18 months showed that autonomous residents were generally healthier than control residents and were less likely to have died since the original study (autonomous = 15 percent; no choice = 30 percent). This is probably the ultimate example of a so-called *hard measure:* a real-life "behavior" that is not measured by self-report.

Incorporating the research of M. M. Baltes, E. Neumann, and S. Zank, "Maintenance and Rehabilitation of Independence in Old Age: An Intervention Program for Staff," 1994, *Psychology and Aging, 9,* pp. 179–188.

Nevertheless, entering a nursing home does not necessarily signify the end of personal autonomy, friendships, or contact with others. If a nursing home has a well-qualified staff, is not overcrowded, and has a low resident-to-staff ratio, it may provide a comforting atmosphere in which residents can take on new activities, forge new relationships with residents and staff, and actively participate in decisions regarding their lifestyles. However, research has shown that if staff members are not aware of an elderly resident's capabilities, they may provide unnecessary care giving and encourage declines in previously practiced independent behaviors (Baltes & Wahl, 1992). *Independent behaviors* are those behaviors autonomously performed by an individual which do not require direct assistance from others. The performance of independent behaviors by nursing home residents has been linked to better health and lower incidences of death (Baltes, 1982). *Dependent behaviors* are those behaviors whose performance depends on the assistance of someone else; that is, a person is otherwise helpless without this additional aid.

Recent research by Margret Baltes focused on the role of environmental contexts in influencing behaviors of residents in elder-care facilities. This research attempted to elucidate the aspects of an elderly person's social environment that are involved in the acquisition and maintenance of independent and dependent behaviors. Baltes's (1988) past research has shown that dependency among the elderly tends to occur under four conditions:

1. As a result of physical deficiencies
2. As a result of learned helplessness
3. As a result of underestimating the present capabilities of an elderly person—by others or by the elderly themselves
4. As the result of forfeiting old behaviors in order to strengthen domains where deficits have begun to appear

The fourth condition is known as *selective optimization*, which we discussed in Chapter 29.

SETTINGS AND PARTICIPANTS

In 1994, Baltes, Neumann, and Zank designed an intervention program with the goal of fostering independent behaviors in elderly residents from several institutions. The intervention program was conducted at three different elder-care facilities in Berlin, Germany: a state-operated nursing home; a nursing home run by a Protestant religious group, and a ward for patients with long-term illness in a state geriatric hospital. The three facilities differed in size, location, socioeconomic status (SES) of residents, operating procedures, and patient-to-staff ratio. Describing the latter, the authors state: "In general, in all three homes, on any given morning, two staff members were responsible for about 10 or 12 elderly residents" (Baltes et al., p. 180).

The participant sample was composed of two different groups from each of the three facilities: a total of 106 elderly residents (range 68–91 years) and 27 staff members. On average, the elderly participants possessed some type of health impairment, usually heart disease, skeletal disease, or both. However, the sample did not include any severely impaired individuals, that is, elderly who were bedridden or cognitively incompetent. Table 31.1 lists the various demographic and health characteristics of the elderly sample.

**TABLE 31.1   Demographic and Health
Characteristics of Residents**

VARIABLE	FREQUENCY $N = 106$
Age	
M	83.2
SD	7.9
Gender	
Female	99
Male	7
Disease	
Mean number of diseases	2.7
Cardiovascular	98
Skeletal	65
Liver or stomach	23
Kidney or bladder	17
Diabetes mellitus	19
Lung or bronchitis	10
Psychiatric disorders	42
Physical impairments	10
Mortality rate	
Dead 18 months after posttest	27
Alive 18 months after posttest	70[*]

*Data are missing from this measure due to relocation of several
residents who could not be found for inclusion.

Source: From "Maintenance and rehabilitation of independance in
old age: An intervention program for staff," M. M. Baltes, E. Neumann, and S. Zank, 1994, *Psychology and Aging, 9,* p. 181.

At each elder-care facility, a head researcher told staff members that the purpose
of the intervention program was to improve interpersonal contact and communication
between staff and residents. The real purpose of the program was to see if a training
program could increase independent behaviors. The researcher did not mention anything
about fostering independent behaviors. Staff members were informed about the intervention procedures, which involved videotaping interactions between staff members and
residents.

The group of staff members was divided in half so that 14 members were placed in an
intervention group and 13 members were placed in a control group. The intervention group
was composed of staff members who volunteered to be videotaped; this group participated
in an extensive 10-session training program over a period of several weeks. The control
group was composed of staff members who did not want to be videotaped and were not
included in the training program. Control group members were told that they would be able
to participate in the training program following the completion of the study if they were
interested at that time.

TRAINING PROGRAM

The training program was designed to improve the staff member's knowledge of care giving along three dimensions:

1. Basic communication skills used in interaction with residents and colleagues.
2. Knowledge of recent and informative facts about aging and the influence of the social environment on the development of dependent behaviors in elderly persons. Staff interactions with resident participants were videotaped during this portion of the training program and replayed to discuss different procedures for helping.
3. The management of desired and undesired behaviors through basic behavioral problem solving strategies. During this phase of training, the staff learned methods for the application of nursing care procedures. They also developed a behavior modification program for the elderly residents with whom the staff had interacted in the previous sessions. The program stressed the learning of various target behaviors, which were mainly self-care tasks, such as tooth brushing or, for the men, shaving. Standard reinforcement and shaping principles were used as the primary techniques for behavior modification. You will be familiar with the general procedure in this kind of program from Chapter 16, "Watch Yourself," in which a behavior modification program for children was described. Staff and resident interactions were once again videotaped and the tapes were used in the supervision and evaluation of staff members. The tapes were used for training in this program, but the outcome data were recorded in separate observations.

The last two group sessions were used by the staff to present their behavioral modification programs and to discuss concerns regarding program implementation in the resident settings. Comments on the training program in general were also addressed.

DESIGN, PROCEDURE, AND DATA CODING

Interactions between staff members and elderly residents were recorded by trained observers prior to and after implementing the behavioral modification programs in the elder-care facilities. The research design used here is known as a *pretest-posttest control group design* because it involves at least two groups of participants—intervention and control—who are measured before and after the intervention or treatment. This design allows one to make assertions about the amount and magnitude of change following the intervention. Another advantage of this research design is that the same people are being measured at pretest and posttest and, therefore, the variability owing to individual differences in the sample is reduced. With this variability reduced, it is more likely that the variability observed is related to the variables in the study.

The intervention phase of the study took place during the standard hours of operation in the elder-care facilities. Undergraduate observers used electronic coding devices to record the behaviors of residents and staff. Specifically, they recorded who performed the behavior—resident or staff member, the type of behavior performed, and whether the behavior was performed alone or in the presence of someone, and if so, whom. A staff member had to be within 2 meters of a resident in order to be classified as in the presence of another. These observers were well versed in the use of the coding devices in live settings. They had been trained previously until interrater reliabilities of at least .80 were achieved.

The behaviors of the elderly residents and staff members were grouped into several categories for operational definitions. These categories are listed and briefly defined in Table 31.2. The number of observation sessions that took place and the times when they occurred were the same for both the intervention and the control group. Observational data were always collected for staff member participants interacting with the same residents. The observers were unaware of the group assignment of the staff members. Prior to the initial pretest observations, the undergraduate observers were introduced to the staff members and residents. A manipulation check was performed comparing the data from two early days of the study with two randomly selected days in the second week of observation to ensure that the continued presence of the observer would not serve as a confound,

TABLE 31.2   Behavior Coding Scheme

Type of Behavior

RESIDENTS

Sleeping—Residents were asleep (Code 00)

Constructively engaged behavior—reading, writing, playing a game, conversing, or watching television (Code 01)

Destructively engaged behavior—quarreling, hitting, throwing food, or screaming (Code 02)

Nonengaged behavior—Lying in bed or sitting on a chair and staring at the wall, doing nothing (Code 03)

Independent self-care behavior—getting dressed, using the toilet, eating or attempting to do so without assistance (Code 04)

Dependent self-care behaviors—being dressed, being fed, and so on (Code 05)

STAFF

Engagement-supportive behavior—any encouragement of constructively engaged behaviors or discouragement of nonengaged behaviors (Code 06)

Nonengagement-supportive behavior—any encouragement of nonengaged behaviors or discouragement of engaged behaviors (Code 07)

Independence-supportive behavior—any encouragement of independent self-care behaviors or discouragement of dependent self-care behaviors (Code 08)

Dependence-supportive behavior—any encouragement of dependent self-care behaviors or discouragement of independent self-care behaviors (Code 09)

No Response—Resident not responding (Code 10)

Leaving—Resident leaves staff member's presence (Code 11)

Medical treatment—Resident requires medical treatment (Code 12)

Source: From "Maintenance and rehabilitation of independence in old age: An intervention program for staff," by M. M. Baltes, E. Neumann, and S. Zank, 1994, *Psychology and Aging, 9,* p. 181.

accounting for changes in behavior over time. No such effect was found. However, observations from the first day of study were not included in this manipulation check.

Observation procedures began when a staff member entered a resident's room. Behaviors were recorded in 10-second intervals. If two behaviors occurred at the same time, independent or dependent self-care behaviors were always given priority and coded appropriately. The coding of behaviors alternated so that, for example, a resident's behavior would be coded for 10 seconds and then a staff member's behavior would be coded for 10 seconds. If a staff member did not respond to the behavior of the resident in some fashion during the 10-second interval, or the resident's behavior extended beyond their time interval, the resident's behavior was recoded so that it would not be confused with the behavior of the staff member. Behavioral coding of the resident continued 1 minute after the staff member had departed from the room in order to accommodate unexpected reentry by the staff member. The observer then tracked down the staff member and recorded subsequent interactions with other residents.

RESULTS AND DISCUSSION

We should note that staff members did not spend equal amounts of time with each of the residents in this study. Because the data collectors in this study measured the frequencies of certain behaviors, more behaviors might have been coded for one particular person than for another. For example, if Mildred eats all day long, snacking from a big bag of pretzels which is always at hand, then the frequency of independent self-care behavior might be very high for her. If frequencies of all independent self-care behaviors of all patients are merely added up, Mildred's very high frequency might make it appear that the overall frequency of this behavior was high. To deal with this, the percentage of each of the behaviors found in Table 31.2 was calculated for each resident, and then a mean was taken of these percentages. In this way, Mildred's high score would only be one of the resident scores used to calculate the mean and it would have less influence on the outcome.

It is important to remember that these data collectors were figuratively "hitched" to the staff members; collectors went wherever the staff members went and measured their interactions, however long they were. Imagine that a staff member spends more time interacting with Mildred than she does with Alan or Barney. If so, Mildred's constant pretzel eating might dramatically influence the total frequencies of the behavior among the residents merely because the staff member spends more time with her than with Alan or Barney. Calculating the percentage of time for each behavior observed in each resident and then taking means of these percents would also attenuate the overrepresentation of Mildred's data, which really resulted only from more staff time being spent with her.

We mention this issue because one must be careful in the interpretation of mean percentages. In this instance, we are convinced that it overcomes some methodological problems that might have resulted in one or a few residents contributing more than their share to the outcome data. However, without some kind of logic, mean percentages might make amount of variability within a group appear to be less than it really was.

Figure 31.1 presents the mean percentage of independent and dependent-supportive behaviors exhibited by the staff members at pretest and posttest. It would appear that following the intervention program, staff members who received the extra training encouraged more independent behaviors among the residents than control group members ($p = .01$).

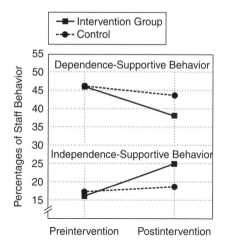

FIGURE 31.1   Changes in Two Staff Behaviors from Pretest to Posttest.

Source: From "Maintenance and rehabilitation of independence in old age: An intervention program for staff," by M. M. Baltes, E. Neumann, and S. Zank, 1994, *Psychology and Aging, 9,* p. 182. Copyright © American Psychological Association. Reprinted with permission.

The control group levels remained fairly constant from pretest to posttest. Even though independence-supportive behavior increased among the intervention group, this figure shows that the staff still spent more of their time providing dependent care for residents ($p = .01$). This difference is likely due to the fact that many patients residing in elder-care facilities require at least some dependent care. However, it is impossible to tell from this figure whether this dependent care was necessary. A statistical analysis did show that staff members from one of the three institutions neither increased their rate of independence-supportive behaviors nor decreased their rate of dependence-supportive behaviors.

Figure 31.2 presents the mean percentage of independent and dependent self-care behavior among the elderly residents. This figure seems to indicate that elderly residents in the intervention group increased the rate of independent self-care behaviors following the intervention program ($p = .01$) and, accordingly, decreased the number of dependent self-care behaviors they previously performed ($p = .01$). Once again, however, this effect was not found for one of the three institutions.

EFFECT SIZE

Baltes et al. (1994) also presented another statistic calculated in their data, the statistic called *effect size.* We have noted in other chapters that standard tests of significance should be viewed critically when the numbers of participants are either very large or very small. With large samples, unimportant differences may be statistically significant and with small samples important differences may not be significant, particularly if there is considerable variability within the sample. The Greek letter gamma (γ) is sometimes used to denote a statistical measure of effect size.

Effect size, in simple terms, is an indication of how far away a finding is from being nothing at all. For example, in a study with a very large sample, a correlation of $r = .05$ might be significant but the effect size would probably be very small. As a rough guide, for the test of a single mean from a single population, an effect size of $\gamma = .20$ can be considered small, $\gamma = .50$ can be considered medium, and $\gamma = .80$ can be considered large. Critical

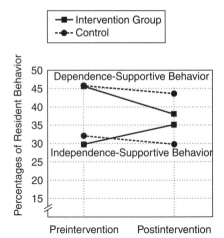

FIGURE 31.2   Changes in Two Resident Behaviors from Pretest to Posttest.

Source: From "Maintenance and rehabilitation of independence in old age: An intervention program for staff," by M. M. Baltes, E. Neumann, & Zank, S., 1994, *Psychology and Aging, 9,* p. 183. Copyright © American Psychological Association. Reprinted with permission.

thinking is still required, however, because the effect size will be large if the proposition being tested is "so obvious as to be useless" (Welkowitz, Ewen, & Cohen, 1988). If we tested to see if the ages of people in geriatric nursing homes was significantly different from that of kindergarten children, the effect size would probably be large but the hypothesis is too obvious to be of any interest.

Older journal articles rarely presented effect sizes for findings but it is becoming more common and some journal editors now insist that this measure be reported. Baltes et al. (1994) reported the effect sizes for the findings. For staff behavior, the difference between dependence- and independence-supportive behavior had an effect size of $\gamma = .88$, but this is only saying that dependence-supportive behavior was more frequent than independence-supportive behavior. Considering the training of the staff, this may be unsurprising. However, the changes in the behaviors over time from pretest to posttest had a moderate effect size of $\gamma = .64$. For resident behavior, the comparison of independent self-care and dependent self-care behaviors had a low to moderate effect size of $\gamma = .39$, and the changes between pretest and posttest times for residents had an effect size of only $\gamma = .19$.

CONCLUSIONS

In spite of the low effect sizes for behavior change in the elderly, this study's findings present several important suggestions for the policies of elder-care facilities. The researchers demonstrated that a relatively simple behavioral-focused intervention might help increase staff knowledge of the abilities of elderly residents and subsequently provide interactions that foster independent behaviors. However, the authors mention that a problem with using a program like the one in this study is that staff members and residents must consent to the methodological procedures and remain tolerant of them for several weeks. Indeed, the authors cite "exhaustion" as the primary reason for not performing a follow-up study on this sample of participants. A follow-up study or studies would have noted the magnitude and duration of the treatment effects due to the intervention. Without a follow-up study it is impossible to know if the intervention program was worth the cost and effort of the researchers and participants.

Another problem the researchers faced was trying to keep the control group from discussing the study with the intervention group and discovering that the study focused on independent behaviors. The authors address this issue by asserting that even if the control group did discover the focus of the study, they would probably have been unable to figure out when to promote independence-supportive behaviors in their interactions with residents and the techniques for doing so.

It is worthy to note that this study was primarily concerned with seeing if the intervention program could break the cycle of dependent care giving and dependence-supportive behaviors present in the elder-care facilities. The techniques learned from the intervention program appear to be successful and may spur further research in this area, assisting in the development of intervention programs that are minimally invasive. It may be that if more elder-care centers promoted independent self-care among residents and provided only the minimum necessary dependent care, some of the negative attitudes about these institutions might be reduced.

CRITICAL THINKING TOOLKIT ITEMS

When means of percentages are presented it may be that some variation is being masked. It may be masked for clear and logical reasons and we believe that this is typically the reason why studies in reputable scientific journals use this tactic. Beyond the journals, beware of assertions underpinned by means of percentages. Someone may be trying to mislead you.

Increasingly it seems that journal articles are reporting effect sizes as part of the data presentation. A large effect size does not, per se, indicate that research is good. If the findings are obvious, effect sizes will probably be large. Effect sizes may be more important as quality indicators when findings are not easily predicted before the study is undertaken. Nevertheless, effect sizes may help you to critically evaluate study findings.

REFERENCES

Baltes, M. M. (1982). Environmental factors in dependency among nursing home residents: A social ecology analysis. In T. A. Wills (Ed.), *Basic processes in helping relationships.* New York: Academic Press.

Baltes, M. M. (1988). The etiology and maintenance of dependency in the elderly: Three phases of operant research. *Behavior Therapy, 19,* 301–319.

Baltes, M. M., Neumann, E., & Zank, S. (1994). Maintenance and rehabilitation of independence in old age: An intervention program for staff. *Psychology and Aging, 9,* 179–188.

Baltes, M. M., & Wahl, H.-W. (1992). The dependency-support script in institutions: Generalization to community settings. *Psychology and Aging, 7,* 409–418.

Langer, E. J., & Rodin, J. (1976). The effects of choice and enhanced personal responsibility for the aged: A field experiment in an institutional setting. *Journal of Personality and Social Psychology, 34,* 191–198.

Seligman, M. E. P. (1975). *Helplessness: On depression, development, and death.* San Francisco: Freeman.

Welkowitz, J., Ewen, R. B., & Cohen, J. (1988). *Introductory statistics for the behavioral sciences.* New York: Harcourt Brace Jovanovich.

CHAPTER 32

TERMINATION OF THE TERMITES

When the term *intelligence quotient,* or its abbreviation *IQ,* is thrown around in everyday conversation, it is often used in reference to a person who performs poorly or commendably in an academic setting. Furthermore, when people are asked to think about someone they know with a high IQ, they frequently envision a nerd adorned with a pocket protector, glasses, and scientific calculator whose hobbies include computer programming, stamp collecting, and chess. By this point, we hope you recognize that these stereotypes are not necessarily accurate; rather, they are more likely to be cultural inventions.

TERMAN GIFTED CHILDREN STUDY

The purpose of this chapter is to present some findings from the most comprehensive and longest study of intellectual giftedness ever performed. The study was pioneered by psychologist Lewis Terman in 1921 and its findings have continued to accumulate to the present day. Terman was avidly interested in studying intellectually gifted children and had done so since his early days as a researcher at Clark University in the early years of the twentieth century. Above all, he wanted to see in what ways gifted children differed from others of the same age who were of lesser ability. Terman was not able to make much headway in this domain until two French psychologists, Alfred Binet and Théodore Simon, developed a standardized intelligence test for children. We now take standardized tests so much for granted that it may be difficult to imagine that standardization of psychological instruments was once a new idea. As you know, a *standardized test* is one that has been given to large groups of people in order to develop norms, or standards, against which future individual test outcomes can be judged. As a faculty member at Stanford University, Terman worked to develop a version of the Binet-Simon test based on American population norms. After several years of recruiting volunteers for this task, the Stanford-Binet Intelligence test was born.

Terman conducted an initial short-term study of very high IQ children while working to standardize the Stanford-Binet. Perhaps the most important finding of this study, which was replicated by Terman's later longitudinal work, was the negation of some unfortunate

Incorporating the research of C. Peterson, M. E. P. Seligman, K. H. Yurko, L. R. Martin, and H. S. Friedman, "Catastrophizing and Untimely Death," 1998, *Psychological Science, 9,* pp. 127–130.

stereotypes about very intelligent children. These stereotypes persist to this day in one form or another despite considerable evidence to the contrary. Highly intelligent children, such as those first studied by Terman, were widely stereotyped as one-sided, physically weak, and socially incompetent. They were supposed to have character defects and perhaps even be mentally unbalanced (Holahan, Sears, & Cronbach, 1995). Terman found that this characterization was not only incorrect, the reverse seemed to be true. The high IQ children were found to excel in personal and social adjustment.

As Terman's preliminary study and the Stanford-Binet IQ test were being finished, war was sweeping across Europe. Terman enlisted in the U.S. Army, where he found application for his psychometric skills. During World War I, he developed an adult intelligence test, known as the Terman Group Test, which was used for identifying army cadets who were supposed to have sufficient intelligence to be placed in command positions.

Following his military service, Terman returned to his primary academic interest—the study of intelligence differences in children. Terman and his research assistants set out to recruit a large sample of young Californians with an IQ of 140 or higher, therefore in the top 1 percent of the U.S. population. The researchers encouraged public school officials and teachers to nominate their youngest and brightest students for eligibility in the Terman study. Students were mainly recruited from public elementary schools, but 309 public high school students were also included in the sample.

One of the problems the researchers encountered following the initial call for participants was that the sample began to deviate more and more from the population they had originally intended to study. Terman had wanted to study children from different geographic, ethnic, and socioeconomic status (SES) backgrounds. However, Terman's final sample was largely restricted to children who were white, urban, and male. There were probably several reasons for this divergence. Once Terman's announcement had gone to the public, enrollment in the study became a sort of contest among local schools to get as many of their students enrolled as possible. Terman too, realized that it would be easier and more cost-effective to include students who were more easily accessible than to search small rural areas for equivalent students. He wanted a large sample. As a consequence, he reluctantly lowered his original IQ score standards (IQ = 140) to include all students who scored at or above 135 on the IQ batteries.

In addition, teacher and school official nominations almost certainly biased the sample because of prevailing attitudes in the early 1920s when the initial recruitment was conducted. Female and minority children frequently were not nominated for reasons of prejudice. Schools containing large percentages of minority students were not even sampled. Some minority students who were tested may not have been native speakers of the English language, hindering their ability to achieve a high score on a test battery that was heavily weighted toward verbal skills.

Terman concluded the recruitment procedures in 1928 and his final sample consisted of 1,528 students. These students later became affectionately known as the "Termites," a label that has stuck with them in the subsequent research literature. Table 32.1 includes some basic demographic characteristics of the Termites.

As you can see from Table 32.1, the Termites came from mostly intact families who were of moderate to high SES. Despite their seemingly low number of professional degrees, the mothers of these children still greatly exceeded the national average for years

TABLE 32.1   Demographic Characteristics of Terman's Sample as of 1922

BIRTHDATE	GENDER
Males (M = January 1910; SD = 3 years, 9 months)	Males (N = 856)
Females (M = October 1910; SD = 3 years, 7 months)	Females (N = 672)

PARENTAL EDUCATION AND TRAINING

Median grade completed = 10th
Bachelor's degree
  Fathers = 29%
  Mothers = 20%

IQ SCORE MEDIAN = 147

Professional Training

	MDs	*PhDs*	*Law degree*
Fathers	N = 47	N = 23	N = 52
Mothers	N = 3	N = 4	N = 1

FAMILY COMPOSITION

Divorced = 10%
Widowed = 12%
Other siblings = 83%

Source: From Holahan, C. K., & Sears, R. R. (1995). *The gifted group in later maturity.* Stanford, CA: Stanford University Press.

of education, as did the fathers. These factors have remained as permanent potential confounds in the interpretation of Termite data, at least when the attempt is made to generalize to other populations. A more comprehensive summary of the demographics of the Terman sample and the evolution of the Terman Gifted Children Study can be found in the book-length monograph by Holahan et al. (1995).

As you already know, the Termites were not a randomly selected sample. Therefore, one must proceed cautiously when making comparisons between this sample and other groups of people. For instance, if you wanted to know if there was a relationship between a person having a high IQ and growing up in a family where both parents were present, you could not answer this question using the Termite data to generalize the findings to the rest of the Californian or U.S. population. The Termites were nothing like a representative sample of these populations. As far as IQ is concerned, the Termites are in the top 1 percent of the standardization population.

Additionally, there is very little variance in IQ among the group members. This lack of variance means that great caution must be exercised using the Termite data alone to draw any conclusions about other factors that might correlate with IQ. In order to find meaning-ful correlates of IQ, the study would have needed to have comparison groups at other IQ levels who were also followed across the life span. To give you another example, the same problem would occur in trying to discover correlates of ethnicity in a sample of people from only one ethnic group.

Despite this, as children the Termites could be compared to other groups of people based on psychological measures other than IQ. This was because these measures were administered to comparable control groups of children, usually classmates of the Termites or other children. There was no reason to believe that the Termites would be homogeneous on these non-IQ instruments when compared to their peers. Indeed, after the data from these measures had been analyzed, the Termites appeared to be similar in variability to the average-intellect peers, except in three particular domains: (1) early onset of intellectual be-havior and interests; (2) mental age as an indicator of knowledge and interests; and (3) vari-ability in academic achievement and nonintellectual pursuits.

The most salient difference found was that the Termites seemed to acquire various be-haviors before their average IQ peers. Reading and speaking in complete sentences tended to emerge earlier in these gifted individuals. They often acquired reading without formal instruction. The Termites also appeared to excel at other nonacademic activities, though to a lesser extent. Because the tests administered to the Terman sample contained a heav-ily weighted verbal component, these individuals can be seen as verbally advanced when compared to their peers. Secondly, as children the Termites' abilities and interests tended to correspond to those of older individuals. Although this is considered to be a finding of the Termite study, it was probably the logical outcome, given the structure of the IQ test. On the Stanford-Binet, measured intelligence was expressed as a quotient. Mental tasks were arranged like rungs on a ladder. A child would start with tasks that could typically be done by a 2-year-old. If those were completed successfully the child would move on to the tasks typical for 3-year-olds. Following this example, at each level, successful completion moved the child to more difficult items. Mental age was determined as the last set of tasks a child completed before experiencing substantial difficulties. Children who made it to the tasks typical for 10-year-olds had a mental age of 10, no matter how old they actually were in years. The formula for IQ was:

$$IQ = \frac{\text{Mental Age (MA)}}{\text{Chronological Age (CA)}} \times 100$$

The reason for putting chronological age in the denominator was to compare children's mental accomplishments to their age. This makes sense if you consider that a mental age of, say, 12 is easier to interpret if we tell you the individual's chronological age. If an individual is 8 years old with a mental age of 12, the IQ score will be high; if the individual is 16 years old, the IQ score will be low.

You can also see from the formula that an individual with an IQ of 100, will have a mental age and chronological age equal to one another. Because the Termites all had IQs over 135, this means that as 10-year-olds they would have been scoring similarly to the average 13.5-year-old on ability to perform mental tasks (13.5 / 10 = 1.35 × 100 = 135). We do not mean to suggest they would be the same as the average 13.5-year-old in every way. Instead, they would perform like 13.5-year-olds on measures such as verbal ability.

Looking at the formula for IQ, you can see why it might be unsurprising that an outstanding characteristic of the Termites was that they were ahead of their classmates on mental skills and interests. The formulaic definition of IQ requires this—children are ahead of average peers if their mental age is larger than its chronological age.

We should mention in passing that although the old formula can give you initial understanding of the workings of IQ, the formula is no longer used in contemporary IQ tests. IQ is now defined as having a mean of 100 and a standard deviation of 15. One reason for this change is quite easy to see. The old formula cannot work for adults because although their chronological ages may become quite high, their mental performance levels off. If the formula were to be used, the necessity to divide by large chronological ages would result in IQ decreases in all people, starting in early adulthood.

In addition to taking IQ tests, the Termites were rated by their parents and teachers on 25 different personality and behavioral traits. The children also took a variety of personality and achievement tests and responded to surveys regarding their interests, goals, activities, and other preferences. All of these psychological measures were said to have been sophisticated for the time and to have achieved high reliability and validity ratings.

FOLLOW-UP NUMBER 1

As adults, the Termites were a reasonably successful group of individuals. Approximately 70 percent of them were college educated and many of them pursued professional and academic careers. Perhaps surprisingly, over the course of their lifetimes, none of the Termites were identified as certifiable "geniuses." Since Terman's initial sampling in 1921–1922, the Termites have been the focus of numerous follow-up studies occurring at 5- to 10-year intervals until the present. One of these follow-up studies was conducted in 1993 by Howard Friedman and his research team (see Friedman et al., 1993). At the time of this follow-up, many members of the original Termite sample were either deceased or in their 80s. This follow-up study only considered the data of those Termites who were born between 1904 and 1915. This excluded some of the older Termites from the original sample.

Following the assumption that personality traits remain relatively stable throughout an individual's lifetime, the researchers were interested in seeing if any of the personality traits upon which the Termites had been rated by their parents and teachers in 1921 and 1922 would be predictors of the time of death. Data from 1,178 Termites were considered in this analysis. This total excluded individuals who could not be located, who had a large amount of personality data missing, or who had died before 1930. Means for the whole sample were used to replace a score here and there for 63 individuals who were missing data on a few personality measures. Participants who could not be located or had dropped out were found not to be significantly different from the remaining sample in any obvious way.

Parents and teachers rated the Termites, back when they were children, on each of 25 traits, using a 13-point scale. The statistical technique called *factor analysis,* described in Chapter 20, was used to identify meaningful personality dimensions from the childhood ratings. The items that were used to form one of these measures, the conscientiousness scale, had an alpha of .76. A further complex statistical procedure was then used to compute probabilities of survivorship for sex and different child personality measures.

RESULTS

Only two personality variables were found to be associated with time of mortality: conscientiousness-social dependability and cheerfulness-humor-optimism. Termites scoring in the upper quartile (the top 25th percentile) of the sample on the conscientiousness measure lived significantly longer than individuals scoring in the lower quartile on this dimension. Because of the way the analysis was conducted, the significance levels for these two trait clusters are not individually available. Figure 32.1 displays the probability of a 20-year-old dying at a given age as a function of gender and conscientiousness score. As you would guess by looking, these data were transformed from the original data by mathematical procedures that extract the trends evident in a large data set and produce smooth curves representing those trends.

The point where the probability curves cross the .50 threshold is equivalent to the mean age of death for this group. This is because at the point where the probability of death is .50, half of the individuals have died and half have not. In a large group, when all the life spans are averaged, the average age of death is likely to be near the age at which about half are dead and half are still living.

As evident from Figure 32.1, females outlived males and this outcome is recognized as a fairly standard finding in the developmental literature. The figure also shows us that high conscientious individuals tend to outlive low conscientious individuals, with low conscientious males being the group most at risk for earlier death. Similarly, although not shown here, individuals who scored high on the cheerfulness-humor-optimism dimension were more likely to meet a premature death than those who scored low on this measure. This finding may contradict the intuitive stereotype of a cheerful and optimistic person as being healthier than average. The authors speculate that people scoring high on this dimension could be overly optimistic about their own health. Perhaps they do not see a doctor when they experience a health-related problem because they optimistically believe they are going to get better. They might neglect a physician's advice because they cheerfully believe that they will not suffer any consequences. Clearly, being overly optimistic when thinking

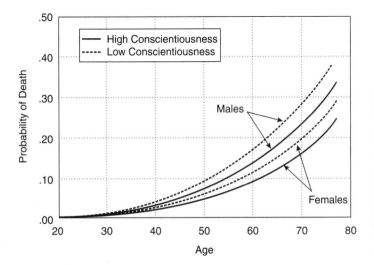

FIGURE 32.1   Probability of a 20-Year-Old Dying at a Given Age as a Function of Gender and Conscientiousness Rating.

Source: From "Does Childhood Personality Predict Longevity?" by H. S. Friedman, J. S. Tucker, C. Thomlinson-Keasey, J. E. Schwartz, D. L. Wingard, & M. H. Criqui, 1993, *Journal of Personality and Social Psychology, 65,* pp. 183. Copyright © 1992 by Joseph Schwartz and Howard S. Friedman. Reprinted by permission.

about one's own health could be devastating, especially because diseases such as cancer and heart disease are often highly treatable if they are diagnosed early. Overly optimistic people might be prone to ignore early symptoms or fail to seek out routine health examinations that could potentially save their lives. We do not mean to suggest that having a cheerful and optimistic personality is remarkably bad, rather that an unrealistic coping style in general might have some adverse consequences, especially for long-term health. Future research will have to be done before this link between cheerfulness-optimism-humor and length of life span can be more thoroughly deciphered.

Although the .50 intersect is not shown in Figure 32.1, if you imagine extending the age scale along the x axis as well as each of the projected curves to show their intersect with that axis, there might be more than a 10-year difference in average life span between the low-conscientious males and the high-conscientious females.

FOLLOW-UP NUMBER 2

In 1998, the vast Termite data archive was once again analyzed, this time by the research team of Peterson, Seligman, Yurko, Martin, and Friedman. The researchers were interested in seeing if prospective data collected from the Termites in 1936 and 1940 on explanatory style would be related to mortality risk and cause of death. Explanatory style can be defined as the nature of a person's cause-and-effect interpretations about the world. This is an attributional style. Attributional styles in general were described in Chapter 14. We will consider three basic explanatory dimensions for the purposes of this article. To help you better understand the way these dimensions operate, imagine that you have recently taken a relatively important examination such as the Graduate Record Exam (GRE) or some other test used to assess your suitability for a graduate school or a job. Pretend that you have just received the scores, which show that you have performed poorly. There are a number of possible explanatory styles you might use to interpret your poor performance.

1. *Internalizing:* It's my own fault for not getting a good score on the exam. I should have studied harder for it.

   vs.

   Externalizing: That test was so unfair; the only reason I didn't do well was because the exam makers like to write trick questions (or the room was too cold, or a barking dog kept me up all night, etc.).

2. *Globality:* I never do well in any aspect of life and this exam is one more example of my inadequacy. I might as well have skipped college.

   vs.

   Specificity: I did really poorly on that one exam, and it probably will hurt my chances of getting into the school and program I want. But I am smart and hardworking and I know I can find something else that I will enjoy.

3. *Stability:* I have done poorly this time so I can never do well on that exam in the future, no matter how hard I study or how many times I take the test.

   vs.

   Instability: I did really badly on the exam, but it was just a one-time thing. I know I can do better if I work at the math section and retake it.

Previous research has shown that when applied to bad academic events, the explanatory style of internalizing (It is my fault), globality (It is this way with every domain in my life), and stability (It has always been, and will always be, this way) were related to poor academic outcomes among college students, even when depression and initial ability were controlled (Peterson & Barrett, 1987). Furthermore, the explanatory styles of globality and stability have been found to predict health problems (Peterson & Bossio, 1991).

The Termites originally answered a variety of open-ended questions relating to their personalities in 1936 and 1940. Two examples of the types of questions quoted from were: (from 1936) "Have any disappointments, failures, bereavements, uncongenial relationships with others, etc., exerted a prolonged influence on you?"; and (from 1940) "What do you regard as your most serious fault of personality or character?" (Peterson et al., 1998, p. 128). A head researcher compiled a list of all the Termites' responses to questions such as these, which described negative situations. A group of independent raters then coded each of the Termites' responses on a 7-point scale using the Content Analysis of Verbatim Explanations, or CAVE (Peterson, Schulman, Castellon, & Seligman, 1992). The CAVE is a standardized instrument that can be used to score explanatory style from open-ended responses to questionnaires. Each individual rater was unaware of the other raters' evaluations. Reliability ratings for statements containing internal, global, and stable attributions were all above .70. The mean CAVE ratings for these statements were 4.49, 4.46, and 4.52, respectively.

The researchers obtained death certificates for the deceased Termites, which contained information regarding each individual's age and cause of death. Cause of death was classified into five broad categories: cancer, cardiovascular disease, accident or violence, other, and unknown. For those Termites whose death certificates could not be obtained (approximately 20 percent), the researchers contacted relatives and asked them about the cause of death; otherwise the category "unknown" was coded. Data from 1,179 participants was examined in the analysis. Table 32.2 lists the number of deaths among the Termites and their corresponding categorical causes.

RESULTS

In an approach similar to that used for the conscientiousness data above, relationships were sought between explanatory style, cause of death, age of death, and gender using a complex

TABLE 32.2   Number and Cause of Death of Deceased Termites after 1930

CAUSE OF DEATH	MALES	FEMALES
Cancer ($N = 148$)	85	63
Cardiovascular disease ($N = 159$)	109	50
Accidents or violence ($N = 57$)	40	17
Other (known) ($N = 87$)	50	37
Unknown ($N = 38$)	24	14

Source: From Peterson, C., Seligman, M. E. P., Yurko, K. H., Martin, L. R., & Friedman, H. S. (1998). Catastrophizing and untimely death. *Psychological Science, 9,* 127–130.

statistical technique. Only globality as an explanatory style was related to length of life span ($p < .01$). The probability of a 20-year-old dying at a given age as a function of gender and global explanatory style is shown in Figure 32.2.

As in Figure 32.1, the .50 probability threshold is equal to the average age of death. Individuals residing in the upper or lower quartiles on this dimension were labeled as high or low respectively. As you can see, men whose responses were rated as being in the upper quartile for globality were the most likely to die. When cause of death and explanatory style were analyzed, globality was significantly related to deaths caused by accident or violence ($p < .01$) and deaths of unknown origin ($p < .01$). Globality did not significantly predict any of the other causes of death listed in Table 32.2. The researchers also conducted a separate overall analysis in which they controlled for the number of people who had committed suicide or died accidentally. Globality as an explanatory style still predicted premature mortality among the Termites ($p < .05$) and, overall, was a better predictor of mortality among men ($p < .05$).

The researchers were interested in seeing if the males who scored high on the globality dimension were different in other ways from males low on this dimension. Correlational analyses revealed that men who scored high on globality as an explanatory style were significantly more likely to have mental health problems by follow-up in 1950 ($r = .14$, $p < .001$) and lower levels of psychological adjustment ($r = -.11$, $p < .02$). When these two outcomes were controlled for, globality was still a significant predictor of premature mortality, suggesting that these two factors were not confounds.

The authors speculate that globality may be related to untimely death because it is an explanatory style that generalizes across many different situations. Individuals who think globally about bad events are likely to feel that bad outcomes pervade their lives, occurring in home, work, and other contexts. High globality thinkers have been shown to put themselves more at risk for making poor decisions and exercising poor problem-solving procedures, as well as withdrawing from social contacts (Peterson, Maier, & Seligman, 1993). This may be one reason why individuals who score high on this dimension are

FIGURE 32.2   Probability of a 20-Year-Old Dying at a Given Age as a Function of Gender and Global Explanatory Style.

Source: From "Catastrophizing and Untimely death," by C. Peterson, M. E. P. Seligman, K. H. Yurko, L. R. Martin, & H. S. Friedman, 1998, *Psychological Science, 9,* pp. 129. Copyright © American Psychological Society. Reprinted with permission.

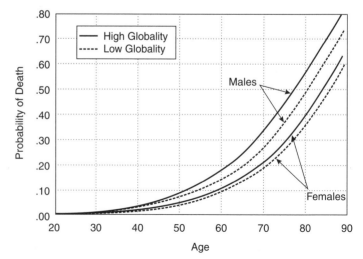

more likely to die from accidental deaths or unknown causes that may have resulted from accidents.

DISCUSSION

When thinking critically about these two Termite studies it is important to remember that they are based on two different measures. In the first follow-up, parent and teacher ratings of the Termites were made when most of the children were still in elementary school. The second follow-up examined self-reported data from questionnaires administered to the Termites in 1936 and 1940. You may be wondering about the quality of these data given that measurement of psychological characteristics was in its infancy as a scientific field when these instruments were designed. This is a hard question to answer. One would have to examine the original items to find evidence of their validity. In fact, the authors of the first follow-up study stated that parental and teacher reports were used instead of self-report personality measures because the personality tests available in 1921 and 1922 were shown to be problematic. You might wonder how much self-report personality tests would have been improved by 1936 and 1940 when they were once again used for data collection and responsible for the findings in the second follow-up. We are confident that Terman and subsequent researchers used the best methods of data collection available to them. We also feel that archival responses to open-ended questionnaires may provide a more valid measure of explanatory style because the Termites only had to answer questions. The questions and answers can be carefully re-analyzed whereas numerical scores from Likert-type scales might mask or distort the actual feelings of the respondents.

We believe that one of the most surprising findings to come out of these two follow-up studies is that the researchers were able to find any significant correlations at all. Given the enormous magnitude of this study, which spanned over three quarters of a century, and the persistent measurement of these gifted individuals, one might expect to find nonsignificant relationships among all personality measures. As you remember from the discussion on correlations in Chapter 2, behavior is multidetermined and we are amazed that any single psychological variable can account for a detectable amount of the variation in length of life span. One of the things that distinguishes the two Termite follow-ups we have discussed in this chapter from other correlational studies is that one outcome being measured is death. In contrast to outcome measures discussed in other chapters, this variable is extremely concrete: A person is either dead or alive. There can be no real dispute over operational definitions when it comes to death.

After reading this chapter, you may now be wondering about the power of personality. After all, a few personality traits observed in children and adolescents have been shown to predict the timing of death. Does this mean we should tell people who have a global explanatory style to stop interpreting the world the way they do, otherwise they'll die earlier than the average person? The answer we hope you arrive at is No. If you got that, you got our answer. It is at least as important to have reasons. At the least, you have learned that you cannot make statements of causation when referring to correlational data. Behavior is multidetermined. Nonetheless, the results of these studies are interesting and future research from the Termite archive, as well as other sources, may be able to construct a more robust picture of outcomes associated with personality across the life span.

CRITICAL THINKING TOOLKIT ITEMS

Longitudinal studies always lose participants as they unfold. If the reasons for participant loss are not explained, later data collections may be affected by a sample that becomes increasingly unrepresentative of the initial group. Data from later samples may lack some external validity as a result of many dropouts.

REFERENCES

Friedman, H. S., Tucker, J. S., Thomlinson-Keasey, C., Schwartz, J. E., Wingard, D. L., & Criqui, M. H. (1993). Does childhood personality predict longevity? *Journal of Personality and Social Psychology, 65,* 176–185.

Holahan, C. K., Sears, R. R., & Cronbach, L. J. (1995). *The gifted group in later maturity.* Stanford, CA: Stanford University Press.

Peterson, C., & Barrett, L. (1987). Explanatory style and academic performance among university freshman. *Journal of Personality and Social Psychology, 53,* 603–607.

Peterson, C., & Bossio, L. M. (1991). *Health and Optimism.* New York: Free Press.

Peterson, C., Maier, S. F., & Seligman, M. E. P. (1993). *Learned helplessness: A theory for the age of personal control.* New York: Oxford University Press.

Peterson, C., Schulman, P., Castellon, C., & Seligman, M. E. P. (1992). CAVE: Content analysis of verbatim explanations. In C. P. Smith (Ed.), *Motivation and personality: Handbook of thematic content analysis* (pp. 383–392). New York: Cambridge University Press.

Peterson, C., Seligman, M. E. P., Yurko, K. H., Martin, L. R., & Friedman, H. S. (1998). Catastophizing and untimely death. *Psychological Science, 9,* 127–130.

NAME INDEX

SUBJECT INDEX

job club, 276

latency, 102
learned helplessness, 99, 140
learning goal, 141
locus of control, 284
longitudinal study, 26, 70, 302

major histocompatibility complex
  (MHC), 246
maltreatment of children, 90, 111
marginal findings, 51
Marital Comparison Level Index
  (MCLI), 286
marital satisfaction, 225, 283
marriage, 223
mastery orientation, 141
maternal employment, 68
maternal instinct, 31
maturation, 110
mean utterance length (MLU), 174
median, 81
memory, 117
memory capacity, 308
menarche, 189
metacognition, 98
mid-career assessment, 274
Miller Marital Locus of Control Scale
  (MMLOC), 286
Minnesota Twin Study, 120
monozygotic twins, 120
multidetermination, 239
Multidimensional Motivational
  Instrument (MMI), 151
mutation, 215

National Educational Longitudinal
  Study (NELS), 149
negative correlations, 13
negative findings, 62
neglect, 113, 114, 201
Nonverbal Test of Intelligence
  (TONI II), 174

obesity, 130
object permanence, 42
operational definition, 3
Oppositional Defiant Disorder (ODD),
  161
optimization, 291

parental investment, 237
parity, 19

partial interval recording system, 164
participant attrition, 103
passive consent for research
  participation, 195
Penn Interactive Peer Play Scale
  (PIPPS), 114
performance goal, 141
phenotype matching, 39
pilot test, 7
placenta, 22
positive correlations, 12
post-traumatic stress disorder (PTSD),
  264
predictive validity, 151
primary aging, 221
primary preventative programs, 204
protective hypothesis, 56
proximate explanations, 245
psychometrics, 32
pubertal timing, 181
punishment, 87

quasi-experiment, 54, 83, 146

random assignment, 54
random selection, 54
reinforcement, 160
reliability, 32, 114
representation of mental events, 45
research artificiality, 40
researcher expectations, 29

sample size, 28, 193
Schaie's most efficient design, 302
secondary aging, 221
secure attachment, 59
self-evaluation, 162
self-management, 162
sensitive care, 56
sensitive period, 29, 56
sensitive periods in language
  development, 172
sexual infidelity, 239
single subject designs, 161
sleep deprivation, 232
sleeper effect, 62
social learning, 66
social referencing, 77
Social Rhythm Metric (SRM), 225
Social Skills Rating System (SSRS),
  115
socioeconomic status (SES), 15, 73, 89,
  95, 112, 133

sociometric rating, 115
soft measures, 32
spanking, 93
standard deviation (SD), 103
standard scores, 186
standardized test, 320
Stanford Binet Form L-M, 123
strange situation, 57
stranger anxiety, 83
stratified sample, 151
stress, 265
subject variables, 15
survival of the fittest, 236
Systematic Screening for Behavior
  Disorders (SSBD), 161

tabula rasa, 20
Tanner stages, 185
television and obesity, 132
temperament, 15, 86
teratogen, 22
test-retest reliability, 151
Tests, 33
Tests in Print IV, 33
threshold, 95
time-lag design, 303
time out from reward, 87
token economy, 162
treatment integrity, 165

ultimate explanations, 245
unemployment, 275

validity, 33
variance and parenting, 192
violation-of-expectation method, 43

Wechsler Adult Intelligence Scale
  (WAIS), 123, 174
Wechsler Intelligence Scale for
  Children-Revised (WISC-R), 123,
  174, 208
wild boy of Aveyron, 172
Wisconsin Maternity Leave and Health
  Project (WMLH), 226
Woodcock-Johnson Psycho-educational
  Battery, 208

Z scores, 186, 307
zygote, 22